SCIENCE CURRICULUM TOPIC STUDY

GREEN HILL SCHOOL
EDUCATION DEPARTMENT

This material is partially supported with funding from the National Science Foundation under the Teacher Professional Continuum—Category III Grant no. ESI-0353315 "Curriculum Topic Study—A Systematic Approach to Utilizing National Standards and Cognitive Research," awarded to the Maine Mathematics and Science Alliance. Any opinions, findings, conclusions, or recommendations expressed in this material are those of the author and do not necessarily reflect the views of the National Science Foundation.

SCIENCE CURRICULUM TOPIC STUDY

PAGE KEELEY

Foreword by Harold Pratt

Bridging the Gap Between Standards and Practice

A JOINT PUBLICATION

CORWIN PRESS

NSTApress®
NATIONAL SCIENCE TEACHERS ASSOCIATION

CORWIN PRESS
A SAGE Publications Company
Thousand Oaks, California

For information:

Corwin Press
A Sage Publications Company
2455 Teller Road
Thousand Oaks, California 91320
www.corwinpress.com

Sage Publications Ltd.
1 Oliver's Yard
55 City Road
London, EC1Y 1SP
United Kingdom

Sage Publications India Pvt. Ltd.
B-42, Panchsheel Enclave
Post Box 4109
New Delhi 110 017 India

Printed in the United States of America.

Library of Congress Cataloging-in-Publication Data

Keeley, Page.
Science curriculum topic study: Bridging the gap between standards and practice / Page Keeley.
     p. cm.
Includes bibliographical references and index.
ISBN 1-4129-0891-4 (cloth) — ISBN 1-4129-0892-2 (pbk.)
     1. Science—Study and teaching (Secondary)—United States. 2. Curriculum planning—United States. I. Title.
Q183.3.A1K44 2005
507'.1'273—dc22   2004024592

This book is printed on acid-free paper.

05   06   07   08   09   10   9   8   7   6   5   4   3   2

Acquisitions Editor:	Rachel Livsey
Editorial Assistant:	Phyllis Cappello
Production Editor:	Diane S. Foster
Copy Editor:	Carla Freeman
Typesetter:	C&M Digitals (P) Ltd.
Proofreader:	Kevin Gleason
Indexer:	Judy Hunt
Cover Designer:	Michael Dubowe

Contents

List of Curriculum Topic Study Guides

Curriculum Topic Study Guides

Diversity of Life
Animal Life
Behavioral Characteristics of Organisms
Biodiversity
Biological Classification
Characteristics of Living Things
Fungi and Microorganisms
Plant Life

Ecology
Biomes
Cycling of Matter in Ecosystems
Decomposers and Decay
Ecological Succession
Ecosystems
Flow of Energy Through Ecosystems
Food Chains and Food Webs
Habitats and Local Environments
Human Impact on the Environment
Interdependency Among Organisms
Populations and Communities

Biological Structure and Function
Cells
Chemistry of Life
DNA
Food and Nutrition
Health and Disease
Human Body Systems
Infectious Disease
Life Processes and Needs of Organisms
Photosynthesis and Respiration
Regulation and Control
Senses

Life's Continuity and Change
Adaptation
Biological Evolution

Origin of Life
Reproduction, Growth, and Development
  (Life Cycles)
Variation

Matter
Acids and Bases
Behavior and Characteristics of Gases
Chemical Bonding
Chemical Properties and Change
Classifying Matter
Conservation of Matter
Density
Elements and the Periodic Table
Liquids
Mixtures and Solutions
Nuclear Chemistry
Particulate Nature of Matter
  (Atoms and Molecules)
Physical Properties and Change
Properties of Matter
Solids
States of Matter

Earth
Air and Atmosphere
Earth History
Earthquakes and Volcanoes
Earth's Gravity
Earth's Natural Resources
Landforms
Oceanography
Plate Tectonics
Processes That Change the Surface of the Earth
Rocks and Minerals
Seasons
Soil
Solar Energy

(Continued)

Fossil Evidence
Human Evolution
Mechanism of Inheritance (Genetics)
Mutations
Natural and Artificial Selection

Astronomy
Earth, Moon, Sun System
Gravity in Space
Historical Episodes in Astronomy
Motion of Planets, Moons, and Stars
Origin and Evolution of the Universe
Scale, Size, and Distance in the Universe
Solar System
Space Technology and Exploration
Stars and Galaxies
The Universe

Energy, Force, and Motion
Chemical Energy
Conservation of Energy
Describing Position and Motion
Electrical Charge and Energy
Electromagnetic Spectrum
Electromagnetism
Energy
Energy Resources and Use
Energy Transformation
Forces
Gravitational Force
Heat and Temperature
Kinetic and Potential Energy
Laws of Motion
Magnetism
Motion
Nuclear Energy
Pressure and Buoyancy
Relativity
Sound
Visible Light, Color, and Vision
Waves
Work, Power, and Machines

Inquiry and the Nature of Science and Technology
Communicating With Drawings, Maps, and Physical Models
Communication in Science
Controlling Variables
Correlation
Data Collection and Analysis
Evidence and Explanation
Experimental Design
Graphs and Graphing

Structure of the Solid Earth
Water Cycle
Water in the Earth System
Weather and Climate
Weathering and Erosion

Identifying and Avoiding Bias
Inquiry Skills and Dispositions
Mathematical Modeling
Mathematics in Science and Technology
The Nature of Scientific Thought and Development
Observation, Measurement, and Tools
Science and Technology
Science as a Human Endeavor
Science as Inquiry
Scientific and Logical Reasoning
Scientific Sampling
Scientific Values and Attitudes
Summarizing and Representing Data
Technological Design
Technology
Understandings About Scientific Inquiry
Understandings About Technology
Use of Computers and Communication Technologies

Implications of Science and Technology
Agricultural Science and Technology
Biotechnology
Environmental Impacts of Science and Technology
Historical Episodes in Science
Human Population Growth and Impact
Materials and Manufacturing Science and Technology
Medical Science and Technology
Personal and Community Health
Pollution
Risks and Benefits of Science and Technology
Science and Technology in Society

Unifying Themes
Constancy, Equilibrium, and Change
Models
Scale
Systems

Foreword

More than 10 years ago, a new vision and guide for reform in science education appeared in the form of national standards. Several important documents followed the lead of the mathematics community a few years earlier. The forerunner of the movement in science was the eloquent and somewhat revolutionary *Science for All Americans* from Project 2061 at the American Association for the Advancement of Science (AAAS). This was followed in 1993 by the *Benchmarks for Science Literacy*, derived from *Science for All Americans*, and it provided standards for four grade-level spans. In early 1996, the National Research Council (NRC) released the *National Science Education Standards*.

With this repertoire of resources, the science education community seemed armed and ready to make major improvements in science teaching and learning. But it has been slow in happening. There are many reasons for this, but one significant one is the lack of clarity on how to use the standards. These were new documents; new in concept, with a new approach to what content should be taught and how it should be presented. We had not been confronted with standards before; they were new, and we didn't know their role and how to use them.

As a member of the content working group for the *National Science Education Standards* and later the staff responsible for producing the standards, I learned, along with my colleagues, that our first, and sometimes our most important task was to introduce the concept of what a standard was and what it wasn't. It was easier to say what they weren't than what they were. Standards were not behavioral objectives so familiar to many educators. They were not a curriculum to replace the ones in place in most states or local districts. Describing how to use them was more difficult; none of us at that time had ever used them to guide curriculum development, select the content for a lesson, or determine the contents of an assessment instrument.

Since the advent of the standards, much has been written about the use of the standards but often in a self-serving manner, to rationalize the content in a local curriculum guide, commercial textbook, or exam. Too often the use is after the fact; a look back to see whether there is a match, alignment, or even just a reference in the standards, after limited or little attention to using them as a guide for the work from the beginning. This book turns that around and places the standards and their supporting documents squarely at the heart of the improvement effort through a process called Curriculum Topic Study (CTS).

By developing the CTS, the author provides the first comprehensive and detailed guide for using standards as the starting point to improve the quality of a wide range of science education activities for multiple audiences, which include K–12 teachers, preservice teachers, preservice higher-education faculty, professional developers, curriculum developers, and science education specialists. These audiences will benefit from the CTS study processes, in their goal to improve their own understanding of science content, identify and clarify the "big ideas" for their instruction that come from their state or local standards, identify potential learning difficulties and misconceptions associated with a topic, apply effective teaching strategies to the ideas or skills associated with a topic, and improve coherence of topic development within a grade or across grades in a vertical curriculum.

Although the above examples do not begin to do justice to the multiple uses the CTS process provides science educators, one result of using the study process is notable enough to merit an elaboration. The results of the Third International Mathematics and Science Study (TIMSS) and other analyses have pointed out the lack of coherence in the U.S. curriculum, resulting in the "mile wide and inch deep" characterization. Much of this is the result of continuing to write curriculum and teach as we always have and then look to see whether our topic is mentioned in one of the standards. The result is a padded, incoherent, and less effective curriculum.

The question that is not asked that CTS requires of the user is, "How much of what I have included is not in the big ideas in the standards?" The author has designed the CTS process to create coherence by asking and helping the user answer questions from the start, such as, "What are the big ideas I should include? At what level? How are they connected to the other ideas in the curriculum? And how can I most effectively help students learn them? The answers to these and many more essential questions are available through a well-developed study process, supported by vignettes from users and a set of study guides on 147 science topics.

By helping the reader answer these important questions and many more, the author and her team have given the standards, whether they are the national standards listed above or the state or local standards in immediate use by the reader, new vitality and enhanced value in our effort to improve the quality of science teaching and learning.

Harold Pratt
President, 2001–2002
National Science Teachers Association

Preface

OVERVIEW

To become an accomplished science teacher in today's classroom environment requires a specific set of abilities and knowledge that combine deep understanding of science content, pedagogy, and familiarity with standards and research on student learning. Teachers with these abilities and knowledge are grounded in science content, the vision of national science standards, and cognitive research. They combine this interconnected knowledge base with the wisdom achieved through their practice to provide all students the opportunity to learn and enjoy science. Accomplished teachers recognize that achieving science literacy for all students requires substantive changes in the science content taught, how and when it is taught, and the need for continuous professional development connected to their work. These are teachers who deliberately seek out ways to gain new knowledge and the ability to implement their local and state standards by "standing on the shoulders of giants"— in other words, drawing upon and using the collective consensus-driven work of hundreds of educators, scientists, researchers, and science education specialists who developed the national standards and contributed to the research base on student learning. They see standards and accountability testing not as the end points in and of themselves, but as ways to help teachers stay on the path to achieving science literacy for all. While they recognize the imperative of meeting their states' articulated standards, their overarching goal is not to raise test scores and teach only to the standards listed in their state standards documents. Their ultimate goal is to ensure that all students develop a deep understanding of the important interconnected knowledge and skills of science identified in the national standards and that they can draw upon these knowledge and skills when needed.

Who are these teachers? Several are Maine, New Hampshire, and Vermont teachers, along with science specialists and colleagues I have had the honor and pleasure of trying out the Curriculum Topic Study (CTS) tools and processes with in the Northern New England Co-Mentoring Network, funded by the National Science Foundation (NSF), the Maine Governor's Academy for Science Education Leadership, and various other professional development projects. I have seen these teachers and leaders significantly transform their beliefs and knowledge about science teaching and learning and professional development through the use of CTS practical tools and processes for putting the vision of the standards and the findings from cognitive research into practice in the classroom and professional development settings. CTS has moved national standards documents, as well as state standards and frameworks, beyond rhetoric and off the shelf and into the hands and minds of science education professionals who use them regularly and purposefully in their practice.

As a result of seeing the impact of using the CTS process with educators I have worked with, combined with the encouragement of my national professional development colleagues, a proposal was submitted to the NSF's Teacher Professional Continuum Program. This proposal, *Curriculum Topic Study: A Systematic Approach to Utilizing National Standards and Research,* was awarded to the Maine Mathematics and Science Alliance (MMSA) in May 2004. The MMSA and our partner for the proposal, WestEd, are working with several national organizations, teachers, and teacher educators over the next 4 years to develop CTS into a set of science, mathematics, and professional development materials that will be available nationally. In addition to this book on science curriculum topic study, mathematics curriculum topic study and a facilitator's guide to using curriculum topic study will be produced for the science and mathematics education community during the period of the NSF-funded grant. There is also a companion Web site at www.curriculumtopicstudy.org. The NSF-funded Curriculum Topic Study Project will provide the "missing link" for implementing national standards and utilizing cognitive research to help teachers and professional developers improve and deepen their understanding of science teaching and learning.

By using CTS to understand the important concepts, skills, and instructional implications within the topics they teach, teachers at all levels of experience, from preservice to accomplished teacher leaders and professional developers, can improve their practice in order to positively impact student learning. It is hoped that this book will provide the bridge as well as the solid support structures that all teachers need to make substantive changes in their practice, while engaging in opportunities for continuous, intellectual professional growth.

KNOWLEDGE BASE

The CTS approach was adapted from the author's experiences working with the American Association for the Advancement of Science's (AAAS) Project 2061, using a procedure for the study of a single benchmark. The original procedure utilized Project 2061's resources, including *Science for All Americans, Benchmarks for Science Literacy,* and *Atlas of Science Literacy.* This study procedure was modified and expanded to create a set of study guides, with preselected readings linked to a specific purpose, used in a process called "Curriculum Topic Study." CTS focuses on topics, instead of a single learning goal, and includes additional reference materials, such as the *National Science Education Standards,* a sourcebook for cognitive research, an adult science content trade book authored by credible scientists, and numerous Web resources.

This book leverages and extends the work of AAAS/Project 2061 and the National Research Council's (NRC) national science education standards development and distribution by building a bridge between the dissemination of standards and their purposeful use. It is an example of how professional developers have been able to draw upon the excellent research and development work done by AAAS and the NRC and connect it to the immediate needs and contextual issues of teachers and professional developers. CTS draws upon the current knowledge base on effective professional development for science teachers—addressing the need for greater focus on relevant content, standards, and research in how students learn.

NEED

Engaging science educators in scholarly thought and purposeful use of standards and research on student learning is key to improving student achievement. National and state standards and an expanding body of cognitive research have been available to teachers since the start of the "standards-based" wave of science education reform. However, a systematic, flexible process and unified set of tools to collectively and deliberately utilize them in practice have been missing.

In addition, the new "highly qualified teacher" requirements set by the "No Child Left Behind" legislation make this a critical time for teachers to have the tools and processes they need to continuously develop as professionals. In this No Child Left Behind age of standards and high stakes accountability, it is not enough to be guided only by a list of state standards.

If your goal is to become a standards- and research-based educator, you need the right tools and processes to reach your goal. Rich explanations of content and learning goals, background information on instructional implications that impact student learning, specific examples of the content in a learning goal, and vignettes that make standards and research come to life are needed to help teachers implement standards and research. This book is intended to fill that need by providing you with an intellectually rigorous and invigorating process for examining the science topics you teach so that you can make well-informed decisions to improve your students' learning.

AUDIENCE

The primary audience for this book is K–12 teachers, preservice teachers, preservice higher-education faculty, professional developers, and science education specialists. Other audiences that may find sections of the book and the CTS process useful include administrators, scientists working on curriculum development and science education reform projects, parents (especially homeschoolers), museum and science center educators, standards revision committees, and curriculum and assessment developers.

ORGANIZATION

The book is divided into six chapters. Chapter 1 provides an introduction to CTS and a description of the knowledge and research base that anchors the development and design: standards, research, professional development theory and practice, and science teachers and teaching. It includes a rationale for the importance of studying a curricular topic and why topics were chosen as the focus.

Chapter 2 takes the reader on a "tour" of a CTS guide. It describes the different features of a CTS guide and provides descriptions of the resources that are used in the process.

Chapter 3 describes the ways users of CTS engage in the process. It describes how to get started and defines the different purposes and outcomes a user must identify before beginning the process. It describes an instructional model for adult learning used in the process, based on the learning cycle. Individual and group use are addressed, and guiding questions are provided to accompany the resources.

Chapter 4 describes the various contexts for professional use in which CTS can be used. Embedded throughout this section are various examples and tools that can be used by teachers, such as improving content knowledge, curriculum, instruction, assessment, and professional development and leadership.

Chapter 5 describes how CTS has been used in actual practice. Real-life vignettes are described that illuminate the different ways CTS users have been informed by the process.

Chapter 6 is the core of the book. It contains the 147 CTS guides arranged in 11 different categories. The study guides are reproducible for use with groups. The Resource sections A and B contain additional resources that complement CTS as well as some of the worksheet templates described in the chapters.

HOW TO USE THIS BOOK

The primary goal in writing this book was to provide educators with ready-to-use study guides that utilize a common template to identify vetted sections in the content, standards, and research resources for reading about, studying, and reflecting on a science topic. It is an essential companion to help you utilize the standards you may already have access to as well as help you incorporate the use of other professional science education resources as you build your professional science teaching library. For educators who are familiar with the CTS approach, you can immediately access and use the guides in Chapter 6. For others, it is helpful to read Chapters 1 through 5 first, to get a clear sense of how and why the guides were developed, and ways to use them effectively. This is not intended to be a "How to" book for professional developers who are interested in ways to facilitate use of CTS in their professional development settings. This book will be developed in the second year of the Curriculum Topic Study Project. In the meantime, professional developers can use this book to learn about the process and practice using it. Higher-education faculty can encourage their students to use this book to plan their lessons and gain a deeper understanding of standards- and research-based teaching and learning in preparation for the reality of teaching.

CTS provides tools and processes to use in improving teachers' understanding of the topics they teach. It is not a "How to" book about curriculum, instruction, and assessment. It is intended to be used to deepen teachers' understanding of how to use standards and research within the context in which they are working. Rather than providing the answers, CTS promotes inquiry among educators in discovering new knowledge about teaching and learning connected to the content they teach.

ACKNOWLEDGMENTS

This book is the pinnacle of working with teachers and professional developers in New England and nationally. In 2000, the first Maine Governor's Academy for Science Education Leadership was developed by the Maine Mathematics and Science Alliance, with support from TERC's Eisenhower Regional Alliance for Science and Mathematics Reform, to support science teacher leaders in Maine. The first set of CTS tools were developed for leaders in the Governor's Academy, who helped me think through their development and use. I want to thank all of the Governor's

Academy Fellows for their contribution to the evolution of this project. I would especially like to thank Steve Deangelis, Anita Bernhardt, and Nancy Chesley, for sticking by me right up to the deadline for submitting this manuscript. This book would not have been possible without your friendship, professional contributions, and unwavering support.

The Northern New England Co-Mentoring Network (NNECN), an NSF-funded science and mathematics mentoring project, has been a major test bed for this project. I wish to thank all of the mentors and their mentees in our network for piloting many of the guides and processes used in this book. In particular, I would like to thank Judith Allard for her high school and preservice insights. Instrumental is my NNECN partner, Susan Mundry, who encouraged me to "go national" with these tools. Susan: You are my mentor and inspiration, and I remain indebted to your support and confidence in my work. Your wisdom and contributions to sections of this book are gratefully acknowledged.

Hundreds of teachers have piloted and field-tested the CTS tools and processes, and I remain indebted to all of you. In particular, I would like to thank Sharon Gallant, Kate Slattery, Andrew Njaa, Mary Whitten, Nancy Chesley, Barbara Fortier, Wes Marble, Jim Chandler, Sandra Ferland, and Laurie Olmstead for your help right up to the manuscript submission deadline in refining the field-test products.

The guidance and support from my MMSA colleagues helped me refine the processes for professional development and shape the ideas for this book. Thank you to Lynn Farrin and Henrietta List for being my sounding board and contributing your teacher and professional developer wisdom. I also wish to thank Deb McIntyre, Beth Small, and Cheryl Rose for their help in reviewing the manuscript. I am extremely grateful to my director, Dr. Francis Eberle, for his unconditional support in allowing me the time and freedom to publish my first book and his affirmation that this work can make a difference for Maine and beyond. I am indebted to my dear friend Janre Mullins, for her "comma coaching" as well as clever and kind words of encouragement throughout this process. You are my pillar of support! I also wish to thank Jan Spencer for her help in pulling together the resources I needed, and her humor when times got rough. Thank you to Nate Keeley for your multitalented work in creating the graphics and developing the CTS Web site, and taking an avid interest in your mom's work! And of course this book would not have been possible without the dedicated, hard work of Brianne Van Den Bossche, project assistant extraordinaire!

I wish to thank all my other professional colleagues for their support and contributions—there are too many to name all individually. In particular, I would like to thank Soren Wheeler for his extraordinary knowledge, way with words, and advice for shaping sections of the book. Thank you to Joyce Tugel and Mark Kaufman for helping me build a professional community of CTS users in New England. Many thanks go to Dr. Richard Audet, at Roger Williams University, for your collaboration and connection to the higher education community. I would also like to gratefully acknowledge Project 2061 and my colleagues in the early days of the Project 2061 Science Literacy Leaders group for pushing my thinking about the multifaceted components that contribute to science literacy and the critical importance of studying standards and research. Many thanks go to Claire Reinburg and David Beacom for having the insight to copublish this book with the National Science Teachers Association (NSTA), reaching thousands of committed NSTA members. I would be remiss if I didn't go all the way back to my days as a fellow in the first National

Academy for Science Education Leadership and acknowledge my role models and mentors Susan Loucks-Horsley, Susan Mundry, Kathy Stiles, Nancy Love, and Nancy Kellogg for guiding me along the path of leadership and vision that made this book possible.

I gratefully acknowledge my editor, Rachel Livsey, for keeping me on track and helping me navigate new waters in the publishing world. I also wish to thank CeCe Sisneros, at Corwin Press, my very first contact at Corwin, who provided encouragement and support throughout this project and others. Finally, I would like to thank my NSF Program Officer, Dr. Michael Haney, for his role in the NSF Teacher Professional Continuum Program support for this book and the two others that will follow.

The contributions of the following reviewers are gratefully acknowledged:

Cary Sneider
Vice President for Educator Programs
Museum of Science, Boston
Boston, MA

Douglas Llewellyn
St. John Fisher College
Rochester, NY

Sandra K. Enger
Associate Professor of Science Education
The University of Alabama in Huntsville
Huntsville, AL

Susan B. Koba, PhD
Project Director, Urban Systemic Program
Omaha Public Schools
Omaha, NE

Nancy Kellogg
Colorado Professional Development Coordinator
Center for Learning and Teaching in the West
Boulder, CO

Katherine E. Stiles
Senior Research Associate and Project Director
WestEd
Tucson, AZ

Janet Crews
Teacher
Wydown Middle School
Clayton, MO

About the Author

**Page Keeley** is the Senior Program Director for Science at the Maine Mathematics and Science Alliance (MMSA). Her work at the MMSA involves leadership and professional development for teachers and leaders in Maine and nationally, as well as the development of materials and tools to support science teaching and learning. She is the principal investigator and project director of three NSF-funded projects, including *Curriculum Topic Study; The Northern New England Co-Mentoring Network;* and *PRISMS: Phenomena and Representations for the Instruction of Science in Middle Schools.* She serves on several national advisory boards for science education and consults with schools and organizations throughout New England and nationally. She was a fellow in the first cohort of the National Academy for Science Education Leadership and serves as a mentor and learning colleague for new fellows. She has taught inquiry science as an adjunct instructor for the University of Maine.

Prior to working at the MMSA, Page taught as a middle school and high school science teacher for 15 years. During that time, she served as president of her state science teachers association and served two terms on the Executive Board of the National Science Teachers Association. She received the Presidential Award for Excellence in Secondary Science Teaching in 1992, the Milken National Educator Award in 1993, and was the AT&T Maine Governor's Fellow for Technology in 1994. Prior to teaching, she worked as a research assistant in immunodeficiency diseases at the Jackson Laboratory in Bar Harbor, Maine. She received her undergraduate degree in life sciences at the University of New Hampshire and her master's in science education at the University of Maine.

This book is dedicated to David, Nate, Chris, Bill, and Peter.
Thank you for being a supportive husband, loving sons, and wonderful brothers.
And to Mom and Dad—your smiles from heaven shine down on everything I do.

1

Introduction to Curriculum Topic Study

Before I plan a lesson, I use Curriculum Topic Study to study the research on students' thinking and their possible misconceptions. I start with these student preconceptions in mind whenever I teach a new topic.

Curriculum Topic Study has helped me understand standards-based concepts I haven't thought about or used since I was in college, like energy transformation. Now I know where to turn to refresh my knowledge of the concepts that make up the topics in my curriculum.

Curriculum Topic Study helped our committee look at the topics in our curriculum across grade spans to identify gaps, redundancy, new contexts, and make sure we are teaching important ideas at a level developmentally appropriate for each grade. Without this tool, we would have been shooting in the dark.

Our lesson study group uses Curriculum Topic Study to research the topic we chose for our lesson. Doing this step first has made a big difference in designing our research lesson so we don't have to start from scratch. Our topic study results help us decide what goals to focus on in crafting the lesson and provide a filter for us to fine-tune our observations.

Curriculum Topic Study has given us a common set of understandings and neutral, third-party perspective to work from at our science department meetings. Our discussions have changed from "What I do" to "This is what the standards and research point out."

I can't imagine designing a workshop for our elementary science teachers without studying the science topic first. Yesterday, we examined a new FOSS kit on Electricity and Magnetism, and I felt much better prepared to explain how the lessons aligned with standards and research and how conceptual ideas flowed from one activity to the next.

WHAT IS CURRICULUM TOPIC STUDY (CTS)?

All of the above quotes came from science educators who use Curriculum Topic Study in their work as teachers, mentors, professional developers, and as members of collaborative learning communities. Curriculum Topic Study, referred to in this book by its acronym, CTS, is a methodical study process and a set of tools and strategies—organized around 147 curriculum topics—designed to help educators improve the teaching and learning of science.

Through the CTS process, educators can

- Improve their understanding of the science content they teach
- Identify K–12 "big ideas," implications for effective instruction, and images of effective practice
- Clarify concepts and specific ideas and skills in a learning goal from their state or local standards
- Identify a cluster of related learning goals that make up a curricular topic
- Improve coherency of topic development within a grade as well as K–12 vertical articulation
- Identify potential learning difficulties, developmental considerations, and misconceptions associated with a topic
- Examine and apply effective strategies for teaching concepts and skills associated with a topic
- Improve their ability to identify relevant connections among concepts and skills within and across topics
- Increase opportunities for students of all levels and backgrounds to achieve learning goals articulated in district, state, and national standards

The CTS process guides individuals or groups through a systematic study of readings from a core set of professional science education resources. These readings are identified and screened in advance, then organized in "Curriculum Topic Study Guides" (see example in Figure 1.1). The specific features and uses of CTS guides are described in Chapter 2.

There are 147 CTS guides in Chapter 6, ranging from specific topics such as Density to broader topics such as Properties of Matter. The majority of the study guides address K–12 topics. Guides that address very sophisticated content, such as Nuclear Energy, are designed to be used only with upper grade levels.

For each topic, CTS guides list relevant professional readings from sources that include national standards documents, trade books written by scientists, research summaries, and K–12 conceptual strand maps (see Figure 1.2). Optional readings, videos, and Web-based material that are not part of the core set of science education resources can also be used to supplement the study of a topic. CTS users can use their own materials or search for supplementary material by topic on the CTS Web site at www.curriculumtopicstudy.org.

Figure 1.1   Example of a CTS Guide

Standards- and Research-Based Study of a Curricular Topic

STATES OF MATTER

Section and Outcome	Selected Sources and Readings for Study and Reflection Read and examine *related parts of:*
I. Identify Adult Content Knowledge	**IA:** *Science for All Americans* ▸ Chapter 4, Structure of Matter, pages 46–49 **IB:** *Science Matters: Achieving Scientific Literacy* ▸ Chapter 7, *The States of Matter*, pages 95–99
II. Consider Instructional Implications	**IIA:** *Benchmarks for Science Literacy* ▸ 4D, *Structure of Matter*, general essay, page 75; grade span essays, pages 76–79 **IIB:** *National Science Education Standards* ▸ Grades K–4, Standard B essay, pages 123, 126 ▸ Grades 5–8, Standard B essay, page 149 ▸ Grades 9–12, Standard B essay, pages 177–178
III. Identify Concepts and Specific Ideas	**IIIA:** *Benchmarks for Science Literacy* ▸ 4D, *Structure of Matter*, pages 76–80 **IIIB:** *National Science Education Standards* ▸ Grades K–4, Standard B, *Properties of Objects and Materials*, page 127 ▸ Grades 5–8, Standard B, *Properties and Changes of Properties in Matter*, page 154 ▸ Grades 9–12, Standard B, *Structure and Properties of Matter*, pages 178–179; *Conservation of Energy and the Increase in Disorder*, page 180
IV. Examine Research on Student Learning	**IVA:** *Benchmarks for Science Literacy* ▸ 4B, *Water Cycle*, page 336 ▸ 4D, *Structure of Matter*, pages 336–337 **IVB:** *Making Sense of Secondary Science: Research Into Children's Ideas* ▸ Chapter 9, *Solids, Liquids, and Gases*, pages 79–84 ▸ Chapter 11, *Development of Particle Ideas About Materials*, pages 92–94; *Particle Ideas About Change of State*, pages 94–95 ▸ Chapter 12, *Water as a Liquid*, page 98; *Freezing Water and Melting Ice*, page 98; *Boiling Water*, pages 98–99; *Evaporation*, pages 99–100; *Condensation*, page 100 ▸ Chapter 13, *Existence of Air*, pages 104–105
V. Examine Coherency and Articulation	**V:** *Atlas of Science Literacy* ▸ *States of Matter*, pages 58–59
VI. Clarify State Standards and District Curriculum	**VIA:** *State Standards:* Link Sections I–V to learning goals and information from your state standards or frameworks that are informed by the results of the topic study. **VIB:** *District Curriculum Guide:* Link Sections I–V to learning goals and information from your district curriculum guide that are informed by the results of the topic study.

Visit www.curriculumtopicstudy.org for updates or supplementary readings, Web sites, and videos.

Figure 1.2 Types of Readings and Their Sources

Type of Resource	Source
Adult science literacy description	*Science for All Americans*, American Association for the Advancement of Science Project 2061
Adult science trade book	*Science Matters*, by Robert Hazen and James Trefil
National, state, and local standards	*Benchmarks for Science Literacy*, American Association for the Advancement of Science Project 2061 *National Science Education Standards*, National Research Council State Standards or Frameworks and/or local curriculum standards or frameworks
Research summaries	*Benchmarks for Science Literacy*, Chapter 15, American Association for the Advancement of Science Project 2061 *Making Sense of Secondary Science: Research into Children's Ideas*, by Rosalind Driver, Ann Squires, Peter Rushworth, and Valerie Wood-Robinson, University of Leeds, England
Conceptual strand maps	*Atlas of Science Literacy*, American Association for the Advancement of Science Project 2061

CTS promotes effective and efficient use of science professional readings. While these readings are to some extent accessible, educators would typically have to sift through an enormous amount of unfamiliar, and often daunting, material from disparate sources. Indeed, teachers who have not used professional science education resources extensively may not even know where to look for the information they are seeking. CTS guides identify the purpose of different resources and explicitly link relevant parts to topics of study that are useful from the teachers' perspective. CTS guides do the groundwork for the busy educator, providing a one-page study guide to relevant results from an enormous range of readings vetted in advance and organized for each topic.

The *National Science Education Standards* (National Research Council [NRC], 1996) and *Benchmarks for Science Literacy* (American Association for the Advancement of Science [AAAS], 1993) have provided a carefully crafted description of the ideas and skills all students should achieve by the time they graduate. *Atlas of Science Literacy* (AAAS, 2001) further clarified and supported those documents by detailing how those ideas and skills connect and develop from kindergarten to graduation. States and districts have modeled their own standards after these national documents, and stakeholders at every level are learning how to evaluate, modify, and develop assessments, curricula, and instructional materials to reflect this vision of science literacy. Many teachers have seen or own a copy of national standards or *Atlas*, and the research on student learning is growing and becoming increasingly accessible.

Yet for all of the thought that went into national standards and all of the research on how students learn, just having the documents is not enough to truly impact student learning. In particular, this means being able to relate them to state and local standards and their own curricular and instructional challenges. CTS provides

Figure 1.3   CTS Professional Science Education Resources

Curriculum Topic Study Resources
• *Science for All Americans*
• *Science Matters*
• *Benchmarks for Science Literacy*
• *National Science Education Standards*
• *Making Sense of Secondary Science*
• *Atlas of Science Literacy*
• *State Standards or Frameworks and Curriculum Guides*
• *Optional: Additional Supplementary Resources (Videos, Journal Articles, Web Sites, Trade Books.)*

this deliberate process, which uses a collective set of common resources (see Figure 1.3) to help users become well-informed science educators who can move beyond paying lip service to the label of "standards- and research-based."

CTS is not a replacement for formal science content coursework, but it can help teachers learn content at the same time that they are studying the pedagogical implications of teaching that content. This can be particularly helpful to elementary teachers, who are expected to teach all content areas and seldom have substantive coursework in all the sciences. CTS can also help teachers translate formal science course content into content that is appropriate for students at different grade levels, an essential step for teachers that content courses largely overlook.

> What has been missing is a *systematic, deliberate* process to help educators intellectually engage with national standards and research on student learning so that they can make effective use of them.

Educators across all 50 states who use CTS will know how and understand why it is important to use the national standards and cognitive research to support implementation of their states' standards and why one is not a replacement for the other. CTS provides the guidance, tools, and strategies educators need to be able to utilize professional resources and research in their practice. It moves standards off the shelf and into the hands and minds of teachers, leaders, and professional developers, who use them on a regular basis to improve teaching and learning of science topics.

> CTS helps educators make the bridge between national standards and research and their local efforts to help all students achieve high standards.

WHY STUDY A CURRICULUM TOPIC?

While national, state, and local standards drive curriculum, instruction, and assessment, the content taught in schools is typically organized in the curriculum by topics. It is essential for educators to make a bridge between these topics and the specific, research-based ideas and skills laid out in national, state, and local standards. To do this, they must understand the content and pedagogical implications of those specific ideas and skills. CTS provides a deliberate process to accomplish this. As the following quote by a former director of the National Science Foundation's (NSF) Elementary, Secondary, and Informal Education Division indicates, teachers who are unfamiliar with the topics they teach tend to rely on textbooks, teach in a more didactic way, and often fail to make connections between important ideas in science:

> [When] teachers cover topics about which they are well-prepared, they encourage student questions and discussions, spend less time on unrelated topics, permit discussions to move in new directions based on student inter-est, and generally present topics in a more coherent way, all strategies described as standards-based teaching. However, when teachers teach topics about which they are less well-informed, they often discourage active participation by students, keep any discussion under tight rein, rely more on presentation than on student discussions, and spend time on tangential issues. (Kahle, 1999)

A plethora of general professional resources for teachers are available in schools, districts, and professional development settings. *Concept-Based Curriculum and Instruction* (Erickson, 1998); *Understanding by Design* (Wiggins & McTighe, 1998); *Enhancing Professional Practice: A Framework for Teaching* (Danielson, 1996); *Classroom Instruction That Works* (Marzano, Pickering, & Pollock, 2001); *Mapping the Big Picture* (Jacobs, 1997); and *Differentiated Instructional Strategies* (Gregory & Chapman, 2002) are examples of the many tools schools and teachers are using. These "one-tool-fits-all disciplines" can be useful to teachers who know the content and structure of their disciplines well and are familiar with the cognitive research base on student learning in science. But they fall short for novice teachers, elementary teachers who teach all content areas, and others who may not have a sufficient knowledge base in the discipline they teach.

For example, in *Understanding by Design,* the authors encourage teachers to use misconceptions to construct questions or tasks for assessment purposes (Wiggins & McTighe, 1998). What if teachers do not know what misconceptions are likely? What if teachers hold similar misconceptions about the content? CTS provides content-specific tools to identify those misconceptions. CTS provides the content-specific knowledge needed to make the general tools embraced by school districts useful and effective.

In addition to adding content specificity to the general resources used in schools, teachers and professional developers who utilize CTS in a deliberate and systematic way will benefit by:

- Developing deeper understanding of the specific content that makes up student learning goals in a science topic area
- Clarifying the "big ideas," central concepts and skills, and specific ideas associated with a topic
- Improving articulation and coherency of topic development within grade levels as well as K–12
- Effectively using the research base to identify potential learning difficulties, developmental considerations, and misconceptions associated with a topic

- Applying effective instructional strategies for teaching and assessing concepts and skills associated with a topic
- Improving ability to identify connections within and across topics
- Increasing opportunities for students of all levels and backgrounds to achieve science learning goals articulated in district, state, and national standards
- Using a common language and knowledge base about teaching and learning science topics regardless of geographic location or curriculum used
- Promoting collegiality among groups of colleagues engaged in intellectual discourse about science teaching and learning
- Providing a greater content focus to professional development activities

Such a study process is right in line with current thinking about designing learning experiences, such as "backwards design." Backwards design, used in Wiggins and McTighe's (1998) popular *Understanding by Design*, begins by identifying evidence of meeting desired standards before planning teaching and learning experiences. The backwards design model suggests four filters for determining what is worth teaching and understanding in a topic. Three of these filters include examining (1) the extent to which the "big ideas" in a topic are addressed, (2) the extent to which the ideas and processes in a topic reside at the heart of the discipline, and (3) the extent to which abstract and counterintuitive ideas need to be uncovered, including students' misconceptions about ideas related to the topic.

> By taking the time to study a topic before planning a unit or lesson, teachers build a deeper understanding of the content, connections, and effective ways to help students achieve understanding of the most important ideas and skills in that topic.

Although they can be powerful, these filters assume that teachers are comfortable with the content, know what the "big ideas" are, can make the connections that reflect the knowledge structure of the discipline and support student learning, and are aware of the misconceptions students may have. Unfortunately, this is rarely the case. In reality, many teachers missed the "big ideas" in their own education. Many elementary teachers have limited science backgrounds, and middle and high school science teachers often specialize in particular disciplines. Teachers are often not aware of the misconceptions their students hold, and in many cases they harbor those very same misconceptions. The critical, and often overlooked, first step in any effective design involves having a clear understanding of the specific ideas and skills that students should learn and the pedagogical implications for how students learn them. A careful study of a topic, using standards and research, clarifies the "end in mind" and provides a framework for planning and instructional design that maintains content fidelity and takes student thinking and developmental levels into account. CTS combines the wisdom of teacher practice with the recommendations from standards and research and serves as the essential first step in effective planning and design.

> CTS provides the process to help teachers identify what they need to know about the science they need to teach, helping them align curriculum and plan instruction and assessment that are congruent with the collective wisdom reflected in the standards and the research base on learning.

All too often, teachers strike out on their own, when a wealth of information and resources, carefully thought through by distinguished scientists and educators, sits at their fingertips.

Even those teachers who understand the science behind the topics they teach can benefit from CTS. Knowing the content is distinct from knowing how to organize and represent it for student learning. Indeed, familiarity with the content of a topic can make it more difficult to identify difficulties a novice learner is likely to have. Designing learning experiences and facilitating learning requires pedagogical content knowledge. Teachers with this special knowledge of teaching and content understand what makes the learning of specific topics easy or difficult for learners, and they can develop strategies for representing and formulating content to make it accessible to learners (Shulman, 1986). Through CTS, teachers with strong content backgrounds can gain new insights about specific ideas that may have been overlooked, relevant connections within and across topics, relevant contexts for learning, developmental considerations for introducing new ideas, and effective instructional strategies. Thus CTS can help teachers deepen and extend their pedagogical content knowledge.

Outside of the work done by the AAAS Project 2061 to promote K–12 science literacy, to date there has been little systematic, widespread work in professional development to help teachers understand standards and research on student learning. Pre- and inservice efforts to support teachers' content knowledge place little emphasis on helping teachers become aware of the intersections between the topics they teach, standards, research on learning and student misconceptions, and how ideas and skills connect as they develop over time. Teachers may have copies of standards or occasionally come across a research article, but a process for using them has been missing.

> Without a process to compare current practice with standards and research, teachers are likely to continue doing what they have always been doing. Recall the old adage, "If you always do what you've always done, you'll always get what you've always gotten."

Now CTS brings this process to teachers at all levels of the science teaching professional continuum and engages them in classroom applications of standards and research. In today's climate of accountability, teachers assume more personal responsibility for their own learning. Rather than waiting for the system to provide more effective professional development opportunities, science educators can use CTS to continue to grow and improve as teachers, enhancing student learning of the most important ideas in science.

WHY FOCUS ON TOPICS?

To understand why this book focuses on "topics," it is important to clarify what is meant by the word. In the context of CTS, *topics* are the broad organizers for ideas and skills in a curriculum; they do not describe the end point of instruction. Learning goals provide the description of what students should know and be able to do after instruction, but they are sorted into topics within the curriculum (see Figure 1.4).

> Because curriculum and instruction are organized around topics, CTS uses topics as the focus for looking at sets of ideas and skills taught within a single lesson or a broader curricular unit.

Making this distinction clear, and making the bridge between learning goals and topics, is one of the main goals of CTS. Rather than focusing on teaching a topic per se, CTS helps teachers think about the organization of curriculum, instruction, and assessment around a connected set of specific ideas and skills. CTS guides range in grain size from a specific idea, such

Figure 1.4   Topics as Organizers

Topics as Organizers for Curriculum and Instruction
• Teachers design instruction by organizing the science concepts and skills they teach by unit topics.
• Curriculum materials and district curriculum guides are often organized by topics. Yet the standards and results of research describing the cognitive difficulties students face are organized by concepts.
• Topics provide a framework for integrating disciplinary knowledge, scientific processes, nature of science, understandings of science as inquiry, and implications of science and technology.

as Conservation of Matter, to a broader topic, such as Properties of Matter (which subsumes Conservation of Matter as a "subtopic"). For a topic to be included in a CTS guide, it must be considered critical content in science and be linked to specific learning goals articulated in national standards, *National Science Education Standards (NSES)* and *Benchmarks*.

CTS does not include contextual themes as topics for learning. Topics such as Ponds, Butterflies, Flight, Rain Forests, and Dinosaurs are common curricular themes. They can be used to develop, practice, and apply ideas and skills, but they are not by themselves critical content. A risk in teaching contextual themes is that teachers can fail to conscientiously develop the important ideas and skills and instead teach mostly facts associated with the context. For example, students doing a unit on "Dinosaurs" may end up learning little more than vocabulary and facts about dinosaurs. The CTS study guide on *Fossil Evidence* would help teachers focus on developing interrelated ideas and skills about changes in life forms and environments over time, even though they may use "Dinosaurs" as a context.

There are 147 topics included in this book (see Chapter 6). But this does not imply that all of these topics should be taught in the K–12 science curriculum. The Third International Mathematics and Science Study (TIMSS) shows that American teachers cover too many topics a "mile wide and an inch deep," resulting in little conceptual understanding for students (Schmidt, McKnight, & Raizen, 1997). The list of CTS guides includes both traditional topics that might appear in textbooks or curriculum guides, and topics used to organize national and state standards and frameworks. Many of these topics have overlapping ideas and skills, and some are completely subsumed in others. The intent of CTS is to provide enough examples of common topics so that teachers can find CTS guides that address the topics they are currently teaching, consolidate topics for deeper understanding, and improve their understanding of how students best learn the ideas in the topics they teach. Furthermore, because CTS examines topics from a K–12 perspective, it allows teachers to eliminate unnecessary redundancy while planning purposeful reiteration for ideas that need to be revisited in different contexts at increasing levels of sophistication. This careful examination of a topic, in contrast to covering a "checklist of standards," promotes the coherency that is lacking from current attempts at "standards-based" curriculum, instruction, and assessment.

THE UNDERLYING KNOWLEDGE AND RESEARCH BASE

The CTS approach was adapted from the Project 2061 study of a benchmark, a powerful approach to understanding single benchmarks as a learning goal for science literacy. In working with groups of teachers and science education leaders throughout New England, it became clear that although it is important to examine a single learning goal in certain cases, teachers often needed to examine learning goals more comprehensively rather than focusing on a single learning goal, as the Project 2061 process does. It was also clear that teachers benefited from working with a range of standards documents, including both *Benchmarks* and *NSES* together. In addition, teachers benefited from looking beyond standards documents to resources for learning content and research on how students learn specific ideas. Based on these experiences, CTS expanded the study process to include content resources, *Benchmarks* and *NSES*, state standards or local curriculum, Rosalind Driver's research compendia, and *Atlas* to get a complete picture of a science curricular topic.

> National standards have been around for almost a decade, yet studies such as the NRC (2002) report, *Investigating the Influence of Standards,* show that standards have not made a significant impact where it matters most—the classroom.

Clearly, translating standards into classroom practice is a challenge yet to be overcome. At the same time, there is a shift toward providing transformative professional development and supporting resources that reflect the current knowledge base on how teachers and students learn. In 2000, the NRC released *How People Learn* (Bransford, Brown, & Cocking), which is raising awareness among science educators of the need to understand the ideas students bring to their learning.

CTS—by virtue of its focus on the structure of scientific content, research into students' conceptions, and pedagogical strategies linked to specific ideas and skills—can help address the findings from *How People Learn* that distinguish expert teachers from novices (see Figure 1.5). There is a strong link between teacher expertise, which involves both content and pedagogical content knowledge, and student achievement. Because teacher expertise has such a demonstrated impact on student learning, it stands to reason that processes that develop science teachers' knowledge and skills, such as CTS, are a sound investment toward improving student achievement in science.

National, State, and Local Standards

The term *standards* (sometimes referred to as *benchmarks, learning results, performance indicators,* and so on) conveys different meanings to different people. CTS defines standards as a set of outcomes that define the ideas and skills that students should learn, and provide a vision for achieving science literacy for all students. A misperception by many educators is that the standards themselves are a curriculum. Curricular decisions at the state and local level are *informed* by standards, but there are a variety of ways to organize the ideas and skills in standards into a curriculum.

The national "content" standards used in CTS include *Benchmarks* and the *NSES.* Project 2061 led the national effort to define goals for science literacy in the late 1980s with the development of *Science for All Americans* (AAAS, 1990). Rather than a "list" of standards, *Science for All Americans* provides a narrative description of the

Figure 1.5   Characteristics of Expert Teachers

Expert Teachers
• Know the structure of the knowledge in their disciplines.
• Know the conceptual barriers that are likely to hinder learning.
• Have a well-organized knowledge of concepts and inquiry procedures and problem-solving strategies (based on pedagogical content knowledge).

SOURCE: Bransford et al. (1999), *How People Learn.*

interconnected web of understanding that all adult Americans should possess after their K–12 education. This narrative account reflects a strong consensus among respected scientists and educators. Based on cognitive research and the expertise of teachers and teacher educators, *Benchmarks* was developed in 1993. Specific learning goals were developed for the K–2, 3–5, 6–8, and 9–12 grade spans—steps along the way to achieving the vision of science literacy laid out in *Science for All Americans.* *Benchmarks* also includes rich descriptions of the content, context, and instructional implications of those learning goals.

In 1991, the NRC agreed to coordinate the development of the *NSES,* which was released in 1996. The NRC took a collaborative and systemic approach to describe standards for all aspects of the science education system. The content standards in the *NSES* drew upon the previous work of Project 2061 to describe fundamental concepts, principles, and abilities at K–4, 5–8, and 9–12 grade spans. Since that time, states and local districts have been developing their own content standards.

Science educators face numerous challenges in the current standards-based teaching and learning environment, ranging from implementing new curricula to the high-stakes accountability requirements mandated by the "No Child Left Behind" legislation. Educators face the daunting task of applying local, state, or national standards in their own curricular, instructional, and assessment contexts. Local districts and states have spent considerable funds, time, and energy in developing their standards. There has been a flurry of activity in aligning curricula, instruction, and assessment to standards. But there is a missing link in the chain that connects standards to efforts to implement new policies, programs, and practices. Little time has been spent helping educators interpret the content, curricular, and instructional meaning of the standards. Interpretation has been left to individual teachers. As a result, consistency and coherency—and what counts as "alignment"—vary across classrooms, districts, and states. CTS provides a more reliable way to analyze and interpret standards. Using a science analogy, Copernicus did not change the motions of the earth and sun; he just provided a more accurate interpretation of those motions. CTS can provide a more accurate and consistent interpretation of standards, resulting in standards-based teaching that actually reflects the intent of the standards.

> Through CTS, teachers will develop a better understanding of standards and become personally involved in their use. Standards can then become living documents translated into classroom practice.

CTS will help educators recognize the role of standards, both national and state, as central pieces in their local science education system.

Cognitive Research

Research into student learning—both in general and with regard to specific ideas—is another fundamental feature of CTS. In *Learning Science and the Science of Learning,* Harold Pratt (2002) described the importance of using the research base on learning:

> As science teachers and science educators, we approach teaching curriculum development, and assessment with our current conceptions about how the world of the classroom works, namely, how teachers should teach and how students learn. Our job as professionals is to find ways to take our current conceptions about learning and place them against new research, concepts, and information about learning as a way of examining and improving our practice. (p. xiii)

For teachers using CTS, awareness of the conceptions that students bring to the classroom and the developmental implications associated with the specific ideas they need to teach has proven a powerful learning experience.

The research literature on students' science conceptions has been growing, even since the publication of *Benchmarks* and the *NSES.* However, much of it has been difficult for teachers to find and access. In fact, many teachers are not aware that there are resources readily available that summarize the research base. Each CTS guide links the topic to relevant research summaries. CTS uses two research compendia to provide concise, accessible summaries of the research that has been done around specific ideas in different curricular topics. In Chapter 15, *Benchmarks* contains research linked to the learning goals in other chapters. CTS also draws upon the work of notable researchers, such as Rosalind Driver, published after *Benchmarks.* In *Making Sense of Secondary Science,* research findings are arranged in three sections: life and living processes, materials and their properties, and physical processes (Driver, Squires, Rushworth, & Wood-Robinson 1994). New research articles, linked to the CTS guides, are also posted and updated on the CTS Web site.

> Research has shown that teaching is unlikely to be effective unless it takes learners' ideas into account. By identifying these ideas, teachers are able to recognize opportunities and design interventions that help their students bridge their current understandings to the scientific view.

CTS is also informed by research on adult learning. Engaging teachers in CTS by surfacing their initial ideas related to a topic, followed by a systematic study and discussion of standards and research, reflects the constructivist theory of learning. In constructivism, learners construct knowledge by modifying or rejecting existing ideas (Bransford et al., 2000). In CTS, teachers interact with the information in the standards and research tools, and filter them through their everyday experiences with students. Furthermore, the collaborative learning environment created when teachers engage together in CTS reflects how people learn through interaction with one another, so that they can make sense of new concepts and ideas (Jonassen, 1994). Another important aspect of learning is personal reflection. Effective teacher-learners use metacognitive strategies during a topic study to monitor their own ideas and thought processes, compare and contrast them with those of others, and provide reasons why they accept them (Loucks-Horsley, Love, Stiles, Mundry, & Hewson, 2003). CTS is designed to take account of all these insights into adult learning.

Changes in Professional Development

The seminal publication for professional development in science and mathematics, *Designing Professional Development for Teachers of Science and Mathematics*, has informed the work of CTS as a tool for transformative teacher learning (Loucks-Horsley et al., 2003). The changes in science education and professional development described in this book create an urgent need for new teacher learning tools and materials focused on content. Some of these changes described by Loucks-Horsley et al. and the connection to CTS are as follows:

1. **The knowledge base about learning, teaching, the nature of science, and professional development is growing.** Our current knowledge base about teachers and teaching and learners and learning has expanded exponentially since the rise of standards. The findings from *How People Learn* and recent papers in professional journals have increased our knowledge of how students learn specific ideas, the misconceptions they are likely to hold, and the developmental implications for introducing ideas in different grades. This literature reveals more about what constitutes and supports transformative learning for teachers and helps educators recognize the importance of developing not only content knowledge, but pedagogical content knowledge as well. Consequently, teachers need tools, such as CTS, to move beyond personal and management concerns in order to successfully implement new practices.

2. **Standards are more widely consulted as school districts shape their visions of teaching and learning.** Standards are now commonplace in most schools, but implementation is still a struggle. Most state standards were developed through a process that consulted and rewrote the learning goals in national standards using performance verbs and broader descriptions of content. Like a childhood game of telephone, by the time these standards reached the teachers, their clarity and specificity were lost, leaving enough ambiguity for most teachers to continue doing what they were doing before, while being able to claim that they were meeting the standards. There is growing recognition that national science standards are essential to understanding the specific intent of state standards. Through CTS, teachers can clarify the meaning and intent of their state standards, recognize the authentic changes they demand, and increase the coherency and consistency of their implementation.

3. **Content and pedagogical content knowledge are playing a greater role in professional development programs**. Professional development for science teachers has shifted from a schoolwide focus on generic opportunities to learn with all the other disciplines to opportunities that are directly connected to the content they teach. CTS reflects this shift by helping individuals and groups of teachers focus on the specific science content they teach and gain knowledge about how students interact with the content.

4. **"Job-embedded," "practice-based," and "collegial" forms of professional development are more widely accepted, researched, and practiced.** Teachers can embed CTS into their daily practice and preparation for instruction. Furthermore, CTS is well suited to collegial structures such as study groups, lesson study, and looking at student work. By using CTS up front, teachers will be grounded in a common understanding. Teachers who experience CTS together draw upon the same knowledge base and use common language in their professional conversations about teaching and learning science.

Reading Research

The CTS process involves a substantial amount of reading and analysis, producing an apparent contradiction to the principle of "active learning" in professional development. An NSF *Foundations Series* research monograph examined ways in which a constructivist paradigm can facilitate teachers' learning from and with text material as part of a strategy called "Gathering and Making Sense of Information" (NSF, 2002). The theoretical rationale and empirical support for this strategy supports the CTS process as an effective strategy for both individual learning and learning within a community.

Selected readings from science trade books, standards, and research source materials can be an integral part of constructing a personal understanding of content, standards-based reform, and the use of cognitive research findings. Recent research on reading, in particular, helps us understand how the CTS process can become an active and socially constructed process:

> Reading researchers have argued that reading does not need to occur as an isolated, or even individual activity. First, reading should be purposeful. In other words, teachers should read either to address questions that *they* feel the need to know more about or because their concerns could not be resolved through discussion. Reading can also be a catalyst for other experiences. Indeed, reading can fulfill many functions while teachers inquire into any topic (Siegel, Borasi, & Fonzi, 1998). Readings can provide background information, raise questions for further inquiry about a topic, synthesize different points of view, and offer models for teachers' own practice. Reading is not a passive or straightforward matter of decoding or extracting information from text (e.g., Pearson & Fielding, 1991; Rosenblatt, 1994). Rather, readers construct meaning in interaction with the text, their own background and interests, and their purposes for reading the text. Furthermore, such construction of meaning can be even more productive when it is augmented by interactions with other learners so that different interpretations can be shared and discussed. (NSF, 2002)

> Readings in the CTS guides come from research studies, from the collective wisdom of the hundreds of researchers, scientists, and educators who contributed to national standards, and from science trade books by highly respected scientists. Thus they are automatically grounded in research and accurate science.

Reading and analyzing text in a social context led by a skilled facilitator is preferred, but CTS can also be useful as a stand-alone process for individual teachers, particularly teachers in isolated areas or those constrained by limited release time for workshops. Through CTS, those teachers can still take charge of their own professional development.

Science Teachers and Teaching

Standards and research provide a sound, theoretical foundation and vision for student and teacher learning, but the rubber meets the road in the classroom. What does it take to be effective in this new vision of science teaching? What do teachers need to know and be able to do to be effective?

Content Knowledge

Research studies that examined the relationship between teacher qualifications and background and student achievement in science found high school science teachers with standard certifications in their fields of instruction (usually indicating coursework in both subject matter and education methods) had higher-achieving students than teachers teaching without certification in their subject areas (Darling-Hammond, 2000; Monk, 1994).

> Science content—including an understanding of the central facts, principles, ideas, and important generalizations within a discipline and how they are organized—is at the heart of effective teaching, and thus student learning.

However, the current reality is that many classrooms lack a "highly qualified" teacher. Most preservice education students do not have basic knowledge of science disciplines as they begin their teacher preparation programs (Zembal-Saul, Blumenfeld, & Krajcik, 2000). Unfortunately, many students, especially students in high-poverty and high-minority settings, do not have teachers with a major or minor in their subject matters. Most elementary teachers did not major or minor in science. Even at the secondary level, where teachers are more likely to have majored in science, it is hard for teachers to keep up with recent developments in the biological, space, earth, and physical sciences that have expanded our horizons and influenced the school curriculum. In addition, a secondary teacher with background in one science discipline (e.g., chemistry) is often called upon to teach other sciences (e.g., physics, earth, or life). Furthermore, it is clear that requiring more content courses alone does not necessarily translate into better understanding of the discipline and how to represent it effectively for learners (Zembal-Saul et al., 2000). Ongoing professional development—especially programs that focus on content and how to teach it—coupled with tools like CTS, can close the gap between what teachers know and what they need to know (Loucks-Horsley et al., 2003).

Effective teaching reflects an understanding not only of the content but also the structure of the content—how ideas interconnect and build on one another. For example, to understand how the eye works, students need to understand that "something can be seen when light waves emitted or reflected by it enter the eye," yet they may struggle with the idea of light traveling if they do not already understand the precursor idea that "light travels and can be absorbed, redirected, bounced back or allowed to pass through objects" (AAAS, 2001, p. 65). Teachers who know the content and how the content builds from understanding of many topics are better able to diagnose and address confusions. They know the next best question to ask when students are engaged in inquiry.

CTS is designed to help teachers identify the content they need to understand in order to teach ideas at a level appropriate for their students. Two resources used in CTS for the purpose of improving teachers' content knowledge are *Science for All Americans* (AAAS, 1990) and *Science Matters* (Hazen & Trefil, 1991). The former describes the specific ideas and skills that a scientifically literate adult should have. Science literacy is important for every adult who will encounter science in his or her daily life, including teachers of every subject area and grade level. Reading *Science for All Americans* is also helpful for teachers who already have a background in a science discipline, as it describes how ideas come together in an integrated picture of science. *Science Matters* is a science adult trade book, written by two credible, respected scientists. Often when teachers do not understand a topic they need to teach, they turn to a textbook. But textbook language is stilted and technical.

> Many of the same misconceptions that research has documented for K–12 students can be found in prospective and practicing science teachers.

Trade books such as *Science Matters* explain science in vivid and comprehensible ways. Together, these resources are used in CTS to help teachers (both with and without a content background) to improve their understanding of the ideas and skills in the topics they teach. Teacher content knowledge is also linked to the research base on students' ideas. Providing opportunities for teachers to examine their own conceptions of the content can help teachers change instructional strategies that may unintentionally convey inaccurate ideas about the topics they teach.

Pedagogical Content Knowledge

Teaching for understanding requires more than content knowledge:

> [Teachers] also must be skilled in helping students develop an understanding of the content, meaning that they need to know how students typically think about particular concepts, how to determine what a particular student or group of students thinks about those ideas, and how to help students deepen their understanding. (Weiss, Pasley, Smith, Banilower, & Heck, 2003, p. 28)

These skills constitute a teacher's specialized professional knowledge, called *pedagogical content knowledge* (PCK). PCK is an understanding of what makes the learning of specific topics easy or difficult for learners and knowledge of ways of representing and formulating subject matter to make it comprehensible to learners (Cochran, DeRuiter, & King, 1993; Fernández-Balboa & Stiehl, 1995; Shulman, 1986; Van Driel, Verloop, & DeVos, 1998). Developing this special knowledge of teaching PCK is contingent on a teacher's subject matter knowledge (Clermont, Krajcik, & Borko, 1993). What is the important content, and what should children at the different grade or age levels know with respect to the content? What common misunderstandings do students have with respect to the content? Knowing the answers to these questions sets the course for making important pedagogical choices in the classroom to guide learning. The *NSES* emphasizes the importance of this type of knowledge:

> Effective teaching requires that teachers know what students of certain ages are likely to know, understand, and be able to do; what they will learn quickly; and what will be a struggle. Teachers of science need to anticipate typical misunderstandings and to judge the appropriateness of concepts for the developmental level of their students. In addition, teachers of science must develop understanding of how students with different learning styles, abilities, and interests learn science. Teachers use all of that knowledge to make effective decisions about learning objectives, teaching strategies, assessment tasks, and curriculum materials. (NRC, 1996)

This is where CTS comes in and why it is called the "missing link." It provides the process to help teachers think about how to create meaningful and appropriate learning opportunities for students. Examining the essays in *Benchmarks* and *NSES* and utilizing the research summaries helps teachers identify topic-specific strategies that support student learning in science. These strategies can include use of particular representations, phenomena, and inquiry-based activities that directly challenge students' misconceptions. Such strategies also include knowing how to sequence those experiences in such a way as to scaffold students' developing understanding. In a similar vein, *Atlas* provides a graphic representation for teachers to examine students' growth of understanding as ideas begin in K–2 and become increasingly sophisticated by the end of high school. It also provides a way for teachers to think about the interconnections among and across the various topics they teach.

Beliefs About Teaching and Learning

CTS draws out teachers' knowledge and beliefs about a topic and how students learn it, and it helps them connect new ideas gained through CTS with their previous ideas and beliefs. One way teachers change or reinforce their beliefs is through discourse in a social setting. Having an opportunity to present one's own ideas after studying a topic, as well as hearing and reflecting on the ideas of others, is an empowering experience. This kind of learning is highly personal. Perhaps most important, it can resolve the dissonance between long-held beliefs and new thinking, resulting in changed practice (Mezirow, 1997).

> The benefit of discourse with others, which is encouraged through the CTS process, facilitates meaning making and leads to changes in long-held beliefs.

Cognitive research on how people learn has begun to influence beliefs about teaching and learning. A significant shift seen among science teachers who have used CTS is in how they see their own role as teachers. More and more, the teachers are moving away from seeing teaching as telling to seeing it as facilitating learning. They are moving away from the idea that only some children can learn to embracing the belief that all children can learn challenging content. Driver (1989) noted children's prior knowledge of phenomena is an important part of how they come to understand science. Children often interpret phenomena from a "commonsense" point of view that can lead to misconceptions. Effective teaching involves changing beliefs that knowledge is passed on from the teacher to recognizing that engaging students in rethinking their ideas results in increased learning.

Having a Professional Knowledge Base

A teacher's role as a facilitator of learning of all students is complex and demanding (Loucks-Horsley et al., 2003). It is enhanced when teachers operate from a body of specialized professional knowledge that is based on research on how to teach and how people learn (Stigler & Hiebert, 1999). CTS provides such a professional knowledge base. Teachers who use it can describe or defend their choices of instructional strategies in the context of the research. One notable observation made while working with teachers who have used CTS is hearing how their conversations became more grounded in the research. For example, teachers are frequently heard to say, "According to the research, it is common for students to have trouble with this concept. What can we do differently to help them?" As they engaged in conversations about what is important to teach, they would say, "Let's look at the standards."

With regard to learning, the national standards and research on cognition point to the importance of learning environments that draw upon learners' prior knowledge and help them make connections between what they know and what they are learning. This sometimes involves helping the learner to discard old ideas that no longer work and accept new ones in order to move to deeper understanding of the knowledge base of science teaching. Furthermore, knowledge is socially constructed, requiring learners to interact actively with others and with the ideas and phenomena they are learning (Bransford et al., 2000).

The Teacher Professional Continuum

Learning to teach can be regarded as a continuum of professional experiences (Bransford et al., 2000). And research on professional development is linked to this concept of a professional continuum (see Figure 1.6). This continuum begins with teachers' experiences as they progress through their K–12 education, and it builds to include preservice programs, induction, professional development, and other life and professional activities. Studies show that teachers develop differently and have different attitudes, knowledge, skills, and behaviors at various points during their careers. Characteristics that change include the nature of their concerns about teaching, their instructional behaviors, their understanding of how students learn science, and their perceptions of themselves, their work, and their profession. As teacher characteristics change, their needs change accordingly.

NSF's Teacher Professional Continuum Program, which provided funding for the development of CTS, is designed to provide support for a comprehensive, coherent, and integrated sequence of lifelong learning for teachers (NSF, 2003). In response, CTS advocates personalized support that addresses the unique needs of an individual teacher as well as a learning community and moves them along a path of learning. "Becoming an effective science teacher is a continuous process that stretches from pre-service experiences in undergraduate years to the end of a professional career" (NRC, 1996). CTS is a tool designed to address this continuous learning by helping educators at all career stages evolve in the science teaching profession.

> CTS is designed to be a tool that considers teachers' professional development, inservice, and professional growth opportunities in light of their career stages.

Figure 1.6   The Teacher Professional Continuum Program

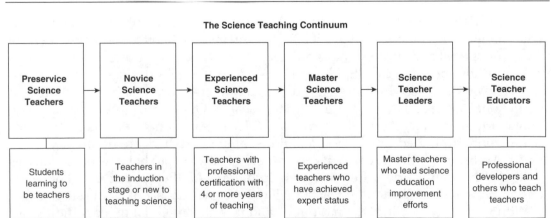

The Science Teaching Continuum

Preservice Science Teachers	Novice Science Teachers	Experienced Science Teachers	Master Science Teachers	Science Teacher Leaders	Science Teacher Educators
Students learning to be teachers	Teachers in the induction stage or new to teaching science	Teachers with professional certification with 4 or more years of teaching	Experienced teachers who have achieved expert status	Master teachers who lead science education improvement efforts	Professional developers and others who teach teachers

2

Examining the Components of a Curriculum Topic Study Guide

THE CTS STUDY GUIDE

At the core of the Curriculum Topic Study process is the CTS guide. Figure 2.1 shows an example of a CTS guide on the topic of "Cells." There are currently 147 CTS guides in Chapter 6, representing a full range of specific to broad content- and skill-based science topics across the disciplines of science. Teachers select, examine, study, and reflect on these prescreened readings to improve their understanding of teaching and learning related to the topic. Teachers may choose any of the sections or all of them, depending on their purpose. Teachers who have used the standards and research remark how easily and quickly they can find readings

> Each CTS guide identifies a particular topic in science and links six purposeful outcomes to selected readings from the nationally available source materials.

relevant to the topics they teach when they use the study guides. CTS guides do the time-consuming work of searching for the right information for busy teachers!

Sections and Outcomes

Each CTS guide uses a standard template divided into two corresponding parts. The left-hand side, labeled "Section and Outcome," contains the Roman-numeral-numbered Sections I–VI and is titled with the user outcome for that section. The following describes each of the sections and their outcomes:

19

Figure 2.1   Example of a CTS Study Guide

Standards and Research-Based Study of a Curricular Topic

CELLS

Section and Outcome	Selected Sources and Readings for Study and Reflection Read and examine *related parts* of:
I. Identify Adult Content Knowledge	**IA:** *Science for All Americans* ▸ Chapter 5, *Cells,* pages 62–64 **IB:** *Science Matters: Achieving Scientific Literacy* ▸ Chapter 15, *The Ladder of Life,* pages 206–219
II. Consider Instructional Implications	**IIA:** *Benchmarks for Science Literacy* ▸ 5C, *Cells,* general essay, page 110; grade span essays, pages 111–113 **IIB:** *National Science Education Standards* ▸ Grades K–4, Standard C, essay, pages 127–128 ▸ Grades 5–8, Standard C, essay, pages 155–156 ▸ Grades 9–12, Standard C, essay, pages 181, 184
III. Identify Concepts and Specific Ideas	**IIIA:** *Benchmarks for Science Literacy* ▸ 5C, *Cells,* pages 111–114 **IIIB:** *National Science Education Standards* ▸ Grades K–4, Standard C, *The Characteristics of Organisms,* page 129 ▸ Grades 5–8, Standard C, *Structure and Function in Living Systems,* pages 156–157 ▸ Grades 9–12, Standard C, *The Cell,* pages 184–185; *The Molecular Basis of Heredity,* page 185; *Matter, Energy, and Organization in Living Systems,* page 186
IV. Examine Research on Student Learning	**IVA:** *Benchmarks for Science Literacy* ▸ 5C, *Cells,* page 342 **IVB:** *Making Sense of Secondary Science: Research Into Children's Ideas* ▸ Chapter 1, *Cell Theory,* page 25
V. Examine Coherency and Articulation	**V:** *Atlas of Science Literacy* ▸ *Cell Functions,* pages 72–73 ▸ *Cells and Organs,* pages 74–75
VI. Clarify State Standards and District Curriculum	**VIA:** *State Standards:* Link Sections I–V to learning goals and information from your state standards or frameworks that are informed by the results of the topic study. **VIB:** *District Curriculum Guide:* Link Sections I–V to learning goals and information from your district curriculum guide that are informed by the results of the topic study.
Visit www.curriculumtopicstudy.org for updates or supplementary readings, Web sites, and videos.	

• **Section I. Identify Adult Content Knowledge:** This section helps users identify what all adults (including teachers) should know and be able to do to be considered literate in science. It also provides explanations of science ideas encountered in the media, public issues, and other popular science venues.

• **Section II. Consider Instructional Implications:** This section helps users identify important considerations for K–12 or grade span instruction, provides a broad overview of the big ideas, concepts, and skills for K–12 students related to the topic, and suggests effective instructional strategies and contexts.

- **Section III. Identify Concepts and Specific Ideas:** This section helps users identify the concepts, specific ideas, level of sophistication, and appropriate terminology related to a topic at different grade levels.

- **Section IV. Examine Research on Student Learning:** This section identifies relevant research so that users can examine developmental considerations, possible misconceptions and their sources, intuitive ideas and lines of reasoning, and difficulties encountered by students in understanding the specific ideas within the topic.

- **Section V. Examine Coherency and Articulation:** This section helps users examine the K–12 conceptual growth in understanding as a coherent flow of ideas builds in sophistication over time. Studying the K–12 growth of understanding will help users identify important prerequisites for learning and examine connections between ideas within and across topics that can promote student understanding.

- **Section VI. Clarify State Standards and District Curriculum:** This section helps the user clarify the meaning and intent of their state standards or learning goals in their district curriculum by linking the information in the previous five sections to the local context in which the user works. It also helps the user identify important ideas in science that may be missing at the state or local level but should be addressed along with their standards.

Selected Readings

The right-hand side of a CTS guide, titled "Selected Sources and Readings for Study and Reflection," lists readings from the CTS set of resources for study and reflection. Each section provides relevant selections from two choices of source material. Users may choose to read both choices of source material or focus on only one. For example, in Sections II and III, the user may decide to use only the *National Science Education Standards (NSES)* (National Research Council, 1996) instead of *Benchmarks for Science Literacy (Benchmarks)* (American Association for the Advancement of Science [AAAS], 1993), or vice versa. Figure 2.2 shows the links between the outcomes and the source material for reading, study, and reflection.

CTS Supplementary Material

A searchable database on the Web site allows the CTS user to search by topic for videos, journal articles, books, CD-ROMs, and Internet sites that supplement sections of a CTS guide. For example, if a user searches the database for supplements to the *Photosynthesis and Respiration* study guide, they will be shown a chapter from Isaac Asimov's classic book, *Photosynthesis*, titled "The Great Cycle," which can be used with Section I to improve adult understanding of the link between photosynthesis and respiration. They would also find a video from the Harvard Smithsonian's Private Universe Project that reveals students' misconceptions about the transformation of matter resulting from photosynthesis, which can be used to supplement Section IV.

> At the bottom of each study guide is a link to the CTS Web site, www.curriculumtopicstudy.org, where users can find optional readings and media resources to supplement individual CTS guides.

Figure 2.2 Links Between Outcomes and Source Material

If your outcome for studying a topic is to:	Then you would read the related parts of:
I. Identify adult content knowledge	*Science for All Americans* and/or *Science Matters*
II. Identify instructional implications	*Benchmarks for Science Literacy* essays and/or *National Science Education Standards* content standard essays and vignettes
III. Identify concepts and specific ideas	*Benchmarks for Science Literacy* bulleted learning goals and/or *National Science Education Standards* bulleted learning goals
IV. Examine research on student learning	*Benchmarks for Science Literacy* Chapter 15 research summaries and/or *Making Sense of Secondary Science* research summaries
V. Examine coherency and articulation	*Atlas of Science Literacy* strand maps and narratives
VI. Clarify state standards and district curriculum	Your state standards or frameworks document and/or Your district curriculum guide or the guide to your curriculum materials

COMMON RESOURCES FOR STUDY AND REFLECTION

A special feature of the CTS approach is that it uses a common collection of nationally available source materials, including several that are considered essential "tools of the science teaching profession."

All professionals—lawyers, doctors, mechanics, accountants—have their own career-specific reference tools that inform their practice. Science educators need their unique professional libraries as well. The set of books used for CTS can be considered science teachers' "tools of the trade." The six source materials for CTS, listed in Figure 2.3, make up the "suite of tools" commonly used by the science education community.

Building a Professional Collection: Experts at Your Fingertips!

The source materials used in CTS have been available to science educators for several years. In a perfect world, every science teacher would be provided with

Figure 2.3   CTS Source Material

Bibliography of Source Materials for Science Curriculum Topic Study

American Association for the Advancement of Science. (1990). *Science for all Americans.* New York: Oxford University Press.

American Association for the Advancement of Science. (1994). *Benchmarks for science literacy.* New York: Oxford University Press.

American Association for the Advancement of Science. (2001). *Atlas of science literacy.* Washington DC: AAAS. (Copublished with NSTA Press, Arlington, VA)

National Research Council. (1996). *National science education standards.* Washington DC: National Academy Press.

Driver, R., Squires, A., Rushworth, P., & Wood-Robinson, V. (1994). *Making sense of secondary science: Research into children's ideas.* New York: Routledge Press.

Hazen, R. & Trefil, J. (1991). *Science matters: Achieving scientific literacy.* New York: Anchor Books.

---

a set of national standards and the other common resources used in CTS. Yet in our experience, many teachers do not even know about some of these materials (often, it is only this lack of awareness that prevents teachers from owning their own copies). National programs like the National Science Teacher Association's (NSTA) Building a Presence have made considerable effort to place copies of the national standards in the schools. Preservice teachers are often required to purchase some of these books for their courses. For teachers who do not own their own copies and may not have funds available, several of these materials are available online (see Resource A).

Teachers and school districts that have used CTS usually purchase selected resources or the full set, realizing how important it is for CTS to be used regularly in their schools or by individuals. CTS gets the standards and research documents into the hands of teachers and into schools, where they are deliberately and routinely used. The advantage of the CTS design is that teachers can select only those resources they need, based on their purpose and availability of the source materials.

> Many teachers and schools have the national standards, but they "sit on the shelf" because they have never had a process for using them.

A good justification for having the resources used in CTS is that you will have experts at your fingertips at all times! Teachers who have used CTS refer to the use of the tools as "standing on the shoulders of giants." Because the standards and resources such as *Atlas of Science Literacy (Atlas)* (AAAS, 2001) were developed through peer review, discussion, and consensus by leading science educators from K–12 schools, universities, science organizations, and governmental agencies, they reflect the best thinking available about what is important to learn in science and how and when to effectively teach it. The research summaries have been conducted by some of the

> Imagine being able to vicariously turn to advice from leading experts whenever you need it! That is what CTS does: It provides users with an external perspective derived from some of the best thinking in the science education world.

world's leading science education researchers, who have dedicated their work to understanding how students learn. *Science for All Americans (SFAA)* (AAAS, 1990) and *Science Matters: Achieving Scientific Literacy (Science Matters)* (Hazen & Trefil, 1991) are both authored by highly respected scientists devoted to promoting science literacy for all. CTS shifts the burden from relying solely on our own intuition and experience to providing sound recommendations and information that users can combine with the wisdom of their own practice. Teachers we have worked with remark, "Now that I have these resources and the CTS to use them, I can't imagine being a science teacher without them!"

Descriptions of the Common Resources Used in CTS

Some of these resources, such as the *NSES,* are more familiar to teachers than others. *Atlas* and several of the optional supplements on the Web site have been published more recently. Resources used in CTS are available through the NSTA bookstore (see Resource A) or major booksellers like Amazon.com or Barnes and Noble. You can check the CTS Web site at www. curriculumtopicstudy.org for links to some of the books or suggestions for ordering them. The following is a description of the collection of resources used in the CTS guides and the corresponding section(s) in which they are used:

> A key feature of CTS is its flexibility: You can use as many or as few of the resources as your purpose and access demands.

IA: *Science for All Americans*

SFAA, authored by James Rutherford and Andrew Ahlgren for the AAAS, was first published in 1989. It represents the first phase of AAAS's science reform initiative, Project 2061. *SFAA* is a seminal document that defines the enduring, interconnected knowledge *all adults* should have acquired after their K–12 education to ensure basic science literacy. Science literacy as described in *SFAA* includes science, mathematics, technology, and social sciences and the interconnections among them. It reflects the belief that:

> The scientifically literate person is one who is aware that science, mathematics, and technology are interdependent human enterprises with strengths and limitations; understands key concepts and principles of science; is familiar with the natural world and recognizes both its diversity and unity; and uses scientific knowledge and scientific ways of thinking for individual and social purposes. (AAAS, 1990, p. 4)

SFAA softens the boundaries between traditional content domains and emphasizes the big ideas and connectedness of science topics, which come together to form a complete picture of science literacy. The scientific terminology used in *SFAA* is the terminology all adults are expected to be familiar with to understand science, mathematics, and technology in their everyday lives.

Teachers who have used *SFAA* praise its eloquent and easy-to-read prose. Teachers who have never used it before quickly embrace it and have commented that it is a book you can open up and start reading anywhere, for pleasure as well as professional use.

IB: Science Matters: Achieving Scientific Literacy

Science Matters, authored by two scientists, Robert Hazen and James Trefil, in 1991, describes the knowledge needed to be an informed, decision-making citizen around issues related to science in the public arena. It differs from *SFAA* because it does not describe the knowledge that culminates from a K–12 education. Some of the concepts described in *Science Matters* exceed basic literacy and come from postsecondary education and life experience. The authors describe the knowledge adults should have as "a grasp of an eclectic mix of facts, vocabulary, and principles. It is not the specialized knowledge of the experts, nor does it rely on jargon and complex mathematics" (Hazen & Trefil, 1991, p. 44). The descriptions are interesting and comprehensible to those who have limited or no science backgrounds. It avoids the stilted, fragmented descriptions typical in textbooks, where novice teachers often get their information. Several teachers have commented that *Science Matters* is so easy to understand that they use some of the same descriptions and interesting examples with their middle and high school students, instead of the textbook descriptions.

IIA, IIIA, IVA: Benchmarks for Science Literacy

Benchmarks followed *SFAA* in 1993 and corresponds to the sections in *SFAA*. It describes the specific steps along the way to achieving the literacy described in *SFAA* by listing specific goals for student learning at K–2, 3–5, 6–8, and 9–12. These benchmarks are specific ideas and skills that all students should learn at different grade levels. *Benchmarks* was based on the work of six different school district teams, with input from hundreds of educators, scientists, university faculty, and science education specialists. They represent our first coherent set of "standards." Since *Benchmarks* was published, many schools have used it to design their curricula and course syllabi, and it has informed the early development of state standards and frameworks. Each section begins with a general essay, which gives a broad overview of the ideas students should learn and types of instructional opportunities and contexts that would effectively impact learning. Furthermore, each grade-level list of benchmarks is accompanied by essays, which discuss difficulties students might face as well as suggestions for instruction at that specific grade level. Chapter 15 in *Benchmarks* contains summaries of research linked to each section in *Benchmarks*.

In our experience, teachers have found *Benchmarks* to be an invaluable resource because of the specificity and clarity of the goals for learning it describes. Until using CTS, many teachers weren't even aware of the research summaries in *Benchmarks*; now they use them on a regular basis. See Chapter 7 for additional resources developed by Project 2061 that complement *Benchmarks* and *SFAA*.

IIB and IIIB: The National Science Education Standards

The *NSES,* released in 1996, is similar to *Benchmarks* in presenting a vision of science literacy for all students. *Benchmarks* was used extensively to develop the *NSES* content standards, which were developed through the leadership of the National Research Council. The *NSES* includes six systemic categories of standards for science education; of these, only the content standards are used in

CTS. The *NSES* divides grade spans by K–4, 5–8, and 9–12 and includes some of the traditional domains, such as physical, life, and earth and space science. Each content standard has a descriptive essay that describes student learning, experiences, inquiry connections, and potential misconceptions. There are several vignettes that help illuminate the topics.

IVB: Making Sense of Secondary Science: Research Into Children's Ideas

Making Sense of Secondary Science, by Rosalind Driver, Ann Squires, Peter Rushworth, and Valerie Wood-Robinson, is a comprehensive summary of research into students' ideas in life and physical sciences, with some earth and space science. The summaries, which were first published in 1994 by Driver's research group at the University of Leeds, in England, followed the release of *Benchmarks* and extended the research findings in *Benchmarks'* Chapter 15. References to the original studies are provided. The book is arranged by topics and corresponds to the topics in the CTS guides. Driver's book is a useful resource that helps science teachers deepen their understanding of how students think about major ideas in science and how these ideas affect their learning. Driver explains,

> In planning teaching it is useful for teachers to think in terms of helping pupils to make a number of "small steps" towards the big ideas. The sequencing of these "small steps" can be informed by what is known about the progression of children's understanding. However, it is important to bear in mind that some of these "small steps" may, in themselves, present learners with difficulty. (Driver et al., 1994, p. 13)

Teachers who are aware of the importance of identifying students' potential misconceptions as a way to bridge students' ideas with correct scientific ones have found this book to be one of the most powerful resources in the CTS collection. In our work with schools, this previously unfamiliar book has become a widely used resource when combined with CTS.

V: Atlas of Science Literacy

Atlas was published in 2000, as a joint publication of AAAS and the NSTA. *Atlas* is a collection of conceptual strand maps, based on *Benchmarks* and *SFAA,* which show how students' ideas progress from K–12. The maps graphically depict connections among the ideas in *Benchmarks.* For any particular topic, a map reveals the important connections to other topics and the conceptual strands or "storylines" that are part of that topic. For any individual benchmark idea, the maps show both the prerequisites to that idea and the later ideas that build on it. The maps can be very helpful in pointing out the intended level of sophistication of a benchmark. Seeing a benchmark idea as part of a K–12 strand helps educators clarify its intended meaning and get a sense of what it is trying to achieve.

The *Atlas* maps referenced in the CTS guides cover only half of the ideas and skills in *Benchmarks* and *SFAA.* For this reason, there are some topics that do not have an associated map in Section V. A second volume of *Atlas* is currently in development. The CTS Web site, at www.curriculumtopicstudy.org, will provide updated links to Section V of the CTS guides when the next version of *Atlas* becomes available.

VI: State Standards or District Curriculum Guides

These are your own individual state standards or frameworks as well as your K–12 scope and sequence guides or curriculum program manuals and teacher guides. Because we recognize the importance of being able to link back to your local or state context and align your findings from CTS with local and state accountability factors, educators in each state and across districts combine the CTS common resources with ones that are unique to their states, districts, or school settings.

3

Engaging in Curriculum Topic Study

GETTING STARTED

While the CTS guides are at the heart of the CTS approach, the process for using the guides is also important. How do you get started using CTS? Educators who are familiar with the CTS resources and process can go directly to Chapter 6, select a CTS guide, and get started with minimal direction. If you are new to CTS, we suggest starting with a few introductory steps to become acquainted with the materials and the process.

Gathering Your Resources

Figure 3.1 lists the complete set of common resources used in CTS. Your access to the resources will determine which CTS purposes and outcomes you can focus on. If you do not have your own personal copies of these resources, check with your colleagues, science department, or school or district professional library to see whether you can borrow them. In our work with new users of CTS, they have been surprised to find that several of these resources, *Benchmarks for Science Literacy (Benchmarks)* (American Association for the Advancement of Science [AAAS], 1993) and *National Science Education Standards (NSES)* (National Research Council, 1996) in particular are "gathering dust" somewhere on shelves in their schools or districts.

Figure 3.1   Materials Used With CTS

Bibliography and URL's of
Source Materials for Science Curriculum Topic Study

American Association for the Advancement of Science. (1990). *Science for all Americans.* New York: Oxford University Press. Available at www.project2061.org

American Association for the Advancement of Science. (1994). *Benchmarks for science literacy.* New York: Oxford University Press. Available at www.project2061.org

American Association for the Advancement of Science. (2001). *Atlas of science literacy.* Washington DC: NSTA Press.

National Research Council. (1996). *National science education standards.* Washington DC: National Academy Press. Available at www.nap.edu

Driver, R., Squires, A., Rushworth, P., & Wood-Robinson, V. (1994). *Making sense of secondary science: Research into children's ideas.* New York: Routledge Press.

Hazen, R., & Trefil, J. (1991). *Science matters: Achieving scientific literacy.* New York: Anchor Books.

These national standards are available online, along with *Science for All Americans* (AAAS, 1990) and selected strand maps from *Atlas of Science Literacy* (AAAS, 2001). In many schools we have worked with, administrators have recognized the power of these tools and purchased sets for their schools, committees, and even individual teachers. These resources comprise one of the best professional development investments in science teaching and learning a school administrator or educator can make.

> To get the most out of the CTS process, it is critical that you have at least one of the resources used in Sections II and III of the CTS study guides: *Benchmarks for Science Literacy* or *National Science Education Standards*

If you are using CTS in a group setting, it is not necessary for each individual to have copies of all the books. Furthermore, depending on the group's or facilitator's preference, you can choose to provide either *Benchmarks* or *NSES,* or both. If you are using *Benchmarks,* we strongly recommend that you also use *Science for All Americans.* We recommend the following set of shared books for every group of five teachers:

- One copy of *Science for All Americans* and/or one copy of *Science Matters* (Hazen & Trefil, 1991)
- Two copies of *Benchmarks* and/or two copies of *NSES*
- One copy of *Making Sense of Secondary Science* (Driver, Squires, Rushworth, & Wood-Robinson, 1994)
- One copy of *Atlas of Science Literacy*
- One or more copies of your state standards or frameworks and/or local district curriculum guide

In addition to gathering the resources you have available, a few basic materials are helpful: Post-It Notes for inserting page markers or making notes, highlighters for marking handouts, paper and pen for recording your notes, and chart paper and markers for recording group ideas. If you are doing CTS as a group, prepare copies of the CTS guide and any necessary worksheet templates for the participants in your group (see Resource B). You might want to have at least one computer to transcribe ideas. If you have a computer connected to the Internet, you can download the worksheet templates contained in Resource B from the CTS Web site at www.curriculum-topicstudy.org, so that you can directly enter CTS results in an expanding Word document. Access to the Web site allows you to copy and paste information from the online resources, saving the time and effort of rewriting important information.

Experienced CTS users may wish to include additional supplementary material. For example, you might include a recent journal article about student learning to supplement Section IV or an Annenberg video showing instruction targeted at a specific idea for Section II. Some supplementary materials are listed on the CTS Web site.

Becoming Familiar With the CTS Guides and Resources

This book provides all the materials you need to familiarize yourself with CTS. Read Chapter 2 to become familiar with the features of a CTS guide and to get a sense for the content, origins, and uses of each of the resources. Then select a CTS guide from Chapter 6 and examine how the resources are linked to the outcomes. Open one of your resources and try locating the identified section for reading listed on the CTS guide. Choose a vignette from Chapter 5 to get a sense of how the CTS process links to the work of science educators.

> If you are new to CTS, we recommend you become familiar with the CTS guide and resources before you begin a topic study.

Read the Chapter 2 summaries of the resources to become familiar with or refresh your knowledge of their origins and use. Spend some time examining each of the resources to see how they are arranged. Read the introductions or prefaces in each book to learn more about their underlying philosophies or purposes and how their contents are arranged. If you are new to *Science for All Americans, Benchmarks,* and *NSES,* we recommend using Richard Audet and Linda Jordan's book, *Standards in the Classroom: An Implementation Guide for Teachers of Science and Mathematics* (2003), to become better acquainted with these national standards resources. The book contains "Discovery Guides" that introduce the features of the CTS resources. Figure 3.2 shows an example of a Discovery Guide for *Science for All Americans* (p. 19).

Defining Your Purpose and Choosing Your Outcomes

At this point, you are ready to start the study of a curriculum topic. What is your purpose for doing a CTS? There are two general purposes: (1) to learn how to use the process or (2) to apply findings from CTS to a particular aspect of your work as a science educator. Applications of CTS are listed in Figure 3.3. Examples are described in more detail in Chapter 4 and illuminated in the Chapter 5 vignettes.

Once you have chosen a curriculum topic that is relevant to your work, you should decide on your purpose or desired outcome. What do you want to learn? The specific outcomes are listed by section in the left column of the CTS guide. The selected readings on the right column of the guide are matched to the outcomes. Do you want to improve your content knowledge of the topic? Gain a better understanding of effective, topic-specific instructional strategies? Gain a K–12 "big

Figure 3.2   Science Discovery Guide: *Science for All Americans*

19	Chapter 2: Exploration

EXPLORATION 2.3   Science Discovery Guide: *Science for All Americans*

These are sources of information that you need to complete the Discovery Guide. You should complete each of the discovery tasks and identify the page(s) where you located the information.	• American Association for the Advancement of Science. (1990). *Science for all Americans.* New York: Oxford University Press. • www.project2061.org

PAGE(S)	1. What national organization spearheaded the preparation of this document? Who participated in writing it? When was it published?
PAGE(S)	2. Why do you think that the particular title, *Science for All Americans,* was chosen for this book?
PAGE(S)	3. When *SFAA* uses the expression "science literacy," what is the intended meaning?
PAGE(S)	4. Each chapter of SFAA is built around a set of Recommendations. Select a single idea from a chapter that relates directly to what you teach. Summarize the major points in the section. Do you agree with what SFAA recommends all high school graduates should know about this concept? Explain.
PAGE(S)	5. Find the chapter titled Common Themes. Describe the four big ideas that pervade all of science, mathematics, and technology.
PAGE(S)	6. Which of the Principles of Learning do you regard as the most important? Why?
PAGE(S)	7. What are the major differences between the type of teaching and learning suggested in this document and what you typically see and use in your school?
PAGE(S)	8. What chapters in *SFAA* would be of special interest to a person with an interest in the history of science, mathematics, and technology?

SOURCE: Reprinted with permission from Audet, R., & Jordan, L. (2003). *Standards in the classroom: An implementation guide for teachers of science and mathematics.* Thousand Oaks, CA: Corwin Press.

Figure 3.3 Examples of the Variety of CTS Applications

Examples of CTS Applications

- Learning new content or refreshing an existing knowledge base
- Choosing content to design course syllabi
- Translating university course content into appropriate K–12 experiences
- Developing or reviewing a K–12 curriculum scope and sequence
- Making relevant interdisciplinary connections
- Analyzing curriculum materials
- Implementing new curricula
- Developing instructional materials
- Examining or choosing instructional strategies
- Deepening understanding of inquiry and technological skills and understandings of inquiry, the nature of science, and technology
- Clarifying learning goals
- Structuring knowledge in a topic
- Developing formative and summative assessments
- Analyzing assessment tasks and student work
- Designing content-specific professional development
- Mentoring new teachers
- Designing preservice courses and practicums
- Reviewing and revising state or district standards

---

picture" of the topic? Understand the meaning and intent of the learning goals that make up the topic? Identify students' misconceptions associated with the topic? Look for connections among ideas in a topic? You might choose one, several, or all of the outcomes. The outcomes you choose will determine the resources you will need and the sections you will read.

It is also important to keep the grade or grade span relevant to your work in mind. If your overall purpose demands a K–12 perspective, then you should read all of the grade-level sections. If your overall purpose is focused on a specific grade, you might read only the sections that include that grade. Or if you are an elementary school teacher, you might focus on the K–6 sections.

> However, examining the specific ideas and skills that come before and after the grade or grade span you are studying can provide valuable insights and give you a more coherent picture of how learning builds over time.

PROCESSING INFORMATION FROM CTS SECTIONS

If you are doing a CTS for the first time or you are studying an unfamiliar topic, we recommend doing a full study of all six sections. It is not necessary to have all of the resources to begin with, but for the purpose of explaining the outcomes, we will assume that all of the books are available to you. Begin by recording your initial ideas about the topic, based on your grade or grade span focus.

Activation and Processing Strategies

Figure 3.4 lists examples of important ideas to record before you begin CTS. Establishing your baseline knowledge about the topic is a critical part of engaging in a topic study. It provides focus for your study and a record of initial understandings and beliefs for an individual or group to reflect back. It provides an opportunity to activate thinking about the topic, so that during the readings, you can connect new ideas with old and resolve the dissonance between long-held beliefs and new information.

Figure 3.4   Questions for Recording Initial Beliefs and Understandings of the Topic

Activating Prior Knowledge of a Topic
1. What important ideas or skills make up this topic?
2. What is important for students to know or be able to do?
3. What learning opportunities or teaching strategies are effective with this topic?
4. What difficulties or misconceptions are associated with this topic?
5. What relevant connections can be made within science or in other disciplines?

Another method to use individually or as a group to activate prior knowledge of a topic, focus the study, and reflect on results, is the "K-W-L strategy" (see Figure 3.5). Using a sheet of paper with three columns, or chart paper for group recording, brainstorm a list of what is already known about the topic under "K." Generate questions about things you want to learn about the topic under "W." Use these questions to guide your investigation of the topic as you study the readings. After you complete the study, compare the "K" column with results from the study, and record new ideas under the "L." It is also useful after completing the CTS to examine the "K" list and decide whether there is anything you would change based on your results. For example, you may have found that ideas that were listed as important ideas for students to learn actually exceed the recommended developmental level of the students you work with. After completing the study, you might realize that the ideas you listed are more appropriate at a later grade level. The K-W-L method can also be used with each individual section.

Additional strategies suggested by users for activating prior knowledge, focusing reading, extracting meaning, and reflecting on results will be added to the CTS Web site. The third book in this series (to be published in 2006) will include a discussion of strategies for facilitators to use in group professional development, preservice education, and committee work.

Figure 3.5 K-W-L Strategy

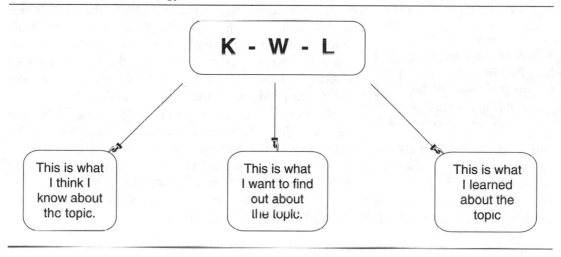

Reading the CTS Sections

CTS is meant to be a flexible process. You should not feel that you have to use *all* the resources. You can begin your study with any section—it is not necessary to go through in a linear fashion starting with Section I. Depending on your preference, time, or the availability of resources, the two resources listed for each section can be used together, or you can focus on only one.

Note a critical point listed at the top of the right-hand column of readings on the CTS study guide (see Figure 3.6).

Figure 3.6 An Important Consideration While Reading Selected Parts

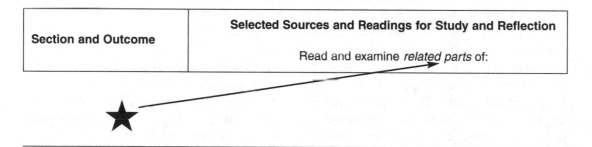

Section and Outcome	Selected Sources and Readings for Study and Reflection
	Read and examine *related parts* of:

We narrowed the selected readings to the pages with relevant information, but there will still likely be some information outside of the topic. For example, in reading the *NSES* essay in Standard B, Physical Science, for the "Properties of Matter" topic, information on force and motion appears on the same page. Although it is part of the Physical Science Standard B, it is not directly relevant to "Properties of Matter." In Section III, pay attention to the learning goals that relate directly to the topic, even though there are others in the section. As you read, continuously scan for and extract the information that is relevant to the topic. Sometimes the relevant information may be only a paragraph or a single sentence. Use the filter of the "topic" as you read.

> As you read the parts identified for each section, be aware that not *everything* you read will be applicable to the topic.

As you become experienced in using CTS, you will be able to identify information that was not in the reading, but which contributes to an understanding of the topic (*Atlas* is very helpful in linking other ideas that may not be included in CTS Sections I–III). The selection of readings in a CTS guide is not meant to imply that they are all-inclusive, but rather that they are central to the topic. When in doubt, use your best judgment to decide whether additional material is related to the topic.

Guiding Questions for Individual Sections of a CTS Guide

As you are becoming familiar with the resources and process of CTS, we suggest you use guiding questions to help focus on connecting the outcome of the reading with the parts relevant to the topic. The chart in Figure 3.7 provides suggestions for general and resource-specific questions to guide reading, study, and analysis. Select the questions that are most relevant to your purpose and the resources you have available. Feel free to develop and add your own questions to this list.

THE CTS LEARNING CYCLE OF INQUIRY, STUDY, AND REFLECTION

In the early 1960s, J. Myron Atkin and Robert Karplus proposed an instructional model for elementary science curricula, based on cognitive science, called the "learning cycle." The original model has undergone several adaptations, including the BSCS 5E model (Bybee, 1997), but the general interpretation and use remain the same. The learning cycle model is designed to bridge prior ideas to the construction and use of new ideas. It provides a structure for a teacher to organize and facilitate learning by determining students' prior knowledge and facilitating a learning path for them to explore new ideas, construct new understandings, discard ideas that are no longer useful, and apply their learning in a meaningful context. This approach to instructional design for students applies to adult learners as well. For adults who engage in CTS, the learning cycle supports a learning environment that is aligned with ideas about changing personal beliefs of teaching and learning.

> CTS is, in essence, an inquiry-based investigation. The topic is the object of the investigation.

What are the essential target learning goals related to a topic? What concepts and ideas are developmentally appropriate? What are the common misconceptions students have? How does the topic connect to other science topics? How do the standards identified by the state or local district match findings from national standards and research? These are questions that CTS can answer. Because CTS is an investigation, it is appropriate to approach it through a research-validated

Figure 3.7   Guiding Questions

Section I: Identify Adult Content Knowledge	
General Questions to Use With Both Resources (IA and IB):	
1. What "big ideas" and major concepts make up this topic? 2. What new content did you learn or improve your understanding of? 3. What examples or contexts were used to explain the ideas? 4. What other new insights about the topic did you gain from this reading?	
Additional Questions to Use With IA: *Science for All Americans* 1. What enduring understandings should all adults, including teachers, know about this topic? 2. What rich interconnections within the topic emerge from the reading? 3. How does the reading help you see what a K–12 education is aiming toward? 4. What technical terminology used in the reading implies the vocabulary all adults should be familiar with?	Additional Questions to Use With IB: *Science Matters* 1. How does the reading clarify the content of the topic? What additional content knowledge did you gain from this reading? 2. How does the reading help you identify the basic ideas underlying the science topic? 3. Are there explanations or vivid examples you can use with students to explain concepts in an interesting, comprehensible, way? 4. Did you find anything that clarifies current science topics in the media or public issues?
Section II: Consider Instructional Implications	
General Questions to Use with Both Resources (IIA and IIB):	
1. What suggestions are provided for effective instruction of the topic? 2. What student learning difficulties, misconceptions, or developmental considerations are mentioned? 3. Does the reading suggest contexts, phenomena, representations, or everyday experiences that are effective in learning the ideas in the topic? 4. What other new insights about the topic did you gain by reading this section?	
Additional Questions to Use With IIA: *Benchmarks for Science Literacy* 1. How does the general essay help you gain a K–12 "big picture view" of the topic? 2. How do the grade-level essays illustrate an increasing sophistication in the content and ways concepts and skills in the topic are taught?	Questions to Use With IIB: *National Science Education Standards* 1. How do the essays and vignettes illustrate the central role inquiry plays in learning the ideas in the topic? 2. What linkages do you find among student learning, teaching, and classroom contexts? 3. How do the grade-level essays compare in sophistication of ideas and contexts for learning?

(Continued)

Figure 3.7 (Continued)

Section III: Identify Concepts and Specific Ideas

General Questions to Use With Both Resources (IIIA and IIIB):

1. Which learning goals align well with the topic?
2. What concepts, specific ideas, or skills make up the learning goals in this topic?
3. How do these goals help you clarify what is important to teach in the topic?
4. How do these goals help you determine what you can eliminate or place less emphasis on?
5. How does the level of sophistication in the learning goals change from one grade span to the next?
6. How do the ideas in the *Benchmarks* compare to the ideas in the *NSES?*
7. How are the *Benchmarks* useful in breaking down the K–4 grade span in the *NSES?*
8. What other new insights in this topic did you gain from reading this section?

Additional Questions to Use With IIIA: *Benchmarks for Science Literacy*	Additional Questions to Use With IIIB: *National Science Education Standards*
1. What is the grain size of the benchmark? Can the benchmark be broken up into smaller ideas? 2. How does the language in the learning goal help you decide what technical terminology in the topic is important?	1. What facts, concepts, principles, or theories are embedded in the standards? 2. How do the organizers used in the standards help you think about how to organize ideas in a topic?

Section IV: Examine Research on Student Learning

General Questions to Use With Both Resources (IVA and IVB):

1. What specific misconceptions or alternative ideas might a student have about this topic?
2. Are there suggestions as to what might contribute to students' misconceptions or difficulties?
3. Which ideas seem to be most resistant to change?
4. Is there an age or grade when students are more likely to learn certain ideas in the topic?
5. How does the research draw attention to important prerequisites?
6. If there is scant research on the topic, can you think about a concept or idea related to the topic you might like to research with your own students?
7. What other new insights about the topic did you gain by reading this section?

Additional Questions to Use With IVA: *Benchmarks for Science Literacy*	Additional Questions to Use With IVB: *Making Sense of Secondary Science*
*Note: It is suggested that CTS users first read "The Role of Research," on pages 327–329, to understand the use of the research base. 1. How can the research be used to clarify the benchmark ideas?	1. Are there examples of questions or tasks that could be used to find out what students know about the topic? 2. Are there suggestions for helping students avoid or overcome misconceptions? 3. Is there a framework or set of rules students use to reason about ideas in the topic?

(Continued)

Figure 3.7 (Continued)

Section V: Examine Coherency and Articulation

Questions to Use With the *Atlas of Science Literacy* (V)

1. How does a map help you trace a concept or skill from its simple beginning to a culminating, interconnected, sophisticated idea?

2. What connections can you identify among concepts or skills in the topic?

3. What connections can you identify to different content areas within and outside of science?

4. What prerequisite ideas can you identify for learning the topic at your grade level?

6. How do the "storylines" or conceptual strands in a map help you think about the way to coherently organize the concepts and skills in a topic?

7. How do the map and its narrative section improve your overall understanding of the topic?

8. How do the skill benchmarks relate to the knowledge benchmarks?

9. What other new insights about the topic did you gain by examining the map?

Section VI: Clarify State Standards and District Curriculum

Questions to Use With Both Resources (VIA and VIB)

1. Which suggestions from Sections II–V align well with your state or district standards or frameworks? Where do you see gaps that need to be addressed?

2. How does the addition of cognitive performance verbs affect the learning of the ideas in the topic? Are the verbs in your state or district standards appropriate for the nature of the content and research-identified difficulty of the ideas in the topic?

3. How can the research findings inform the placement of your state or district standards? Are they appropriately placed, or are there some that may need to be reconsidered?

4. How do the readings improve your interpretation and understanding of the concepts and skills associated with the topic in your standards, curriculum guide, or materials?

Additional Questions to Use With VIA:
State Standards or Frameworks

1. Which learning goals in your state standards are integral to learning the ideas in the topic?

2. How did reading sections I–V help you better understand the meaning and intent of your standards or frameworks?

3. How did your results help make a bridge between a broad content standard and a learning goal?

4. How can the study results help improve K–12 articulation of your standards?

5. How do the end points in the 9–12 section of your standards related to the topic compare with the adult literacy ideas in Section I?

6. How do the results of Sections I–V improve your understanding of students' "opportunity to learn and demonstrate" your state standards?

Additional Questions to Use With VIB:
District Curriculum Guide

1. Which concepts or skills, essential to developing a coherent understanding of the topic, are included in your district curriculum guide or curriculum materials? What gaps would you fill, based on your study?

2. How do the study results help you see why certain lessons in your curriculum program need to be taught and not skipped over?

4. How do the results help you identify the appropriate sequence of instructional opportunities in your curriculum?

5. How do the results help you recognize that some topics need to be revisited within or at different grade levels with new contexts and increasing sophistication of concepts?

instructional model compatible with an inquiry-based investigation. A number of studies have shown that the learning cycle has many advantages when compared with other approaches to instruction, specifically the transmission model (Bybee, 1997). The CTS Learning Cycle of Inquiry, Study, and Reflection is such an instructional model for adult learners. Figure 3.8 compares the learning cycle used for student investigation of a science phenomenon with the learning cycle used for adult investigation of a topic.

Figure 3.8 Comparing and Contrasting Student and Adult Inquiry-Based Investigation Using the Learning Cycle

Student Learning Cycle Investigation of Phenomena	Adult Learning Cycle Investigation of a Curricular Topic
• Students are engaged around a purpose for investigating the phenomenon.	• Adults are engaged around a purpose for investigating a curricular topic.
• Students identify their existing ideas about the phenomenon.	• Adults identify their existing knowledge and beliefs related to the curricular topic.
• Students explore ideas by manipulating materials and gathering evidence.	• Adults explore ideas by interacting with text and gathering evidence.
• Students clarify findings, resolve dissonance, and develop an acceptable scientific explanation of the phenomenon based on evidence.	• Adults clarify readings, resolve dissonance, and develop a standards- and research-based understanding of the topic based on information from the CTS.
• Students use their findings to solve a new problem, ask new questions, provide alternative explanations, or apply knowledge to a novel situation.	• Adults apply their findings from the CTS to an aspect of their work in order to improve student learning.

The learning cycle model is not required in order to engage in CTS, but in our work with teachers, we have found that the purposeful and guided steps of the cycle (see Figure 3.9) provide a structure for teachers to investigate effectively and make sense of the information they uncover. The CTS learning cycle can be used when focusing on just one or several of the CTS sections I–VI, or it can be used with a full study of all six sections. It can be used by an individual or by a group. These steps can be done in an individual study as well. The following describes the six stages in the CTS learning cycle and the embedded processes of reflection, self-assessment, and evaluation that accompany CTS (Figure 3.13, at the end of this list, describes examples of what CTS users and facilitators would do in each stage when using the CTS learning cycle).

Engagement

The topic engagement stage requires the individual or group to think about why they want to engage in a CTS. What is your purpose? What grade levels will you focus on? What are you interested in learning? What topic or topics will you examine? What outcomes (sections of the CTS guide) will fit your purpose? It helps reinforce the purpose for the study and generates interest before beginning the study.

Figure 3.9   The CTS Learning Cycle

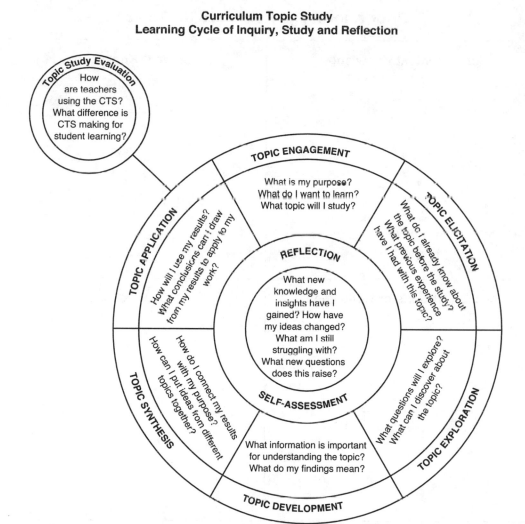

Curriculum Topic Study
Learning Cycle of Inquiry, Study and Reflection

Elicitation

The topic elicitation stage asks learners to activate and identify their current knowledge and beliefs about the topic. It draws on teachers' previous experiences, their beliefs about teaching and student learning, and their prior knowledge. It uses the central question, "What do you know about the topic before engaging in the study?" Depending on whether you decide to do a full topic study or select particular sections, the ideas you might elicit related to the topic include:

- Your content knowledge
- Content or skills important for all students to know
- Effective instructional strategies
- Difficulties or misconceptions related to the topic
- Precursor ideas

Figure 3.10 Four-Square Elicitation Organizer

Prior Knowledge Related to the Topic

Adult Content Knowledge	Student Knowledge
Misconceptions or Difficulties	**Connections**

- Technical terminology and facts
- Connections within and across the content areas of science

A four-square template may be useful in organizing this information visually (see Figure 3.10). A worksheet copy for duplication is provided in Resource B, or you can download a Word version off the CTS Web site.

Exploration

In the topic exploration stage, teachers use the CTS guide to focus on selected readings. This stage is characterized by a preliminary scan of the readings. In-depth reading for meaning comes in the next stage. For now, the purpose is to get a taste of what is in the readings, to raise questions, and acquire a broad perspective of the topic. This is the stage where you might note something that resonates or conflicts with your current understandings that you want to investigate further. By previewing the material, users are, in a sense, testing the ideas they generated during the elicitation stage. Recording thoughts, information, questions, and observations can take many forms, including the addition of information in the four-square graphic provided in Figure 3.10. The exploration stage is also a time to begin making your own meaning out of the information. What is your initial interpretation of what you are reading? This stage is still personal to the learner. Because this is only a preliminary scan, the suggested time limit for this stage is 15 minutes for all six sections, and less if you are focusing only on particular sections.

Development

In the topic development stage, the CTS user is guided through a thorough study of the topic by carefully reading and analyzing all of the appropriate sections in the guide. Teachers process the information as they read. They jot down notes on ideas that are important to understanding the topic. The guide emphasizes that you should read the *related* sections. Readers should be aware that there may be extraneous information included on the pages provided for the resources. As you read, you need to continually filter out information that is not relevant to the topic. For example, if you are exploring the topic of "Cells" and a life science *NSES* essay also includes text related to developing ecological ideas, then you would focus only on what is relevant to "Cells."

If you are working in a group, this stage of the study is a time to clarify your ideas with others and the facilitator in order to develop a shared understanding that can provide common ground for discussions. What does this information mean? Do I interpret it the same way as other people do? This is where collegial discussion and having a skilled facilitator can help participants make formal meaning out of their study. It is also a time when pieces of the study can come together to form a complete picture of the topic. For example, in a group learning situation, participants may decide to engage in a jigsaw, with one person taking responsibility for each particular section. After studying an assigned section, everyone comes back together to share what they have learned and, as a group, construct a full and complete understanding of the topic.

We recommend creating a summary sheet at this stage. The summary concisely organizes the information from the study results following the outline of the CTS guide. It can be used with a full topic study or selected sections. Figure 3.11 shows an example of a Grades 6–12 CTS summary sheet on the topic "Energy Transformation." These summary sheets can be filed as a collection that teachers can use for future applications. In Chapter 5, Vignette #7, *A High School Physics Teacher Uses CTS to Design Energy Lessons Based on Research on Learning*, describes how one teacher used the summary in Figure 3.11.

Synthesis

In this stage, teachers synthesize their summary results and extract findings from their study that are pertinent to their original purpose. If the purpose of a CTS is to develop a set of assessment probes for Grades 3–8 to use with a curricular strand, the CTS users would identify useful findings from Sections II, III, IV, and V that could support that task. Questions that may guide the synthesis work at this stage include:

Figure 3.11 CTS Summary Sheet for *Energy Transformation*

CTS Summary for the CTS Guide: *Energy Transformation*

Section I: Adult Content Knowledge From *SFAA* and *Science Matters*

- Energy appears in many forms.
- One form of energy can change into another.
- All forms of energy involve a system that is capable of exerting a force.
- Most of what happens in the universe involves some type of energy transformation.
- Energy can be stored (potential energy) or moving (kinetic energy).
- Forms of energy include sound, heat, gravitational, chemical, elastic, mechanical, electrical, magnetic, electromagnetic, etc., and they are described in different ways.
- Energy can be measured. This measurement allows us to keep track of how much of one form is converted to another.
- Everything you do or see requires energy.
- Energy follows two basic rules: (1) energy is conserved—it cannot be created or destroyed, only changed from one form to another; and (2) energy always goes from more useful (more concentrated) to less useful (more spread-out) forms.
- Most energy transformations give off heat energy.
- The total amount of energy available for transformation is almost always decreasing.
- Heat tends to diffuse from warmer places to cooler places, usually ending up in more disorder than what you began with.

Section II: Instructional Implications From *Benchmarks* and the *NSES*

General Essay from *Benchmarks:*
- Energy is a mysterious concept for all ages.
- Students will use the term *energy* long before they really understand what energy is.
- Students start at an early age with a basic concept of energy—they think of it as something needed to make things go, run, or happen.
- Many people think of energy as a substance.
- It's a good idea to talk about familiar energy ideas even before students can formally define energy.
- There are three "big ideas" related to energy to develop for student learning: (1) energy transformation, (2) conservation of energy, and (3) in a transformation, some energy is likely to be dissipated as heat.
- Older students will grasp general energy ideas, but even they will have difficulty developing deep understanding.
- Qualitative understandings should take priority over quantitative.

Middle School Essays from *Benchmarks* and *NSES:*
- At this level, the focus is on transfers and transformations.
- Use several examples to trace where energy comes from and goes next.
- There may be confusion in distinguishing between energy and an energy source. Focusing on energy transformation may help address this.
- The basic idea of energy needed for something to occur triggers students' asking about where the energy comes from, and later where it goes.
- Students develop a qualitative idea of energy conservation with a focus on "energy cannot be created or destroyed." Later, this will become quantitative.

(Continued)

Figure 3.11 (Continued)

High School Essays from *Benchmarks* and *NSES*:

- Concepts acquired in middle school can now be revisited and extended to new contexts (e.g. nuclear and living systems).
- Revisiting energy ideas in new ways will help students see how powerful these ideas are.
- A major idea that should first be introduced qualitatively is the idea that the total amount of energy available for transformation is always decreasing, with an emphasis on practical losses through dissipation of heat.

Section III: Concepts and Specific Ideas From *Benchmarks* and the *NSES*

Middle School Learning Goals from *Benchmarks* and *NSES*:

- Energy is a property of many substances and is associated with heat, light, electricity, mechanical motion, sound, nuclei, and the nature of a chemical.
- Energy is transferred in many ways.
- Energy cannot be created or destroyed, only changed from one form into another.
- Most of what goes on everywhere involves some form of energy being transformed into another.

High School Learning Goals from *Benchmarks* and *NSES*:

- The total energy of the universe is constant.
- Energy can be transferred by collisions, by light waves and other radiations, and in many other ways. However, it can never be destroyed.
- All energy can be considered to be either kinetic energy, which is the energy of motion; potential energy, which depends on relative position; or energy contained by a field, such as electromagnetic waves.
- Everything becomes less organized and less orderly over time. In energy transfers, heat spreads out more evenly.

Section IV: Research on Student Learning From *Benchmarks* and *Making Sense of Secondary Science*

- Students' meanings for *energy,* before and even after instruction, may be considerably different from the scientific meaning.
- Common conceptualizations about energy include: Energy is associated only with animate objects; energy is a causal agent stored in certain objects; it is linked with force and motion; and it is a fuel-like substance, ingredient, or product.
- Upper-elementary students tend to associate energy only with living things, in particular with growing, fitness, exercise, and food.
- Even as students develop skill in identifying different forms of energy, in most cases their descriptions of energy change focus only on forms that have perceivable effects.
- Students intuitively reason that energy is lost, rather than using conservation-of-energy ideas.
- It is suggested that to promote learning about energy, more time should be devoted to qualitative questions and students should be advised to explain physical phenomena in their own words.

Section VI: State Standards

Middle School *Learning Results*:

- H1: Analyze the benefits and drawbacks of energy conversions.
- H2: Demonstrate that energy cannot be created or destroyed, but only changed from one form to another.
- H3: Compare and contrast the ways energy travels.

High School *Learning Results*:

- H4: Analyze the relationship between the kinetic and potential energy of a falling object.
- H9: Demonstrate an understanding that energy can be found in chemical bonds and can be used when it is released from those bonds.

What information from the study is relevant to our purpose? How can these ideas be combined to support our work?

If two or more curriculum topics are studied by the group, this is the stage where they can make connections between the two. For example, the study of "Biological Evolution" may be combined with the study of "Earth History." Teachers can merge the results of both topic studies into the larger topic of "Changes Over Time." This stage is also an opportunity to combine content topic studies with cross-cutting categories from the CTS guides on the "Nature of Science and Technology," "Implications of Science and Technology," and "Unifying Themes." For example, study results on the "Solar System" might be combined with results from "Evidence and Explanation," "Historical Episodes in Science," and "Models" to develop a unit on the "Sun-Earth Connection." In this way, the unit could include explanations of our current knowledge in contrast to the historical idea of an earth-centered universe, the role of sunspot data in explaining events on the sun and their effect on earth, and the use of physical models to represent sun-earth phenomena.

Application

In the topic application stage, individuals or groups decide how they are going to apply the information from their study (which has now been filtered for their purpose) to fit their needs. The central question is, "How can I apply these findings to my work?" This stage draws upon evidence (data) gathered from CTS to construct explanations of what needs to be done for a particular purpose. Conclusions are drawn, based on evidence from CTS, about the best ways to improve teaching and learning. These conclusions are applied to the particular situation. For example, the purpose of a group's study might be to improve their current curriculum. After studying the topic of "Human Body Systems," a district curriculum committee might decide to use their results to examine the articulation of K–8 learning goals across grade levels in their curriculum. The study could help them identify redundancy or gaps and arrange a more coherent development of understanding.

Study Reflection and Self-Assessment

This is a critical part of the process, whether the CTS is undertaken by an individual, a pair, a team, or a large group of educators. It is embedded throughout CTS and is connected to the original ideas listed in the elicitation stage. Figure 3.12 shows an example of a reflection summary sheet that can be used to organize information, thoughts, questions, and ideas generated through reflection and self-assessment. A worksheet copy is provided in Resource B and is available as a Word document on the CTS Web site. Questions used to guide reflection and self-assessment might include

> Reflection and self-assessment are at the center of the CTS Learning Cycle of Inquiry, Study, and Reflection.

- What important knowledge have I gained from this process?
- What new insights about teaching and learning have I gained?
- How have my ideas about the content knowledge in the topic changed?
- Are there ideas I am still struggling with?
- How has this changed my beliefs about teaching and learning?
- Are there beliefs I am still resistant to change?

Figure 3.12   Topic Study Reflection: Capturing Your Thoughts

Capture Your Thoughts

★ Important Ideas	👁 Specific Insights
? Questions Raised	⇨ Implications for Action

- What things will I do differently?
- What other questions does this raise?

As mentioned, Figure 3.13 describes examples of what CTS users and facilitators do in each stage when using the CTS learning cycle.

CTS EVALUATION

This formative and summative step is not an actual part of the CTS learning cycle, but is inextricably linked to it. Evaluation should be considered during CTS and after results have been implemented. What kinds of data could you collect to see whether CTS made a difference for teachers' and students' learning? What do the data tell you about the ways teachers are using CTS and its results? What do the data tell you about how students are learning ideas in science? Since the ultimate goal of CTS is to improve science teaching and learning, it is important to take the time to evaluate its impact. The third book in this series, due to be published in 2006, *Facilitator's*

Figure 3.13 Examples of What CTS Users and Facilitators Do During a Group CTS Using the CTS Cycle of Inquiry, Study, and Reflection

Stage	What the CTS User Does	What the CTS Facilitator Does
Topic Engagement	Asks: • What is my purpose? • What grade level(s) will I focus on? • What do I want to find out? • What topic(s) will I study? • What outcomes will I focus on? Thinks about purpose for doing CTS and shows interest in the topic	• Uses a hook to engage the group in the topic (video, student work, presents a dilemma, etc.) • Defines purpose and outcomes • Generates questions • Charts group's responses • Generates interest and curiosity from the group
Topic Elicitation	Asks: • What adult content knowledge should a scientifically literate adult have? • What content or skills are important for all students to know? • What instructional strategies are most effective? • What difficulties or misconceptions related to the topic am I aware of? • What precursor ideas are needed? • What technical terminology and facts are important? • What connections exist within and across the content areas of science? Activates and records current knowledge and beliefs	• Asks elicitation questions • Provides recording worksheets for individual responses • Asks group to share initial ideas • Observes and listens carefully • Safely uncovers knowledge and beliefs of the group • Records ideas on chart • Suspends judgment
Topic Exploration	Asks: • What predictions can I make about what I will learn from this study? • What is my initial interpretation of this study? • What do I see that I want to dig deeper into? • What is resonating with me or causing conflict that I need to revisit? • What questions do I want to explore further? Does a quick scan to get an initial taste of the topic and what it involves, records ideas and questions, begins to make some initial meaning out of the readings	• Directs group to the CTS study guide and selected readings • Provides time for a quick scan • Keeps group on task and encourages them to do a "quick read" and not get bogged down in details • Encourages them to pay attention only to "related parts." • Encourages interaction among the group • Observes and listens during interactions • Suspends judgment
Topic Development	Asks: • What information relates to the topic I am studying? • What are the important ideas? • What do these findings mean? Processes information for meaning, jots down important notes, filters information as to what	• Assigns the group's tasks • Uses jigsaws and other strategies to provide time for reading and processing • Monitors time • May provide optional additional supplements for reading • Encourages collaboration

(Continued)

Figure 3.13 (Continued)

Stage	What the CTS User Does	What the CTS Facilitator Does
	is most relevant, clarifies ideas with others, listens critically to others' ideas, listens to and comprehends clarifications offered by the facilitator, reflects on initial ideas and outcomes, summarizes group's findings	• Asks probing and clarifying questions during group sense making • Provides time and support to work through dissonance • Encourages explanations based on evidence citing • Provides clarifications when needed • Connects new ideas to old and helps reflect on the outcomes • Helps group construct the summary
Topic Synthesis	Asks: • What is my purpose for using these results? • What information from the CTS results will help me with my purpose? • How can I put ideas from different topic studies together? Synthesizes results and extracts relevant information, prepares to apply findings	• Reminds group of their purpose • Encourages group work to extract meaningful information • Helps group connect CTS findings to their purpose • Provides examples
Topic Application	Asks: • How will I use the findings? • What conclusions can I draw from the findings to help me apply them to my work? Thinks about how to use the findings, and draws conclusions and applies them to the particular problem or work that results from defining the purpose	• Refers users to the evidence in drawing their conclusions • Helps support user in thinking about ways to implement findings • Shares examples of ways findings have been applied in the particular curricular, instructional, or assessment context • Encourages reflection and self-assessment after task is completed

Guide to Using Curriculum Topic Study, will provide examples of ways to evaluate CTS in various professional development configurations. Evaluation results of the CTS project funded by the National Science Foundation (NSF) will also be posted on our Web site in 2007.

INDIVIDUAL AND GROUP USE OF CTS

As stated earlier, CTS can serve many purposes for both individual teachers and for groups of teachers in a professional growth setting. Ultimately, the decision of whether to use CTS as an individual or with a group depends on what you want to accomplish. Do you want to build your own capacity for using standards and research, or are you building the capacity of the group you work with? Are you addressing the learning of the students you have, or are you working with

> The flexibility of CTS allows it to be used by an individual, anytime and anywhere, or with a group for a designated purpose.

other teachers across grades to impact all students? Are you intent on building a learning community within the setting you work with? Are you intent on helping others change long-held beliefs and practices? The answers to these questions will help you determine whether you want to use this book for your own individual purposes or as part of a collaborative group.

Individual Use of CTS

Individual teachers use CTS to inform lesson planning, to examine student work or ideas, to help them address confusions that come up in their classroom, or to select the most effective instructional materials and strategies. As individual teachers study a topic, they increase their understanding of what is important to teach about the topic and what their students might find confusing.

Maybe you are switching to teach a different grade level or have just encountered some students who are having difficulty learning a topic. You might be asking yourself, "What is blocking these students from learning?" This is a good time to turn to the CTS process and gain insight from the research to help you make good instructional decisions.

In developing CTS, we encountered many teachers who thought they knew and taught to the standards. While they did know a lot about standards, they discovered through CTS that they could do a much better job of making connections between the topics they teach and the "big ideas" in science. They also found that by studying the common misconceptions students face, they could probe and assess understanding far better. An individual teacher who has this book and the suggested resources, and/or access to the resources on the Internet, has the professional knowledge base needed to enhance their own understanding of the standards and how to teach to them.

For example, a high school biology teacher who uses CTS on a regular basis explained that she backs up and makes sure her students have a grasp of basic fundamental ideas before presenting the content that she finds challenging and interesting. She described how she no longer takes what she learned through her summer research experiences and NSF institutes and teaches it the same way she was exposed to it. Instead, she now takes the time to study the topic and think about how to translate her exciting experiences into learning opportunities that are engaging and challenging, but, most important, appropriate for and comprehensible to her students.

> Teachers with strong science backgrounds have found CTS to be a useful resource in bridging what they know about the content with what is appropriate for their students. It helps them to see that what they perceive as simple ideas may be stumbling blocks for students.

Professional developers also find CTS useful to their work. Professional developers of science who are excellent staff developers and facilitators but lack a strong science content background or are specialized in a particular discipline find that using CTS grounds them in the issues that may come up in regard to the content of a professional development session. Professional developers also need to be able to cite current research or standards recommendations.

Group Use of CTS

Group use of CTS can be as simple as two teachers engaged in a topic study, or it can be a large professional development audience. As noted earlier, learning is enhanced through social engagement about the content.

School- and district-based study groups and other teacher networks are also opportunities for using CTS. Study groups usually identify goals for improved student learning in a particular area and then use CTS to understand what the expectations for students should be at each grade level. They develop a shared vision of the appropriate and effective instruction and assessment practices, and they set goals to implement new practices aligned with what they learned from CTS.

> CTS is often used in settings with groups of teachers who are engaged in professional development, teacher induction/mentoring, committees for school improvement, and curriculum selection and adaptation.

Mentor teachers also use CTS to help beginning teachers plan their lessons and deepen their content and pedagogical content knowledge. They can discuss goals of the lesson and then do a study together on the topic, making adjustments in the lesson plan based on what they learn. CTS can be embedded in virtually any professional development session that seeks to increase teachers' understanding of what content is important, when it should be taught, the common misconceptions students hold about the topics, and what it is important to assess.

The third book in the CTS series, *Facilitator's Guide to Curriculum Topic Study* (anticipated release in 2006), will address facilitating CTS with groups. It will describe various group structures, facilitation techniques for engaging learners, learning strategies, learning designs for CTS, examples of CTS used with various professional development strategies, vignettes that illuminate group use of CTS, and various tools to use with groups.

4

Utilizing Curriculum Topic Study for Different Contexts

C TS is not designed to be a one-size-fits-all approach. It needs to be tailored to fit your purpose and the context you are working in. Context and purpose are intertwined. While not an all-inclusive list, various contexts CTS is used with include

- Science content knowledge
- Curriculum
- Instruction
- Assessment
- Preservice and inservice education and professional development
- Leadership

This chapter presents examples of ways the CTS process and tools are used in the different contexts educators encounter in their work. As you become familiar with CTS, you may find other ways to utilize the process and tools that are not listed here. As we work with educators across the country in the CTS project funded by the National Science Foundation (NSF), we will share examples of various ways educators have used CTS in their contexts, along with additional tools developed by CTS users. These examples will be added on an ongoing basis to the CTS Web site.

Illustrative vignettes based on actual applications of CTS by science educators are included in Chapter 5. These vignettes illuminate ways CTS was used in different contexts. The vignettes also describe the use of several tools and suggestions included in this chapter. Figure 4.1 lists vignettes that correspond to the contexts described in this chapter (several vignettes overlap in context; the chart identifies the contexts most central to the vignette). After you read and examine the contextual suggestions and examples in this chapter, it is helpful to read a corresponding vignette in order to get a fuller picture of what CTS looks like in actual practice.

> CTS is not a rigid, lockstep process. It is meant to be molded and shaped to fit the unique context of each user.

Figure 4.1   Context Examples of Vignettes

Context	Vignette
Content Knowledge	Vignette #1: A High School Integrated Science Teacher Uses CTS to Understand Gravity-Related Content
Curriculum	Vignette #2: An Experienced Middle School Teacher Uses CTS to Revise a Unit on Biological Classification
	Vignette #3: A Team of Primary Teachers Uses CTS to Identify Goals for Learning About Life Cycles
	Vignette #10: A GLOBE Curriculum Developer Uses CTS to Develop Instructional Materials
	Vignette #6: A Fourth-Grade District Team Uses CTS to Examine Alignment of Curriculum, Instruction, and Assessment
Instruction	Vignette #4: A Middle School Teacher Uses CTS to Understand a Difficult Concept to Teach—Density
	Vignette #5: A Teacher Leader Uses CTS to Help Guide Fifth-Grade Teachers' Implementation of the Ecology Content Standards
	Vignette #7: A High School Physics Teacher Uses CTS to Design Energy Lessons Based on Research on Learning
	Vignette #8: An Elementary Teacher Uses CTS to Improve Opportunities to Learn for Her Disadvantaged Students
Assessment	Vignette #6: A Fourth-Grade District Team Uses CTS to Examine Alignment of Curriculum, Instruction, and Assessment
	Vignette #7: A High School Physics Teacher Uses CTS to Design Energy Lessons Based on Research on Learning
Professional Development	Vignette #9: Professional Developers Use CTS to Redesign Their Inquiry-Based Workshops
Leadership	Vignette #5: A Teacher Leader Uses CTS to Help Guide Fifth-Grade Teachers' Implementation of the Ecology Content Standards

CTS AND SCIENCE CONTENT KNOWLEDGE

Science educators recognize the critical importance of having a strong, broad base of scientific knowledge extensive enough to understand the big ideas, concepts, and important fundamental facts of science. This content knowledge base is needed to make conceptual connections within and across science disciplines. Teachers of science continue to learn science throughout their teaching careers (National Research Council [NRC], 1996). Many teachers pursue content learning for their own enjoyment as well as for required certification. Content learning experiences, such as working in a research lab or taking a science course at a university, are valuable, but at times they are impractical for teachers bound by schedule, geographic, and time constraints. While these experiences are important, it is also critical that teachers have opportunities to learn content knowledge in ways that are directly linked to the classroom. In addition, there are times when a teacher may need immediate content support or a refresher for teaching

> "Content that is learned disconnected from how to teach it may provide teachers with more scientific understanding but will not necessarily result in improved student learning. Standards and accountability systems have made us more aware that the content teachers need to learn is the content they will teach" (Loucks-Horsley, Love, Stiles, Mundry, & Hewson, 2003, p. 333).

a concept or skill in science. Opportunities are needed to learn science content knowledge in ways that are linked to the classroom and can be done independently or in groups anytime, anywhere. CTS provides that opportunity as a scholarly, versatile way for teachers to renew their continuous science content learning.

CTS does not replace formal science content coursework. Instead, it offers a systematic way for teachers to identify relevant grade-level content and increase their knowledge of the science ideas as well as understand how the knowledge is structured. CTS is particularly helpful to elementary teachers or other generalists who are expected to teach multiple subjects and have not had substantive coursework in all the areas of science they are expected to teach. High school teachers specialized in a science discipline, such as biology, faced with teaching science outside their area of specialty also benefit from using CTS to enhance their content knowledge. An old adage says, "You don't know what you don't know if you don't have the knowledge to begin with." CTS can help teachers identify the content they need to know more about, which may, in turn, lead them to enroll in university courses or participate in content institutes, research experiences, and other types of content learning. Teachers and other educators who work with teachers as mentors, coaches, and staff developers can use CTS to increase their understanding of the content they help their adult learners with, as well as improve their own content understanding as they design a teacher learning experience.

Using a CTS Guide to Identify the Content Knowledge Needed to Teach a Topic

Section I of a CTS study guide includes readings from *Science for All Americans* (American Association for the Advancement of Science [AAAS], 1990); *Science Matters* (Hazen & Trefil, 1991); and optional supplementary content readings or videos. The focus is on describing what scientifically literate adults should know about a particular topic. (Optional content reading supplements are listed on the CTS Web site at www.curriculumtopicstudy.org.)

Sections II, III, and V provide further clarification of the content at different grade spans. For teachers engaged in formal science content coursework at the university level, these sections help teachers translate the content they learned at an adult level to what is developmentally and conceptually appropriate to teach students. Figure 4.2 shows how selected readings can be used to identify the relevant content in a topic teachers and students need to know.

Figure 4.2 Recording Information from the CTS Guide for Content Knowledge of a Topic

Section	Resource Used	Content Information to Record as You Read
Section I	*Science for All Americans*	• Culminating big ideas in the topic • Important concepts and specific ideas related to the topic • Illustrative examples that clarify the content
	Science Matters	• Information that contributes to understanding the topic in a real-world context • Basic facts, vocabulary, principles, generalizations, or laws associated with the topic • Illustrative examples or analogies that clarify the content
Section II	*Benchmarks for Science Literacy*	• Big ideas that span across grade levels • Grade-level concepts and ideas important for understanding the topic
	National Science Education Standards	• Grade span concepts and ideas important for understanding the topic
Section III	*Benchmarks for Science Literacy* *National Science Education Standards*	• Specific science ideas in the goal statements • Technical terminology used in the goal statements
Section V	*Atlas of Science Literacy*	• Connections between ideas that provide clarification for the content

K-W-L is a strategy used with students to identify the prior knowledge they bring to their learning (K), what they would like to learn (W), and what they learned after an instructional opportunity (L) (see Figure 4.3). This same strategy, described in more detail in Chapter 3, can be used with CTS in a content knowledge context.

> If your purpose for using CTS is to build upon your own content knowledge, it is important to start with what you already know about the topic you select to study.

Before beginning the study, list what you know about the content in the topic. List any specific ideas, concepts, principles, laws, generalizations, illustrative examples, facts, or important terminology associated with the topic. If you are working in a group, individually record your own ideas, share with the group, and then post the group's ideas on a large chart.

Figure 4.3   K-W-L Strategy

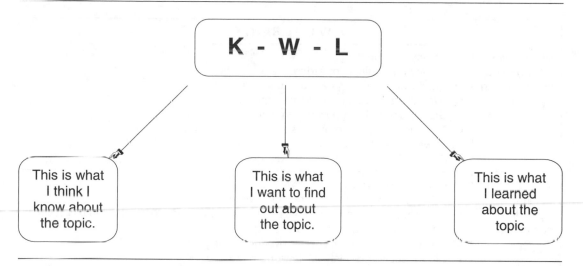

Next, think about what you would like to know, based on the content needs you have for teaching your students or working with other teachers in the topic area. Record your questions and utilize them to guide your study of the content. If you are engaging in the process with a group, collectively agree on 4 to 5 questions that will guide your group's study. After completing the readings and taking notes individually, reflect on your findings and complete the chart by filling in your new learnings about the content. Identify and reflect on any novice understandings, misconceptions, or conceptual gaps you may have had prior to the study. This can also be done with a group, with results posted on a large chart. If there are ideas you want to learn more about that were not addressed in the study, decide whether they are important to pursue through other content resources or discussion within your group. Figure 4.4 shows an example of a teacher's use of K-W-L to examine content ideas about gravity. (This example is illuminated in Vignette #1.)

Using CTS to Examine the Hierarchal Structure of Content Knowledge in a Topic

Knowing the content of a topic is important, but it is not enough by itself. Knowing the organizational structure of ideas within a discipline helps identify the core science ideas at different levels of specificity. This leads to a better understanding of the knowledge that makes up a topic and how it connects with other ideas. *Concept-Based Curriculum and Instruction* defines "Structure of Knowledge and Topic" as follows:

Structure of Knowledge: A schema (visual or verbal) that specifies a cognitive hierarchy and relationship between facts, topics, concepts, generalizations and principles, and theories.

Topic: A category of study that implies a body of related facts to be learned. Study that is focused on topics, without a conceptual lens, results in

Figure 4.4　Example of a Teacher Using K-W-L with a Gravity CTS

K-W-L – GRAVITY	
What I think I **K**now about the content in the topic	• Gravity is a force. • Gravity pulls things toward the center of the earth. • Gravity acts on things without touching them. • Everything on earth experiences gravity. • Gravity depends on how big an object is. • There is no gravity in empty space. • Newton described gravity. • Einstein had something to do with gravity.
What I **W**ant to learn about the content in the topic	• How strong is gravity? • Is there a mathematical formula to calculate gravity? • How small does something have to be before it no longer is affected by gravity? • Does having an atmosphere affect gravity? • Are there new theories or discoveries about gravity? • Did an apple really fall on Newton's head?
What I **L**earned about the content in the topic	• Gravity is universal! Everything in the universe is affected by gravity. • There is a gravitational field that affects space around any mass. • The strength of the gravitational field around an object is proportional to its mass and decreases with distance from its center. • The earth is spherical because of the mutual gravitational attraction toward a common center. • Objects in space are held in orbit by gravity. • An object's weight depends on the local force of gravity. • There is an equal and opposite force to the force the earth's gravity exerts on an object. • Celestial gravity was once thought to be different from earth's gravity. • Galileo did experiments to test the effect of gravity, and his observations allowed others to make predictions about falling objects. • Newton did get his idea from a falling apple (but maybe not on his head!) • Newton's law of universal gravitation states, "Between any two objects there is an attractive force proportional to the product of the two masses divided by the square of the distance between them." • The law of gravity tells us that every object in the universe is exerting a gravitational force on me right now—that includes the person sitting next to me as well as stars and distant galaxies. Gravity is everywhere! • Newton's laws of gravity and motion made the universe predictable and his use of mathematics was a model for other sciences. • Einstein proposed a theory of gravity: the theory of general relativity. • Current theoretical physicists are trying to describe gravitational force in terms of the exchange of particles. • A "g-force" is the same as earth's gravity.

memorization and surface understanding rather than integrated thinking and deep understanding. (Erickson, 1998, p. 168)

These two definitions underscore the importance of knowing the structure of content knowledge in a topic. This is further supported by the research on expert knowledge in *How People Learn:*

Their [experts'] knowledge is not simply a list of facts and formulas that are relevant to their domain; instead their knowledge is organized around core concepts or "big ideas" that guide their thinking about their domains. (Bransford, Brown, & Cocking, 2000, p. 36)

In CTS, the structure of content knowledge in a topic is represented hierarchically by the schema in Figure 4.5. Key words used in the diagram for describing the structure of content knowledge have slightly different meanings to different groups of educators both within and outside the field of science. To be clear about these differences, CTS provides the following operational definitions and examples:

Unifying Concepts: Fundamental and comprehensive non-discipline-specific concepts that provide connections between content standards in science (e.g., models, systems, patterns, change).

Big Ideas: Generalizations, laws, theories, principles, or broad ideas that show relationships among concepts. Big ideas are the essential understandings that often cut across grade spans and inform adult literacy (e.g., organisms depend on other organisms for their needs).

Concepts: Mental constructs made up of one to three words that can be broad or topic specific. Even though factual knowledge may evolve and change, concepts remain universal and timeless. Concepts can begin with very basic ideas and culminate in sophisticated understanding. Students refine and enhance their thinking about concepts over the course of their K–12 experience. Several of the CTS topics are also concepts (e.g., motion, adaptation, ecosystem, weathering).

Subconcepts: Concepts broken down into more specific mental constructs (e.g., horizontal motion, behavioral adaptation, lunar eclipse)

Specific Ideas: Scientific statements about a concept or subconcept that give it meaning. Specific ideas provide specificity for a broad local, state, or national learning goal (e.g., in solids, the atoms or molecules are closely locked in position and can only vibrate; rock is composed of different combinations of minerals).

Facts and Terminology: Definitions, formulas, fragments of specific knowledge, and technical vocabulary. While certain facts and terminology are necessary, when taught and learned in isolation they are less likely to contribute to conceptual understanding (e.g., density equals mass divided by volume; atoms are made up of protons, neutrons, and electrons; photosynthesis; evaporation).

This schema is useful in "unpacking" a topic by identifying the concepts linked to the topic, the specific ideas that describe the concepts, and the important facts and terminology associated with the topic. The opposite of "unpacking" is "putting together." Concepts can be put together to construct larger ideas. The schema shows how concepts in a topic can be used to formulate fundamental and comprehensive "big ideas." These "big ideas" can be integrated into broader unifying concepts in which discipline-specific boundaries are no longer distinct.

> Examining national standards helps educators tease out concepts and specific ideas as well as identify the terminology that is important for students to use with the topic.

Figure 4.6 shows an example of how the topic of "Conservation of Matter" at the middle school level was examined as a hierarchal set of ideas using CTS. A learning goal from the Maine *Learning Results* (Maine Department of Education, 1997) was used to connect the knowledge to a deeper understanding of a state standard, in this

Figure 4.5   Hierarchy of Content Knowledge in a Topic

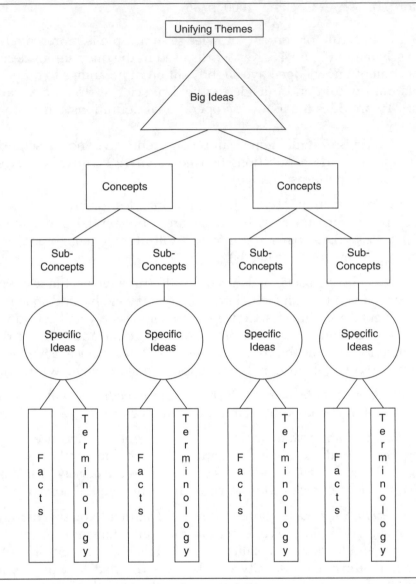

instance, a performance indicator. Readings from Section I and II helped extract the "big ideas." Sections III and V helped the user identify the concepts, subconcepts, and specific ideas. The terminology used in the Section III and VI learning goals was combined with relevant factual knowledge. Overall, the process helped teachers deepen their understanding of the concepts related to the topic of conservation of matter. Taking time to examine the hierarchal structure of knowledge helps move teaching away from an overemphasis on facts and specific ideas to developing the types of "big ideas" that will provide enduring understandings of the content in various contexts.

This process is also helpful to use in constructing questions. Figure 4.7 shows an example of how teachers used this knowledge to construct questions that reflect the hierarchal structure of the knowledge in the topic, ranging from overarching essential questions to specific elicitation of facts. These questions can be used to guide and focus both adult and student content learning and assessment. The CTS

Figure 4.6   Example: Hierarchal Structure of Content Knowledge in a Topic

---

Hierarchy of Content Knowledge in a Topic

Topic: Conservation of Matter

Grade Level: Middle School

Unifying Concepts and Processes:
- Constancy and change
- Systems

Big Ideas:
- Matter is transformed and reused in many ways.
- All visible matter is made up of smaller particles.
- In a closed system, matter may change form, but the total amount remains the same.

Related Concepts:
- Matter
- Atoms
- Interaction
- Conservation of matter
- Systems

Related Subconcepts:
- Solids, liquids, gases, plasma
- Physical and chemical changes
- Mass and volume
- Closed systems

State/District Learning Goal: Maine *Learning Results,* E7: Demonstrate the Law of the Conservation of Matter.

Specific Ideas:
- Matter exists as a solid, liquid, gas, or plasma.
- All matter is made up of atoms.
- The idea of atoms explains conservation of matter: No matter how they interact or are rearranged, the number of atoms stays the same.
- No matter how substances interact or change chemically or physically in a closed system, the mass always remains the same.
- In a closed system, nothing can get in and nothing can get out.

Facts and Terminology:
- The law of conservation of matter.
- An atom is the smallest particle of matter that retains the properties of the matter.
- Matter is anything that has mass and occupies space.
- A system is made up of interconnected parts and/or processes.

---

process helps move the emphasis from overreliance on questions about facts and terminology to questions that utilize the important conceptual ideas needed to develop and demonstrate deeper understanding.

CTS AND CURRICULUM

Curriculum is the way content is designed and delivered. It includes the structure, organization, balance, and presentation of the content in the classroom (NRC, 1996).

Figure 4.7 Levels of Questioning

Topic: CONSERVATION OF MATTER	
Hierarchy of Knowledge	**Hierarchal Question**
Unifying Concepts and Processes: • Constancy and Change • Systems **Big Ideas:** • Matter cannot be created or destroyed in ordinary changes • All matter is made up of smaller particles or atoms • In a closed system, matter may change form but the total amount remains the same **Concepts:** • Matter • Atoms and molecules • Interaction • Conservation of matter • Systems **Subconcepts:** • Solids, liquids, gases, plasma • Physical and chemical changes • Mass and volume • Closed systems **State/District Learning Goals:** Grades 5–8 E7: Demonstrate the law of the conservation of matter **Specific Ideas:** • Matter exists as a solid, liquid, gas, or plasma • All matter is made up of atoms • The idea of atoms explains conservation of matter: No matter how they interact or are rearranged, the number of atoms stays the same • No matter how substances interact or change chemically or physically in a closed system, the mass always remains the same • In a closed system, nothing can get in, and nothing can get out **Facts and Terminology:** • The law of conservation of matter • An atom is the smallest particle of matter that retains the properties of the matter • Matter is anything that has mass and occupies space • A system is made up of interconnected parts and/or processes	• How does conservation of matter demonstrate the ideas of both constancy and change? • How does the idea of systems explain conservation of matter? • Why is it significant that matter cannot be created or destroyed? • Does size make a difference in conservation of matter? • How is it possible that matter in a closed system both changes and remains the same? • What types of things are considered to be matter? • What is the difference between a substance and an atom or molecule of a substance? • How does matter interact with other matter? • What does it mean to "conserve matter"? • What determines a system? • What forms does matter exist in? • What kinds of changes does matter undergo? • How do mass and volume describe matter? • How does a closed system differ from an open system? • What are different ways you can demonstrate conservation of matter? • What forms does matter exist in? • What is all matter made up of? • What happens to the total number of atoms when matter undergoes changes? • What happens to the mass in a closed system when matter changes or interacts with other matter? • What happens to the transfer of matter in a closed system? • What does the law of conservation of matter state? • How do you define an atom? • What is the definition of matter? • What is a system made up of?

Translating science content standards into a K–12, grade span, or single grade-level curriculum is enhanced through the deliberate study and analysis provided by CTS. Contrary to some beliefs and curricular practices, standards are not the curriculum. Standards-based content in the curriculum needs to be well thought out, coordinated, conceptually and contextually organized at the local level, and taught with effective curriculum materials.

Curriculum Coherence and Articulation

Putting together a K–12 science curriculum aligned with standards is not an easy task. It is even more difficult when committee members lack the necessary tools and resources to undertake this arduous work. A curriculum scope and sequence can be compared to a jigsaw puzzle:

> Imagine that we are faced with a pile of jigsaw puzzle pieces and told to put them together. Our first reaction might be to ask for the picture. When we put together a jigsaw puzzle, we usually have a picture to guide us. None of the pieces means anything taken alone; only when the pieces are put together do they mean something. (Beane, 1995, p. 1)

CTS provides the picture needed to put the necessary pieces together in a way that they make sense for students. Examining the concepts and ideas in a topic (Sections III and VI) coupled with recommendations from the standards and the research on student learning (Sections II and IV) is like holding a jigsaw puzzle piece up to see roughly what area of the puzzle you should put it in. After getting some of the initial pieces laid out, the interconnected ideas in Section V add more connections from other topics to the developing curriculum represented by the full puzzle. The CTS results are the "picture" to keep look-

> Putting together curriculum pieces without a "picture" to guide you is a struggle. CTS provides that picture.

ing at to make sure you are putting the right pieces together in the curriculum puzzle. This struggle often results in a pile of disconnected curriculum pieces that fail to come together to form a complete picture in the minds of students.

"A 'coherent' curriculum is one that holds together, that makes sense as a whole; and its parts, whatever they are, are unified and connected by that sense of the whole" (Beane, 1995, p. 3). This involves carefully thinking through the flow of ideas to determine

- The important core set of ideas students should learn, ranging from specific facts, terminology, and ideas to broad concepts, "big ideas" and unifying themes
- The major connections among ideas both within the content domain, across content domains, and across disciplines
- Cross-cutting processes and understandings of inquiry and technological design, the nature and history of science, and personal and social perspectives of science and technology
- Important prerequisites leading to increasing sophistication, by which students eventually come to understand important ideas in science from one grade level to the next and within grade levels

These considerations for coherence and articulation within and across science topics in a K–12 curriculum are represented in Figure 4.8.

Common issues and practices that contribute to a lack of coherence in K–12 science curriculum development in schools that have not used standards- and research-based tools like CTS include

Figure 4.8 Topic Coherence and Articulation

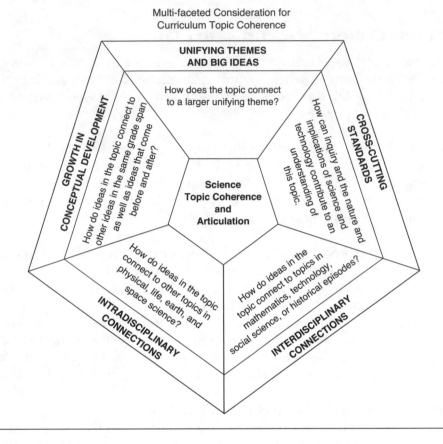

- Too much unnecessary content—a curriculum that mirrors a textbook
- A vague curriculum design that is interpreted and implemented in multiple ways by different teachers
- Use of standards that are too broad—a lack of specific learning goals that make up the standards
- Misinterpretation of the meaning and intent of state standards that guide the local curriculum
- Lack of the necessary tools and the lack of expertise in using them to guide quality and consistency
- Adopting state standards as *the* curriculum
- Topical alignment—lack of depth or relevant match
- Themes emphasized over relevant topics and learning goals
- Concepts and processes delineated and learned in isolation
- A mix-and-match approach to curriculum materials selection that does not consider prior learning
- Lack of the use of cognitive research to determine appropriate developmental levels
- Holding on to "favorite units" that are not conducive to student learning and do not reflect standards and research
- Rushing the curriculum development and alignment process without taking the time to study, analyze, reflect, revisit, and revise

Figure 4.9 provides an example of questions that can be used with CTS to guide development or revision of a science curriculum. Each question includes the section in a CTS guide that addresses the question.

Curriculum committees often spend enormous amounts of time and energy preparing curriculum documents for their schools or districts that describe what should be taught at each grade level.

> Taking the time to identify relevant topics and study them before including them in a grade-level, school, or district curriculum guide can make a significant difference in shaping a curriculum for all students that does not sacrifice substance and content integrity.

> The problem with curriculum is often the "Dusty Binder Effect." This happens when we create elaborate notebooks full of information about what we should teach. We hand this to new teachers or vaguely refer to the existence of such materials. (Gregory & Kuzmich, 2004, p. 78)

Teachers who have used CTS with district curriculum committee members have found the use of short summaries that describe content, specific ideas for students, instructional considerations, research findings, and links to their state standards to be very helpful in giving teachers a summary of cross-grade curriculum topics. Teachers can see how a topic develops in the curriculum over time without having to search and read through all the pages in their curriculum binders. These summaries are provided in the front of their curriculum guides, preceding the grade-level sections. Fig. 4.10 shows an example of a guide created for a district in Maine that showed how the topic of "Rocks and Minerals" developed over multiple grade spans.

Curriculum Selection

CTS is helpful for reviewing and selecting curriculum materials. The results from CTS are used as a lens to examine instructional materials with an eye for determining whether they are informed by standards and research. Often publishers claim their materials are aligned with national standards. Close examination reveals the alignment is frequently "topical," meaning it matches the topic but fails to include the important conceptual ideas articulated in the standards. Furthermore, ideas that are addressed in the material may exceed what research identifies as developmentally appropriate for students.

Consider this example: A curriculum selection committee is looking for materials for their Grade 4 earth science curricular strand. The committee decides to look at an inquiry-based elementary unit called "The Earth Beneath Our Feet." The committee uses the "Structure of the Solid Earth" CTS guide to gain a better sense of the concepts and specific ideas that are appropriate for Grade 4. They find the unit includes ideas about the materials that make up the solid earth: rocks and soil and the processes of weathering and erosion. They also notice that a substantial part of the unit includes the idea of continents as land masses and how they have changed over time. The terminology in the lessons includes words like *lithosphere, plates,* and *subduction.* Playdough models are made by students to investigate what happens when plates collide.

> If the goal of a curriculum selection committee is to select standards-based and research-informed materials, doing a CTS prior to examining and selecting new curriculum can make educators more aware of what to look for in the material.

As the teachers examine the CTS results for Grade 4, they cannot find ideas about plate tectonics. They turn to the CTS guide, "Plate Tectonics," for further clarification.

Figure 4.9   CTS Curriculum Considerations

K–12 Science Curriculum: Questions to Use With CTS to Guide Curriculum Decisions

1. Does your curriculum include all the required state standards (Section VI)?
2. Does your curriculum also include important national standards (Sections III and V)?
3. Does your curriculum reflect a deliberate and careful study of the curricular topic (Sections I–VI)?
4. Does your curriculum break the standards down into *specific* learning goals (Section III)?
5. Is the curriculum organized by relevant science topics rather than by contextual themes or irrelevant topics (list of CTS guides)?
6. Does the curriculum carefully align instruction to the learning goals (Sections II, III, IV, V)?
7. Does the curriculum provide opportunities to learn and demonstrate learning of concepts and skills in different contexts (Sections II and V)?
8. Does the curriculum eliminate wasteful repetition (Sections III and V)?
9. Was deliberate thought given to vertical (K–12) articulation that builds from basic, fundamental ideas to increasing sophistication (Section V)?
10. Was deliberate thought given to horizontal (across grade-level) articulation (Sections III and V)?
11. Does the curriculum make connections across sciences (earth, life, space, physical) each year (Section I and V)?
12. Does the curriculum take in to account and reflect research on developmental, age-appropriate concepts, common misconceptions, and difficulties students have with certain concepts and skills (Sections II and IV)?
13. Are the learning goals carefully sequenced? Was the decision arbitrary or based on prerequisite and connecting ideas (Section V)?
14. Does the curriculum emphasize ideas and thinking over facts and vocabulary (Sections I and III)?
15. Does the curriculum include inquiry as both a means to learn content and an ability/skill (CTS guides in Inquiry and the Nature of Science and Technology)?
16. Does the curriculum attempt to make connections to personal, societal, environmental, and political considerations (CTS guides in Implications of Science and Technology)?
17. Does the curriculum make connections to other disciplines closely linked to science, like mathematics, technology, history, and social science (Section V)?
18. Is process linked to content, as opposed to teaching process skills in isolation (Section II)?
19. Does the curriculum emphasize depth over breadth (Sections I, II, III, and V)?
20. Is the curriculum designed for ALL students (Sections I–VI)?

➔ **If a first-year, beginning teacher were handed the curriculum, how easy would it be to implement it as designed? Is it explicit enough? Is sufficient guidance provided for teachers?**

Note: Sections to refer to in a CTS study guide are referenced in the parentheses.

The CTS reveals that plate tectonics is a sophisticated idea that is not even addressed until the secondary level. Section VI of the CTS showed that although the state Grades 3–5 performance indicator says, "Students will demonstrate how changes happen to the surface of the earth over time," Grade 4 material should focus on developmentally appropriate ideas such as how waves, wind, water, and ice affect the earth's surface by eroding and depositing rock and soil and how larger rocks break up and weather over time.

Figure 4.10   Example of a Maine District's Curriculum Clarification Guide to a Topic

Clarification of a Curricular Topic: Rocks and Minerals

Adult Content Knowledge	K–12 Content Knowledge from *Benchmarks* and *NSES*	Related Research on Student Learning	Implications for Teaching Ideas in the Topic	Connections to Maine's *Learning Results*
Culminating Ideas from *Science for All Americans*: • The earth is mostly rock. • Minerals are made, dissolved, and remade on the earth's surface, in the oceans, and in the hot, high-pressure layers beneath the crust. • Sediments of sand and shells of dead organisms are gradually buried, cemented together by dissolved minerals, and eventually turned into solid rock again. • Sedimentary rock buried deep enough may be changed by pressure and heat, perhaps melting and recrystallizing into different kinds of rock.	**K–2:** • Chunks of rocks come in many sizes and shapes, from boulders to grains of sand and even smaller. • Change is something that happens to many things. **3–4:** • Waves, wind, water, and ice erode rock. • Rock is composed of different combinations of minerals. • Smaller rocks come from the breakage and weathering of bedrock and larger rocks. • Earth materials include solid rocks with different physical and chemical properties that make them useful in different ways, for example, as building materials. **5–8:** • The earth is mostly rock. • Some minerals are very rare, and some exist in great quantities, the ability to recover them is just as important as their abundance. • Some changes in the solid earth can be described as the "rock cycle." Old rocks at the earth's surface weather, forming sediments that are buried, then	**Rocks:** Children have difficulty distinguishing between rocks and minerals. To children: Rocks must be large, heavy, and jagged. Smaller pieces are not called rocks, but rather stones. **Minerals:** Some students suggest that minerals are small, precious stones. **Sedimentary Rocks:** Some students confuse sedimentary rock with being volcanic and that heat is involved in its formation. Layers are sometimes confused with cleavage planes in metamorphic rocks. **Igneous Rocks:** Confusion as to their origin: Some associate igneous with fire. **Metamorphic Rocks:** Some children confuse these rocks with metamorphosis in animals.	**K–12:** • An integrated picture of the earth has to develop over many years, with some concepts being visited over and over again in new contexts and greater detail. Some aspects can be learned in science, others in geography some parts can be purely descriptive, and others must draw on physical principles. **K–2:** • Teaching geological facts serves little purpose at this age. • Young children are naturally interested in soil and rocks and during these years they should be encouraged to observe closely. **3–4:** • Students should become adept at using magnifiers to inspect a variety of rocks. The point is not to classify rigorously, but to make observations of the variety. • Students should now observe elementary processes of the rock cycle: erosion, transport, and deposit. • By observing and carefully describing the properties of many rocks, children will begin to see that some rocks are made of a	**K–2:** E1: Show that large things are made up of small pieces. F3: Observe changes that are caused by water, snow, wind, and ice. **3–4:** F3: Describe differences among rocks, minerals, and soils. **5–8:** F5: Classify and identify rocks and minerals based on their physical and chemical properties, composition, and the processes that formed them F6: Describe the many products used by humans that are derived from materials in the earth's crust. **9–12:** F3: Describe the impact of plate movement and erosion on the rock cycle.

(Continued)

Figure 4.10 (Continued)

Clarification of a Curricular Topic: Rocks and Minerals

Adult Content Knowledge	K–12 Content Knowledge from Benchmarks and NSES	Related Research on Student Learning	Implications for Teaching Ideas in the Topic	Connections to Maine's Learning Results
• Buried rock layers may be forced up again to become land surface and eventually mountains. **Science Matters: Fundamental Ideas for Adult Literacy** • Rocks are categorized into three types: sedimentary, igneous, and metamorphic. Each represents a different complex past. • Each type of rock can be changed from one form to another and then back again: the rock cycle. • All three forms of rock can weather to form more sediment, and all three can be subducted to melt or metamorphose and start the cycle anew.	compacted, heated, and often recrystallized into new rock, which may be forced up again to become land surface and even mountains. • Sediments of sand and smaller particles are gradually buried and are cemented together by dissolved minerals to form solid rock again. • Rock bears evidence of the minerals, temperatures, and forces that created it. • Thousands of layers of sedimentary rock confirm the long history of the changing surface of the earth and the changing life forms whose remains are found in successive layers. The youngest layers are not always found on top, because of folding, breaking, and uplift of layers. **9–12:** • The formation, weathering, sedimentation, and reformation of rock constitute a continuing "rock cycle" in which the total amount of material stays the same as its forms change.	**Mountains:** Some children describe mountains as "high rocks." **Soil:** Some students think of soil as the precursor to rock and that it changes to rock in the sequence: soil-clay-rock.	single substance but most are made of several substances. In later grades, the substances can be identified as minerals. • Understanding rocks and minerals should not be extended to the study of the source of the rocks, such as sedimentary, igneous, and metamorphic, because the origin of rocks and minerals has little meaning to young children. • Playgrounds and nearby vacant lots are convenient study sites to observe a variety of earth materials. **5–8:** • Students investigate the rock cycle as an introductory example of geophysical and geochemical cycles. • It is important to connect formation of sedimentary rock and the fossil record to evidence for evolution of species. **9–12:** • Crustal dynamics and geochemical processes provide a focus for understanding the solid earth. • Knowledge of radioactivity can be used to understand how rocks are dated.	F4: Describe ways scientists measure long periods of time and determine the age of very old objects. F5: Demonstrate how rocks and minerals are used to determine geologic history.

However, this is different from a thorough curriculum materials analysis, which looks more precisely at the extent of alignment and the instructional quality of the lessons (see Resource A for information about curriculum materials analysis procedures that can be used to extend the CTS process). CTS provides a filter to use during initial screening to determine whether materials address standards and research beyond a topical match.

An example of how CTS and a set of tools were used to examine a new elementary science curriculum unit is shown in Figures 4.11 and 4.12. The review committee used the "Visible Light, Color, and Vision" CTS guide to focus their screening of *Science Companion's* "Light" unit (Chicago Science Group, 2004). The committee used a CTS tool called the "CTS Content Summary Guide for Instructional Materials Review" to summarize findings from each of the CTS sections (I–VI) that would be useful in examining the unit (a worksheet copy of this tool is available in Resource B and on the CTS Web site). The summary includes CTS results such as

- Adult concepts that could be explained in the teachers' guide
- Content knowledge for students described in the standards
- Instructional strategies and implications described in the standards and research
- Research-identified difficulties and misconceptions
- Important prerequisites to consider
- Connections to other CTS topics

The short, one-page CTS summary guide shown in Figure 4.11 provides an overview-at-a glance of the things the committee should look for in the "Light" unit that were identified by using the "Visible Light, Color, and Vision" CTS study guide.

A summary review sheet was used to cite preliminary evidence that the "Light" unit was "standards-based" and informed by research on student learning. Each of the five categories is rated to the extent that it matches the results from the CTS with comments that describe the match between a preliminary scan of the material and the CTS summary guide (Figure 4.11). The summary review points out that *Science Companion's* "Light" unit appears to be very well matched to the CTS results. The results initially indicate that the material aligns well with standards, is informed by research, and makes relevant connections to other topics. An example of the summary review is included in Figure 4.12. (A worksheet template for the review summary can be found in Resource B and on the CTS Web site.)

CTS tools are not a replacement for a rigorous and thorough curriculum analysis. Instead, they can help teachers determine whether the development of the instructional material was informed by standards and research. This is an important process for curriculum materials selection committee members charged with determining the validity of the claim "standards- and research-based" materials.

Supporting Curriculum Implementation

Curriculum implementation involves classroom use of new instructional materials selected and organized by a school or district for a particular grade level to use for developing student understanding of specific concepts and skills (Loucks-Horsley et al., 2003).

The CTS process is used before implementing new curricula to improve understanding of the content, understand the meaning and

> Curriculum implementation involves not only knowing about the key features of a new curriculum program and its materials but also knowing the science content in the curriculum program and why it is presented and sequenced the way it is.

Figure 4.11 Visible Light, Color, and Vision CTS Content Summary Guide for Grade 3 Materials Review

CTS Content Summary Guide for Instructional Materials Review

CTS Topic: Visible Light, Color, and Vision   **Grade Level:** 3–5

Concepts for Teacher Background Information (Sec. I, II) • Nature of light • Waves and wave behavior • Electromagnetic spectrum	**Students' Content Knowledge (Sec. III, V, VI)** • Light travels in a straight line until it strikes an object or material. • Light can be reflected, refracted, absorbed, or allowed to pass through an object or material
Instructional Implications (Sec. II, IV) • Use children's curiosity to explore through observing and manipulating common objects: comparing, describing, and sorting to form explanations and communicate through drawings. • Use prisms to see that white light produces a whole "rainbow" of colors. • Wait until middle school for more complex ideas like composition of white light or linking light to wave motion. • Specially designed, explicit instruction can help some students understand vision as "detecting" reflected light. • Encourage experimentation with light to help students begin to understand that phenomona can be observed, measured, and controlled in various ways.	**Student Difficulties and Misconceptions (Sec. II, IV)** • Tendency to identify light with its source or its effects. • Difficult notion of light as something that travels from one place to another; hence difficulty explaining shadows and reflection off objects. • Accept idea that mirrors reflect light but difficulty accepting that ordinary objects reflect light. • Difficulty understanding how we see light: persistent notion of eye seeing without linking it to light reflecting off an object.
Prerequisite Knowledge (Sec. III, V) • Develop idea of light reflection off objects before understanding how objects can be seen by our eyes. • Ideas about light and sight are prerequisite to understanding astronomical phenomena (stars, phases of the moon, eclipses). • How things are seen by their reflected light is necessary before phases of the moon will make sense.	**Connections to Other Topics (Sec. II, V)** • Sun, Earth, Moon System • Stars • Heat • Models

intent of the curricular goals, and be aware of research that may impact student learning. The CTS process builds upon and extends the material presented in the teacher's guide, which varies with different programs in its support for teachers. The CTS groundwork for implementing new curriculum can be done by an individual teacher or with groups of teachers learning how to implement new curricula together. Figure 4.13 shows an example of a CTS customized study guide, used by a FOSS (full option science system) teacher leader that combines the "Magnetism" and the "Electrical Charge and Energy" topic studies. This CTS was used to support a group of fourth-grade teachers in implementing a new FOSS "Magnetism and

Figure 4.12 Summary Review of *Science Companion's®* "Light"

CTS Content Summary Review Match for Instructional Materials

Unit: Light Grade Level: 3–4 Developer: *Science Companion*

Please rate the summary categories, on a scale of 1–5, to the extent that the material showed evidence of matching the findings and recommendations in the CTS Summary Guide: **1-** No evidence; **2-** Minimal evidence; **3-** Sufficient evidence; **4-** Strong evidence; **5-** Strong evidence that includes relevant material that exceeds the CTS findings and recommendations.

Concepts for Teacher Background Information   Evidence: 1   2   3   4 | 5 |

Comments: *The material addressed the CTS-identified adult science literacy concepts teachers should know to teach this concept, and also did a nice job of linking them to students' ideas. The detailed descriptions and illustrations of how light travels are particularly helpful to novices. Misconceptions that students (as well as adults) might have are explained. The material explains the correct ideas about how we see and goes on to provide a biological explanation of vision. There is also a nice summary of the history of physicists' ideas about light that lead up to an explanation of the particle and wave theories of light.*

Students' Content Knowledge   Evidence: 1   2   3   4 | 5 |

Comments: *Cluster 2 develops the idea about light traveling in a straight line and how it moves outward until it strikes an object. Cluster 3 goes on to develop ideas about reflection and connecting it to how we see objects. Cluster 4 builds upon the idea of light interacting with objects by developing ideas about absorption, refraction, or passing right through and classifying materials according to how light interacts with them. Terminology is appropriately used in conjunction with developing the idea. In addition to the ideas from the Grades 3–5 standards, the middle school idea of how we see objects by their reflected light is introduced early on in an appropriate, developmental way. In addition, the listing of the big ideas helps give "bigger" conceptual meaning to the specific ideas developed in the lessons as well as the standards themselves. This material is a strong match to the content in the standards, including our Massachusetts standards.*

Instructional Implications   Evidence: 1   2   3   4 | 5 |

Comments: *The rich, well-designed inquiry-based investigations infused throughout the lessons engage students in observing multiple relevant phenomena and manipulating common objects and material: comparing, describing, and sorting to form explanations and communicate through drawings. The use of the science notebooks encourages students to use their drawings and record observations to support their explanations and conclusions. Students have multiple opportunities to control light and examine its effects. While the Benchmarks suggested using prisms, it wasn't necessary in this unit for the concepts being developed. I particularly liked how the unit explicitly addresses and provides an opportunity for students to try and experience total darkness: It is the lack of this experience that leads many students to develop misconceptions about how we see. Overall, the material is very consistent in addressing the CTS instructional implications.*

Student Difficulties and Misconceptions   Evidence: 1   2   3   4 | 5 |

Comments: *The very first lesson addresses the misconception of identifying light with its source. This is explicitly pointed out in the teacher note. Students have opportunities to distinguish between light emitters and light reflectors. Having direct experiences with darkness helps the students overcome misconceptions associated with how we see. The use of drawings and many opportunities for modeling help students develop the correct conception of light traveling outward from its source and interacting with objects. The material does an excellent job of developing the idea that light reflects off objects other than mirrors by giving students a variety of smooth and bumpy surfaces of different materials, starting with shiny surfaces they could detect and then transferring the ideas to matte surfaces. By not focusing the activities on mirrors, students will be more likely to develop a correct conception of reflection off various surfaces. The unit also points out potential misconceptions that can come from children's literature tied to students' difficulty with understanding how we see, such as the picture of the bat with "rays of light" coming out of its eyes, indicating an inaccurate model of the eye as the activator of vision. Overall, this material does a very good, intentional job of alerting teachers to potential misconceptions and designing activities to address them by helping students construct correct scientific ideas.*

(Continued)

Figure 4.12 (Continued)

Prerequisite Knowledge   Evidence: 1   2   3   4 $\boxed{5}$

Comments: *Although it wasn't mentioned in the CTS findings as a prerequisite, the unit began by activating students' prior knowledge about where light comes from. The second lesson develops precursor ideas about sources of light, necessary knowledge needed before developing ideas about how light travels. It is also evident when looking through the full-year scope and sequence of lessons that the notion of light reflection off objects and how some objects do not allow light to pass through are prerequisite ideas used in the solar system lessons to observe shadows and the changing phases of the moon. Overall, the material does a very good job of identifying and building upon prior knowledge both within this unit and across other units, like the Solar System module.*

Connections to Other Topics   Evidence: 1   2   3   4 $\boxed{5}$

Comments: *The unit does an excellent job of helping students understand the importance of using models to develop ideas. While it does not make connections within this unit to astronomy related ideas, it is evident in the yearlong scope and sequence that light ideas are linked to understanding shadows and the changing phases of the moon. Design technology, while not part of the CTS results, is also a potential connection, through the design and use of periscopes. Overall, this material does a nice job of making connections to other content ideas and skills.*

Electricity" kit-based unit. The teachers were first led through the CTS to develop a common understanding of the content, instructional practices, and research on student learning as it related to the kit. Keeping the results of their CTS in mind, the teachers experienced the different activities, all the while connecting what they were doing to what they learned by doing the CTS. The common understanding gained through the CTS process helped the teachers understand why it is important to maintain the fidelity of the program by strengthening components rather than changing them altogether.

A CTS Curricular Conceptual Storyline includes

- Unifying themes such as the ones listed in the CTS guides section "Unifying Themes" as well as other themes, such as Patterns, Cause and Effect, Structure and Function, Evolution and Equilibrium, Interactions, Change, Diversity, Limits, and so on
- Big ideas
- Major concepts
- Subconcepts
- Inquiry and Technological Skills
- The primary CTS guide related to the unit
- Related CTS guides
- State standards

These storylines are based in part on the work of California's El Centro School District's NSF-funded local systemic change project, VIPS, which created 1- to 2-page storyline guides to help their teachers implement kit-based science programs. Figure 4.15 shows an example of how a CTS user created a conceptual storyline for the GEMS curricular unit, "Real Reasons for Seasons" (Gould, Willard, & Pompea, 2000). First, the CTS study guide "Seasons" was selected as the primary topic study most central to the unit. Sections I, II, III, and V of the CTS guide were used to examine the content of the topic for structure and hierarchy of knowledge (see Figure 4.5).

Figure 4.13   Combined "Customized" CTS Guide for FOSS "Electricity and Magnetism" Kit Grade 4 Implementation

Standards- and Research-Based Study of a Curricular Topic
ELECTRICITY AND MAGNETISM

Section and Outcome	Selected Sources and Readings for Study and Reflection Read and examine *related parts* of:
I. Identify Adult Content Knowledge	**IA:** *Science for All Americans* ▶ Chapter 4, *Forces of Nature*, pages 55–56 **IB:** *Science Matters: Achieving Scientific Literacy* ▶ Chapter 3, *Electricity and Magnetism*, pages 35–45
II. Consider Instructional Implications	**IIA:** *Benchmarks for Science Literacy* ▶ 4G, *Forces of Nature* general essay, page 93; Grade 3–5 essay, page 94 **IIB:** *National Science Education Standards* ▶ Grades K–4, Standard B essay, pages 123, 126
III. Identify Concepts and Specific Ideas	**IIIA:** *Benchmarks for Science Literacy* ▶ 4G, *Forces of Nature* Grades 3–5, page 94 **IIIB:** *National Science Education Standards* ▶ Grades K–4, Standard B, *Light, Heat, Electricity, and Magnetism*, page 127
IV. Examine Research on Student Learning	**IVB:** *Making Sense of Secondary Science: Research Into Children's Ideas* ▶ Chapter 15, *Electricity*, pages 117–125 ▶ Chapter 16, *Magnetism*, pages 126–127
V. Examine Coherency and Articulation	**V:** *Atlas of Science Literacy:* There are no maps for this topic in Volume 1.
VI. Clarify State Standards and District Curriculum	**VIA:** *State Standards:* Link Sections I–V to learning goals and information from your state standards or frameworks that are informed by the results of the topic study. **VIB:** *District Curriculum Guide:* Link Sections I–V to learning goals and information from your district curriculum guide that are informed by the results of the topic study.
Visit www.curriculumtopicstudy.org for updates or supplementary readings, Web sites, and videos.	

The content from the CTS results was applied in the context of the curriculum guide to identify the different levels of knowledge, as shown in Figure 4.14.

Next, the activities in the unit were examined for their flow of ideas, briefly described and grouped in clusters with the subconcepts. The flow chart layout helps teachers see at a glance, without having to scour numerous pages of teacher notes, how the subconcepts related to the concepts, big ideas, and unifying themes and flow as a scaffolded set of activities in the unit. Since inquiry is embedded throughout the activities, specific inquiry skills are identified at the bottom of the storyline page. The topic study that was used to develop the storyline is identified for teachers who wish to do their own complete study of the topic. Related

> Another way CTS can support curriculum implementation is by using a CTS guide to develop a CTS Curricular Conceptual Storyline, a one-page summary of the conceptual flow of a curricular unit.

Figure 4.14   Structure of Knowledge Summary for a CTS Curriculum Storyline

---

CTS Structure of Knowledge Summary for the "Real Reasons for Seasons" Storyline

Unifying Theme: Constancy and Change

Big Ideas (from Section I and II):
The motion of the earth and its position with regard to the sun have noticeable effects; models are representations that help us understand the real thing better; distances in the cosmos are immense.

Concepts (from Section III): Motion, Seasons, Models, Solar Energy, Cycles

Subconcepts:
Earth's revolution, earth's rotation, spherical earth, earth's tilted axis, sun-earth models, sun-earth distance, angle of sunlight, seasonal change, shape of orbits, temperature variation, photoperiods

Learning Goals from Maine's *Learning Results* (Section VI):
MLR 5–8 F1: Demonstrate how earth's tilt on its axis results in the seasons.

MLR 5–8 G5: Describe the motions of moons, planets, stars, solar systems, and galaxies.

Specific Ideas (from Sections II, III, and IV):
- Most objects in the solar system are in regular and predictable motion.
- The regular and predictable motion of the earth explains phenomena, such as the day and year.
- The earth turns daily on an axis tilted relative to the plane of the earth's yearly orbit around the sun.
- The sun is the major source of energy for phenomena on the earth's surface.
- Sunlight falls more intensely on different parts of the earth during the year.
- Seasons result from variations in the amount of the sun's energy hitting the surface due to the tilt of the earth's rotation on its axis and the length of day
- Cycles, such as the seasons, can be described by their length or frequency, what their highest and lowest values are, and when these values occur.
- A sun-earth model is a simplified imitation that can help us understand aspects of the sun-earth system.

---

topic studies are also identified for teachers who wish to further examine other concept- and skill-based topics addressed in the unit. Last, the relevant state standards are identified. These conceptual storylines provide a conceptual road map for teachers implementing a curriculum. In addition, the development of conceptual storylines, following a CTS and identification of the levels of knowledge in a topic, is a significant professional development activity by itself. (See Figure 4.15.)

CTS AND INSTRUCTION

CTS can be used to design new lessons, improve instructional delivery of existing lessons, and review and modify lessons to be more in line with standards and research findings. Standards- and research-based lesson design utilizes the tools and reflective processes of CTS. The CTS process helps teachers improve instruction by helping them

- Improve understanding of the content taught
- Focus on important learning goals
- Choose effective strategies and contexts

Figure 4.15 Example of a Curricular Conceptual Storyline

The "Real Reasons for Seasons" Conceptual Storyline GEMS Unit: Grades 6–8

Unifying Theme: Constancy and Change

Big Ideas: The motion of the earth and its position with regard to the sun has noticeable effects. Models are representations that help us understand the real thing better. Distances in the cosmos are immense.

Major Concepts: Seasons, Motion, Cycles, Models, Solar Energy

Subconcept: Seasonal Change   **Subconcepts:** Spherical Earth, Earth's Revolution, Earth's Rotation, Sun-Earth Distance

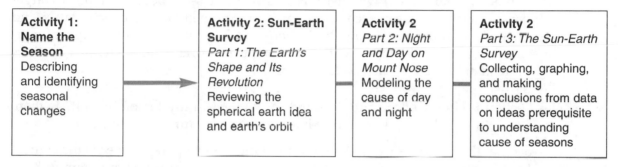

| Activity 1: **Name the Season** Describing and identifying seasonal changes | Activity 2: **Sun-Earth Survey** *Part 1: The Earth's Shape and Its Revolution* Reviewing the spherical earth idea and earth's orbit | **Activity 2** *Part 2: Night and Day on Mount Nose* Modeling the cause of day and night | **Activity 2** *Part 3: The Sun-Earth Survey* Collecting, graphing, and making conclusions from data on ideas prerequisite to understanding cause of seasons |

Subconcept: Sun-Earth Scale Model   **Subconcepts:** Orbits, Sun-Earth Distance

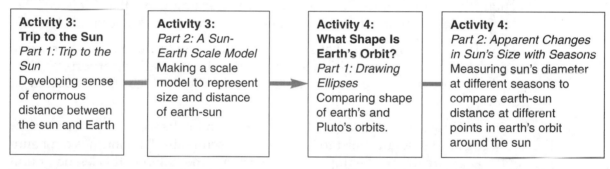

| Activity 3: **Trip to the Sun** *Part 1: Trip to the Sun* Developing sense of enormous distance between the sun and Earth | **Activity 3:** *Part 2: A Sun-Earth Scale Model* Making a scale model to represent size and distance of earth-sun | Activity 4: **What Shape Is Earth's Orbit?** *Part 1: Drawing Ellipses* Comparing shape of earth's and Pluto's orbits. | **Activity 4:** *Part 2: Apparent Changes in Sun's Size with Seasons* Measuring sun's diameter at different seasons to compare earth-sun distance at different points in earth's orbit around the sun |

Subconcepts: Temperature Variation, Photoperiods   **Subconcepts:** Tilted Earth, Angle of Sunlight

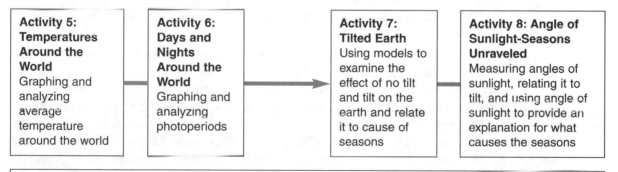

| Activity 5: **Temperatures Around the World** Graphing and analyzing average temperature around the world | Activity 6: **Days and Nights Around the World** Graphing and analyzing photoperiods | Activity 7: **Tilted Earth** Using models to examine the effect of no tilt and tilt on the earth and relate it to cause of seasons | Activity 8: **Angle of Sunlight-Seasons Unraveled** Measuring angles of sunlight, relating it to tilt, and using angle of sunlight to provide an explanation for what causes the seasons |

Skills: Observation, Inference, Data Collection and Analysis, Designing and Making Models, Explanation, Drawing Conclusions

Major CTS Guide Used for Storyline Development: Seasons

Related CTS Guides: Scale, Size, and Distance in Space; Evidence and Explanation; Data Collection and Analysis; Graphs and Graphing; Models; Constancy and Change

Maine's Learning Results: Grades 5–8: The Earth: F1; The Universe: G3, G5; Inquiry and Problem Solving: J2; Scientific Reasoning: K6, K8; Communication: L1, L4

- Identify developmental issues
- Be aware of alternative ideas and misconceptions their students may hold
- See how ideas are connected

Reviewing and Modifying Lessons

Perhaps you have a lesson that works fairly well but could use some improvement. A topic study can provide useful information for improving the lesson's potential to increase student learning. On the other hand, perhaps it is time to let go of the lesson, regardless of whether it is a "favorite" lesson, because it fails to target important ideas and seems contrary to the recommendations of standards and research. How would you know this? Choose a CTS that matches the topic of your lesson. As you study the topic, with a filter of the lesson, ask the following questions as you read and analyze each section of the CTS:

Section I: How well do I understand the content in my lesson or unit? Is there content in the lesson that may be inaccurate, irrelevant, or missing?

Section II: How does this lesson or unit fit into a K–12 perspective? Is the context I am using appropriate? What are the "big ideas" the lesson should aim for?

Section III: Are there specific ideas within the learning goals that I missed? Are there goals in the national standards that I should be addressing in this lesson?

Section IV: Is there research that supports or alerts me to things I might need to know about the lesson or unit? Is the lesson developmentally appropriate? How can I build formative assessment into the lesson to target ideas from research on learning?

Section V: How connected are the learning goals in my lesson or unit? What prior knowledge did students need to have? What essential understandings am I aiming toward? Are there other topics in our curriculum related to this lesson or unit I can connect to?

Section VI: Does this lesson or unit align with the state or district standards?

Answers to these questions based on the CTS results can be used to analyze, revise, refine, or discard any lesson, whether it is teacher developed or a commercial lesson that was not developed based on standards and research on learning. The advantage of using CTS to examine instruction is that changes are based on evidence that comes from standards or research, not individual interpretation. It combines the creativity and wisdom of teachers with generally accepted ideas and practices that ensure greater consistency of opportunity to learn across classrooms. Vignette #2 describes an example of how lessons in a curricular unit were revised (and some discarded) based on using CTS.

Developing a Standards- and Research-Based Lesson

Using a lesson design process with CTS, teachers identify the appropriate learning goal(s) for the topic of the lesson, the research base on student learning that informs the lesson, and effective instructional strategies to help students learn the concepts and skills taught in the lesson. It adds an essential front-end step to the popular "Understanding by Design" backwards planning process (Wiggins & McTighe, 1998). It is not enough to begin with an identification of the learning goals and assessments as the starting point of instructional design. An extra step is needed to understand the learning goals as well as identify important goals that may have been overlooked. CTS helps to frame the backwards design process around accepted standards- and research-based implications for teaching, learning, and assessment, rather than relying on individual teachers' assumptions and interpretations. Steps in developing standards- and research-based lessons using CTS are described in Figure 4.16. The CTS Web site provides examples of standards- and research-based lessons developed by teachers using the CTS lesson design process.

> The CTS lesson design process moves instructional design away from starting with activities and figuring out whether there are learning goals that align with the activity to thinking about the appropriate types of activities and pedagogy that support the specific ideas and research base identified through the CTS.

CTS and Inquiry-Based Instruction

Inquiry is the centerpiece of good science instruction.

For students to understand inquiry and use it to learn science, their teachers need to be well-versed in inquiry and inquiry-based methods. Yet most teachers have not had opportunities to learn science through inquiry or to conduct scientific inquiries themselves. Nor do many teachers have the understanding and skills they need to use inquiry thoughtfully and appropriately in their classrooms. (NRC, 2000, p. 87)

CTS addresses this critical need to understand the abilities of inquiry and be able to design opportunities for students to use inquiry skills. CTS guides include skill-based topics that address a particular aspect of inquiry as well as content knowledge topics. These CTS guides help teachers develop a common understanding of the inquiry skills embedded within inquiry-based lessons.

There are 26 CTS guides in Chapter 6 that address multiple facets of inquiry, the nature of science, and technological design. These guides can be used to design inquiry-based instruction that includes both important skills and content knowledge. The CTS guides range from comprehensive inquiry topics such as "Science as Inquiry" to specific inquiry skills such as "Controlling Variables."

In designing inquiry-based instruction, a "content" CTS guide and a "skill" CTS guide can be studied together to improve understanding about the use of inquiry to develop content understanding. For example, a teacher may use the "Magnetism" CTS guide along with "Experimental Design" to examine an effective way to provide opportunities for students to carry out an investigation to learn important ideas about magnets.

> CTS helps move instruction from an activity focus or a disconnected skill exercise to a richer inquiry experience that involves students in constructing understandings in science through the use of scientifically oriented questions, collection of relevant evidence, evidence-based explanations, logical argument, and scientific communication as well as understanding how scientists study the natural world.

Figure 4.16 Steps to Developing a CTS Standards- and Research-Based Lesson

---

Steps in CTS Standards and Research-Based Lesson Design

1. IDENTIFY A CORE SET OF LEARNING GOALS: Begin by identifying the important learning goals in your state or local standards. Select a curricular topic or topics these learning goals may be organized around in a unit of instruction. (CTS Section VI)

2. STUDY THE GOALS: Carefully study the curricular topic using one or more CTS guides. Keep in mind that some CTS guides can be combined (e.g., combining Cells and Models may be useful in designing a lesson on creating a model of a cell). Take careful notes on specific content knowledge in the learning goals, context, instructional and assessment implications, developmental appropriateness, research-identified misconceptions, prerequisites, and interconnected and contributing learning goals. (CTS Sections I, II, III, IV, V)

3. COMPARE RESULTS AND IDENTIFY GAPS AND EXCESSES: Match the results of your study with your local curriculum guide, existing curriculum materials, preliminary ideas for a new lesson, and state standards. Modify as needed based on the study results. For example, you might find your curriculum materials contain more content than is necessary, mismatch the appropriate level of sophistication, or should include additional important ideas not mentioned in your state standards that provide coherency for the development of a lesson. (CTS Sections III, IV, and VI)

4. IDENTIFY THE MEANS: Decide whether you are going to modify an existing lesson or set of lessons or create a new lesson(s). Determine what kinds experiences or phenomena relate to the topic that can be used to develop understanding. (CTS Sections I, II, and IV)

5. DESIGN INSTRUCTION USING KNOWLEDGE OF EFFECTIVE TEACHING AND LEARNING: Incorporate pedagogical practices informed by standards or research that will help students learn the ideas. No matter how well aligned the content of a lesson is, there is no assurance that students will understand the ideas without appropriate instructional strategies. Be sure to include opportunities to elicit students' existing ideas, including misconceptions, and probe for conceptual understanding throughout the lesson. (CTS Sections II and IV).

6. TRY OUT THE LESSON AND MODIFY AS NEEDED: Try the lesson out, making careful notes of where students are having difficulty and also the strengths of the lesson. Record interesting ideas and statements from students for later reference. Collect student work. Make modifications as needed. Have others try out the lesson and suggest changes as needed.

7. "PUBLISH" YOUR LESSON: Create teaching notes to go with a write-up of your lesson that could be shared with others who may wish to use the lesson. Include findings from the CTS, including the content background, alignment to the learning goals in the topic, your thinking that went into the lesson design, pedagogical strategies, and descriptions of what students would be doing. Include student work if available.

Students learn about magnetism, while concurrently developing the ability to carry out a scientific investigation. The following questions can be used to gather information and reflect on the readings from the sections of the CTS guides that focus on different aspects of inquiry:

Section II: What is this inquiry skill? Why is it important for students to develop this skill? What are the implications for instruction and assessment? How will I design instruction to help students develop this skill?

Section III: What are the specific skills at the designated grade level that students need to develop to be proficient in this aspect of inquiry? Where do these specific skills fit within the context of the lesson?

Section IV: What are the difficulties students might encounter with this particular aspect of inquiry? Are there developmental implications I should be aware of when helping students develop or use this skill? How will I design and monitor their experiences in order to help them work through these difficulties?

Section V: How do the skills related to this aspect of inquiry build over time? Have my students had previous opportunities to use these skills? What precursor skills do I need to consider as I plan instruction?

Section VI: What do my state standards identify as important skills related to this aspect of inquiry? How will my CTS findings be used to design instruction to ensure students have the opportunity to learn and demonstrate these standards?

Initially, the time it takes to do both CTS and instructional planning may appear daunting. However, in the long run, CTS saves time by focusing instruction clearly on learning goals and understandings about how students learn. Designing lessons that fail to meet their targets is both frustrating and an inefficient use of valuable instructional time. CTS-informed lessons are more likely to be effective, since they are clearly designed with standards and research in mind. In the long run, it promotes effective and maximum achievement of student learning. The use of a common knowledge base ensures greater coherence and consistency in using a backwards design planning process for instruction.

> Over time, teachers who use CTS describe it as a naturally integrated process for lesson planning that prevents the backfilling that occurs when instruction fails to reach all students.

CTS AND ASSESSMENT

There are a variety of assessment practices used by teachers, states, and federal agencies to assess student learning and the opportunity to learn. Despite these differences in assessment policies, programs, procedures, and protocols, there is one common, essential key practice that ensures that assessment is used effectively in science. That common key practice is a thorough understanding of both the content in the learning goal to be assessed and the knowledge about student learning related to that content. When teachers do not thoroughly understand the content, learning goals, and cognitive aspects of the topics they teach in science, they not only have difficulty teaching the ideas but also fail to assess ideas appropriately or use assessment results effectively. Likewise, assessment developers who fail to thoroughly examine the specific and relevant ideas in a learning goal, the contexts appropriate for demonstrating understanding and knowledge, and the research on student learning that underlies achievement of the goal may provide assessments that do not effectively assess learning.

> CTS provides tools and processes to help assessment developers become better assessment designers and to help teachers become informed consumers of assessments and assessment data.

CTS can be used with both formative and summative assessment. The first type of assessment is used as feedback for the student or to the teacher to inform instruction and learning. The second type of assessment, summative assessment, measures the extent to which students have achieved the goals for learning. The first step in linking CTS to assessment is to define the purpose and stage in the assessment process:

Diagnostic Stage: What existing conceptions do your students have about the scientific ideas in the topic? Use CTS guide Sections III, IV, and VI to identify concepts and specific ideas in the topic and examine research on how students learn and think about these ideas. This information can be used to elicit teachers' own students' ideas and compare them to the research findings. This information is used to design effective instruction and monitor conceptual change.

Formative Stage: How are your students building their conceptual understanding or skills? How is their understanding progressing during any point in the instructional process? What different paths could I use to differentiate instruction in order to bridge the gap between individuals' alternative ideas and the scientific understandings I want the class to achieve? CTS guides Sections II and IV point out the difficulties students might encounter, effective strategies and contexts, and ideas that may need to be monitored over time. Section V indicates gaps or steps along the way that may need to be revisited or reassessed.

Summative Stage: How can my students demonstrate their understanding of the learning goals after instruction? Did they have the opportunity to learn in order to be successful on the assessment? What should my assessment include? Does my assessment fairly target the learning goals? Are my students able to transfer their knowledge and understanding to a new context, or are they limited by the context they learned the idea in? CTS guide Sections III, V, and VI are used to clarify the specific knowledge and skills intended by a learning goal, recognize important generalizations, rigorously align the assessment, identify appropriate contexts and connections that demonstrate transfer of learning, and ensure and maintain the disciplinary integrity of the science being assessed.

Designing Assessment Probes

There are numerous resources on assessment that help educators design and use assessment to measure student learning but few that help educators design research-based assessments that can identify students' misconceptions before and during instruction.

In CTS, these types of formative assessments are referred to as *probes*, indicating they are used to probe for student understanding.

Assessment probes are used diagnostically and formatively to elicit students' ideas and monitor changes in student thinking. The research on student learning from Section IV of the CTS guide is used to link the ideas to be assessed to the research findings. By using the research, a teacher can determine whether students have the same or similar misconceptions indicated by the CTS results. These types of assessments provide information to the teacher that can be used to design effective instruction that targets students' ideas and encourages conceptual change. It is consistent with research on implications for teaching and learning that says:

The roles for assessment must be expanded beyond the traditional concept of testing. The use of frequent formative assessment helps make students' thinking visible to themselves, their peers, and their teacher. This provides feedback that can guide modification and refinement in thinking. (Bransford et al., 2000, p. 19)

> Because explanation is a hallmark of science, eliciting ideas and analyzing explanations are useful ways to gather information about what students know, may struggle with, or have misconceptions about.

CTS has been used with educators to develop individual or sets of assessment probes that elicit students' preconceptions. Steps in designing CTS probes include:

Step 1: Identify the CTS guide(s) for the unit topic you will be teaching. Decide whether to study the entire topic or a subtopic within the CTS guide.

Step 2: Examine Sections III, V, and VI. Identify and record the scientific concepts in the topic or subtopic that are related to your instructional unit. Beneath these concepts, list the specific ideas, including prerequisite knowledge and related learning goals in your state or district standards.

Step 3: Examine Section IV and the narrative research notes in Section V. Match research findings to the concepts or ideas you identified. Make notes on any contextual issues, relevant phenomena, developmental considerations, strategies, and so on that could be used to inform the design of your assessment probe. Map the research findings to the concepts and ideas in Step 2 (see Figure 4.17).

Step 4: Focus on a concept or an idea and the related research findings. Choose the type of probe that lends itself best to an assessment probe based on the research findings. Justified selected response or justified lists are good formats for probes that specifically target research-identified misconceptions.

Step 5: Develop the stem and distracters to specifically target the research findings and match the developmental level of your students. Suggestions for selected response stems include providing a familiar phenomenon to explain an idea, contrasting opposing views, and asking for a prediction. Justified lists begin with a statement about a scientific idea followed by several examples students select that represent the idea or match the statement. These are useful in determining whether students are able to transfer ideas to other contexts beyond those in which they may have learned the ideas (see Figure 4.18 for an example of an assessment using a justified list).

Step 6: Share your assessment probe(s) with colleagues for constructive feedback, pilot with students, and modify as needed.

Step 7: Administer assessment probe and analyze student data. What do the responses tell you about correct, naive, or erroneous ideas your students have? What are the implications for your curriculum and instruction? What will you do to address these ideas your students have? What else would you like to know?

Examining the research in Section IV revealed that many students learn that sound is caused by vibration in a specific context of musical instruments or other common sound-making objects they can investigate. When given a different type of object, students may fail to generalize the idea that sound comes from the vibrations

Figure 4.17 Mapping Sound Concepts and Ideas for Developing Formative Assessment Probes

Mapping Concepts and Ideas in a Topic to Research Findings

Topic: Sound

Science Concepts and Ideas	Research Findings
★Vibration • Sound is produced by vibrating objects. (*NSES* K–4 p. 127) • The pitch of the sound can be varied by changing the rate of vibration. (*NSES* K–4 p. 127) • Explain ways different forms of energy (such as sound) are produced. (*Maine LR's* 3–4 H2) **Waves** • Vibrations in materials set up wavelike disturbances that spread away from the source. Sound waves are an example. (*BSL* 6–8 p. 90) **Sound Transmission** • Sound waves move at different speeds in different materials. (*BSL* 6–8 p. 90) • Compare and contrast the ways energy travels. (*Maine LR's* 5–8 H3) • Explain or demonstrate how sound waves travel. (*Maine LR's* 9–12 H3) **Energy** • Energy is a property of many substances and is associated with sound. (*NSES* 5–8 p. 155) • Energy (including sound) is transferred in many ways. (*NSES* 5–8 p. 155) • Identify different forms of energy (e.g. sound) (*Maine LR's* 3–4 H1) **Hearing** • Something can be "heard" when sound waves from it enter the ear. (*BSL* 6–8 p. 90)	**Characteristics of Sound** • Confusion about speed/size of vibration: Bigger vibrations thought to be slower than small vibrations: consequently difficulties in understanding pitch and volume. **Sound Production** (Driver pp. 133–135) • Many children explain how sound is produced in terms of the physical properties of the material that produces the sound (plastic or rubber or because it is thick, thin, taut, or hard). • The force needed to produce sound, like a human beating a drum, is another proposed mechanism for sound. • Explanations involving vibration or vibrations being transferred to air increase with age. ★• Children appear to be context bound when using vibration ideas, particularly musical instruments. Children may not have a generalized theory of sound production across contexts, particularly in situations where vibration is not obvious, such as hitting two stones together. **Sound Transmission** (Driver pp. 135–137) • Tendency to think sound needs an unobstructed pathway in order to travel. • Some children may conceptualize sound as an invisible object with dimensions that needs room to move. • Air as a medium is seldom mentioned. • Older students' conceptualizations included: (1) sound as an entity carried by individual molecules through a medium, (2) sound as an entity transferred between molecules in a medium, (3) sound as a substance that "flowed," (4) sound as a substance in the form of some "traveling pattern." • Some recognize sound spreads out from a source, while others think it goes only to the listener. • Difficulties accepting sound absorption. **Hearing** (Driver pp. 45–46) • Some mention sound associated with the ear, but few mentioned actually entering the ear. • Few mention the link between eardrum and the brain. • "Active ear" model, in which the listener is responsible for getting the sound, and "the ear picking up sound" are two models for hearing. • By age 16, students start to mention sound transmission to the ear by air and vibration of eardrum.

★Identifies match between a concept and research finding for development of the "Sound" probe in Figure 4.18

NSES: National Science Education Standards. National Research Council (1996). Washington DC: National Academy Press.

Maine LR: Maine's Learning Results. Maine Department of Education (1997). Augusta, ME: State of Maine Printing Office.

BSL: Benchmarks for Science Literacy. American Association for the Advancement of Science (1993). New York: Oxford University Press.

Driver: *Making sense of secondary science.* Driver, R., Squires, A., Rushworth, P., & Wood-Robinson, V. (1994). New York: Routledge.

Figure 4.18 Assessment Probe on Making Sound

Making Sound

Each of the things listed below makes sounds. Put an X after the things that you think produce sound by vibrations.

_____ Guitar Strings	_____ Drum	_____ Dripping Faucet
_____ Barking Dog	_____ Piano	_____ Screeching Brakes
_____ Radio Speaker	_____ Crumpled Paper	_____ Car Engine
_____ Chirping Cricket	_____ Singer	_____ Popped Balloon
_____ Drum	_____ Wind	_____ Wood Saw
_____ Clapped Hands	_____ Bubbling Water	_____ Rustling Leaves
_____ Hammer	_____ Flute	_____ Thunderstorm
_____ Two Stones Rubbed Together		_____ Snapped Fingers

Explain your thinking. What "rule" or reasoning did you use to decide which objects produce sound by vibrations?

SOURCE: *Probing Students' Ideas in Science*, Volume 1, by Paige Keeley, Francis Eberle, and Lynn Farrin. (in press). Arlington, VA: National Science Teachers Association. Reprinted by permission of the publisher.

of objects. The research points out that students are sometimes "context bound" when learning ideas related to sound. The map in Figure 4.17 shows the link between the research idea of being context bound and the concept of vibration. This information was used to develop a probe, in the form of a justified list, to find out whether students can transfer the idea across contexts. Figure 4.18 is an example of a CTS-developed assessment probe based on using the CTS "Sound."

Developing Culminating Performances

CTS can also be used to develop rich, culminating performance tasks. Resources like *Understanding by Design* (Wiggins & McTighe, 1998) provide guidance to educators on how to design performance tasks that effectively measure student understanding.

Figure 4.19 Dark Moons Task

Dark Moons

Did you ever wonder why you sometimes see no moon at all during the moon's monthly cycle of phases? Have you ever watched as a full moon appears to grow dimmer, seems to partially disappear, and gradually reappears again over the course of several hours in the same evening? Astronomers recognize these as two distinct events. These two different astronomical events that affect the way we see the moon are called new moons and lunar eclipses. In this task, you will work in a small group to become "experts" in distinguishing between these two very different astronomical events.

Your Task:

Working in a small group, research the Internet and other materials to find information about lunar eclipses and new moons. Discuss your research with your group. Work together to come up with a common understanding and explanation of why we can't see the moon's reflected light during a new moon and the change that happens during a lunar eclipse. Work together to design and make a model you can use to explain and show what causes these "dark moons." To complete this task successfully, you must:

1. Design your model from common, available materials (you may not use a commercial model that has already been designed for this purpose).

2. Demonstrate and describe your model to the class. Show how it explains the new moon and the lunar eclipse.

3. Include a description of the position and motions of the earth, moon, and sun as you describe each event using your model.

4. Use your models to show and explain the difference between the two events.

5. Show evidence that each person in your group contributed to the task.

You will present your models to the class to describe and explain each astronomical event and the difference between them. You will also listen to and observe your peer's presentations. After the presentations have been completed, you will individually complete two questions assigned by your teacher to demonstrate your individual understanding of the position and motion of the earth, moon, and sun system.

CTS complements these resources by providing a front-end process to study the learning goals and research in the topic and ensure that the task aligns with the meaning and intent of the learning goal and considers research.

The example in Figure 4.19 shows how the CTS "Earth, Moon, and Sun System" and "Models" were used to develop a classroom performance task, "Dark Moons," which targets ideas related to the position of the moon in relation to the earth and sun as well as how models can be used to demonstrate phenomena. The task developer did a full study of the topic prior to developing the task. The teacher notes that follow demonstrate how the results of the topic study were used to inform the task and create teacher notes that describe the task and the extent to which it aligns with the learning goals (see Figure 4.20).

> CTS is a tool that can help teachers develop a common and shared knowledge base needed to ensure assessments are valid, reliable, and truly reflect the nature of science as a disciplinary body of knowledge, skills, and ways of knowing.

Whether using a culminating classroom performance task or assessments that are part of a district or state assessment program, it is essential that teachers combine their assessment knowledge and practices with a deep understanding of the content knowledge and

Figure 4.20   CTS-Informed Teacher Notes for "Dark Moons" Performance Task

---

Dark Moons: Teacher Notes

Task Summary: This task requires students to examine two different astronomical phenomena related to the "Earth-Moon-Sun system": a new moon and a lunar eclipse. Students draw upon prior instructional experiences and conduct additional research of each phenomenon to prepare and present a model that demonstrates what causes the "dark moon" in each event. The models are also used to show the difference between the two phenomena. This task may be used as an instructional opportunity or as a summative assessment if prior learning opportunities were provided to develop the scientific ideas.

Grade Level: Grades 6–8

Time Required: Varies, approximately three 45-minute class periods, including work outside of classroom time.

Materials Needed: Internet access, astronomy books; materials such as Styrofoam balls and light sources for students who may not have access to materials at home.

Product: Physical model and oral presentation

CTS Guides Used to Inform Task Development: "Earth, Moon, Sun System" and "Models"

CTS Section VI: Alignment to State Standards: Grades 5–8 Maine *Learning Results*:
- Universe Standard G5: *Describe the motion of moons, planets, stars, solar systems, and galaxies.* Description of alignment: Students describe motion within the Earth (planet)-Moon (moon)-Sun (star) system that explain phases of the moon (new moon) and eclipse (lunar eclipse) phenomena.
- Scientific Communication Standard L4: *Make and use scale drawings, maps, and three-dimensional models to represent real objects, find locations, and describe relationships.* Description of alignment: Students make and use a physical model to represent the positional relationship between the earth, moon, and sun in order to demonstrate the phenomena and explain the difference between a new moon and a lunar eclipse.

CTS Section III: Underlying Concepts, Ideas, and Skills in National Standards:
- The 4B(6–8)#5 benchmark describes why we see different phases of the moon. Three fundamental ideas in this benchmark are combined in order for students to understand moon phases:
  1) The moon orbits around the earth once every 28 days.
  2) The light we see from the moon is reflected light from the sun.
  3) How much light (the part of the moon) we see depends on the positions of the earth, moon, and sun.
- Regular and predictable motion is emphasized in the *NSES* 5–8/E3b. Two fundamental ideas are combined in this standard:
  1) Most objects in the solar system are in regular and predictable motion.
  2) Regular and predictable motions explain such phenomena as the day, year, phases of the moon, and eclipses.
- The use of models is a unifying theme in both *Benchmarks* and *NSES*. The *NSES* describe models as representations of real objects or events that provide great explanatory power in understanding how things work. The benchmark 11B(6–8)#3 describes how students select the type of model they will use. This benchmark contains 4 key ideas about model selection:
  1) Different models can be used to represent the same thing.
  2) What kind of a model to use and how complex it should be depends on its purpose.
  3) The usefulness of a model may be limited if it is too simple or if it is needlessly complicated.
  4) Choosing a useful model is one of the instances in which intuition and creativity come into play in science, mathematics, and engineering.

(Continued)

Figure 4.20 (Continued)

CTS Sections II and IV: Instructional Implications and Research on Learning:

- Students are often *told* what causes the phases of the moon, rather than constructing their own understanding through the use of models. One of the reasons this idea is so difficult is students' unfamiliarity with the geometry of light and "seeing." Models can help them see where the light is coming from and how much of it reaches our eyes when it is reflected, depending upon where the reflecting object is in relation to the light source and where we are when we see it. Students need many direct experiences with light and reflection first.

- Eclipse ideas may be more comprehensible to students, but be aware that students often confuse the shadow cast by the earth on the moon during a lunar eclipse as being the explanation for phases of the moon. Research shows that the shadow explanation is the most commonly held adult and child idea for what causes the moon's phases. Therefore, providing an opportunity to see and examine the difference between the two phenomena may help students give up the shadow notion as the explanation for moon phases.

- When using models, it is important for students to understand their limitations. They should examine their models for what approximately represents the objects, the distance, and the motions and what might be misrepresented by their models. This examination of their models can help ensure that students try to make models that represent the actual objects or phenomena as closely as possible and do not perpetuate misconceptions based on a faulty model.

- Making a physical model is not the end point. The importance of making the model is the explanatory power it provides. In this task, the students' explanation of the cause of and difference between the new moon and lunar eclipse that accompanies the use of the model is what provides that explanatory power. Emphasize to students that the value of the model is in providing a scientific explanation for the phenomena they have described.

- Description and explanation are two different things. Be sure students understand that an explanation is based on evidence and reasoning.

---

skills that are being assessed and pedagogical content knowledge based on research on how students think and learn.

CTS AND PRESERVICE AND NOVICE TEACHER SUPPORT

Preservice programs are designed to ensure that teachers have the knowledge and skills they need to be effective when they get into the classroom. Often their science methods course requires them to develop sample lessons for teaching science concepts and engage them as learners in the processes of science. These activities can be enhanced by using CTS to help the preservice teachers learn what content is important to focus on, what is appropriate for students to learn at the different age or grade levels, and what to look for to spot common misconceptions. Some preservice teachers even have the opportunity to teach their sample lesson to their peers. In these cases, consider having all the preservice teachers in the class use CTS to establish criteria of what to look for in the sample lesson and to make suggestions on how to enhance it. Using the CTS process will also help preservice teachers prepare for student teaching.

> Introducing preservice students to the CTS process will give them a lifeline they can use when they enter teaching and confront content they may not understand or see students struggling with content.

As beginning teachers enter the workforce, they have many challenges. They need to learn how to manage their classrooms, learn the ropes of getting things done in their new schools, and get to know the students and their families in their classrooms. As they settle into teaching science, they encounter questions about what to teach, how to reach students who are struggling, and how to best assess learning. They realize that all students learn differently, and need to develop a repertoire of strategies to reach all learners. Ideally, they have mentor teachers who will help them develop and revise lessons and interpret what is happening in the classroom and begin to develop their pedagogical content knowledge. CTS can play a key role for beginning teachers as they become experienced teachers. As they have to make decisions about what content to cover in their texts, they can turn to CTS for guidance from the national standards, and they can use the process to examine their local and state curriculum frameworks to help them make choices. They can use the information from the CTS to communicate with their principals about the instructional choices they are making in the classroom. Rarely do beginning teachers get enough support that is focused on teaching science content. Often their mentor teachers don't have backgrounds in science themselves and can help with general teaching skills but not with content and the pedagogy needed for that content. Even when this is the case, the beginning teacher and mentor can use CTS and learn more about the content and how to teach it. Teachers also need to communicate with parents about what students are expected to know and how they will be assessed.

> CTS provides a research-backed grounding teachers can point to as the rationale for their curricular and assessment practices.

CTS AND LEADERSHIP DEVELOPMENT

In our work supporting the development of all types of educational leaders, we have consistently found that even when leaders have a background in one science discipline, they may not know what content is seen as most important for students to know in the other science disciplines. Yet they are often in the position of observing teachers, leading professional development, selecting curriculum, and informing or making policy.

Section I of the CTS might be regarded as the most important information for school and district leaders to know. It reveals what the basic scientifically literate adult should know in each of the science topic areas. We contend school leadership must strive to recognize and understand these concepts themselves and to ensure that their school programs provide the opportunity for all students to gain understanding of the ideas that are articulated in CTS Sections III and V as the steps along the way to adult scientific literacy.

> Principals, teacher leaders, professional developers, and leaders of reform initiatives in science benefit from a deeper understanding of the standards and research behind the hundreds of science topics that are taught K–12.

Teachers who have assumed leadership positions, such as mentors, coaches, curriculum committee leaders, and professional developers, benefit greatly from using CTS as part of their leadership development process. By using and demonstrating applicability of the CTS process, they become leaders who are "standards- and

> CTS is a tool that not only informs leaders and raises their level of knowledge, but most important, it provides them with a process for developing a common core of understanding within the various groups they work with.

research-based." In their work with other teachers, they share their own opinions less; instead, they engage others in looking at the standards and research to inform decisions and choices. Through CTS, they learn how to teach others what it means to intentionally apply standards and research in the classroom.

Whether leaders are involved in school, district, or state committee work; advisory roles; staff development; standards setting and review; or other science reform efforts that draw upon leadership, CTS is a tool that brings greater continuity, consistency, and coherence to their work.

CTS AND PROFESSIONAL DEVELOPMENT

As previously described, the CTS process increases teachers' understanding of the content in a topic and when and how they should teach it. For example, as a stand-alone strategy, a group of teachers who teach chemistry may use their professional development time to work together on the topic studies in the "Matter" category related to the units in their curriculum. Their goals for the professional development may be to increase their knowledge of when to teach certain concepts, identify necessary prerequisites and connections to other topics, and become aware of some common misconceptions.

> CTS is both a stand-alone professional development strategy and a valuable addition to any other professional development program or strategy.

CTS fits nicely into many other professional development strategies. It provides a focused way to ensure that the professional development session is content driven, and forges a strong link to standards and research.

Embedding CTS in a Variety of Professional Development Strategies

In our work with teachers, schools, and with various teacher enhancement and leadership projects, CTS has been used with the following professional development strategies: study groups, case discussions, curriculum selection and implementation, workshops, examining student work and thinking, lesson study, coaching and mentoring, and demonstration lessons. For each of these strategies, CTS was used to focus the participants' learning experience on science content, standards, and research. Each example is described briefly below.

Study Groups

The purpose of study groups is to examine and solve problems of teaching and learning. Study groups focus on a particular learning need of their students. Often these needs are identified through data such as state or local assessment results. These needs may be related to difficult concepts in the curriculum or processes of science they struggle with. One study group identified that students had problems understanding the concept of controlling variables. The teachers got together to study why this concept was so hard for the students. They used the CTS "Experimental Design" and found out that the research shows that student familiarity with the topic of the given experiment influences the likelihood that they will control variables—and that students are more likely to control the variables they believe will affect the outcome of the experiment. As a result, they decided to change the way they introduce investigations in all science labs.

Case Discussions

Case discussions are a relatively new area of professional development. Teachers read and discuss cases—often depicting topics that are difficult to learn or teachers who face dilemmas in the classroom. We have used CTS as a reference for discussing the case. For example, teachers read the case or view the video and have a short discussion. They complete a CTS on the content in the case, which is then used to continue the case discussion, informed by what the standards or research have to say about the content or pedagogical issue in the case. An example of a CTS-based case discussion and guide can be found on the CTS Web site.

Curriculum Selection and Implementation

As groups of teachers engage in curriculum selection and implementation processes, there is extensive opportunity to use CTS. Groups selecting curriculum and instructional materials want to choose those materials that align best with their standards and the research. As committees review materials, CTS can guide them to evaluate how well the material addresses the topics deemed important in the standards. Figures 4.11 and 4.12 show examples of one way CTS was used to inform curriculum selection. CTS is used to help teachers understand the underlying standards and research base of the curriculum they are using, including why the lessons are designed the way they are and what content is important. As the group moves into implementation of the new curriculum, they can continue to use CTS; for example, when they encounter areas of student confusion, they can use the process to learn what research on student learning says about students' common misconceptions about topic. Professional developers can use existing CTS guides to develop customized CTS guides to accompany specific curriculum programs for the purposes of understanding the content and pedagogy during curriculum implementation. For example, Figure 4.13 shows an example of a customized CTS guide used to help fourth-grade teachers implement a new science kit program. CTS-developed storylines (Figure 4.15) can also be developed for use in supporting curriculum implementation.

Workshops

In workshops too, especially those focused on increasing teachers' content and pedagogical content knowledge, CTS is used to help teachers see the big picture of why certain topics are taught in certain ways at particular grade levels. Whether the workshop is a hands-on experience or learning about a new instructional technique, CTS provides the specific content focus and research grounding that is sometimes missing from workshops.

Examining Student Work and Thinking

More and more teachers are engaged in examining student work and thinking as part of their ongoing professional development. But what should teachers look for when examining student work or listening to students' thinking in the classroom? Teachers who conduct CTS on the topics of the student work learn what to look for. Especially helpful to this process are the CTS sections on goals for content learning and the research on children's ideas. Conversations about student work are much richer when participants have a common understanding of the learning goals and opportunities for students to learn and demonstrate their understanding. Developing and using CTS assessment probes (such as the example in Figure 4.17) can stimulate discussions about student learning across multiple grade levels and move the emphasis from strictly scoring to also learning about students' thinking for the purpose of improving teaching and learning.

Lesson Study

Lesson Study in the United States uses or adapts a structured professional development strategy used in Japan through which teachers collaboratively develop research-based lessons and study how the lesson enhances student learning. A key feature of lesson study is studying and researching a lesson that is directly related to learning goals in local, state, or national standards. The CTS process provides a means for teachers to study what standards and research say about the topic of the lesson, including student difficulties and misconceptions to be aware of. The process grounds teachers in a common knowledge base and provides a lens through which they can observe the impact of the lesson on student learning.

Mentoring, Coaching, and Demonstration Lessons

Mentoring, coaching, and demonstration lessons often involve planning lessons, observing novice or veteran teachers teach the lessons, and then discussing how they can be enhanced. Using CTS as part of these professional development strategies—especially in the lesson-planning and debriefing processes—helps to keep the discussion and learning focused on the standards and the teaching, not on the teacher. CTS was used as the centerpiece tool in the NSF-funded Northern New England Co-Mentoring Network, at www.nnecn.org. Mentors and mentees who have used CTS significantly shift the level of discourse from their own individual perspectives to a shared, common language and understanding about science.

The trends in teacher professional development indicate that more and more teachers want learning opportunities that focus directly on their practice: the content they teach and how to best teach it. CTS is a powerful tool for making professional development more connected to these goals. The third book in this series will be designed for professional developers and facilitators of CTS. The book will contain strategies, tools, and vignettes for using CTS with the 18 professional development strategies described in *Designing Professional Development for Teachers of Science and Mathematics* (Loucks-Horsley et al., 2003). Information on this book as well as opportunities for professional developer training are available on the CTS Web site.

5

Images From Practice

Vignette #1: A High School Integrated Science Teacher Uses CTS to Understand Gravity-Related Content

I was worried when our school made the decision to require an integrated science course for all incoming freshmen. I have been teaching freshman and sophomore biology for 20 years, and the thought of teaching physics concepts was quite intimidating to me! I haven't had a physics course or any professional development in physical science since I attended college 25 years ago. Even then, I took only one introductory course to meet my requirements.

As I looked through the course syllabus and the objectives for the physics component, I noticed gravity was one of the concepts addressed. What do I know about gravity besides "What goes up must come down"? Where could I learn more about this concept?

One of the teachers in our science department introduced us to CTS after attending a leadership institute in Boston. Our department has been using it regularly to examine the content we teach. I decided to use the CTS guide "Gravity" to help me understand the gravity-related content I need to know to teach the course. When I had used CTS with other topics, it helped me uncover what is appropriate for my students, and it gave me an overall picture of the content, how it is structured, and how narrow or broad the focus should be.

I started by using K-W-L to list the ideas I thought I knew about gravity (see Figure 3.5). I thought gravity was related to weight and that astronauts were weightless in space when they "floated" around in the space shuttle; therefore I believed there was no gravity unless they were on or near a planet or moon. I remembered this from watching the images of the Apollo astronauts "bouncing" on the moon where gravity was only one sixth of earth's. I wondered whether having an atmosphere had anything to do with gravity. I wanted to find out more about the nature of this force and the math involved. I also wanted to learn more about the historical findings related to gravity and whether there were other theories I needed to be aware of.

As I read *Science for All Americans* (American Association for the Advancement of Science, [AAAS] 1990), I was surprised to find out that gravity exists everywhere in the universe. If I had the misconception that there is no gravity in space, then maybe my students would think this too. As I thought about this, I realized it could be due to the way the word "weightless" is used in the media. The strength of the force of gravity between two objects depends on the mass of the objects and the distance between them. It really doesn't matter how small an object is or whether there is an atmosphere; if it has mass, then it is affected by gravity. I never thought about why the earth was spherical—now I know gravity is involved in shaping the earth. This also explains for me why the other planets and moons are spheres: Gravity is everywhere.

Science Matters (Hazen & Trefil, 1991) also added to my understanding of gravity. Reading about the historical development of scientists' understanding of gravity was very interesting, particularly the fact that gravity in space and gravity on earth were once thought of as distinctly different. My original ideas about gravity were much like the historical view. And yes, Newton did contemplate gravity by watching an apple fall! The way *Science Matters* described the mathematical relationship in words, rather than a formula, helped me understand the proportionality and inverse-square relationship. Newton's laws of motion combined with the law of gravity help me appreciate the elegance of science and its explanatory power. Gravity is one of the oldest "big ideas" in science that explains so many things!

I used Sections III and V of the CTS guide to check the learning goals for middle school and high school to make sure I understood the content appropriate for students, in light of what I had learned. *Atlas of Science Literacy* (AAAS, 2001) emphasized the high school level idea of gravity as an attractive force between masses and that the larger the mass, the greater its force of attraction will be. The further the distance between the two masses, the less the attraction. This qualitative idea is simpler than the relationship described in *Science Matters,* but I feel comfortable knowing I can go further in introducing the math and the inverse-square relationship if my students grasp this idea first. The middle school ideas are a simpler version of what I read in *Science for All Americans* and *Science Matters,* which I feel I understand much better now. After doing parts of the topic study to refresh my content understanding, a lot of pieces have come together for me so that I understand gravity better. If I were to pick one idea from my K-W-L chart that I would like to explore further, it would be current theories of gravity. I think I might go online or talk with the physics teacher to find out more, in case my students' questions take us there. I realize there are many more details I can learn, but for now, I feel more comfortable with this abstract topic.

Vignette #2: An Experienced Middle School Teacher Uses CTS to Revise a Unit on Biological Classification

I teach a seventh-grade unit on "Classification of Life." For 15 years, I have been following the sequence in my textbook: the need for classification, ways to classify various things, Linnaeus's system, the five kingdoms and major subgroupings, and using field guides and taxonomic keys. The overarching question for my unit has been, "How do we classify and identify organisms?" I usually supplement my text with activities that match the content. Our state standards include classification, so I felt I was on the right track. For a culminating performance task, I had my students create and describe a system for classifying a variety of candy bars, develop a dichotomous key to identify and name the candy bars using made-up Latin names, and compare their systems with their classmates' systems. This has always been a fun project that my students enjoy immensely, especially because they get to eat the candy bars!

This year, I used the CTS guide "Biological Classification" to examine my unit prior to teaching it. After attending a conference where I learned about CTS and how it can help teachers revise their units so they are more standards based, I decided to try it out. I started with Section I of the CTS guide by reading *Science for All Americans*. As I read, I noticed the focus was not on classification per se, but rather on the broader concept of the diversity of life. Some of what I had always known and taught was mentioned, such as the idea of a hierarchy of groups and subgroups based on similarities and differences; but the specific nomenclature of kingdom, phylum, class, order, family, genus, and species wasn't emphasized. I read, "When scientists classify organisms, they consider details of anatomy to be more relevant than behavior or general appearance" (AAAS, 1990, p. 60). As I pondered this, I wondered whether the candy bar performance task could be leading my students to think that classification is based on behavior (e.g., melts in your hand) and outward appearances (color, texture, shape).

The reading from *Science Matters* gave me pause to rethink the content and activities I was using. I spend, on average, a week providing activities in which my students use taxonomic keys to practice identifying and naming various organisms. *Science Matters* pointed out that "taxonomy—giving things names—is important to science but is not essential to achieving scientific literacy" (Hazen & Trefil, 1991, p. 219). Could I be placing too much emphasis on taxonomy at the expense of helping students explicitly recognize that there are similarities and differences within the diversity of living things? I always thought taxonomy was a major part of biologists' work. This certainly changed for me when I read, "Aside from occasional regroupings (particularly of fossils), the job of classifying living things is no longer considered to be a major research area in biology" (p. 220). Why then, am I placing so much emphasis on it with my students? Does my unit reflect changes in modern science?

Next, I turned to Section II in the CTS guide and skimmed the general and grade-level essays in *Benchmarks,* Chapter 5, Section A: The Diversity of Life (AAAS, 1993). Using diversity of life as the major organizing concept, I could see that one of the main goals of my unit should be to help students understand the relatedness among organisms. The essay also pointed out a progression in developing the idea of similarities and differences—starting with external features and behaviors, moving to using internal structures and processes, then to cellular activity, then to molecular structure. I started to realize that my unit was more focused on facts and terminology about classification and less on developing student understanding of the bigger idea of relatedness.

The middle school *Benchmarks* essay affirmed what I had read in *Science for All Americans*. I need to spend more time emphasizing the importance of looking at internal structures and functions. Patterns of development could also be used to show similarities and differences. *Benchmarks* also pointed out that this is a time when students should move from invented systems of classification to biological systems. As I reflected on this recommendation, I realized I was doing a lot of the former. Perhaps I should talk with the fifth-grade teacher to find out whether invented systems were covered earlier so I could build upon their prior experiences with invented systems to develop ideas about scientific systems.

Using Section II, I realized that in order to align with the suggestions in the *Benchmarks,* I should focus more on examining living things or representations of them and less on objects. I need to make sure my students know the distinction between plants and animals, and discover for themselves that some organisms do not fall easily into these categories. I will help them realize that we need to consider the internal anatomical features and that this is more helpful in determining how closely related different organisms are than behavior or the obvious external features they had been using. I will explicitly emphasize these ideas and connect them to the purpose for classification systems with more of an emphasis on phylogeny than taxonomy.

Once my students understand this, I can go further if the time and interest is there, but I should probably stop at the molecular level. If I develop the idea of anatomical similarities, then students can build on that in high school by seeing how the similarity in DNA often matches anatomical similarities between organisms. I think I will have this conversation with the high school biology teacher.

A quick skim through the "Life Science" essays provided more food for thought. I like the way the K–4 essay helped me understand how elementary students classify things. At this level, it is okay to use obvious features. The *National Science Education Standards (NSES)* (National Research Council [NRC], 1996) describes how younger children use mutually exclusive rather than hierarchal categories. I need to be aware of this and make sure my seventh graders move beyond two groups to using three or more. I found a Grades 5–8 learning goal that reinforces the importance of teaching the specific idea that although organisms may look different, there is a unity among them when we examine internal structures. The wording in the *NSES* goal helped me better understand the idea in *Benchmarks*. Like *Benchmarks,* the *NSES* also includes the ideas of similarity in chemical processes that occur in cells. The *NSES* also adds the idea of evidence of common ancestry at the middle grade level, which can be inferred through fossils. I am beginning to see how I can connect learning about cell processes, like photosynthesis, to classification and relatedness among different organisms, topics I tend to treat separately. I can also include fossil organisms and not just use examples from present-day living things. The evidence for similarity within the diversity of life, as seen through the use of classification systems, begins to be explained through the big idea of evolution when students are in middle school. I am starting to see how a small, once separate topic like classification is now part of the much larger, connected topic of evolution, a major unifying theme and big idea in biology.

Section IV of the CTS guide helped me become aware of ideas my students may hold that I had not considered previous to using CTS. The research indicates that with age, there is a shift from obvious features to biological ones. By middle school, students can use hierarchal groupings, but they may need to be asked to do so, whereas high school students may use them without prompting. I guess I shouldn't expect my seventh graders will automatically do this once they have been introduced to and used hierarchal grouping. An interesting research finding is on the different meanings students hold for animals and plants. I think I will use an assessment probe to find out whether my students have a restricted meaning for the classification category of animal prior to and after instruction.

I was really interested in the research on how students classify plants. I hadn't realized that students have more difficulty classifying plants into categories than animals and that they tend to focus more on individual features, such as the shape of a leaf or the flower, rather than on the whole plant. Looking back, I think the activity our students do in elementary school classifying leaves might contribute to that idea. I need to draw upon their prior experience in that activity and point out that leaves are just one part of a plant that we look at. I also realize I focus too much on animal classification. I think I will broaden my examples to include multiple kingdoms, so that my students will see that using anatomical characteristics for grouping applies to all organisms. I will keep these difficulties in mind as I monitor my students' learning, and I will consider them in the development of my assessments.

In Section V of the CTS guide, I used a map from *Atlas of Science Literacy* to examine connections I could make in my unit. I noted that the map used was called "Biological Evolution" and there were no strands specifically titled "Classification." As I looked at the titles of the two strands, "Evidence From Existing Organisms" and "Fossil Evidence," it became clearer to me that I should focus on this permeating idea of relatedness, past and present, and the ways we can determine these relationships. I saw connections to ideas about similarities in human development and other vertebrates, similar cell functions, and differences between plant and animal cells. I can clearly see how the evidence we gather in middle school about the relatedness of seemingly different organisms will become more sophisticated in high school, when the idea of similar DNA sequences is added.

Finally, I used Section VI to put all the pieces together and see how the national documents and research findings could help me clarify what my students are being held accountable for in my state standards. It was an eye-opener for me when I read the two state goals: "Compare systems of classifying organisms including systems used by scientists" and "Decipher the system for assigning a scientific name to every living thing." The lightbulb went off as I realized I was focusing too much on taxonomic terms and using classification to identify and name organisms, rather than developing the idea that a scientific system is used to organize patterns of relatedness based on internal anatomical features and patterns of development. Once I develop this idea, terminology like genus and species will make more sense to students.

I included the idea of hierarchy in my original unit, but I placed too much emphasis on knowing the names of the different taxonomic categories, rather than on the purpose for having those categories. I wasn't making the connection between the systems my students developed initially, based on obvious features or habitats, to the systems used by scientists. The reasons why the latter is more useful in looking for patterns of relatedness somehow got lost. Some of my activities seemed to be for "activity's sake," and they didn't lead to the bigger idea of relatedness. While I will still have my students examine how we assign scientific names and use a key to identify organisms, I will cut back on several redundant activities to place more emphasis on the idea of relatedness. As far as that candy bar activity—it was fun, but comparing similarities among different candy bars is a contrived, nonscientific context that doesn't encourage any connection to inferring evolutionary relationships through similarities. It also doesn't model authentic, inquiry-based use of a classification system by using present-day organisms and fossils as examples.

I realize now that I can also help students discover how classification systems change as biologists obtain new knowledge about structure and function in living things. I think I will bring in an old 1928 biology text to show students that there were only two kingdoms recognized at that time: plants and animals. Protozoa belonged to the animal kingdom, and fungi belonged to the plant kingdom. I am curious what my students will think the reasons are for having such a limited system and why it is different today. Recently, several students asked me about the newer, three-domain system of eukarya, eubacteria, and archaea. While a detailed explanation of the molecular relationships is more appropriate for high school, I could use this as an example of how some biologists use a different classification system based on relationships. I don't want my students to think that there is only one accepted system used by all scientists.

For 15 years, I taught what I thought were the big ideas and essential concepts and skills, based on the way I was taught, the way my textbook presented the content, and the topical match in my state standards. I now realize that I should be emphasizing that classification systems are just a framework used to organize and examine patterns of similarity, based on the current scientific knowledge available. Classification, by itself, is not the big idea. It is a framework that students, as well as biologists, can use to examine diversity. Now that I better understand the teaching implications of biological classification and where it fits in to a larger schema of learning, my new unit will be called "Patterns of Similarity in the Diversity of Life," and my new overarching question will be: How can similarities and differences be used to explain life's diversity? I feel a sense of renewal in using CTS to examine my teaching, and I am excited to make well-informed changes. I feel confident that the standards-based changes I am going to make will benefit my students in achieving a connected and deeper understanding of science. After all, isn't that the ultimate purpose of teaching standards-based science?

Vignette #3: A Team of Primary Teachers Uses CTS to Identify Goals for Learning About Life Cycles

A traditional science unit for the primary grades in the fall is life cycles, specifically the life cycle of a monarch butterfly. Excitement mounts in the classroom as students bring in the yellow and black monarch caterpillars found on the plentiful milkweed plants in my New England state. These caterpillars are carefully placed in aquariums and supplied daily with fresh milkweed leaves. As they grow, our students record observations in their science journals. We have developed many engaging activities over the years related to the monarch butterfly and have even involved our students in Monarch Watch, a program from the University of Kansas that enlists schoolchildren from across the country in tracking monarch migrations. Nonfiction books about monarch butterflies are shared with our students, as are many fictional stories about butterflies. Art is also integrated into the unit, with orange, yellow, and black paint being in particular demand. Butterfly puppets are created to act out the storylines found in the literature. Tic-tacs are used to show the egg stage of the life cycle in an art activity recreating the egg, caterpillar, and butterfly stages of the monarch. Worksheets reinforce the stages of this cycle. One video enthusiast on our team actually taped a monarch butterfly emerging from its chrysalis, and that has become a classic shown to each succeeding group of second graders. At the end of the unit, our students are proud that they can recite the three stages of the butterfly life cycle, and they have their artwork to support it.

Due to the increased emphasis on accountability in all curriculum areas, we decided to do a CTS of "Reproduction, Growth, and the Development (Life Cycles)," to verify our team's already secure knowledge that we are targeting the specific concepts implied in our state's K–2 performance indicator: "Explain, draw, or otherwise demonstrate the life cycle of an organism" (Maine Department of Education, 1997, p. 68). We decided to use the CTS process to guide an investigation of the national documents for information about relevant and developmentally appropriate concepts for Grades K–2 and up to Grade 4 so we could consider our role in developing the basic concepts required for students to be successful in second grade and the immediate grades ahead.

We started with Section II and decided to focus on using just the *NSES*, expecting tight alignment. The statements in the essay, "During elementary grades, children build understanding of biological concepts through direct experience with living things, their life cycles, and their habitats" (NRC, 1996, p. 127) and "An understanding of the life cycles of organisms begins with questions" (p. 128), affirmed our hands-on, inquiry approach to investigating the life cycle of the monarch butterfly. It also mentioned that young children have difficulty in defining *life*. This prompted us to be sure we take time to help students understand the difference between living and nonliving, since developing an understanding of life cycles implies that students know what "life" is. This led us to discuss the importance of embedding formative assessment strategies to find out whether our students thought the egg and chrysalis were living. Weren't we surprised when we went out on the playground and interviewed a few of our former students. Most of them said the chrysalis was not living, but comes alive when it hatches into a butterfly! We have been teaching life cycles, yet our students have not connected the idea of changes in "living" things to the cycle. How could it be a cycle of life if our students thought that one of the stages was nonliving?

Examining national goals and specific ideas for K–4 in Section III directed us to the K–4 section on the "Life Cycle of Organisms." Here we found the basic concept the team has been trying to develop, that "plants and animals have life cycles that include being born, developing into adults, reproducing, and eventually dying. The details for this life cycle are different for different organisms" (NRC, 1996, p. 129). This was an indication to us that the concept, which should be emerging for young students, is one that may include the life cycle of the monarch but should not be restricted to the monarch—we need to make sure students can generalize the idea of life cycles to a variety of animals and plants. We talked about how we need to be explicit about this and investigate other examples, making the connection that they all go through a cycle, even though it varies. We admitted that we never addressed the idea of dying—we addressed only the "life" component of the life cycle.

In Section IV, we examined Rosalind Driver's research on teaching and learning (Driver, Squires, Rushworth, & Wood-Robinson, 1994). We discovered an interesting item about children's understanding of death: that lower-elementary children understand that death is irreversible and inevitable but think that it is caused by an external agent and not caused by the cessation of bodily functions. This research finding provides a rationale for including death as a component of the life cycle, but teachers need to be aware of this research. Other research findings show that children struggle with the notion of continuity of life and think that living things develop from nonliving, such as "Larvae change into pupae, which are dead, and then we get butterflies." This is exactly what we learned from our playground interviews. Now we know we need to take time to develop the notion that from egg to adult, all the stages are living, including eggs, pupae, and chrysalises.

We used Section VI to reflect back to the performance indicator in our state standards. It became obvious to us that if the organism selected as an item for testing was not the monarch, then there was a high risk that the students would not be able to meet the state standards. We need to be sure we do not focus on only one context and that our students can transfer ideas about life cycles to other organisms. The wording of the indicator implied a general knowledge of life cycles rather than the cycle of a specific organism.

At the conclusion of the CTS, our team discussed how we would revise our unit, based on our findings. First, we want to start with developing a conception of life and comparing nonliving and living things. A second revision in the unit relates to the subject of death as a natural component to the life cycle. While the team members need to be aware that children think of death as caused by an external agent and not a natural function, the discussion of the life of the butterfly after it leaves our playground and makes the journey south and its role in the emergence of a new generation of monarchs, which lay the eggs the following summer, enlarges the span of the life cycle for the students. The fact that some students want to know whether the butterflies they release will be back suggests that a discussion of a life cycle as cyclical and not linear is imperative.

A third revision to the unit involves the connection between the characteristics of the life cycle of the monarch and the life cycles of other organisms. A significant flaw in the original unit as designed is the narrow focus on the monarch. We were teaching a monarch butterfly unit—not a life cycle unit. Monarchs should be the context in which the team members teach broader ideas. This connection takes the solitary focus away from the monarch and directs it toward the big idea that should be evolving for students: All organisms have life cycles, and there are common elements, as well as differences, across the range of organisms.

A fourth consideration that evolved from the CTS study is that students need more than one exposure to the idea of life cycles. For connections to evolve, students need to have direct experiences with many organisms so that a coherent pattern of life, development and change, growth, death, and the continuation of life determines the continued existence of the diversity of species on earth. Summarily, the topic study provided guidance through a process that resulted in a significant increase in understanding about the limitations of the originally designed unit and guidance about the direction the unit should take in future implementation.

Vignette #4: A Middle School Teacher Uses CTS to Understand a Difficult Concept to Teach: Density

The concept of density has been a difficult one for my eighth-grade students to understand. Each year, I spend a significant amount of time contemplating which instructional strategies and experiences will lead students to construct a successful mental model of density. I look through old lessons, search for new ones, and review notes that I had scratched from previous years. During this review process, I ask myself several questions. Why spend the time developing students' ideas about density if students do not seem to be able to really understand it? Is density too abstract for this age group to understand? Is understanding density an integral part of understanding other ideas in science? Are there different contexts that I can use to introduce and revisit density? I have debated this line of thinking for years, formulating ideas based on my individual experience but lacking the tools to help me examine my questions in a deeper way.

Over the past 2 years, I have participated in a mentoring program that showed me how to utilize the CTS process to examine the content and instructional implications of a curriculum prior to teaching a topic. The tools provided a standards- and research-based perspective to help me study the concept of density and answer some of the lingering questions that remain year after year when I teach this concept. Using CTS has helped me see density in a different light, giving me new insights into the topic and ways to help my students construct meaning of this difficult concept. Because I am the only eighth-grade teacher in my school, having this tool to help me gather information from "other experts" gave me another perspective to examine my teaching.

Although density is listed as only one learning goal in our state's Grades 5–8 Structure of Matter standards, I discovered, by using the "Density" topic study, there are many other interrelated and parallel concepts connected to this idea. Section III led me to a learning goal in the *NSES* that describes density as a characteristic property of a substance that is independent of the amount of sample, the same as boiling point and solubility. This helped me see that I should provide opportunities for my students to discover that other physical properties depend on the type of matter, not the amount, and make the link to density as well. *Benchmarks* contains the idea that equal volumes of different substances usually have different masses, but they never use the word *density*. To me, this is an indication that I should develop the idea of mass and volume relationships before introducing the technical term density and D = M/V.

One of my CTS professional development sessions showed us how to use the Structure of Knowledge (See Figure 4.5) to unpack learning goals in a topic as well as identify the bigger ideas. If I take density as a concept, related concepts include mass and volume. Subconcepts include qualitative density comparison and quantitative density determination. The specific idea is that density is a specific property of matter that describes a proportional relationship between mass and volume. At the factual level is the formula D = M/V. Moving upward from the concept of density is the bigger idea described in the *NSES* that substances have characteristic properties that are independent of the amount of the sample. This leads to the bigger unifying theme of constancy and change: Even though the amount of matter changes, the density stays the same. This really helped me see that I was mostly emphasizing ideas at the factual level and not helping students progress toward the bigger idea.

Before working out the sequencing of density experiences for my students this year, I reviewed the misconception research in Part IV of the topic study. Studying this pointed out to me that children at an early age (5–7 years) seem to have an understanding that something can be "heavy for its size." Older children (aged 8–10) talk about "feeling weight" and begin to relate one material's heaviness to another. These children also state that something floats because it is "lighter" than water. Older students (aged 14–22) are often able to state that density is the "compactness" of particles but have incomplete or inaccurate explanations of density, many of which are due to their misunderstanding of volume and the nature of particles, particularly the idea that there is empty space between atoms and molecules.

From my own experiences, I have noted that students think of less dense objects as having more air inside of them, causing them to float or layer on top of another substance. When working with volumes, I have seen that students do not understand solids are in cubic units and have difficulty making the necessary measurements in their work. My students also fail to recognize that milliliters are the parallel measurements for cubic units of solids. They seem to have difficulty with the idea that different shapes of the same amount of solid or the same amount of liquid in a different-shaped container have the same volume. Because my state standards require that students have both a qualitative and quantitative understanding of density, the research helped me see that I need to spend more time developing the concept of volume and its measurement. Once my students can grasp the volume ideas, I think I will have them compare the mass of a compacted versus uncompacted volume of the same substance, such as an aluminum foil ball, to develop a representation of what it means for the same type of material to be "denser." I will carefully connect this model to their previous understandings about the space between particles in different states of matter and ask them to use their mental model to compare the density of a gas to a liquid of the same substance.

I know my students have had a number of opportunities this year and in prior years to find the mass of various objects. If I could connect the new density experiences with their previous experiences with mass, I could help my students attain understanding and conceptual development at a higher level. For example, I will have them compare the volumes of two different masses of the same substance and have them think about why the density doesn't change. I will also have them compare a less dense object of high mass with a denser object with a low mass to answer the essential question, "Does size matter?" which is connected to the bigger idea I want to develop. As an assessment, I may try to use an open-ended task: "Which material is denser, rice or sand, and how do you know?" I will give them two different volumes, one twice as heavy as the other, and have them make predictions based on "felt weight." As my students solve the question and explain how they got their answers, I will be able to observe how they apply their understanding of volume and mass relationships in a new context.

Reading the vignette "Funny Water" in the *NSES* helped me reflect on my students' prior experiences in fifth grade with floating and sinking. I wonder whether it is more difficult to make the transition to solid objects using mass and volume measurements rather than how solid objects float in water. I noticed the CTS supplements listed on the CTS Web site had an article from the National Science Teachers Association journal, *The Science Teacher*, for the "Density" guide, addressing this difficulty. I will try to find a copy of it so I can further understand this challenge. I'll try to build upon the fifth-grade experience, while at the same time using the strategies described in the vignette to help students construct their own ideas first. As in the ending of the vignette, some students may still be puzzled, but I feel they will be more likely to grasp the ideas once I have taken the guesswork out of how to design my activities.

It is now evident to me that developing students' ideas about density involves making connections to several related topic areas, such as properties of matter, particulate matter, and measurement. As a follow-up, I am going to do a topic study on "Observation, Measurement, and Tools," so I can be more deliberate about connecting the process of relative comparisons and quantitative determinations of density to understanding what density is and its relationship to bigger ideas.

Vignette #5: A Teacher Leader Uses CTS to Help Guide Fifth-Grade Teachers' Implementation of the Ecology Content Standards

As a teacher leader on special assignment in my district, I have been facilitating grade-level curriculum meetings of our fifth-grade teachers during our monthly early release days. The group of teachers I work with have been "merged" from two other schools and felt it was important to clarify and establish common, coherent curricular goals that would unify student experiences in their nine classrooms. The teachers have been doing curriculum work over the course of the school year and were already familiar with the process of CTS. At our last meeting, they asked for help in the area of ecology, one of the 13 broad content standards in the state's *Learning Results* (Maine Department of Education, 1997). All expressed concerns with the enormity of the ecology content standard—it was overwhelming!

The teachers recognized that ecology units were taught in a number of different ways, depending on the individual teacher's interest, the materials that were available, and which interdisciplinary theme was emphasized for the year. The group wanted guidance in clarifying the state's standards as well as identifying the major concepts and other specific ideas that lead to a coherent understanding. Using this knowledge, they would examine curriculum materials and experiences and select ones that appropriately matched the learning goals.

Knowing I had only 3 hours to work with the group next month, I started by having the teachers share what they currently taught in their ecology units. As a group, they generated a large list of concepts, ideas, vocabulary, activities, contexts for learning, and interdisciplinary connections. The list included items such as food chains, food webs, producers, consumers, predator/prey relationships, chemical details of photosynthesis, owl pellets, biomes, recycling, water monitoring, pollution, local habitat plot studies, raising salmon, and composting. This allowed everyone to become familiar with colleagues' practices and gave us a baseline to refer to at the next session.

I chose the CTS study guide "Ecosystems" and assigned the readings to be done before our next meeting. As a group, we created an initial concept web on the major ideas in ecology before beginning the study of ecosystems (see Figure 5.1). I reviewed the purpose of the CTS and emphasized the importance of recording notes for each section, focusing on Grade 5 but also being aware of precursor knowledge from Grades 3–4, as well as identifying where students will be going next with their knowledge in middle school.

The teachers came back the next month and shared their insights gleaned from the topic study. Initially, the discussion centered around the concepts and specific ideas the study brought forth as potentially difficult or misunderstood by students, such as the idea about soil as being the only place where decomposition takes place, due to worms, and the misconception that energy "adds up'" through an ecosystem—viewing the top predator as "keeper of all of the energy" and thus the most powerful. They discussed the importance of helping students recognize the role of the sun, as linked to the producers in the food chains and food webs. They noted that the specific chemical details of photosynthesis could wait until later in middle school when students have a better understanding of atoms and molecules.

Three "big ideas" began to be identified by the teachers through the topic study: (1) Energy flows through an ecosystem; (2) matter is constantly being transformed in an ecosystem; and (3) organisms in an ecosystem are dependent on each other as well as on physical resources. I put up the chart they generated at the last session and their initial group concept map. They

Figure 5.1 Concept Map Before CTS

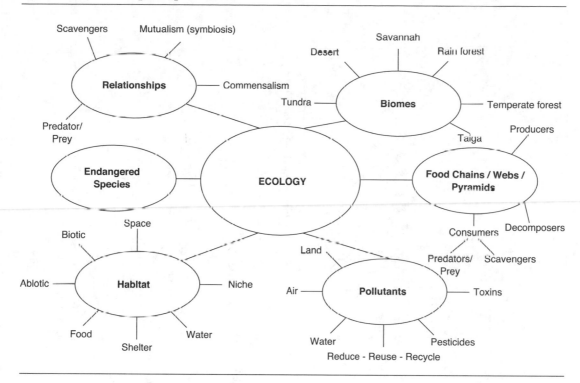

discussed how these concepts of energy flow, matter cycling, and interdependency should be explicitly developed, and they made note of the gaps and underdeveloped ideas that currently existed in their units. They agreed that they were teaching isolated ideas and doing a lot of fun activities without developing the key concepts and big ideas related to ecosystems.

To help the teachers get a better sense of how the concepts of energy flow and transformation of matter are key to understanding ecosystems, I showed the teachers video clips from the Annenberg CPB series, *Essential Life Science*. These were recommended on the CTS Web site as supplements to several of the CTS guides. Each video uses scientists to help build content understanding of the central ideas, as well as student interviews that probe students' thinking around the featured concept. This was particularly useful in helping the teachers connect what they read in Section IV, the research, to real students' difficulties and common conceptions. As they watched the video and connected it to the topic study, they realized they were teaching food chains and food webs as "Who eats who," rather than focusing on flow of energy and matter. Several admitted that they, just like the students on the videos, did not fully understand the differences in the way matter and energy flowed through an ecosystem. They probably perpetuated misunderstandings by treating matter and energy ideas the same way. As a result, students were unable to connect the idea of energy to food; and they were unable to recognize that food is the fuel for the "passage and transformation" of matter from one organism to the next.

Teachers remarked that the items in their initial list and their initial concept map of the "Ecology" unit lacked the interconnected ideas of matter, energy, and interdependency that they now have. They were used to teaching ideas in smaller segments—inadvertently creating a piecemeal understanding of ecology. They created a new concept map to reflect their findings from the CTS (see Figure 5.2). Now that they know how to use CTS, they are eager to review other units for alignment with standards and work to develop more coherence in their science curriculum.

Figure 5.2   After CTS

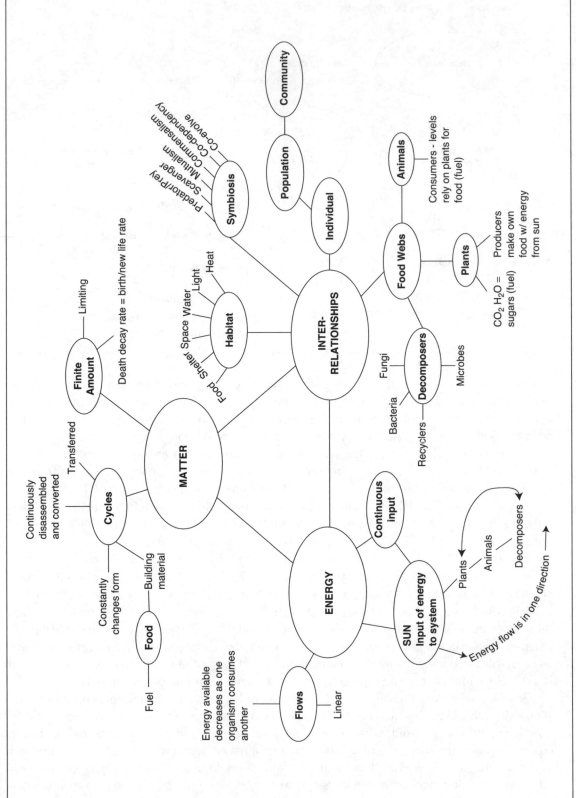

Vignette #6: A Fourth-Grade District Team Uses CTS to Examine Alignment of Curriculum, Instruction, and Assessment

Our fourth-grade district team met to examine the results of a districtwide performance task that required our students to construct an explanation of the phases of the moon. Local assessment results from last year showed low performance on the task. We decided as a group to do a CTS, hoping it might help us shed light on why our students are having difficulty on our district-designed assessment. We used the "Earth, Moon, Sun System" CTS guide, focusing on the ideas that related to moon phases.

The topic study was a major eye-opener for us. As we examined and discussed the instructional implications and learning goals in Sections II and III, we realized we were asking our students for explanations of a phenomenon before they were cognitively ready to grasp the idea of the moon's position in relation to the earth and the sun. The national standards pointed out that instruction should start with observations before explanation. We were surprised to see that both *Benchmarks* and the *NSES* waited on explanations of the moon phases until middle school, yet we had aligned our fourth-grade curriculum and assessment without realizing the standards' recommendations. We all came to the profound realization that we were teaching a rather complex, sophisticated idea before our students were ready. Instead, at our grade level, we should be spending time having our students make systematic observations of the moon and notice the patterns. Explanations come much later!

Examining the national standards helped us see that ideas such as "The moon orbits the earth" need to be developed first. When we talked about this, we all agreed that we never even thought about making sure students had that idea first. We were surprised when we read the *Benchmarks* essay in Section II that pointed out that "how things are seen by their reflected light is a difficult concept for students at this age, but is probably necessary for them to learn before phases of the moon will make sense" (AAAS, 1993, p. 63). As we examined our science curriculum, we realized our students had no prior opportunities to learn about light reflection and that this may have posed a difficulty for them.

Section IV of the CTS showed us the different frameworks identified by researchers that students use to explain phases of the moon, starting from simple ideas in early years, like clouds blocking parts of the moon, to the common conception held by many students and adults that the earth's shadow caused the difference in the moon's appearance. The shadow explanation was common in the examples of student work we examined. We hadn't realized before now that this was an intuitive idea likely to be held by our students. We had been blaming our students for not learning the material we taught them rather than understanding that it was our curriculum, instruction, and assessment that needed to change!

Section V showed a conceptual strand on "Phases of the Moon." Here it was clearly evident that the explanation for the causes of the moon phases should wait until middle school, after students had the precursor idea that "the moon looks a little different every day but looks the same again about every 4 weeks" (AAAS, 1993, p. 62). We found several contributing ideas about the motion of the earth, moon, and sun system that could be appropriately developed now, to prepare students later on in middle school for the more complicated positional relationship.

When we used Section VI to reflect back on our state standards, the district curriculum guide, and our performance task, we looked at each other in amazement. As a fourth-grade district team, we had misinterpreted the state learning goal: "Students will explore the relationship between the earth and its moon" (Maine Department of Education, 1997, p. 71). Our curriculum and assessment should have been designed for our students to discover the cyclic patterns of the changing moon, based on observation, and demonstrate an understanding of those cyclic patterns. We will also develop the idea of the moon orbiting the earth and that light from the sun is reflected off the moon toward earth, which is why we see parts of the moon at night. We will model the latter phenomenon with flashlights and balls. As a result of our study of the national standards, our fourth-grade teachers will make necessary changes to our curriculum and assessment that better align with the intent of our state standard. Curriculum review and revision are necessary if our students are to achieve the standards. It is so easy to misinterpret the wording of a broad state standard! Our next step will be to meet with the middle school teachers and discuss the revision to our K–8 curriculum and how they may build upon the ideas appropriate for fourth graders so they are ready to be fairly assessed on their explanations of moon phases by the end of middle school.

Vignette #7: A High School Physics Teacher Uses CTS to Design Energy Lessons Based on Research on Learning

I teach a Grade 11 Heterogeneous Physics class. Energy is a major topic in our Physics syllabus. This year, I combined a study of the CTS guides on "Energy" and "Evidence and Explanation" to design a series of inquiry-based lessons to help students develop an accurate conception of energy. The goals for the lessons included (a) using student-generated questions to conceptualize and carry out an investigation into what energy is and how energy can be transformed from one form into another, (b) using evidence gathered from in-class experimentation and outside resources to develop a conceptual model of energy and its transformation, and (c) communicating and justifying proposed explanations in a manner consistent with student-collected evidence and being open to modifying explanations as new evidence is developed.

These are important goals for my students because, as Section I of the "Energy" topic study revealed, the concept of energy is central and has integral connections to every branch of science. *Science for All Americans* describes this central notion of energy: "Most of what goes on in the universe—such as the collapsing and exploding of stars, biological growth and decay, the operation of machines and computers—involves one form of energy being transformed into another" (AAAS, 1990, p. 50). *Science Matters* states that "everything you do or see requires energy, and that energy follows two basic rules" (Hazen, & Trefil, 1991, p. 20).

The inquiry approach is particularly important because I want my students to understand that science is not a static body of knowledge that can simply be passed on in total from me to them. I want them to see that new knowledge is built on existing knowledge—this lesson was designed to let my students connect "new" knowledge to what they already know. I want my students to be clear that knowing a technical term is not equivalent to demonstrating understanding of a concept, so the design of the lesson de-emphasizes the use of "technical vocabulary."

I started by studying Sections II, III, and IV in the "Energy" guide. I felt it was important to be aware of the middle school ideas, since it is likely that some of my students may still be thinking about energy at that level. I made the following CTS summary notes of the important points to pay attention to in designing and implementing my lesson (see Figure 3.11).

The lesson I designed and implemented, informed by CTS, is an introduction to energy that lasts for three 84-minute blocks. In the first class, I started by working with the class as a large group to identify some of their current conceptions about energy, keeping in mind what I read in the CTS. I listed their ideas and then I asked the students to look at the list and recognize the diversity of things on the list, while at the same time noticing there are some patterns to be discerned.

Following this opportunity to make their initial ideas about energy known, I had my students use some pictures from the *Minds on Physics* text (Leonard, Dufresne, Gerace, & Mestre, 1999) as prompts to get them talking about what it means to "have energy." This worked well, as heated disagreements ensued over a number of the scenarios. It was obvious that the discussions were creating dissonance with many of the students' own ideas. That dissonance helps to create an atmosphere where the students see the need for further investigation. We followed the small-group discussion with the generation of the questions the students wanted answered. That concluded the work we accomplished in the first class period. Between the first and second classes, the students were asked to gather information from whatever outside sources they chose to help answer their groups' questions.

During the second class period of the lesson, the students were able to work in groups, with any materials I could provide, to gather data that would help them to answer their energy questions. As I worked with the groups while they were using the information they had gathered and the results of their experiments to put together their presentations, I was also continuously assessing each student's understanding of energy and transformation, keeping in mind the potential for misconceptions noted in Section IV. This type of formative assessment is ongoing throughout the lesson, but when the students are doing group work—where they verbalize their thoughts, defend their own beliefs, and challenge their classmates' thinking—I find it particularly easy to get a clear picture of my students' understanding. I then use that picture, combined with CTS findings, to inform my instruction from that point on.

During the third class of the lesson, research groups shared, discussed, and evaluated what they had found. An interesting interchange happened when a student made the statement, "We also found out that energy can't be created or destroyed." This led several students to state that they still thought it was possible to "stop or kill energy." Another student then raised the possibility that energy can be created when you rub two sticks together to make a fire. "Anna" then responded to "Tim" that "the energy does come from somewhere, from your muscles." This exchange of ideas is important for several reasons. First, it illustrates to me the growth in how I teach and the resulting changes in my students' understanding that are reflected in the CTS. Ten years ago, I would have been standing at the blackboard writing and saying, "Energy can not be created or destroyed." My students would have written down what I wrote, memorized it, and probably not asked a question about it. They could have stated the law of conservation of energy, but did they understand it and could they apply it? It takes time, creativity, and flexibility to make inquiry work and to study a topic like energy so you know where to go with questions and student difficulties.

The predominant misconception, confirmed by my readings in Section IV, that students have when they enter the study of energy is the idea that energy is a tangible substance, almost like a fuel, that can be used up. This is understandable when you think about the way the word *energy* is used in everyday language. Because all students come into the study of energy with some deep-rooted conceptions (some of the misconception variety), it is important to set up a class scenario that allows the students to express their conceptions, gather data and information, identify inconsistencies, question each other and the teacher, and modify their mental models based on this work. It is virtually impossible to unseat student misconceptions by merely stating what you as the teacher think they should believe! My hope is that a lesson such as I have described serves the dual purposes of helping my students learn how to gather information and make scientific judgments about what that information means, as well as creating a mental model of energy transformations that is accurate and enduring, all supported by the CTS information.

Vignette #8: An Elementary Teacher Uses CTS to Improve Opportunities to Learn for Her Disadvantaged Students

I teach third grade in an elementary school where there is a small population of socially and economically disadvantaged students. These students stood apart from the others in ways that seemed subtle to the average observer but were obvious to those students, their classmates, and teachers. Jelly sandwiches for lunch instead of ham and cheese, apartment numbers for addresses instead of house numbers, and their clothes. These particular students were the ones who could not write about family vacations, trips to the beach, or the museum. Their lack of real-world experiences became an issue when they did not have the background experiences or the follow-up experiences to complement the opportunities that I could offer in the classroom.

When I assigned projects, I could see that the differences in access to culturally enriching experiences played into the variety of options available to my students. For example, last year I taught a unit on rocks. I asked the students to bring in a collection of 10 rocks with a description of each one. Family trips to the Boston Museum of Science and a stopover in the gift shop produced some dazzling collections. The backyard and playground collections were not as dazzling. The resources available to describe the exotic rocks from the museum were obviously more detailed than the ones describing the common rocks found in the unpaved driveways.

I wanted to do something to level the playing field for my students, not by bringing the level of the advantaged students down, but by raising the level of access to the less advantaged students. My units have always been designed to provide vicarious experiences of scientific phenomena to my students, through books, films, and so on. I had inadvertently encouraged my students to look beyond their own environment for knowledge, but the world beyond was not available to some of my students, except through books and TV. How could I use their world to develop important science ideas and skills?

I decided to use a new tool that had been introduced at one of our district science workshops. This tool was the CTS. I hoped this tool would help me target appropriate learning goals and guide my design of a unit about rocks that would afford equal access to ideas and resources for all my students, since the standards were designed for all. I decided to complete all sections of the CTS. I needed a full review of the topic for my own background, and a full CTS would ground my unit in the larger context of building toward adult science literacy, educational research, and national standards. I selected two CTS guides, "Rocks and Minerals" and "Processes That Change the Surface of the Earth." As I completed Section I, identifying and clarifying my own knowledge, I found that the details of the three types of rocks, sedimentary, igneous, and metamorphic, was information that adults should have, yet this was the target goal for my original third-grade unit.

Section II revealed ideas and information that enlightened and inspired me! The *NSES* K–4 essay described how "during the first years of school, students should be encouraged to observe closely the objects and materials in their environment, note their properties, distinguish one from another and develop their own explanations of how things become the way they are" (NRC, 1996, p. 130). I started to see that as students became more familiar with their environment, they could begin to observe changes. I found out that the local environment was an ideal study site, not just one relegated to those students who were confined to it by social and economic circumstances. I could rationalize the careful observation of local environments because I knew the history of science education in my building. Distant and exotic locations had been the focus of study in science, including deserts, the polar regions, rain forests, and the Grand Canyon.

CTS also helped me see that teaching and learning about the three types of rocks served little purpose at this age. The *NSES* essay stated, "Understanding rocks and minerals should not be extended to the study of the source of the rocks, such as sedimentary, igneous, and metamorphic, because the origin of rocks and minerals has little meaning to young children" (NRC, 1996, p. 130). As I read this piece of information, I thought back to the glitzy rock collections from the Boston Museum and the descriptions written by these children taken from the rock guides purchased at the museum gift shop and realized how little these children actually learned from that exercise. After reading Section II, I knew that I could begin to promote equal access to appropriate learning objects and resources for all my students.

In Section III, I looked for specific learning goals. I found my starting place in the K–2 *Benchmarks*, because I knew my students would need the prerequisite experiences that were lacking at their previous grade levels. I want students to begin looking closely at rocks, understanding that they come in many shapes and sizes. I want the children to start noticing that change happens in the environment, and, from the Grades 3–5 *Benchmarks*, that wind and water can also cause changes. I want to provide guidance to help them write rich descriptions of the properties of the rocks they collected rather than copy a description of a rock they bought from a guidebook. I decided I would provide all students with a science notebook, some colored pencils, and magnifying glasses to use in school and to borrow in order to encourage detailed drawings of the rocks they collected. I would also promote the value of the local environment as a study site by setting aside a spot for frequent visits and providing guidance to help students notice, describe, and record the changes that were taking place at their site.

In the research referenced in Section IV, I found that students of all ages think that the earth is as it has always been. I decided I could begin to address this misconception through books and videos in my classroom, a resource available to all my students. I also found they had a hard time accepting that freezing water could break rock. I also found that there were many rock- and soil-related terms used incorrectly by students and that rocks implied "large," whereas stones implied "small." I wanted to be very careful not to contribute to those misunderstandings and decided to learn more about the specific scientific meanings of words myself before I started designing and teaching the unit.

In the *Atlas for Science Literacy* reference in Section V, I found that the concepts of change and the properties of rocks were inextricably linked. I could envision a study of a local site and a simultaneous investigation of the changes that take place at the site and of the properties of the rocks found there. I would also be careful not to bring in the cause of earthquakes and volcanoes or the scientific terms for the three types of rocks and an explanation of their origin— these can wait until middle school.

Section VI brought me back to my own state standards. I looked at both the K–2 and Grades 3–4 in order to evaluate the prerequisite experiences in which my students might need to engage in a successful study of rocks and minerals. I found that a rich study of rocks and minerals can occur at a site that is not exotic and out of reach for my less advantaged students. The study can emphasize careful observation and detailed journal entries, addressing important communication skills. I can also tie in the concept that processes are changing the features of the earth and that my students can observe some of those changes in their own backyards. The resources available to all are the ones they should have been looking at all the time. Without CTS, I would still be teaching a rock unit based on classifying three types of rock with samples they didn't collect themselves or of which they really didn't understand the origin and formation.

Vignette #9: Professional Developers Use CTS to Redesign Their Inquiry-Based Workshops

For 12 years, I have worked as a professional developer for a statewide science education program. I support K–12 teachers in teaching science through inquiry. I got turned on to the power of inquiry when I was a scientist working in a research lab. The culture in the lab was to learn through investigation and to apply scientific knowledge to solve health problems. As much as I loved this work, I always wanted to teach, so I decided to get a teacher credential and later brought my enthusiasm for "hands-on/minds-on" learning to the classroom as a high school biology teacher. Five years later, I started leading workshops in the summer for other teachers to share my love of inquiry. That led to moving into a full-time career as a professional developer.

As a professional developer with a background in the life sciences, I am most comfortable working with teachers in this content, but it is rare for me to work only with biology or life sciences teachers. More often, my coworkers and I are working with secondary teachers across the physical, life, and earth science disciplines and with groups of elementary or middle school teachers who are responsible for a broad range of content.

In our workshops, my coworkers and I combine a variety of hands-on experiences with investigations from the teachers' own materials as much as possible. We engage the teachers in inquiry experiences, where they explore phenomena, generate questions, and conduct investigations. The teachers work in groups to generate hypotheses, inquire, and write up the results of their inquiry. My coworkers and I model the role of the teacher in the classroom as we work with the teachers. We visit the table groups, ask good questions, and try to push the thinking in the groups. Our evaluations are always very positive, and teachers return to our workshops to explore new inquiry topics.

In the past year, our project decided to do a more in-depth evaluation of what teachers learn from our workshops. We hired an outside evaluator to research what teachers learned and what changes they made in their practice. The evaluator provided evidence that most teachers we worked with learned the stages of science inquiry and how to implement them in the classroom, and some reported teaching science lessons in a more investigation-oriented fashion. While these results were a start, what was missing from the evaluation was any evidence that the teachers involved were making any connection between using more inquiry and changes in student learning and understanding. We were surprised. Wasn't that the whole point? Were our workshops focusing too heavily on the process of science and what students do in the classroom, and not connecting enough to the content of science and the big ideas that are important for students to learn?

We decided we needed to investigate how our professional development programs could focus more closely on student learning. We learned about the CTS process at a session at the National Science Teachers Association national convention and wondered whether it would help us in rethinking the design for our workshops—especially in helping teachers to focus on the important content students needed to know. We looked through the materials and saw that the process provided reading links to the research and national standards documents on many of the topics we cover in our workshops. We decided to try the CTS process to analyze our workshop design. We chose to do a topic study on photosynthesis because it is a very common topic in middle and high school curriculum and one we often build into our workshops.

We gathered in a meeting room at 3 p.m. on a Wednesday afternoon, fortified with coffee, tea, and cookies. As suggested by one of the developers of the process, we started by brainstorming the key learning goals we believe teachers should focus on when teaching this topic at different grade levels. We said that at the 9–12 level, we would want students to understand photosynthesis as an energy conversion process; another person thought it was important for students to understand different types of plants. At the middle grade level, the group said students should know the roles played by carbon dioxide, water, sugar, oxygen, and sunlight and have a basic understanding of how photosynthesis works. At the elementary level, we said children should understand that plants need food, just like people. Following the process, we then turned to look at what *Benchmarks* and the *NSES* had to say about what students should know and understand about photosynthesis. As we read, we saw there were some differences between what we thought the major learning goals would be and what the national standards suggest. For example, in *Benchmarks for Science Literacy,* an understanding of photosynthesis is developed in service of understanding the big idea of flow of matter and energy. While several of our initial goals touched on what was in *Benchmarks,* only the first, understanding photosynthesis as an energy conversion process, came close to getting at the overall concept we want students to understand.

We read *Benchmarks* and *Atlas of Science Literacy* and discovered that students at the elementary level should understand that both plants and animals need to take in water and that animals need to take in food and also that plants need light. As students move into middle school, they should understand the general distinction among organisms is that plants use sunlight to manufacture their own food and animals consume food. Building on their understanding of plants' use of sunlight as the energy source to make their food, students will develop an understanding that plants use the energy from the sun to make sugar from carbon dioxide and water. We also noticed that students in Grades 3–5 need to understand that air is "there"—it surrounds us—for them to be able to understand later that plants take something out of the air to make their food. The middle-grade ideas build toward the secondary level, where we discovered students should understand that plants interact with the earth by taking carbon dioxide from the atmosphere, using it to make sugar, and releasing oxygen back into the air. The understanding of these interactions contributes to students' understanding of the cycling of matter and the flow of energy, and are the big ideas that are important for students to develop.

We talked briefly about how some of the units we use with teachers for the upper-elementary level involve growing plants with and without sun but that most focus on the plant and not its interaction with its environment nor on understanding plants as matter. In addition, since our focus had been on the inquiry process, we paid more attention to making sure the teachers could set up and support the plant growth and investigation than on the questions and ideas they would need to raise with the students to help them connect their experiment to the cycling of matter and the flow of energy.

Returning to our goal of redesigning the workshop to focus more on student learning, we scanned Section IV, the research on how children learn the concepts and what they find confusing. This was revealing: With regard to our topic of photosynthesis, we learned that students have difficulty learning this process because they think about food in the everyday way, not in the biological way. The way our group worded our learning goal would even add to this confusion. Children have been found to see all food as something an organism takes in, so the idea of producing food, as in the case of photosynthesis, is somewhat foreign and hard to understand. According to the research in *Benchmarks,* there is also confusion about what matter is: Children think about animals and plants as being made of very different matter that is not "transformable" into the other. Other common confusions were identified that make it hard for children to understand what happens to matter and energy in organisms.

Two hours later, we began to see how this information could help shape our thinking for our next workshops. We identified two major areas that we needed to design into our workshops. First, we decided to build in time for the teachers to develop their own understanding of the big idea and its associated concepts in the standards and how the topics they teach fit into those. We brainstormed the idea of having teachers develop a concept map on the topics of the workshop and then having them do some of the reading we did in the standards. They will then return to their concept map and reconfigure it or add to it based on what they read. Later in the workshop, after the teachers have experienced an investigation designed to develop understanding of the concepts, we will invite them to go back to their concept maps to identify the specific activities they find useful in addressing the concepts. We will also give them time to talk with another teacher about the questions they have about using the ideas in their own classrooms.

Second, we decided we need to provide specific ways for the teachers to assess students' knowledge and ideas against the concepts in the map. Do their students have some of the common confusions cited in the research? Are these getting in the way of learning? We came up with the idea of having the teachers work in groups to identify the ideas children seem to struggle with when learning about photosynthesis. We will then engage the teachers in reading some of the cognitive research on students' ideas in this area. We will discuss why it would be important for teachers to understand some of the common misunderstandings students have even before they start a lesson.

Then they will return to the lists they made to see what is confirmed in the research and discuss the instructional strategies suggested in the research that will help to clear up the confusions. We will then present several classroom-based assessment strategies for assessing students' prior knowledge that can be used in the classroom every day.

We have only just begun using the CTS process to enhance the professional development programs we offer. We intend to continue doing topic studies in all of the topic areas in which we offer workshops. We plan to build CTS into what we do with the teachers, so that they become aware of the research on learning and the content and learning goals recommended by national standards. In our prior work, we were missing the storyline that built to the big ideas. CTS is helping us close that gap, so that the inquiry methods we teach are strongly connected to building student understanding of the concepts that are most important to know.

Vignette #10: A GLOBE Curriculum Developer Uses CTS to Develop Instructional Materials

In response to an announcement of funding opportunity from the National Science Foundation (NSF), I wrote a proposal to develop new materials for the GLOBE program. GLOBE is a project that partners students and researchers in investigations of atmosphere, hydrology, soils, land cover, and phenology. Classes collect data in the area of study using protocols developed by research teams. The scientists use the data in their research of earth systems.

The proposal suggested the development of four classroom units. Two themes would form the focus of the units: coastal biodiversity and urban atmosphere. Each theme would have one unit for high school and one for middle school. Although GLOBE had educational activities associated with the investigation areas, the theory on which the proposal was based was that instructional materials were needed that provided a conceptual whole, were aligned with national standards, and were thus differentiated between middle school and high school. One key tool for delineating these units was the CTS process.

Beginning with the examples provided in the proposal, through the teamwork done with teachers in the unit development process, and finally in the proposed professional development to be used by GLOBE in sharing the materials with other teachers, the CTS process has been utilized.

When writing the proposal, I felt a sample outline of the proposed units was needed to give clarity to the process and product designed. To prepare for outlining the coastal biodiversity lesson, a CTS was done on "Biodiversity." This process first identified the important concepts and big ideas. Next, it helped sequence the steps to building the concepts for K–12. Finally, it identified the potential misconceptions students might bring to the topic. From this teasing apart of the middle and high school levels ideas that should be addressed, a sequence of tentative instructional activities was developed.

The proposal was funded by the NSF. A team of teachers from around the country were selected as codevelopers. A commercially available module was selected with which to integrate the new GLOBE units. Each module was selected based on its alignment with the targeted concepts and its instructional design. Each team of teachers was first skilled in the implementation of the selected module by its developer. They were also given background on the tentative GLOBE protocols that might be included in their final units. During implementation, discussions were held to identify how the field measurements from GLOBE would integrate into the existing modules.

Teams then gathered to design the modules. At the start of the designing workshop, each team did a CTS. Beginning with a reading in *Science for All Americans,* each team outlined the culminating ideas that make up the topic. In their reading from Section I, the biodiversity team identified two ideas to focus on: Variations in genetic sequences express themselves as variations in structure by which scientists classify organisms; and a broad variation in structures of organisms assures that some will survive despite changing conditions.

Examining the readings in Section II and III, the teams could identify how these culminating ideas broke into stepping-stones toward them. Teams worked to determine which of the grade span standards were addressed by the existing curriculum modules and which would best be addressed by collecting the GLOBE measurements. This process provided the teams with focus for the new GLOBE units. For high school, this was determined to be the benchmark:

> The variation of organisms within a species increases the likelihood that at least some members of the species will survive under changed environmental conditions, and a great diversity of species increases the chance that at least some living things will survive in the face of large changes in the environment. (AAAS, 1993, p. 105)

As a final step, teams read the selections on research on student learning in Section IV. These possible problems students might have in learning the concepts identified would provide direction in creating the activities, assessments, and coaching to teachers.

Completing the CTS in preparation for writing the GLOBE units allowed the codevelopment teams to closely delineate the focus of the unit. This, in turn, provided a strong base for eliciting an essential question, creating a summative assessment, and building the instructional sequence.

6

The Curriculum Topic Study Guides

ORGANIZATION OF CTS GUIDES

This chapter contains the complete set of science Curriculum Topic Study Guides. The organization and use of these guides are described in Chapter 2. The guides are arranged in 11 categories, representing major domains in science. Within each category, the individual CTS guides are arranged by alphabetical order. The guides within a category reflect a particular focus for the study. Taking the time to become familiar with the focus of a category will help you understand what to expect from the readings. For example, in the category "Diversity of Life," a topic study guide on "Animal Life" is used to understand the diversity of animals on earth. Many ideas relate to animals, including animal habitats, animal cells, animal life cycles, and so on. These would be addressed under topics within the categories of "Ecology," "Biological Structure and Function," and "Life's Continuity and Change" respectively, even though they are related to the topic of "Animal Life." It is important to keep in mind that topics are interconnected, just as learning goals are. Two or more topics can be studied together to create a more comprehensive understanding of a general topic.

Topics also come in different grain sizes, ranging from specific concepts (e.g., "Conservation of Matter") to much broader topics (e.g., "Properties of Matter"). Broad topics like "Energy" may subsume multiple CTS topics. It is up to the user to decide how broad or specific you want your topic study to be. For that reason, a full range of grain sizes is available to the CTS user.

DESCRIPTIONS OF THE CTS CATEGORIES

The following section describes the 11 different categories of CTS guides (see "List of Curriculum Topic Study Guides" at the beginning of this book). The primary domain is listed for each category as well as the number of guides in each category. The overview describes the major emphasis of the category in terms of the focus on ideas that are developed by using the different CTS guides in the respective category. The CTS guides follow each category description, arranged in alphabetical order by category.

Diversity of Life

Primary Domain: Life Science

Number of CTS Guides: 7

Overview: The primary focus of this section is the variety of life forms on earth. Ideas such as the patterns of similarities and differences among different living things, their unique features and characteristics, and ways organisms can be classified are developed through a study of the topics in this section.

Standards- and Research-Based Study of a Curricular Topic

ANIMAL LIFE

Section and Outcome	Selected Sources and Readings for Study and Reflection Read and examine *related parts* of:
I. Identify Adult Content Knowledge	**IA:** *Science for All Americans* ▸ Chapter 5, *Diversity of Life*, pages 60–61 **IB:** *Science Matters: Achieving Scientific Literacy* ▸ Chapter 15, *The Five Kingdoms*, pages 220–221
II. Consider Instructional Implications	**IIA:** *Benchmarks for Science Literacy* ▸ 5A, *Diversity of Life* general essay, page 101; grade span essays, pages 102–105 **IIB:** *National Science Education Standards* ▸ Grades K–4, Standard C essay, pages 127–128 ▸ Grades 5–8, Standard C essay, pages 155–156 ▸ Grades 9–12, Standard C essay, pages 181, 184
III. Identify Concepts and Specific Ideas	**IIIA:** *Benchmarks for Science Literacy* ▸ 5A, *Diversity of Life*, pages 102–105 **IIIB:** *National Science Education Standards* ▸ Grades K–4, Standard C, *The Characteristics of Organisms*, page 129; *Life Cycles of Organisms*, page 129 ▸ Grades 5–8, Standard C, *Diversity and Adaptations of Organisms*, page 158 ▸ Grades 9–12, Standard C, *Biological Evolution*, page 185; *The Behavior of Organisms*, page 187
IV. Examine Research on Student Learning	**IVA:** *Benchmarks for Science Literacy* ▸ 5A, *Meaning of Word "Animal" and "Plant,"* page 341 **IVB:** *Making Sense of Secondary Science: Research Into Children's Ideas* ▸ Chapter 1, *Concept of "Animal,"* pages 22–23
V. Examine Coherency and Articulation	**V:** *Atlas of Science Literacy* ▸ *Natural Selection*, pages 82–83
VI. Clarify State Standards and District Curriculum	**VIA:** *State Standards:* Link Sections I–V to learning goals and information from your state standards or frameworks that are informed by the results of the topic study. **VIB:** *District Curriculum Guide:* Link Sections I–V to learning goals and information from your district curriculum guide that are informed by the results of the topic study.
Visit www.curriculumtopicstudy.org for updates or supplementary readings, Web sites, and videos.	

Standards- and Research-Based Study of a Curricular Topic

BEHAVIORAL CHARACTERISTICS OF ORGANISMS

Section and Outcome	Selected Sources and Readings for Study and Reflection Read and examine *related parts* of:
I. Identify Adult Content Knowledge	**IA:** ***Science for All Americans*** ▸ Chapter 5, *Diversity of Life,* pages 60–61 ▸ Chapter 6, *Human Identity,* pages 72–73 ▸ Chapter 6, *Learning,* pages 78–80
II. Consider Instructional Implications	**IIA:** ***Benchmarks for Science Literacy*** ▸ 5A, *Diversity of Life* general essay, page 101; grade span essays, pages 102–105 ▸ 6A, *Human Identity* general essay, page 128; grade span essays, pages 128–130 ▸ 6D, *Learning* general essay, page 139; grade span essays, pages 140–142 **IIB:** ***National Science Education Standards*** ▸ Grades K–4, Standard C essay, pages 127–129 ▸ Grades 5–8, Standard C essay, pages 155–156 ▸ Grades 9–12, Standard C essay, pages 181, 184
III. Identify Concepts and Specific Ideas	**IIIA:** ***Benchmarks for Science Literacy*** ▸ 5A, *Diversity of Life,* pages 102–105 ▸ 6A, *Human Identity,* pages 128–130 ▸ 6D, *Learning,* pages 140–142 **IIIB:** ***National Science Education Standards*** ▸ Standard C, Grades K–4, *The Characteristics of Organisms,* page 129; *Organisms and Their Environments,* page 129 ▸ Standard C, Grades 5–8, *Regulation and Behavior,* page 157 ▸ Standard C, Grades 9–12, *The Behavior of Organisms,* page 187
IV. Examine Research on Student Learning	**IVA:** ***Benchmarks for Science Literacy*** ▸ 5A, *Classification of Organisms,* page 340 **IVB:** ***Making Sense of Secondary Science: Research Into Children's Ideas*** ▸ Chapter 4, *Responding to the Environment,* pages 41–47
V. Examine Coherency and Articulation	**V:** ***Atlas of Science Literacy*** ▸ *Heredity and Experience Shape Behavior,* pages 96–97
VI. Clarify State Standards and District Curriculum	**VIA:** ***State Standards:*** Link Sections I–V to learning goals and information from your state standards or frameworks that are informed by the results of the topic study. **VIB:** ***District Curriculum Guide:*** Link Sections I–V to learning goals and information from your district curriculum guide that are informed by the results of the topic study.
Visit www.curriculumtopicstudy.org for updates or supplementary readings, Web sites, and videos.	

Standards- and Research-Based Study of a Curricular Topic

BIODIVERSITY

Section and Outcome	Selected Sources and Readings for Study and Reflection Read and examine *related parts* of:
I. Identify Adult Content Knowledge	**IA:** *Science for All Americans* ▸ Chapter 5, *Diversity of Life*, pages 60–61 ▸ Chapter 10, *Explaining the Diversity of Life*, pages 157–159 **IB:** *Science Matters: Achieving Scientific Literacy* ▸ Chapter 15, *The Organization of Life*, pages 219–220 ▸ Chapter 17, *Extinction*, pages 255–257
II. Consider Instructional Implications	**IIA:** *Benchmarks for Science Literacy* ▸ 5A, *Diversity of Life* general essay, page 101; grade span essays, pages 102–105 ▸ 10H *Explaining the Diversity of Life* general essay, page 254; grade span essay, page 254 **IIB:** *National Science Education Standards* ▸ Grades K–4, Standard C essay, pages 127–128 ▸ Grades 5–8, Standard C essay, pages 155–156 ▸ Grades 9–12, Standard C essay, pages 181, 184
III. Identify Concepts and Specific Ideas	**IIIA:** *Benchmarks for Science Literacy* ▸ 5A, *Diversity of Life*, pages 102–105 ▸ 10H *Explaining the Diversity of Life*, pages 254–255 **IIIB:** *National Science Education Standards* ▸ Grades K–4, Standard C, *The Characteristics of Organisms*, page 129; *Organisms and Their Environments*, page 129 ▸ Grades 5–8, Standard C, *Diversity and Adaptations of Organisms*, page 158 ▸ Grades 9–12, Standard C, *Biological Evolution*, page 185
IV. Examine Research on Student Learning	**IVA:** *Benchmarks for Science Literacy* ▸ 5A, *Diversity of Life*, pages 340–341 **IVB:** *Making Sense of Secondary Science: Research Into Children's Ideas* ▸ Chapter 1, *The Concept of "Animal,"* pages 22–23; *The Concept of "Plant,"* page 23 ▸ Chapter 6, *Microbes as Living Things*, pages 54–55
V. Examine Coherency and Articulation	**V:** *Atlas of Science Literacy* ▸ *Biological Evolution*, pages 80–81 ▸ *Natural Selection*, pages 82–83
VI. Clarify State Standards and District Curriculum	**VIA:** *State Standards:* Link Sections I–V to learning goals and information from your state standards or frameworks that are informed by the results of the topic study. **VIB:** *District Curriculum Guide:* Link Sections I–V to learning goals and information from your district curriculum guide that are informed by the results of the topic study.
Visit www.curriculumtopicstudy.org for updates or supplementary readings, Web sites, and videos.	

Standards- and Research-Based Study of a Curricular Topic

BIOLOGICAL CLASSIFICATION

Section and Outcome	Selected Sources and Readings for Study and Reflection Read and examine *related parts* of:
I. Identify Adult Content Knowledge	**IA:** *Science for All Americans* ▸ Chapter 5, *Diversity of Life,* pages 60–61 **IB:** *Science Matters: Achieving Scientific Literacy* ▸ Chapter 15, *Organization of Life,* pages 219–221
II. Consider Instructional Implications	**IIA:** *Benchmarks for Science Literacy* ▸ 5A, *Diversity of Life* general essay, page 101; grade span essays, pages 102–105 **IIB** *National Science Education Standards* ▸ Grades K–4, Standard C essay, pages 127–128 ▸ Grades 5–8, Standard C essay, pages 155–156 ▸ Grades 9–12, Standard C essay, pages 181,184
III. Identify Concepts and Specific Ideas	**IIIA:** *Benchmarks for Science Literacy* ▸ 5A, *Diversity of Life,* pages 102–105 **IIIB:** *National Science Education Standards* ▸ Grades K–4, Standard C, *Characteristics of Organisms,* page 129 ▸ Grades 5–8, Standard C, *Diversity and Adaptations of Organisms,* page 158 ▸ Grades 9–12, Standard C, *Biological Evolution,* page 185
IV. Examine Research on Student Learning	**IVA:** *Benchmarks for Science Literacy* ▸ 5A, *Classification of Organisms,* page 340 ▸ 5A, *Meaning of the Words "Animal" and "Plant,"* page 341 **IVB:** *Making Sense of Secondary Science: Research Into Children's Ideas* ▸ Chapter 1, *The Concept of "Animal,"* pages 22–23; *The Concept of "Plant,"* pages 23–24; *Classification,* pages 24–25; *The Concept of "Species,"* page 25
V. Examine Coherency and Articulation	**V.** *Atlas of Science Literacy* ▸ *Biological Evolution,* pages 80–81
VI. Clarify State Standards and District Curriculum	**VIA:** *State Standards:* Link Sections I–V to learning goals and information from your state standards or frameworks that are informed by the results of the topic study. **VIB:** *District Curriculum Guide:* Link Sections I–V to learning goals and information from your district curriculum guide that are informed by the results of the topic study.
Visit www.curriculumtopicstudy.org for updates or supplementary readings, Web sites, and videos.	

Standards- and Research-Based Study of a Curricular Topic

CHARACTERISTICS OF LIVING THINGS

Section and Outcome	Selected Sources and Readings for Study and Reflection Read and examine *related parts* of:
I. Identify Adult Content Knowledge	**IA:** *Science for All Americans* ▸ Chapter 5, *Diversity of Life*, pages 60–61; *Cells*, pages 62–64 **IB:** *Science Matters* ▸ Chapter 15, *The Chemical Factories of Life*, pages 213–219
II. Consider Instructional Implications	**IIA:** *Benchmarks for Science Literacy* ▸ 5A, *Diversity of Life* general essay, page 101; grade span essays, pages 102–105 ▸ 5C, *Cells* general essay, page 110; grade span essays, pages 111–113 **IIB:** *National Science Education Standards* ▸ Grades K–4, Standard C essay, pages 127–129 ▸ Grades 5–8, Standard C essay, pages 155–156 ▸ Grades 9–12, Standard C essay, pages 181, 184
III. Identify Concepts and Specific Ideas	**IIIA:** *Benchmarks for Science Literacy* ▸ 5A, *Diversity of Life*, pages 102–105 ▸ 5C, *Cells*, pages 111–114 **IIIB:** *National Science Education Standards* ▸ Grades K–4, Standard C, *The Characteristics of Organisms*, page 129; *Life Cycles of Organisms*, page 129 ▸ Grades 5–8, Standard C, *Structure and Function in Living Systems*, pages 156–157; *Reproduction and Heredity*, page 157; *Regulation and Behavior*, page 157 ▸ Grades 9–12, Standard C, *The Cell*, pages 184–185; *Matter, Energy, and Organization in Living Systems*, page 186
IV. Examine Research on Student Learning	**IVA:** *Benchmarks for Science Literacy* ▸ 5A, *Living and Nonliving*, page 341 **IVB:** *Making Sense of Secondary Science: Research Into Children's Ideas* ▸ Chapter 1, *The Concept of Living*, pages 17–21 ▸ Chapter 3, *Growth as a Criterion of Life*, page 36 ▸ Chapter 4, *Behavior as a Criterion of Life*, page 41 ▸ Chapter 5, *Reproduction as a Criterion of Life*, page 48 ▸ Chapter 20, *Energy and Living Things*, pages 143–144
V. Examine Coherency and Articulation	**V:** *Atlas of Science Literacy*: ▸ *Cell Functions*, pages 72–73 ▸ *Flow of Energy in Ecosystems*, pages 78–79
VI. Clarify State Standards and District Curriculum	**VIA:** *State Standards:* Link Sections I–V to learning goals and information from your state standards or frameworks that are informed by the results of the topic study. **VIB:** *District Curriculum Guide:* Link Sections I–V to learning goals and information from your district curriculum guide that are informed by the results of the topic study.

Visit www.curriculumtopicstudy.org for updates or supplementary readings, Web sites, and videos.

Standards- and Research-Based Study of a Curricular Topic

FUNGI AND MICROORGANISMS

Section and Outcome	Selected Sources and Readings for Study and Reflection Read and examine *related parts* of:
I. Identify Adult Content Knowledge	**IA:** *Science for All Americans:* ▸ Chapter 5, *Diversity of Life,* pages 60–61 **IB:** *Science Matters: Achieving Scientific Literacy* ▸ Chapter 15, *Single-Celled Organisms,* page 221
II. Consider Instructional Implications	**IIA:** *Benchmarks for Science Literacy* ▸ 5A, *Diversity of Life* general essay, page 101; grade span essays, pages 102–105 ▸ 5C, *Cells* general essay, page 110, grade span essays, pages 111–113 **IIB:** *National Science Education Standards* ▸ Grades K–4, Standard C essay, pages 127–128 ▸ Grades 5–8, Standard C essay, pages 155–156 ▸ Grades 9–12, Standard C essay, pages 181, 184
III. Identify Concepts and Specific Ideas	**IIIA:** *Benchmarks for Science Literacy* ▸ 5A, *Diversity of Life,* pages 102–105 ▸ 5C, *Cells,* pages 111–114 **IIIB:** *National Science Education Standards* ▸ Grades K–4, Standard C, *The Characteristics of Organisms,* page 128 ▸ Grades 5–8, Standard C, *Structure and Function in Living Systems,* page 156; *Diversity and Adaptations of Organisms,* page 158 ▸ Grades 9–12, Standard C, *The Cell,* pages 184–185; *Biological Evolution,* page 185; *The Behavior of Organisms,* page 187
IV. Examine Research on Student Learning	**IVB:** *Making Sense of Secondary Science: Research Into Children's Ideas* ▸ Chapter 6, *Microbes,* pages 54–58
V. Examine Coherency and Articulation	**V:** *Atlas of Science Literacy* ▸ *Cell Functions,* pages 72–73 ▸ *Cells and Organs,* pages 74–75
VI. Clarify State Standards and District Curriculum	**VIA:** *State Standards:* Link Sections I–V to learning goals and information from your state standards or frameworks that are informed by the results of the topic study. **VIB:** *District Curriculum Guide:* Link Sections I–V to learning goals and information from your district curriculum guide that are informed by the results of the topic study.
Visit www.curriculumtopicstudy.org for updates or supplementary readings, Web sites, and videos.	

Standards- and Research-Based Study of a Curricular Topic

PLANT LIFE

Section and Outcome	Selected Sources and Readings for Study and Reflection Read and examine *related parts* of:
I. Identify Adult Content Knowledge	**IA:** ***Science for All Americans*** ▸ Chapter 5, *Diversity of Life*, pages 60–61 **IIB:** ***Science Matters: Achieving Scientific Literacy*** ▸ Chapter 15, *The Five Kingdoms*, page 220
II. Consider Instructional Implications	**IIA:** ***Benchmarks for Science Literacy*** ▸ 5A, *Diversity of Life*, general essay, page 101; grade span essays, pages 102–105 **IIB:** ***National Science Education Standards*** ▸ Grades K–4, Standard C essay, pages 127–128 ▸ Grades 5–8, Standard C essay, pages 155–156 ▸ Grades 9–12, Standard C essay, pages 181, 184
III. Identify Concepts and Specific Ideas	**IIIA:** ***Benchmarks for Science Literacy*** 5A, *Diversity of Life*, pages 102–105 **IIIB:** ***National Science Education Standards*** ▸ Grades K–4, Standard C, *The Characteristics of Organisms*, page 129; *Life Cycles and Organisms*, page 129 ▸ Grades 5–8, Standard C, *Diversity and Adaptations of Organisms*, page 158 ▸ Grades 9–12, Standard C, *The Cell*, page 184; *Biological Evolution*, page 185; *The Behavior of Organisms*, page 187
IV. Examine Research on Student Learning	**IVA:** ***Benchmarks for Science Literacy*** 5A, *Meaning of Words "Animal" and "Plant,"* page 341 **IVB:** ***Making Sense of Secondary Science: Research Into Children's Ideas*** ▸ Chapter 1, *Concept of "Plant,"* page 23
V. Examine Coherency and Articulation	**V:** ***Atlas of Science Literacy*** ▸ *Natural Selection*, pages 82–83
VI. Clarify State Standards and District Curriculum	**VIA:** ***State Standards:*** Link Sections I–V to learning goals and information from your state standards or frameworks that are informed by the results of the topic study. **VIB:** ***District Curriculum Guide:*** Link Sections I–V to learning goals and information from your district curriculum guide that are informed by the results of the topic study.
	Visit www.curriculumtopicstudy.org for updates or supplementary readings, Web sites, and videos.

Ecology

Primary Domain: Life Science

Number of CTS Guides: 11

Overview: The primary focus of this section is the relationship between organisms and their environments. Ideas such as the types of relationships among organisms, physical conditions that describe an organism's environment, interactions between organisms and their physical surroundings, and the transfer of matter and energy between organisms and their environments are developed through a study of the topics in this section.

Standards- and Research-Based Study of a Curricular Topic

BIOMES

Section and Outcome	Selected Sources and Readings for Study and Reflection Read and examine *related parts* of:
I. Identify Adult Content Knowledge	**IA:** *Science for All Americans* ▸ Chapter 5, *Interdependence of Life*, page 65

II. Consider Instructional Implications	**IIA:** *Benchmarks for Science Literacy*
	    ▸ 5D, *Interdependence of Life* general essay, page 115; grade span essays, pages 116–117
	
	IIB: *National Science Education Standards*
	    ▸ Grades K–4, Standard C essay, pages 127–129
	    ▸ Grades 5–8, Standard C essay, page 155

III. Identify Concepts and Specific Ideas	**IIIA:** *Benchmarks for Science Literacy*
	    5D, *Interdependence of Life,* pages 116–117
	
	IIIB: *National Science Education Standards*
	    ▸ Grades K–4, Standard C, *Organisms and Their Environments*, page 129
	    ▸ Grades 5–8, Standard C, *Populations and Ecosystems*, pages 157–158

IV. Examine Research on Student Learning	**IVB:** *Making Sense of Secondary Science: Research Into Children's Ideas* ▸ Chapter 7, *Environments*, page 63
V. Examine Coherency and Articulation	**V:** *Atlas of Science Literacy:* There are no maps for this topic in Volume I.
VI. Clarify State Standards and District Curriculum	**VIA:** *State Standards:* Link Sections I–V to learning goals and information from your state standards or frameworks that are informed by the results of the topic study. **VIB:** *District Curriculum Guide:* Link Sections I–V to learning goals and information from your district curriculum guide that are informed by the results of the topic study.
Visit www.curriculumtopicstudy.org for updates or supplementary readings, Web sites, and videos.	

Standards- and Research-Based Study of a Curricular Topic

CYCLING OF MATTER IN ECOSYSTEMS

Section and Outcome	Selected Sources and Readings for Study and Reflection Read and examine *related parts* of:
I. Identify Adult Content Knowledge	**IA:** *Science for All Americans* ▸ Chapter 5, *Flow of Matter and Energy*, pages 66–67 **IB:** *Science Matters: Achieving Scientific Literacy* ▸ Chapter 18, *Nutrients and the Carbon Cycle*, pages 265–267
II. Consider Instructional Implications	**IIA:** *Benchmarks for Science Literacy* ▸ 5E, *Flow of Matter and Energy* general essay, page 118; grade span essays, pages 119–121 **IIB:** *National Science Education Standards* ▸ Grades K–4, Standard C essay, pages 127–129 ▸ Grades 5–8, Standard C essay, pages 155–156 ▸ Grades 9–12, Standard C essay, page 181; Standard F essay, pages 193, 197
III. Identify Concepts and Specific Ideas	**IIIA:** *Benchmarks for Science Literacy* ▸ 5E, *Flow of Matter and Energy*, pages 119–121 **IIIB:** *National Science Education Standards* ▸ Grades K–4, Standard C, *Organisms and Their Environments*, page 129 ▸ Grades 5–8, Standard C, *Populations and Ecosystems*, pages 157–158 ▸ Grades 9–12, Standard C, *The Interdependence of Organisms*, page 186; *Matter, Energy, and Organization in Living Systems*, pages 186–187
IV. Examine Research on Student Learning	**IVA:** *Benchmarks for Science Literacy* ▸ 5D, *Relationships Between Organisms*, page 342 ▸ 5E, *Flow of Matter and Energy*, pages 342–343 **IVB:** *Making Sense of Secondary Science: Research Into Children's Ideas* ▸ Chapter 2, *Food Chains and Ecological Cycles*, pages 34–35 ▸ Chapter 7, *Cycling of Matter Through Ecosystems*, page 65
V. Examine Coherency and Articulation	**V:** *Atlas of Science Literacy* ▸ *Flow of Matter in Ecosystems*, pages 76–77
VI. Clarify State Standards and District Curriculum	**VIA:** *State Standards:* Link Sections I–V to learning goals and information from your state standards or frameworks that are informed by the results of the topic study. **VIB:** *District Curriculum Guide:* Link Sections I–V to learning goals and information from your district curriculum guide that are informed by the results of the topic study.
	Visit www.curriculumtopicstudy.org for updates or supplementary readings, Web sites, and videos.

Standards- and Research-Based Study of a Curricular Topic

DECOMPOSERS AND DECAY

Section and Outcome	Selected Sources and Readings for Study and Reflection Read and examine *related parts* of:
I. Identify Adult Content Knowledge	**IA:** ***Science for All Americans*** ▸ Chapter 5, *Flow of Matter and Energy*, page 66 **IB:** ***Science Matters: Achieving Scientific Literacy*** ▸ Chapter 18, *Energy and the Food Web*, pages 263–265
II. Consider Instructional Implications	**IIA:** ***Benchmarks for Science Literacy*** ▸ 5D, *Interdependency of Life* general essay, page 115; grade span essays, pages 116–117 ▸ 5E, *Flow of Matter and Energy* general essay, page 118; grade span essays, pages 119–121 **IIB:** ***National Science Education Standards*** ▸ Grades K–4, Standard C essay, pages 127–129 ▸ Grades 5–8, Standard C essay, pages 155–156 ▸ Grades 9–12, Standard C essay, pages 181, 184
III. Identify Concepts and Specific Ideas	**IIIA:** ***Benchmarks for Science Literacy*** ▸ 5D, *Interdependency of Life*, pages 116–117 ▸ 5E, *Flow of Matter and Energy*, pages 119–121 **IIIB:** ***National Science Education Standards*** ▸ Grades K–4, Standard C, *Organisms and Their Environments*, page 129 ▸ Grades 5–8, Standard C, *Populations and Ecosystems*, pages 157–158 ▸ Grades 9–12, Standard C, *The Interdependence of Organisms*, page 186; *Matter, Energy, and Organization in Living Systems*, pages 186–187
IV. Examine Research on Student Learning	**IVA:** ***Benchmarks for Science Literacy*** ▸ 5E, *Decay*, page 343 **IVB:** ***Making Sense of Secondary Science: Research Into Children's Ideas*** ▸ Chapter 7, *Decay*, pages 63–65
V. Examine Coherency and Articulation	**V:** ***Atlas of Science Literacy*** ▸ *Flow of Matter in Ecosystems*, pages 76–77
VI. Clarify State Standards and District Curriculum	**VIA:** *State Standards:* Link Sections I–V to learning goals and information from your state standards or frameworks that are informed by the results of the topic study. **VIB:** *District Curriculum Guide:* Link Sections I–V to learning goals and information from your district curriculum guide that are informed by the results of the topic study.
Visit www.curriculumtopicstudy.org for updates or supplementary readings, Web sites, and videos.	

Standards- and Research-Based Study of a Curricular Topic

ECOLOGICAL SUCCESSION

Section and Outcome	Selected Sources and Readings for Study and Reflection Read and examine *related parts* of:
I. Identify Adult Content Knowledge	**IA:** *Science for All Americans* ▸ Chapter 5, *Interdependence of Life,* pages 65–66
II. Consider Instructional Implications	**IIA:** *Benchmarks for Science Literacy* ▸ 5D, *Interdependence of Life* general essay, page 115; grade span essays, pages 116–117 **IIB:** *National Science Education Standards* ▸ Grades K–4, Standard C essay, pages 127–129 ▸ Grades 5–8, Standard C essay, pages 155–156 ▸ Grades 9–12, Standard C essay, page 181
III. Identify Concepts and Specific Ideas	**IIIA:** *Benchmarks for Science Literacy* ▸ 5D, *Interdependence of Life,* pages 116–117 **IIIB:** *National Science Education Standards* ▸ Grades K–4, Standard C, *Organisms and Their Environments,* page 129 ▸ Grades 5–8, Standard C, *Populations and Ecosystems,* pages 157–158 ▸ Grades 9–12, Standard C, *The Interdependence of Organisms,* page 186
IV. Examine Research on Student Learning	**IVA:** *Benchmarks for Science Literacy* ▸ 5D, *Interdependence of Life,* page 342
V. Examine Coherency and Articulation	**V:** *Atlas of Science Literacy:* There are no maps for this topic in Volume 1.
VI. Clarify State Standards and District Curriculum	**VIA:** *State Standards:* Link Sections I–V to learning goals and information from your state standards or frameworks that are informed by the results of the topic study. **VIB:** *District Curriculum Guide:* Link Sections I–V to learning goals and information from your district curriculum guide that are informed by the results of the topic study.
Visit www.curriculumtopicstudy.org for updates or supplementary readings, Web sites, and videos.	

Standards- and Research-Based Study of a Curricular Topic

ECOSYSTEMS

Section and Outcome	Selected Sources and Readings for Study and Reflection Read and examine *related parts* of:
I. Identify Adult Content Knowledge	**IA:** ***Science for All Americans*** ▶ Chapter 5, *Interdependence of Life*, pages 64–66; *Flow of Matter and Energy*, pages 66–67 **IB:** ***Science Matters: Achieving Scientific Literacy*** ▶ Chapter 18, *Ecosystems*, pages 260–276
II. Consider Instructional Implications	**IIA:** ***Benchmarks for Science Literacy*** ▶ 5D, *Interdependence of Life* general essay, page 115; grade span essays, pages 116–117 ▶ 5E, *Flow of Matter and Energy* general essay, page 118; grade span essays, pages 119–121 **IIB:** ***National Science Education Standards*** ▶ Grades K–4, Standard C essay, pages 127–129 ▶ Grades 5–8, Standard C essay, pages 155–156 ▶ Grades 9–12, Standard C essay, page 181
III. Identify Concepts and Specific Ideas	**IIIA:** ***Benchmarks for Science Literacy*** ▶ 5D, *Interdependence of Life*, pages 116–117 ▶ 5E, *Flow of Matter and Energy*, pages 119–121 **IIIB:** ***National Science Education Standards*** ▶ Grades K–4, Standard C, *Organisms and Their Environments*, page 129 ▶ Grades 5–8, Standard C, *Populations and Ecosystems*, pages 157–158 ▶ Grades 9–12, Standard C, *The Interdependence of Organisms*, page 186; *Matter, Energy, and Organization in Living Systems*, page 186
IV. Examine Research on Student Learning	**IVA:** ***Benchmarks for Science Literacy*** ▶ 5D, *Interdependence of Life*, page 342 ▶ 5E, *Flow of Matter and Energy*, pages 342–343 **IVB:** ***Making Sense of Secondary Science: Research Into Children's Ideas*** ▶ Chapter 7, *Ecosystems*, pages 59–69
V. Examine Coherency and Articulation	**V:** ***Atlas of Science Literacy*** ▶ *Flow of Matter in Ecosystems*, pages 76–77 ▶ *Flow of Energy in Ecosystems*, pages 78–79
VI. Clarify State Standards and District Curriculum	**VIA:** *State Standards:* Link Sections I–V to learning goals and information from your state standards or frameworks that are informed by the results of the topic study. **VIB:** *District Curriculum Guide:* Link Sections I–V to learning goals and information from your district curriculum guide that are informed by the results of the topic study.

Visit www.curriculumtopicstudy.org for updates or supplementary readings, Web sites, and videos.

Standards- and Research-Based Study of a Curricular Topic

FLOW OF ENERGY THROUGH ECOSYSTEMS

Section and Outcome	Selected Sources and Readings for Study and Reflection Read and examine *related parts* of:
I. Identify Adult Content Knowledge	**IA:** *Science for All Americans* ▶ Chapter 5, *Flow of Matter and Energy*, pages 66–67 **IB:** *Science Matters: Achieving Scientific Literacy* ▶ Chapter 18, *Energy and the Food Web*, pages 263–265
II. Consider Instructional Implications	**IIA:** *Benchmarks for Science Literacy* ▶ 5E, *Flow of Matter and Energy* general essay, page 118; grade span essays, pages 119–121 **IIB:** *National Science Education Standards* ▶ Grades K–4, Standard C essay, pages 127–129 ▶ Grades 5–8, Standard C essay, pages 155–156 ▶ Grades 9–12, Standard C essay, pages 181, 184; Standard F essay, pages 193, 197
III. Identify Concepts and Specific Ideas	**IIIA:** *Benchmarks for Science Literacy* ▶ 5E, *Flow of Matter and Energy*, pages 119–121 **IIIB:** *National Science Education Standards* ▶ Grades K–4, Standard C, *Organisms and Their Environments*, page 129 ▶ Grades 5–8, Standard C, *Populations and Ecosystems*, pages 157–158 ▶ Grades 9–12, Standard C, *The Interdependence of Organisms*, page 186; *Matter, Energy, and Organization in Living Systems*, page 186
IV. Examine Research on Student Learning	**IVA:** *Benchmarks for Science Literacy* ▶ 5E, *Flow of Matter and Energy*, pages 342–343 **IVB:** *Making Sense of Secondary Science: Research Into Children's Ideas* ▶ Chapter 2, *Food Chains and Ecological Cycles*, pages 34–35 ▶ Chapter 7, *Nutrition and Energy Flow*, pages 59–60; *Food Chains and Webs*, pages 60–62
V. Examine Coherency and Articulation	**V:** *Atlas of Science Literacy* ▶ *Flow of Energy in Ecosystems*, pages 78–79
VI. Clarify State Standards and District Curriculum	**VIA:** *State Standards:* Link Sections I–V to learning goals and information from your state standards or frameworks that are informed by the results of the topic study. **VIB:** *District Curriculum Guide:* Link Sections I–V to learning goals and information from your district curriculum guide that are informed by the results of the topic study.
Visit www.curriculumtopicstudy.org for updates or supplementary readings, Web sites, and videos.	

Standards- and Research-Based Study of a Curricular Topic

FOOD CHAINS AND FOOD WEBS

Section and Outcome	Selected Sources and Readings for Study and Reflection Read and examine *related parts* of:
I. Identify Adult Content Knowledge	**IA:** *Science for All Americans* ▸ Chapter 5, *Flow of Matter and Energy*, pages 66–67 **IB:** *Science Matters: Achieving Scientific Literacy* ▸ Chapter 18, *Energy and the Food Web*, pages 263–265
II. Consider Instructional Implications	**IIA:** *Benchmarks for Science Literacy* ▸ 5D, *Interdependence of Life* general essay, page 115; grade span essays, pages 116–117 ▸ 5E, *Flow of Matter and Energy* general essay, page 118; grade span essays, pages 119–121 **IIB:** *National Science Education Standards* ▸ Grades K–4, Standard C essay, pages 127–129 ▸ Grades 5–8, Standard C essay, pages 155–156
III. Identify Concepts and Specific Ideas	**IIIA:** *Benchmarks for Science Literacy* ▸ 5A, *Diversity of Life*, Grades 6–8, page 104 ▸ 5D, *Interdependence of Life*, pages 116–117 ▸ 5E, *Flow of Matter and Energy*, pages 119–121 **IIIB:** *National Science Education Standards* ▸ Grades K–4, Standard C, *Organisms and Their Environments*, page 129 ▸ Grades 5–8, Standard C, *Populations and Ecosystems*, pages 157–158 ▸ Grades 9–12, Standard C, *The Interdependence of Organisms*, page 186
IV. Examine Research on Student Learning	**IVA:** *Benchmarks for Science Literacy* ▸ 5E, *Flow of Matter and Energy*, pages 342–343 **IVB:** *Making Sense of Secondary Science: Research Into Children's Ideas* ▸ Chapter 2, *Food Chains and Ecological Cycles*, pages 34–35 ▸ Chapter 7, *Nutrition and Energy Flow*, pages 59–60; *Food Chains and Webs*, pages 60–62; *Communities, Populations, and Competition Between Organisms*, pages 62–63
V. Examine Coherency and Articulation	**V:** *Atlas of Science Literacy* ▸ *Flow of Matter in Ecosystems*, pages 76–77 ▸ *Flow of Energy in Ecosystems*, pages 78–79
VI. Clarify State Standards and District Curriculum	**VIA:** *State Standards:* Link Sections I–V to learning goals and information from your state standards or frameworks that are informed by the results of the topic study. **VIB:** *District Curriculum Guide:* Link Sections I–V to learning goals and information from your district curriculum guide that are informed by the results of the topic study.

Visit www.curriculumtopicstudy.org for updates or supplementary readings, Web sites, and videos.

Standards- and Research-Based Study of a Curricular Topic

HABITATS AND LOCAL ENVIRONMENTS

Section and Outcome	Selected Sources and Readings for Study and Reflection Read and examine *related parts* of:
I. Identify Adult Content Knowledge	**IA:** ***Science for All Americans*** ▸ Chapter 5, *Interdependence of Life,* pages 64–65
II. Consider Instructional Implications	**IIA:** ***Benchmarks for Science Literacy*** ▸ 5D, *Interdependence of Life* general essay, page 115; grade span essays, pages 116–117 **IIB:** ***National Science Education Standards*** ▸ Grades K–4, Standard C essay, pages 127–129 ▸ Grades 5–8, Standard C essay, pages 155–156
III. Identify Concepts and Specific Ideas	**IIIA:** ***Benchmarks for Science Literacy*** ▸ 5D, *Interdependence of Life,* pages 116–117 **IIIB:** ***National Science Education Standards*** ▸ Grades K–4, Standard C, *Organisms and Their Environments,* page 129 ▸ Grades 5–8, Standard C, *Populations and Ecosystems,* pages 157–158
IV. Examine Research on Student Learning	**IVA:** ***Benchmarks for Science Literacy*** ▸ 5D, *Habitat,* page 342 **IVB:** ***Making Sense of Secondary Science: Research Into Children's Ideas*** ▸ Chapter 7, *Environments,* page 63
V. Examine Coherency and Articulation	**V:** ***Atlas of Science Literacy:*** There are no maps for this topic in Volume 1.
VI. Clarify State Standards and District Curriculum	**VIA:** ***State Standards:*** Link Sections I–V to learning goals and information from your state standards or frameworks that are informed by the results of the topic study. **VIB:** ***District Curriculum Guide:*** Link Sections I–V to learning goals and information from your district curriculum guide that are informed by the results of the topic study.
Visit www.curriculumtopicstudy.org for updates or supplementary readings, Web sites, and videos.	

Standards- and Research-Based Study of a Curricular Topic

HUMAN IMPACT ON THE ENVIRONMENT

Section and Outcome	Selected Sources and Readings for Study and Reflection Read and examine *related parts* of:
I. Identify Adult Content Knowledge	**IA:** *Science for All Americans* ▸ Chapter 3, *The Human Presence*, pages 32–33 ▸ Chapter 5, *Flow of Matter and Energy*, page 67 ▸ Chapter 8, *Agriculture*, page 109; *Materials*, page 112; *Energy Sources*, page 115 **IB:** *Science Matters: Achieving Scientific Literacy* ▸ Chapter 18, *Humans and the Environment*, pages 267–276
II. Consider Instructional Implications	**IIA:** *Benchmarks for Science Literacy* ▸ 5D, *Interdependence of Life* general essay, page 115; grade span essays, pages 116–117 **IIB:** *National Science Education Standards* ▸ Grades K–4, Standard C essay, pages 127–129; Standard F essay, pages 138–139 ▸ Grades 5–8, Standard C essay, pages 155–156; Standard F essay, pages 167–168 ▸ Grades 9–12, Standard F essay, page 193
III. Identify Concepts and Specific Ideas	**IIIA:** *Benchmarks for Science Literacy* ▸ 5D, *Interdependence of Life*, pages 116–117 **IIIB:** *National Science Education Standards* ▸ Grades K–4, Standard C, *Organisms and Their Environments*, page 129; Standard F, *Changes in Environments*, page 140 ▸ Grades 5–8, Standard C, *Populations and Ecosystems*, pages 157–158; Standard F, *Populations, Resources, and Environments*, page 168; *Natural Hazards*, pages 168–169 ▸ Grades 9–12, Standard C, *The Interdependence of Organisms*, page 186; Standard F, *Population Growth*, page 198; *Environmental Quality*, page 198; *Natural and Human Induced Hazards*, pages 198–199
IV. Examine Research on Student Learning	**IVA:** *Benchmarks for Science Literacy* ▸ *Relationships Between Organisms*, page 342 **IVB:** *Making Sense of Secondary Science: Research Into Children's Ideas* ▸ Chapter 7, *Pollution*, pages 68–69
V. Examine Coherency and Articulation	**V:** *Atlas of Science Literacy:* There are no maps for this topic in Volume 1.
VI. Clarify State Standards and District Curriculum	**VIA:** *State Standards:* Link Sections I–V to learning goals and information from your state standards or frameworks that are informed by the results of the topic study. **VIB:** *District Curriculum Guide:* Link Sections I–V to learning goals and information from your district curriculum guide that are informed by the results of the topic study.

Visit www.curriculumtopicstudy.org for updates or supplementary readings, Web sites, and videos.

Standards- and Research-Based Study of a Curricular Topic

INTERDEPENDENCY AMONG ORGANISMS

Section and Outcome	Selected Sources and Readings for Study and Reflection Read and examine *related parts* of:
I. Identify Adult Content Knowledge	**IA:** *Science for All Americans* ▸ Chapter 5, *Interdependence of Life,* pages 64–66 **IB:** *Science Matters: Achieving Scientific Literacy* ▸ Chapter 18, *Ecosystems,* pages 260–263
II. Consider Instructional Implications	**IIA:** *Benchmarks for Science Literacy* ▸ 5D, *Interdependence of Life* general essay, page 115; grade span essays, pages 116–117 **IIB:** *National Science Education Standards* ▸ Grades K–4, Standard C essay, pages 127–129 ▸ Grades 5–8, Standard C essay, pages 155–156 ▸ Grades 9–12, Standard C essay, page 181
III. Identify Concepts and Specific Ideas	**IIIA:** *Benchmarks for Science Literacy* ▸ 5D, *Interdependence of Life,* pages 116–117 **IIIB:** *National Science Education Standards* ▸ Grades K–4, Standard C, *Organisms and Their Environments,* page 129 ▸ Grades 5–8, Standard C, *Populations and Ecosystems,* pages 157–158 ▸ Grades 9–12, Standard C, *The Interdependence of Organisms,* page 186
IV. Examine Research on Student Learning	**IVA:** *Benchmarks for Science Literacy* ▸ 5D, *Interdependence of Life,* page 342 **IVB:** *Making Sense of Secondary Science: Research Into Children's Ideas* ▸ Chapter 7, *Communities, Populations, and Competition Between Organisms,* pages 62–63
V. Examine Coherency and Articulation	**V:** *Atlas of Science Literacy* ▸ *Flow of Matter in Ecosystems,* pages 76–77
VI. Clarify State Standards and District Curriculum	**VIA:** *State Standards:* Link Sections I–V to learning goals and information from your state standards or frameworks that are informed by the results of the topic study. **VIB:** *District Curriculum Guide:* Link Sections I–V to learning goals and information from your district curriculum guide that are informed by the results of the topic study.
Visit www.curriculumtopicstudy.org for updates or supplementary readings, Web sites, and videos.	

Standards- and Research-Based Study of a Curricular Topic

POPULATIONS AND COMMUNITIES

Section and Outcome	Selected Sources and Readings for Study and Reflection Read and examine *related parts* of:
I. Identify Adult Content Knowledge	**IA:** ***Science for All Americans*** ▸ Chapter 5, *Interdependence of Life*, page 65 **IB:** ***Science Matters: Achieving Scientific Literacy*** ▸ Chapter 18, *The House of Life*, pages 260–262
II. Consider Instructional Implications	**IIA:** ***Benchmarks for Science Literacy*** ▸ 5D, *Interdependence of Life* general essay, page 115; grade span essays, pages 116–117 **IIB:** ***National Science Education Standards*** ▸ Grades K–4, Standard C essay, pages 127–129; Standard F essay, pages 138–139 ▸ Grades 5–8, Standard C essay, pages 155–156; Standard F essay, pages 167–168 ▸ Grades 9–12, Standard C essay, page 184; Standard F essay, page 193
III. Identify Concepts and Specific Ideas	**IIIA:** ***Benchmarks for Science Literacy*** ▸ 5D, *Interdependence of Life,* pages 116–117 **IIIB:** ***National Science Education Standards*** ▸ Grades K–4, Standard C, *Organisms and Their Environments,* page 129; Standard F, *Characteristics and Changes in Populations,* page 140 ▸ Grades 5–8, Standard C, *Populations and Ecosystems,* pages 157–158; Standard F, *Populations, Resources, and Environments,* page 168 ▸ Grades 9–12, Standard C, *The Interdependence of Organisms,* page 186; Standard F, *Population Growth,* page 198
IV. Examine Research on Student Learning	**IVA:** ***Benchmarks for Science Literacy*** ▸ 5D, *Relationships Between Organisms,* page 342 **IVB:** ***Making Sense of Secondary Science: Research Into Children's Ideas*** ▸ Chapter 7, *Communities, Populations, and Competition Between Organisms,* pages 62–63
V. Examine Coherency and Articulation	**V:** ***Atlas of Science Literacy:*** There are no maps for this topic in Volume 1.
VI. Clarify State Standards and District Curriculum	**VIA:** ***State Standards:*** Link Sections I–V to learning goals and information from your state standards or frameworks that are informed by the results of the topic study. **VIB** ***District Curriculum Guide:*** Link Sections I–V to learning goals and information from your district curriculum guide that are informed by the results of the topic study.
Visit www.curriculumtopicstudy.org for updates or supplementary readings, Web sites, and videos.	

Biological Structure and Function

Primary Domain: Life Science

Number of CTS Guides: 11

Overview: The primary focus of this section is form and function in living organisms. Ideas such as complementary aspects of structure and function, requirements for life, structures and life processes at various levels of organization from molecules to organisms, and illness and disease are developed through a study of the topics in this section.

Standards- and Research-Based Study of a Curricular Topic

CELLS

Section and Outcome	Selected Sources and Readings for Study and Reflection Read and examine *related parts* of:
I. Identify Adult Content Knowledge	**IA:** ***Science for All Americans*** ▸ Chapter 5, *Cells*, pages 62–64 **IB:** ***Science Matters: Achieving Scientific Literacy*** ▸ Chapter 15, *The Ladder of Life*, pages 206–219
II. Consider Instructional Implications	**IIA:** ***Benchmarks for Science Literacy*** ▸ 5C *Cells* general essay, page 110; grade span essays, pages 111–113 **IIB:** ***National Science Education Standards*** ▸ Grades K–4, Standard C essay, pages 127–128 ▸ Grades 5–8, Standard C essay, pages 155–156 ▸ Grades 9–12, Standard C essay, pages 181, 184
III. Identify Concepts and Specific Ideas	**IIIA:** ***Benchmarks for Science Literacy*** ▸ 5C, *Cells*, pages 111–114 **IIIB:** ***National Science Education Standards*** ▸ Grades K–4, Standard C, *The Characteristics of Organisms*, page 129 ▸ Grades 5–8, Standard C, *Structure and Function in Living Systems*, pages 156–157 ▸ Grades 9–12, Standard C, *The Cell*, pages 184–185; *The Molecular Basis of Heredity*, page 185; *Matter, Energy, and Organization in Living Systems*, page 186
IV. Examine Research on Student Learning	**IVA:** ***Benchmarks for Science Literacy*** ▸ 5C, *Cells*, page 342 **IVB:** ***Making Sense of Secondary Science: Research Into Children's Ideas*** ▸ Chapter 1, *Cell Theory*, page 25
V. Examine Coherency and Articulation	**V:** ***Atlas of Science Literacy*** ▸ *Cell Functions*, pages 72–73 ▸ *Cells and Organs*, pages 74–75
VI. Clarify State Standards and District Curriculum	**VIA:** ***State Standards:*** Link Sections I–V to learning goals and information from your state standards or frameworks that are informed by the results of the topic study. **VIB:** ***District Curriculum Guide:*** Link Sections I–V to learning goals and information from your district curriculum guide that are informed by the results of the topic study.
Visit www.curriculumtopicstudy.org for updates or supplementary readings, Web sites, and videos.	

Standards- and Research-Based Study of a Curricular Topic

CHEMISTRY OF LIFE

Section and Outcome	Selected Sources and Readings for Study and Reflection Read and examine *related parts* of:
I. Identify Adult Content Knowledge	**IA:** *Science for All Americans* ▸ Chapter 5, *Diversity of Life*, pages 60–61; *Cells*, pages 62–64 **IB:** *Science Matters: Achieving Scientific Literacy* ▸ Chapter 15, *Molecules of Life*, pages 207–213; *Protein Structures*, pages 221–222
II. Consider Instructional Implications	**IIA:** *Benchmarks for Science Literacy* ▸ 5C *Cells* general essay, page 110; 6–8 and 9–12 grade span essays, pages 112–113 **IIB:** *National Science Education Standards* ▸ Grades 5–8, Standard C essay, pages 155–156 ▸ Grades 9–12, Standard C essay, pages 181, 184
III. Identify Concepts and Specific Ideas	**IIIA:** *Benchmarks for Science Literacy* ▸ 5C, *Cells* 6–8 and 9–12, pages 112–114 **IIIB:** *National Science Education Standards* ▸ Grades 5–8, Standard C, *Structure and Function in Living Systems*, pages 156–157 ▸ Grades 9–12, Standard C, *The Cell*, pages 184–185; *The Molecular Basis of Heredity*, page 185; *Matter, Energy, and Organization in Living Systems*, page 186
IV. Examine Research on Student Learning	**IVA:** *Benchmarks for Science Literacy* ▸ 5E, *Organisms as Chemical Systems*, page 342 **IVB:** *Making Sense of Secondary Science: Research Into Children's Ideas* ▸ Chapter 1, *Cell Theory*, page 25 ▸ Chapter 2, *Food: What Is It?* pages 27–28; *Dietary Components*, pages 28–29
V. Examine Coherency and Articulation	**V:** *Atlas of Science Literacy* ▸ *DNA and Inherited Characteristics*, pages 68–69 ▸ *Cell Functions*, pages 72–73 ▸ *Flow of Matter in Ecosystems*, pages 76–77 ▸ *Flow of Energy in Ecosystems*, pages 78–79
VI. Clarify State Standards and District Curriculum	**VIA:** *State Standards:* Link Sections I–V to learning goals and information from your state standards or frameworks that are informed by the results of the topic study. **VIB:** *District Curriculum Guide:* Link Sections I–V to learning goals and information from your district curriculum guide that are informed by the results of the topic study.
Visit www.curriculumtopicstudy.org for updates or supplementary readings, Web sites, and videos.	

Standards- and Research-Based Study of a Curricular Topic

DNA

Section and Outcome	Selected Sources and Readings for Study and Reflection Read and examine *related parts* of:
I. Identify Adult Content Knowledge	**IA:** ***Science for All Americans*** ▸ Chapter 5, *Heredity,* pages 61–62; *Cells,* pages 62–64 **IB:** ***Science Matters: Achieving Scientific Literacy*** ▸ Chapter 16, *DNA and RNA: Messengers of the Code,* pages 227–234
II. Consider Instructional Implications	**IIA:** ***Benchmarks for Science Literacy*** ▸ 5B *Heredity* general essay, page 106; 6–8 and 9–12 grade span essays, page 108 ▸ 5C, *Cells* 9–12 grade span essay, page 113 ▸ 6B, *Human Development* 9–12 grade span essay, page 134 **IIB:** ***National Science Education Standards*** ▸ Grades 5–8, Standard C essay, pages 155–156 ▸ Grades 9–12, Standard C essay, pages 181, 184
III. Identify Concepts and Specific Ideas	**IIIA:** ***Benchmarks for Science Literacy*** ▸ 5B *Heredity,* page 108 ▸ 5C, *Cells,* page 113 ▸ 6B, *Human Development,* page 134 **IIIB:** ***National Science Education Standards*** ▸ Grades 5–8, Standard C, *Reproduction and Heredity,* page 157 ▸ Grades 9–12, Standard C, *The Cell,* page 184; *The Molecular Basis of Heredity,* page 185
IV. Examine Research on Student Learning	**IVA:** ***Benchmarks for Science Literacy*** ▸ 5B, *Heredity,* page 341
V. Examine Coherency and Articulation	**V:** ***Atlas of Science Literacy*** ▸ *DNA and Inherited Characteristics,* pages 68–69 ▸ *Variation in Inherited Characteristics,* pages 70–71
VI. Clarify State Standards and District Curriculum	**VIA:** ***State Standards:*** Link Sections I–V to learning goals and information from your state standards or frameworks that are informed by the results of the topic study. **VIB:** ***District Curriculum Guide:*** Link Sections I–V to learning goals and information from your district curriculum guide that are informed by the results of the topic study.

Visit www.curriculumtopicstudy.org for updates or supplementary readings, Web sites, and videos.

Standards- and Research-Based Study of a Curricular Topic

FOOD AND NUTRITION

Section and Outcome	Selected Sources and Readings for Study and Reflection Read and examine *related parts* of:
I. Identify Adult Content Knowledge	**IA:** ***Science for All Americans*** ▸ Chapter 5, *Cells,* pages 62–63; *Flow of Matter and Energy,* pages 66–67 ▸ Chapter 6, *Physical Health,* pages 80–82 **IB:** ***Science Matters: Achieving Scientific Literacy*** ▸ Chapter 15, *The Power Plant,* pages 217–219
II. Consider Instructional Implications	**IIA:** ***Benchmarks for Science Literacy*** ▸ 5C, *Cells* general essay, page 110; grade span essays, pages 111–113 ▸ 5E, *Flow of Matter and Energy* general essay, page 118; grade span essays 119–121 ▸ 6E, *Physical Health* general essay, page 143; grade span essays, pages 144–146 **IIB:** ***National Science Education Standards*** ▸ Grades K–4, Standard C essay, pages 127–128, Standard F essay, pages 138–139 ▸ Grades 5–8, Standard C essay, pages 155–156, Standard F essay, pages 167–168 ▸ Grades 9–12, Standard C essay, pages 181, 184, Standard F essay, pages 193, 197
III. Identify Concepts and Specific Ideas	**IIIA:** ***Benchmarks for Science Literacy*** ▸ 5C, *Cells,* pages 111–114 ▸ 5E, *Flow of Matter and Energy,* pages 119–121 ▸ 6E, *Physical Health,* pages 144–146 **IIIB:** ***National Science Education Standards*** ▸ Grades K–4, Standard C, *The Characteristics of Organisms,* page 129; Standard F, *Personal Health,* pages 139–140 ▸ Grades 5–8, Standard C, *Structure and Function in Living Systems,* pages 156–157; Standard F, *Personal Health,* page 168 ▸ Grades 9–12, Standard C, *The Cell,* page 184; *Matter, Energy, and Organization in Living Systems,* pages 186–187; Standard F, *Personal and Community Health,* page 197
IV. Examine Research on Student Learning	**IVA:** ***Benchmarks for Science Literacy*** ▸ 5E, *Food,* page 342, *Plant and Animal Nutrition,* pages 342–343 ▸ 6C, *Digestive System,* page 345 ▸ 6E, *Health,* page 346; *Nutrition,* page 346 **IVB:** ***Making Sense of Secondary Science: Research Into Children's Ideas*** ▸ Chapter 2, *Nutrition,* pages 27–35 ▸ Chapter 3, *Conditions for Growth,* pages 37–38
V. Examine Coherency and Articulation	**V:** ***Atlas of Science Literacy*** ▸ *Flow of Matter in Ecosystems,* pages 76–77 ▸ *Flow of Energy in Ecosystems,* pages 78–79 ▸ *Maintaining Good Health,* pages 88–89; note the conceptual strand *Diet and Exercise*
VI. Clarify State Standards and District Curriculum	**VIA:** ***State Standards:*** Link Sections I–V to learning goals and information from your state standards or frameworks that are informed by the results of the topic study. **VIB:** ***District Curriculum Guide:*** Link Sections I–V to learning goals and information from your district curriculum guide that are informed by the results of the topic study
Visit www.curriculumtopicstudy.org for updates or supplementary readings, Web sites, and videos.	

Standards- and Research-Based Study of a Curricular Topic

HEALTH AND DISEASE

Section and Outcome	Selected Sources and Readings for Study and Reflection Read and examine *related parts* of:
I. Identify Adult Content Knowledge	**IA:** *Science for All Americans* ▸ Chapter 6, *Basic Functions*, pages 76–78; *Physical Health*, pages 80–82; *Mental Health*, pages 82–84 ▸ Chapter 8, *Health Technology*, pages 123–126 **IB:** *Science Matters: Achieving Scientific Literacy* ▸ Chapter 15, *Immunology*, pages 222–223
II. Consider Instructional Implications	**IIA:** *Benchmarks for Science Literacy* ▸ 6C, *Basic Functions* general essay, page 135; grade span essays, pages 136–138 ▸ 6E, *Physical Health* general essay, page 143; grade span essays, pages 144–146 ▸ 6F, *Mental Health* general essay, page 147; grade span essays, pages 148–149 ▸ 8F, *Health Technology* general essay, page 204; grade span essays, pages 205–207 **IIB:** *National Science Education Standards* ▸ Grades K–4, Standard F essay, pages 138–139 ▸ Grades 5–8, Standard C essay, pages 155–156; Standard F essay, pages 167–168 ▸ Grades 9–12, Standard F essay, pages 193, 197
III. Identify Concepts and Specific Ideas	**IIIA:** *Benchmarks for Science Literacy* ▸ 6C, *Basic Functions*, pages 136–138 ▸ 6E, *Physical Health*, pages 144–146 ▸ 6F, *Mental Health*, pages 148–149 ▸ 8F, *Health Technology*, pages 205–207 **IIIB:** *National Science Education Standards* ▸ Grades K–4, Standard F, *Personal Health*, pages 139–140 ▸ Grades 5–8, Standard C, *Structure and Function in Living Systems*, pages 156–157; Standard F, *Personal Health*, page 168; *Risks and Benefits*, page 169 ▸ Grades 9–12, Standard F, *Personal and Community Health*, page 197
IV. Examine Research on Student Learning	**IVA:** *Benchmarks for Science Literacy* ▸ 6 *The Human Organism*, pages 344–346 **IVB:** *Making Sense of Secondary Science: Research Into Children's Ideas* ▸ Chapter 6, *Microbes and Disease*, pages 55–56
V. Examine Coherency and Articulation	**V:** *Atlas of Science Literacy* ▸ *Disease*, pages 86–87 ▸ *Maintaining Good Health*, pages 88–89 ▸ *Coping with Mental Distress*, pages 90–91 ▸ *Diagnosis and Treatment of Mental Disorders*, pages 92–93
VI. Clarify State Standards and District Curriculum	**VIA:** *State Standards:* Link Sections I–V to learning goals and information from your state standards or frameworks that are informed by the results of the topic study. **VIB:** *District Curriculum Guide:* Link Sections I–V to learning goals and information from your district curriculum guide that are informed by the results of the topic study.
Visit www.curriculumtopicstudy.org for updates or supplementary readings, Web sites, and videos.	

Standards- and Research-Based Study of a Curricular Topic

HUMAN BODY SYSTEMS

Section and Outcome	Selected Sources and Readings for Study and Reflection Read and examine *related parts* of:
I. Identify Adult Content Knowledge	**IA:** ***Science for All Americans*** ▸ Chapter 6, *Human Identity,* pages 72–73; *Human Development,* pages 73–76; *Basic Functions,* pages 76–78 **IB:** ***Science Matters: Achieving Scientific Literacy*** ▸ Chapter 15, *The Organization of Life,* pages 219–220
II. Consider Instructional Implications	**IIA:** ***Benchmarks for Science Literacy*** ▸ 6A *Human Identity* general essay, page 128; grade span essays, pages 128–130 ▸ 6B, *Human Development* general essay, page 131; grade span essays, pages 132–134 ▸ 6C, *Basic Functions* general essay, page 135; grade span essays, pages 136–138 **IIB:** ***National Science Education Standards*** ▸ Grades K–4, Standard C essay, pages 127–128; Standard F essay, pages 138–139 ▸ Grades 5–8, Standard C essay, pages 155–156; Standard F essay, pages 167–168 ▸ Grades 9–12, Standard C essay, pages 181, 184; Standard F essay, pages 193, 197
III. Identify Concepts and Specific Ideas	**IIIA:** ***Benchmarks for Science Literacy*** ▸ 6A, *Human Identity,* pages 128–130 ▸ 6B, *Human Development,* pages 132–134 ▸ 6C, *Basic Functions,* pages 136–138 **IIIB:** ***National Science Education Standards*** ▸ Grades K–4, Standard C, *The Characteristics of Organisms,* page 129 ▸ Grades 5–8, Standard C, *Structure and Function in Living Systems,* pages 156–157; *Reproduction and Heredity,* page 157; *Regulation and Behavior,* page 157 ▸ Grades 9–12, Standard C, *The Cell,* pages 184–185; *Behavior of Organisms,* page 187
V. Examine Research on Student Learning	**IVA:** ***Benchmarks for Science Literacy*** ▸ 6, 6B, and 6C, *The Human Organism,* pages 344–345 **IVB:** ***Making Sense of Secondary Science: Research Into Children's Ideas*** ▸ Chapter 1, *Organization of the Body: Structure and Function,* page 26 ▸ Chapter 2, *Human Digestion and Assimilation,* pages 29–30 ▸ Chapter 4, *The Nervous System,* pages 46–47; *Muscles and Skeleton,* page 47
V. Examine Coherency and Articulation	**V:** ***Atlas of Science Literacy*** ▸ *Cells and Organs,* pages 74–75
VI. Clarify State Standards and District Curriculum	**VIA:** ***State Standards:*** Link Sections I–V to learning goals and information from your state standards or frameworks that are informed by the results of the topic study. **VIB:** ***District Curriculum Guide:*** Link Sections I–V to learning goals and information from your district curriculum guide that are informed by the results of the topic study.
Visit www.curriculumtopicstudy.org for updates or supplementary readings, web sites, and videos	

Standards- and Research-Based Study of a Curricular Topic

INFECTIOUS DISEASE

Section and Outcome	Selected Sources and Readings for Study and Reflection Read and examine *related parts* of:
I. Identify Adult Content Knowledge	**IA:** ***Science for All Americans*** ▸ Chapter 6, *Basic Functions*, pages 76–78; *Physical Health*, page 81 ▸ Chapter 8, *Health Technology*, pages 123–126 ▸ Chapter 10, *Discovering Germs*, pages 159–160 **IB:** ***Science Matters: Achieving Scientific Literacy*** ▸ Chapter 15, *Single-Celled Organisms*, page 221; *Immunology*, pages 222–223
II. Consider Instructional Implications	**IIA:** ***Benchmarks for Science Literacy*** ▸ 6C, *Basic Functions* general essay, page 135; grade span essays, pages 136–138 ▸ 6E, *Physical Health* general essay, page 143; grade span essays, pages 144–146 ▸ 8F, *Health Technology* general essay, page 204; grade span essays, pages 205–207 ▸ 10I *Discovering Germs* general essay, page 256; grade span essay, page 257 **IIB:** ***National Science Education Standards*** ▸ Grades K–4, Standard F essay, pages 138–139 ▸ Grades 5–8, Standard C essay, pages 155–156, Standard F essay, pages 167–168 ▸ Grades 9–12, Standard F essay, pages 193, 197
III. Identify Concepts and Specific Ideas	**IIIA:** ***Benchmarks for Science Literacy*** ▸ 6C, *Basic Functions*, pages 136–138 ▸ 6E, *Physical Health*, pages 144–146 ▸ 8F, *Health Technology*, pages 205–207 ▸ 10I, *Discovering Germs*, page 257 **IIIB:** ***National Science Education Standards*** ▸ Grades K–4, Standard F, *Personal Health*, pages 139–140 ▸ Grades 5–8, Standard C, *Structure and Function in Living Systems*, pages 156–157; Standard F, *Personal Health*, page 168 ▸ Grades 9–12, Standard F, *Personal and Community Health*, pages 197–198
IV. Examine Research on Student Learning	**IVA:** ***Benchmarks for Science Literacy*** ▸ 6E, *Germs*, page 345, *Causes of Illness*, pages 345–346 **IVB:** ***Making Sense of Secondary Science: Research Into Children's Ideas*** ▸ Chapter 6, *Microbes and Disease*, pages 55–56
V. Examine Coherency and Articulation	**V:** ***Atlas of Science Literacy*** ▸ *Disease*, pages 86–87 ▸ *Maintaining Good Health*, pages 88–89
VI. Clarify State Standards and District Curriculum	**VIA:** ***State Standards:*** Link Sections I–V to learning goals and information from your state standards or frameworks that are informed by the results of the topic study. **VIB:** ***District Curriculum Guide:*** Link Sections I–V to learning goals and information from your district curriculum guide that are informed by the results of the topic study.

Visit www.curriculumtopicstudy.org for updates or supplementary readings, Web sites, and videos.

Standards- and Research-Based Study of a Curricular Topic

LIFE PROCESSES AND NEEDS OF ORGANISMS

Section and Outcome	Selected Sources and Readings for Study and Reflection Read and examine *related parts* of:
I. Identify Adult Content Knowledge	**IA:** *Science for All Americans* ▸ Chapter 5, *Cells,* pages 62–64; *Flow of Matter and Energy,* pages 66–67 **IB:** *Science Matters: Achieving Scientific Literacy* ▸ Chapter 15, *The Ladder of Life,* pages 206–219
II. Consider Instructional Implications	**IIA:** *Benchmarks for Science Literacy* ▸ 5C *Cells* general essay, page 110; grade span essays, pages 111–113 ▸ 5E, *Flow of Matter and Energy* grade span essays, pages 119–121 **IIB:** *National Science Education Standards* ▸ Grades K–4, Standard C essay, pages 127–128 ▸ Grades 5–8, Standard C essay, pages 155–156 ▸ Grades 9–12, Standard C essay, pages 181,184
III. Identify Concepts and Specific Ideas	**IIIA:** *Benchmarks for Science Literacy* ▸ 5C, *Cells,* pages 111–114 ▸ 5E, *Flow of Matter and Energy,* pages 119–121 **IIIB:** *National Science Education Standards* ▸ Grades K–4, Standard C, *The Characteristics of Organisms,* page 129 ▸ Grades 5–8, Standard C, *Structure and Function in Living Systems,* pages 156–157; *Reproduction and Heredity,* page 157; *Regulation and Behavior,* page 157 ▸ Grades 9–12, Standard C, *The Cell,* pages 184–185; *Matter, Energy, and Organization in Living Systems,* pages 186–187; *The Behavior of Organisms,* page 187
IV. Examine Research on Student Learning	**IVA:** *Benchmarks for Science Literacy* ▸ 5C, *Cells,* page 342 ▸ 5E, *Flow of Matter and Energy,* page 342 **IVB:** *Making Sense of Secondary Science: Research Into Children's Ideas* ▸ Chapter 1, *The Concept of "Living,"* pages 17–21 ▸ Chapter 2, *Nutrition,* pages 27–35 ▸ Chapter 3, *Growth,* pages 36–40 ▸ Chapter 4, *Behavior as a Criterion for Life,* page 41 ▸ Chapter 5, *Reproduction as a Criterion for Life,* page 48
V. Examine Coherency and Articulation	**V.** *Atlas of Science Literacy* ▸ *Cell Functions,* pages 72–73 ▸ *Flow of Matter in Ecosystems,* pages 76–77 ▸ *Flow of Energy in Ecosystems,* pages 78–79
VI. Clarify State Standards and District Curriculum	**VIA:** *State Standards:* Link Sections I–V to learning goals and information from your state standards or frameworks that are informed by the results of the topic study. **VIB:** *District Curriculum Guide:* Link Sections I–V to learning goals and information from your district curriculum guide that are informed by the results of the topic study.
	Visit www.curriculumtopicstudy.org for updates or supplementary readings, Web sites, and videos.

Standards- and Research-Based Study of a Curricular Topic

PHOTOSYNTHESIS AND RESPIRATION

Section and Outcome	Selected Sources and Readings for Study and Reflection Read and examine *related parts* of:
I. Identify Adult Content Knowledge	**IA:** *Science for All Americans* ▶ Chapter 5, *Flow of Matter and Energy*, pages 66–67 **IB:** *Science Matters: Achieving Scientific Literacy* ▶ Chapter 15, *The Power Plant*, pages 217–219 ▶ Chapter 18, *Energy and the Food Web*, pages 263–265; *Nutrients and the Carbon Cycle*, pages 265–267
II. Consider Instructional Implications	**IIA:** *Benchmarks for Science Literacy* ▶ 5C, *Cells* general essay, page 110; grade span essays, pages 111–113 ▶ 5E, *Flow of Matter and Energy* general essay, page 118; grade span essays, pages 119–121 **IIB:** *National Science Education Standards* ▶ Grades K–4, Standard C essay, pages 127–129 ▶ Grades 5–8, Standard C essay, pages 155–156 ▶ Grades 9–12, Standard C essay, pages 181; Vignette, *Photosynthesis*, pages 194–196
III. Identify Concepts and Specific Ideas	**IIIA:** *Benchmarks for Science Literacy* ▶ 5C, *Cells*, pages 111–114 ▶ 5E, *Flow of Matter and Energy*, pages 119–121 **IIIB:** *National Science Education Standards* ▶ Grades K–4, Standard C, *The Characteristics of Organisms*, page 129; *Organisms and Their Environments*, page 129 ▶ Grades 5–8, Standard C, *Populations and Ecosystems*, pages 157–158 ▶ Grades 9–12, Standard C, *The Cell*, page 184; *The Interdependence of Organisms*, page 186; *Matter, Energy, Organization in Living Systems*, pages 186–187
IV. Examine Research on Student Learning	**IVA:** *Benchmarks for Science Literacy* ▶ 5E, *Flow of Matter and Energy*, pages 342–343 **IVB:** *Making Sense of Secondary Science: Research Into Children's Ideas* ▶ Chapter 2, *Food: What Is It?* pages 27–28; *Human Digestion and Assimilation*, pages 29–30; *Plant Nutrition*, pages 30–32; *Photosynthesis*, pages 32–33; *Gas Exchange by Plants*, pages 33–34 ▶ Chapter 7, *Nutrition and Energy Flow*, pages 59–60; *Cycling of Matter Through the Ecosystem*, page 65; *Gas Exchange and Balance*, page 66; *Respiration*, pages 66–68 ▶ Chapter 13, *Gases Involved in Life Processes*, pages 110–111
V. Examine Coherency and Articulation	**V:** *Atlas of Science Literacy* ▶ *Flow of Matter in Ecosystems*, pages 76–77 ▶ *Flow of Energy in Ecosystems*, pages 78–79
VI. Clarify State Standards and District Curriculum	**VIA:** *State Standards:* Link Sections I–V to learning goals and information from your state standards or frameworks that are informed by the results of the topic study. **VIB:** *District Curriculum Guide:* Link Sections I–V to learning goals and information from your district curriculum guide that are informed by the results of the topic study.

Visit www.curriculumtopicstudy.org for updates or supplementary readings, Web sites, and videos.

Standards- and Research-Based Study of a Curricular Topic

REGULATION AND CONTROL

Section and Outcome	Selected Sources and Readings for Study and Reflection Read and examine *related parts* of:
I. Identify Adult Content Knowledge	**IA:** *Science for All Americans* ▸ Chapter 5, *Cells,* pages 62–64 ▸ Chapter 6, *Basic Functions,* pages 76–78 **IB:** *Science Matters: Achieving Scientific Literacy* ▸ Chapter 15, *Neurobiology,* page 222
II. Consider Instructional Implications	**IIA:** *Benchmarks for Science Literacy* ▸ 5C *Cells* general essay, page 110; grade span essays, pages 111–113 ▸ 6B, *Basic Functions* general essay, page 135; grade span essays, pages 136–138 **IIB:** *National Science Education Standards* ▸ Grades K–4, Standard C essay, pages 127–128 ▸ Grades 5–8, Standard C essay, pages 155–156 ▸ Grades 9–12, Standard C essay, pages 181, 184
III. Identify Concepts and Specific Ideas	**IIIA:** *Benchmarks for Science Literacy* ▸ 5C, *Cells,* pages 111–114 ▸ 6B, *Basic Functions,* pages 136–138 **IIIB:** *National Science Education Standards* ▸ Grades K–4, Standard C, *The Characteristics of Organisms,* page 129 ▸ Grades 5–8, Standard C, *Structure and Function in Living Systems,* pages 156–157; *Regulation and Behavior,* page 157 ▸ Grades 9–12, Standard C, *The Cell,* pages 184–185; *The Behavior of Organisms,* page 187
IV. Examine Research on Student Learning	**IVA:** *Benchmarks for Science Literacy* ▸ 5C, *Cells,* page 342 ▸ 6C, *Nervous System,* page 345 **IVB:** *Making Sense of Secondary Science: Research Into Children's Ideas* ▸ Chapter 4, *The Nervous System,* pages 46–47; *Muscles and Skeleton,* page 47; *The Responses of Plants,* page 47
V. Examine Coherency and Articulation	**V:** *Atlas of Science Literacy* ▸ *Cell Functions,* pages 72–73 ▸ *Cells and Organs,* pages 74–75
VI. Clarify State Standards and District Curriculum	**VIA:** *State Standards:* Link Sections I–V to learning goals and information from your state standards or frameworks that are informed by the results of the topic study. **VIB:** *District Curriculum Guide:* Link Sections I–V to learning goals and information from your district curriculum guide that are informed by the results of the topic study
Visit www.curriculumtopicstudy.org for updates or supplementary readings, Web sites, and videos.	

Standards- and Research-Based Study of a Curricular Topic

SENSES

Section and Outcome	Selected Sources and Readings for Study and Reflection Read and examine *related parts* of:
I. Identify Adult Content Knowledge	**IA:** *Science for All Americans* ▸ Chapter 6, *Basic Functions,* pages 76–78; *Learning,* pages 78–79 **IB:** *Science Matters: Achieving Scientific Literacy* ▸ Chapter 15, *The Organization of Life,* pages 219–220
II. Consider Instructional Implications	**IIA:** *Benchmarks for Science Literacy* ▸ 6C, *Basic Functions* general essay, page 135; grade span essays, pages 136–138 ▸ 6D, *Learning* general essay, page 139, grade span essays, pages 140–142 **IIB:** *National Science Education Standards* ▸ Grades K–4, Standard C essay, pages 127–128; Standard F essay, pages 138–139 ▸ Grades 5–8, Standard C essay, pages 155–156; Standard F essay, pages 167–168 ▸ Grades 9–12, Standard C essay, pages 181, 184; Standard F essay, pages 193, 197
III. Identify Concepts and Specific Ideas	**IIIA:** *Benchmarks for Science Literacy* ▸ 6C, *Basic Functions,* pages 136–138 ▸ 6D, *Learning,* pages 140–141 **IIIB:** *National Science Education Standards* ▸ Grades K–4, Standard C, *The Characteristics of Organisms,* page 129 ▸ Grades 5–8, Standard C, *Structure and Function in Living Systems,* pages 156–157; *Regulation and Behavior,* page 157 ▸ Grades 9–12, Standard C, *Behavior of Organisms,* page 187
IV. Examine Research on Student Learning	**IVA:** *Benchmarks for Science Literacy* ▸ 6C, *Nervous System,* page 345 **IVB:** *Making Sense of Secondary Science: Research Into Children's Ideas* ▸ Chapter 4, *Vision,* pages 41–45; *Hearing,* pages 45–46
V. Examine Coherency and Articulation	**V:** *Atlas of Science Literacy* ▸ *Cells and Organs,* pages 74–75
VI. Clarify State Standards and District Curriculum	**VIA:** *State Standards:* Link Sections I–V to learning goals and information from your state standards or frameworks that are informed by the results of the topic study. **VIB:** *District Curriculum Guide:* Link Sections I–V to learning goals and information from your district curriculum guide that are informed by the results of the topic study.

Visit www.curriculumtopicstudy.org for updates or supplementary readings, Web sites, and videos.

Life's Continuity and Change

Primary Domain: Life Science

Number of CTS Guides: 10

Overview: The primary focus of this section is how organisms maintain certain characteristics as well as change during their lifetimes and over several generations. Ideas such as biological evolution and the evidence that supports it, heredity, and the mechanism and changes in the cycle of life from birth to death are developed through a study of the topics in this section.

Standards- and Research-Based Study of a Curricular Topic

ADAPTATION

Section and Outcome	Selected Sources and Readings for Study and Reflection Read and examine *related parts* of:	
I. Identify Adult Content Knowledge	**IA:**	***Science for All Americans*** ▸ Chapter 5, *Heredity,* page 62; *Evolution of Life,* pages 67–69
	IB:	***Science Matters: Achieving Scientific Literacy*** ▸ Chapter 17, *Natural Selection,* pages 248–250
II. Consider Instructional Implications	**IIA:**	***Benchmarks for Science Literacy*** ▸ 5F, *Evolution of Life* general essay, page 122; grade span essays, pages 123–124
	IIB:	***National Science Education Standards*** ▸ Grades K–4, Standard C essay, pages 127–129 ▸ Grades 5–8, Standard C essay, pages 155–156 ▸ Grades 9–12, Standard C essay, pages 181, 184
III. Identify Concepts and Specific Ideas	**IIIA:**	***Benchmarks for Science Literacy*** ▸ 5F, *Evolution of Life,* pages 123–125
	IIIB:	***National Science Education Standards*** ▸ Grades K–4, Standard C, *The Characteristics of Organisms,* page 129, *Organisms and their Environments,* page 129 ▸ Grades 5–8, Standard C, *Diversity and Adaptations of Organisms,* page 158 ▸ Grades 9–12, Standard C, *Biological Evolution,* page 185
IV. Examine Research on Student Learning	**IVA:**	***Benchmarks for Science Literacy*** ▸ 5D, *Habitat,* page 342 ▸ 5F, *Adaptation,* page 344
	IVB:	***Making Sense of Secondary Science: Research Into Children's Ideas*** ▸ Chapter 1, *Adaptation,* page 26 ▸ Chapter 5, *Adaptation,* pages 52–53
V. Examine Coherency and Articulation	**V:**	***Atlas of Science Literacy*** ▸ *Biological Evolution,* pages 80–81 ▸ *Natural Selection,* pages 82–83; note the conceptual strand on *Variation and Advantage.*
VI. Clarify State Standards and District Curriculum	**VIA:**	***State Standards:*** Link Sections I–V to learning goals and information from your state standards or frameworks that are informed by the results of the topic study.
	VIB:	***District Curriculum Guide:*** Link Sections I–V to learning goals and information from your district curriculum guide that are informed by the results of the topic study.
Visit www.curriculumtopicstudy.org for updates or supplementary readings, Web sites, and videos.		

Standards- and Research-Based Study of a Curricular Topic

BIOLOGICAL EVOLUTION

Section and Outcome	Selected Sources and Readings for Study and Reflection Read and examine *related parts* of:
I. Identify Adult Content Knowledge	**IA:** ***Science for All Americans*** ‣ Chapter 5, *Evolution of Life,* pages 67–69 ‣ Chapter 6, *Human Identity,* page 72 ‣ Chapter 10, *Explaining the Diversity of Life,* pages 157–159 **IB:** ***Science Matters: Achieving Scientific Literacy*** ‣ Chapter 17, *Evolution,* pages 243–259
II. Consider Instructional Implications	**IIA:** ***Benchmarks for Science Literacy*** ‣ 5F, *Evolution of Life* general essay, page 122; grade span essays, pages 123–124 ‣ 6A, *Human Identity,* 9–12 grade span essay, page 130 ‣ 10H, *Explaining the Diversity of Life* general essay, page 254; grade span essay, page 254 **IIB:** ***National Science Education Standards*** ‣ Grades K–4, Standard C essay, pages 127–128 ‣ Grades 5–8, Standard C essay, pages 155–156 ‣ Grades 9–12, Standard C essay, pages 181, 184; Vignette *Fossils,* pages 182–183
III. Identify Concepts and Specific Ideas	**IIIA:** ***Benchmarks for Science Literacy*** ‣ 5F, *Evolution of Life,* pages 123–125 ‣ 6A, *Human Identity,* pages 128–130 ‣ 10H, *Explaining the Diversity of Life,* pages 254–255 **IIIB:** ***National Science Education Standards*** ‣ Grades K–4, Standard C, *The Characteristics of Organisms,* page 129 ‣ Grades 5–8, Standard C, *Diversity and Adaptations of Organisms,* page 158 ‣ Grades 9–12, Standard C, *Biological Evolution,* page 185
IV. Examine Research on Student Learning	**IVA:** ***Benchmarks for Science Literacy*** ‣ 5F, *Evolution of Life,* pages 343–344 **IVB:** ***Making Sense of Secondary Science: Research Into Children's Ideas*** ‣ Chapter 1, *The Concept of Species,* page 25; *Adaptation,* page 26 ‣ Chapter 5, *Adaptation,* pages 52–53; *Chance in Inheritance,* page 53
V. Examine Coherency and Articulation	**V:** ***Atlas of Science Literacy*** ‣ *Biological Evolution,* pages 80–81 ‣ *Natural Selection,* pages 82–83
VI. Clarify State Standards and District Curriculum	**VIA:** ***State Standards:*** Link Sections I–V to learning goals and information from your state standards or frameworks that are informed by the results of the topic study. **VIB:** ***District Curriculum Guide:*** Link Sections I–V to learning goals and information from your district curriculum guide that are informed by the results of the topic study.
Visit www.curriculumtopicstudy.org for updates or supplementary readings, Web sites, and videos.	

Standards- and Research-Based Study of a Curricular Topic

FOSSIL EVIDENCE

Section and Outcome	Selected Sources and Readings for Study and Reflection Read and examine *related parts* of:
I. Identify Adult Content Knowledge	**IA:** *Science for All Americans* ▸ Chapter 4, *Processes That Shape the Earth,* page 46 ▸ Chapter 5, *Evolution of Life,* pages 67–69 ▸ Chapter 10, *Extending Time,* pages 151–152 **IB:** *Science Matters: Achieving Scientific Literacy* ▸ Chapter 17, *Fossils and Evolution,* pages 252–258
II. Consider Instructional Implications	**IIA:** *Benchmarks for Science Literacy* ▸ 4C, *Processes That Shape the Earth* 6–8 grade span essay, page 73 ▸ 5F, *Evolution of Life* general essay, page 122; grade span essays, pages 123–124 ▸ 10D, *Extending Time* general essay, page 246; grade span essay, page 246 **IIB:** *National Science Education Standards* ▸ Grades K–4, Standard C essay, pages 127–128; Standard D essay, page 130 ▸ Grades 5–8, Standard C essay, pages 155–156; Standard D essay, page 159 ▸ Grades 9–12, Standard C essay, pages 181, 184; Standard D essay, page 188; Vignette *Fossils,* pages 182–183
III. Identify Concepts and Specific Ideas	**IIIA:** *Benchmarks for Science Literacy* ▸ 4C, *Processes That Shape the Earth,* 6–8 grade span essay, page 73 ▸ 5F, *Evolution of Life,* pages 123–125 ▸ 10D, *Extending Time,* 9–12 grade span essay, page 246 **IIIB:** *National Science Education Standards* ▸ Grades K–4, Standard D, *Properties of Earth Materials,* page 134 ▸ Grades 5–8, Standard C, *Diversity and Adaptations of Organisms,* page 158; Standard D, *Earth's History,* page 160 ▸ Grades 9–12, Standard C, *Biological Evolution,* page 185; Standard D, *The Origin and Evolution of the Earth System,* pages 189–190
IV. Examine Research on Student Learning	**IVA:** *Benchmarks for Science Literacy* ▸ 4C, *Processes That Shape the Earth,* page 336 ▸ 5F, *Evolution of Life,* pages 343–344
V. Examine Coherency and Articulation	**V:** *Atlas of Science Literacy* ▸ *Changes in the Earth's Surface,* pages 50–51; note the conceptual strand *Rocks and Sediments* ▸ *Biological Evolution,* pages 80–81; note the conceptual strand *Fossil Evidence*
VI. Clarify State Standards and District Curriculum	**VIA:** *State Standards:* Link Sections I–V to learning goals and information from your state standards or frameworks that are informed by the results of the topic study. **VIB:** *District Curriculum Guide:* Link Sections I–V to learning goals and information from your district curriculum guide that are informed by the results of the topic study.
Visit www.curriculumtopicstudy.org for updates or supplementary readings, Web sites, and videos.	

Standards- and Research-Based Study of a Curricular Topic

HUMAN EVOLUTION

Section and Outcome	Selected Sources and Readings for Study and Reflection Read and examine *related parts* of:
I. Identify Adult Content Knowledge	**IA:** *Science for All Americans* ▸ Chapter 5, *Evolution of Life,* pages 67–69 ▸ Chapter 6, *Human Identity,* pages 72–73 **IB:** *Science Matters: Achieving Scientific Literacy* ▸ Chapter 17, *Human Evolution,* page 258
II. Consider Instructional Implications	**IIA:** *Benchmarks for Science Literacy* ▸ 5F, *Evolution of Life* general essay, page 122; grade span essays, pages 123–124 ▸ 6A, *Human Identity,* Grades 6–8 and 9–12 grade span essays, pages 129–130 **IIB:** *National Science Education Standards* ▸ Grades K–4, Standard C essay, pages 127–128 ▸ Grades 5–8, Standard C essay, pages 155–156 ▸ Grades 9–12, Standard C essay, pages 181, 184
III. Identify Concepts and Specific Ideas	**IIIA:** *Benchmarks for Science Literacy* ▸ 5F, *Evolution of Life,* pages 123–125 ▸ 6A, *Human Identity,* pages 129–130 **IIIB:** *National Science Education Standards* ▸ Grades K–4, Standard C, *The Characteristics of Organisms,* page 129 ▸ Grades 5–8, Standard C, *Diversity and Adaptations of Organisms,* page 158 ▸ Grades 9–12, Standard C, *Biological Evolution,* page 185
IV. Examine Research on Student Learning	**IVA:** *Benchmarks for Science Literacy* ▸ 5F, *Evolution of Life,* pages 343–344
V. Examine Coherency and Articulation	**V:** *Atlas of Science Literacy* ▸ *Biological Evolution,* pages 80–81
VI. Clarify State Standards and District Curriculum	**VIA:** *State Standards:* Link Sections I–V to learning goals and information from your state standards or frameworks that are informed by the results of the topic study. **VIB:** *District Curriculum Guide:* Link Sections I–V to learning goals and information from your district curriculum guide that are informed by the results of the topic study.
Visit www.curriculumtopicstudy.org for updates or supplementary readings, Web sites, and videos.	

Standards- and Research-Based Study of a Curricular Topic

MECHANISM OF INHERITANCE (GENETICS)

Section and Outcome	Selected Sources and Readings for Study and Reflection Read and examine *related parts* of:
I. Identify Adult Content Knowledge	**IA:** *Science for All Americans* ▶ Chapter 5, *Heredity*, pages 61–62 **IB:** *Science Matters: Achieving Scientific Literacy* ▶ Chapter 16, *Code of Life*, pages 224–242
II. Consider Instructional Implications	**IIA:** *Benchmarks for Science Literacy* ▶ 5B, *Heredity* general essay, page 106; grade span essays, pages 107–108 **IIB:** *National Science Education Standards* ▶ Grades K–4, Standard C essay, pages 127–128 ▶ Grades 5–8, Standard C essay, pages 155–156 ▶ Grades 9–12, Standard C essay, pages 181, 184; Vignette *Genetics*, pages 64–66
III. Identify Concepts and Specific Ideas	**IIIA:** *Benchmarks for Science Literacy* ▶ 5B, *Heredity*, pages 107–109 **IIIB:** *National Science Education Standards* ▶ Grades K–4, Standard C, *Life Cycles of Organisms*, page 129 ▶ Grades 5–8, Standard C, *Reproduction and Heredity*, page 157 ▶ Grades 9–12, Standard C, *The Cell*, pages 184–185; *The Molecular Basis of Heredity*, page 185
IV. Examine Research on Student Learning	**IVA:** *Benchmarks for Science Literacy* ▶ 5B, *Heredity*, page 341 **IVB:** *Making Sense of Secondary Science: Research Into Children's Ideas* ▶ Chapter 5, *The Mechanism of Inheritance*, pages 51–52
V. Examine Coherency and Articulation	**V:** *Atlas of Science Literacy* ▶ *DNA and Inherited Characteristics*, pages 68–69 ▶ *Variation in Inherited Characteristics*, pages 70–71
VI. Clarify State Standards and District Curriculum	**VIA:** *State Standards:* Link Sections I–V to learning goals and information from your state standards or frameworks that are informed by the results of the topic study. **VIB:** *District Curriculum Guide:* Link Sections I–V to learning goals and information from your district curriculum guide that are informed by the results of the topic study.
Visit www.curriculumtopicstudy.org for updates or supplementary readings, Web sites, and videos.	

Standards- and Research-Based Study of a Curricular Topic

MUTATIONS

Section and Outcome	Selected Sources and Readings for Study and Reflection Read and examine *related parts* of:
I. Identify Adult Content Knowledge	**IA:** ***Science for All Americans*** ▸ Chapter 5, *Heredity,* pages 62; *Cells,* page 64; *Evolution of Life,* page 69 **IB:** ***Science Matters: Achieving Scientific Literacy*** ▸ Chapter 17, *The Mechanism for Change,* pages 250–251
II. Consider Instructional Implications	**IIA:** ***Benchmarks for Science Literacy*** ▸ 5B, *Heredity* general essay, page 106; 6–8 and 9–12 grade span essays, page 108 ▸ 5C, *Cells,* 9–12 grade span essay, page 113 ▸ 5F, *Evolution of Life,* 9–12 grade span essay, page 124 **IIB:** ***National Science Education Standards*** ▸ Grades 5–8, Standard C essay, pages 155–156 ▸ Grades 9–12, Standard C essay, pages 181, 184
III. Identify Concepts and Specific Ideas	**IIIA:** ***Benchmarks for Science Literacy*** ▸ 5B, *Heredity,* 6–8 and 9–12 grade span essays, pages 108–109 ▸ 5C, *Cells,* 9–12, page 114 ▸ 5F, *Evolution of Life,* 9–12 grade span essays, page 125 **IIIB:** ***National Science Education Standards*** ▸ Grades 5–8, Standard C, *Reproduction and Heredity,* page 157 ▸ Grades 9–12, Standard C, *The Cell,* pages 184–185; *The Molecular Basis of Heredity,* page 185; *Biological Evolution,* page 185
IV. Examine Research on Student Learning	**IVA:** ***Benchmarks for Science Literacy*** ▸ 5B, *Heredity,* page 341 ▸ 5F, *Natural Selection,* page 343 **IVB:** ***Making Sense of Secondary Science: Research Into Children's Ideas*** ▸ Chapter 5, *The Mechanism of Inheritance,* pages 51–52; *Sources of Variation,* page 52
V. Examine Coherency and Articulation	**V:** ***Atlas of Science Literacy*** ▸ *DNA and Inherited Characteristics,* pages 68–69 ▸ *Variation in Inherited Characteristics,* pages 70–71 ▸ *Natural Selection,* pages 82–83
VI. Clarify State Standards and District Curriculum	**VIA:** ***State Standards:*** Link Sections I–V to learning goals and information from your state standards or frameworks that are informed by the results of the topic study. **VIB:** ***District Curriculum Guide:*** Link Sections I–V to learning goals and information from your district curriculum guide that are informed by the results of the topic study.
Visit www.curriculumtopicstudy.org for updates or supplementary readings, Web sites, and videos.	

Standards- and Research-Based Study of a Curricular Topic

NATURAL AND ARTIFICIAL SELECTION

Section and Outcome	Selected Sources and Readings for Study and Reflection Read and examine *related parts* of:
I. Identify Adult Content Knowledge	**IA:** *Science for All Americans* ▶ Chapter 5, *Heredity,* pages 61–62; *Evolution of Life,* pages 67–69 ▶ Chapter 8, *Agriculture,* pages 108–109 ▶ Chapter 10, *Explaining the Diversity of Life,* pages 157–159 **IB:** *Science Matters: Achieving Scientific Literacy* ▶ Chapter 17, *Natural Selection,* pages 248–250
II. Consider Instructional Implications	**IIA:** *Benchmarks for Science Literacy* ▶ 5B, *Heredity* 6–8; 9–12 grade span essays, page 108 ▶ 5F, *Evolution of Life* general essay, page 122; grade span essays, pages 123–124 ▶ 8A, *Agriculture* general essay, page 183; 9–12 grade span essay, page186 ▶ 10H, *Explaining the Diversity of Life* general essay, page 254; grade span essay, page 254 **IIB:** *National Science Education Standards* ▶ Grades K–4, Standard C essay, pages 127–128 ▶ Grades 5–8, Standard C essay, pages 155–156 ▶ Grades 9–12, Standard C essay, pages 181, 184
III. Identify Concepts and Specific Ideas	**IIIA:** *Benchmarks for Science Literacy* ▶ 5B, *Heredity,* pages 108–109 ▶ 5F, *Evolution of Life,* pages 123–125 ▶ 8A, *Agriculture,* pages 184–186 ▶ 10H, *Explaining the Diversity of Life,* pages 254–255 **IIIB:** *National Science Education Standards* ▶ Grades K–4, Standard C, *The Characteristics of Organisms,* page 129 ▶ Grades 5–8, Standard C, *Diversity and Adaptations of Organisms,* page 158 ▶ Grades 9–12, Standard C, *Biological Evolution,* page 185
IV. Examine Research on Student Learning	**IVA:** *Benchmarks for Science Literacy* ▶ 5,F *Natural Selection,* page 343; *Adaptation,* page 344 **IVB:** *Making Sense of Secondary Science: Research Into Children's Ideas* ▶ Chapter 1, *The Concept of Species,* page 25; *Adaptation,* page 26 ▶ Chapter 5, *Adaptation,* pages 52–53
V. Examine Coherency and Articulation	**V:** *Atlas of Science Literacy* ▶ *Biological Evolution,* pages 80–81 ▶ *Natural Selection,* pages 82–83
VI. Clarify State Standards and District Curriculum	**VIA:** *State Standards:* Link Sections I–V to learning goals and information from your state standards or frameworks that are informed by the results of the topic study. **VIB:** *District Curriculum Guide:* Link Sections I–V to learning goals and information from your district curriculum guide that are informed by the results of the topic study.

Visit www.curriculumtopicstudy.org for updates or supplementary readings, Web sites, and videos.

Standards- and Research-Based Study of a Curricular Topic

ORIGIN OF LIFE

Section and Outcome	Selected Sources and Readings for Study and Reflection Read and examine *related parts* of:
I. Identify Adult Content Knowledge	**IA:** *Science for All Americans* ▸ Chapter 5, *Evolution of Life,* page 68 **IB:** *Science Matters: Achieving Scientific Literacy* ▸ Chapter 17, *Chemical Evolution,* pages 245–247
II. Consider Instructional Implications	**IIA:** *Benchmarks for Science Literacy* ▸ 5F, *Evolution of Life* general essay, page 122; 9–12 grade span essay, page 124 **IIB:** *National Science Education Standards* ▸ Grades 9–12, Standard C essay, pages 181, 184
III. Identify Concepts and Specific Ideas	**IIIA:** *Benchmarks for Science Literacy* ▸ 5F, *Evolution of Life,* 9–12, page 125 **IIIB:** *National Science Education Standards* ▸ Grades 9–12, Standard C, *Biological Evolution,* page 185; Standard D, *The Origin and Evolution of the Universe,* page 190
IV. Examine Research on Student Learning	**IV:** No related research in either resources.
V. Examine Coherency and Articulation	**V:** *Atlas of Science Literacy* ▸ *Biological Evolution,* pages 80–81
VI. Clarify State Standards and District Curriculum	**VIA:** *State Standards:* Link Sections I–V to learning goals and information from your state standards or frameworks that are informed by the results of the topic study. **VIB:** *District Curriculum Guide:* Link Sections I–V to learning goals and information from your district curriculum guide that are informed by the results of the topic study.
Visit www.curriculumtopicstudy.org for updates or supplementary readings, Web sites, and videos.	

Standards- and Research-Based Study of a Curricular Topic

REPRODUCTION, GROWTH, AND DEVELOPMENT (LIFE CYCLES)

Section and Outcome	Selected Sources and Readings for Study and Reflection Read and examine *related parts* of:
I. Identify Adult Content Knowledge	**IA:** *Science for All Americans* ▸ Chapter 6, *Human Development*, pages 73–76 **IB:** *Science Matters: Achieving Scientific Literacy* ▸ Chapter 16, *Sex: A Good Idea*, pages 235–238
II. Consider Instructional Implications	**IIA:** *Benchmarks for Science Literacy* ▸ 6B, *Human Development* general essay, page 131; grade span essays, pages 132–134 **IIB:** *National Science Education Standards* ▸ Grades K–4, Standard C essay, pages 127–128 ▸ Grades 5–8, Standard C essay, pages 155–156 ▸ Grades 9–12, Standard C essay, pages 181,184
III. Identify Concepts and Specific Ideas	**IIIA:** *Benchmarks for Science Literacy* ▸ 5B, *Heredity*, 6–8 and 9–12, pages 108–109 ▸ 6B, *Human Development*, pages 132–134 **IIIB:** *National Science Education Standards* ▸ Standard C, Grades K–4, *The Life Cycle of Organisms*, page 129 ▸ Standard C, Grades 5–8, *Reproduction and Heredity*, page 157 ▸ Standard C, Grades 9–12, *The Cell*, pages 184–185; *Molecular Basis of Heredity*, page 185
IV. Examine Research on Student Learning	**IVA:** *Benchmarks for Science Literacy* ▸ 6B, *Human Development*, page 344 **IVB:** *Making Sense of Secondary Science: Research Into Children's Ideas* ▸ Chapter 3, *Growth*, pages 36–40 ▸ Chapter 5, *Reproduction as a Criterion of Life*, page 48; *Human Reproduction*, pages 48–49; *Continuity of Life*, pages 49–50; *Biological Principles of Reproduction*, pages 50–51
V. Examine Coherency and Articulation	**V.** *Atlas of Science Literacy* ▸ *DNA and Inherited Characteristics*, pages 68–69; note the conceptual strands on *Sexual Reproduction* and *Cells and Development*
VI. Clarify State Standards and District Curriculum	**VIA:** *State Standards:* Link Sections I–V to learning goals and information from your state standards or frameworks that are informed by the results of the topic study. **VIB:** *District Curriculum Guide:* Link Sections I–V to learning goals and information from your district curriculum guide that are informed by the results of the topic study.
Visit www.curriculumtopicstudy.org for updates or supplementary readings, Web sites, and videos.	

Standards- and Research-Based Study of a Curricular Topic

VARIATION

Section and Outcome	Selected Sources and Readings for Study and Reflection Read and examine *related parts* of:
I. Identify Adult Content Knowledge	**IA:** *Science for All Americans* ▸ Chapter, 5 *Heredity,* pages 61–62 **IB:** *Science Matters: Achieving Scientific Literacy* ▸ Chapter 17, *Natural Selection,* pages 248–250
II. Consider Instructional Implications	**IIA:** *Benchmarks for Science Literacy* ▸ 5B, *Heredity* general essay, page 106; grade span essays, pages 107–108 **IIB:** *National Science Education Standards* ▸ Grades K–4, Standard C essay, pages 127–128 ▸ Grades 5–8, Standard C essay, pages 155–156 ▸ Grades 9–12, Standard C essay, pages 181, 184; Vignette *Fossils,* pages 182–183
III. Identify Concepts and Specific Ideas	**IIIA:** *Benchmarks for Science Literacy* ▸ 5B *Heredity,* pages 107–109 **IIIB:** *National Science Education Standards* ▸ Grades K–4, Standard C, *Life Cycles of Organisms,* page 129 ▸ Grades 5–8, Standard C, *Reproduction and Heredity,* page 157 ▸ Grades 9–12, Standard C, *The Molecular Basis of Heredity,* page 185
IV. Examine Research on Student Learning	**IVA:** *Benchmarks for Science Literacy* ▸ 5B, *Heredity,* page 341 **IVB:** *Making Sense of Secondary Science: Research Into Children's Ideas* ▸ Chapter 5, *Variation and Resemblance,* page 51; *Sources of Variation,* page 52
V. Examine Coherency and Articulation	**V:** *Atlas of Science Literacy* ▸ *Variation in Inherited Characteristics,* pages 70–71 ▸ *Natural Selection,* pages 82–83; note the conceptual strand *Variation and Advantage*
VI. Clarify State Standards and District Curriculum	**VIA:** *State Standards:* Link Sections I–V to learning goals and information from your state standards or frameworks that are informed by the results of the topic study. **VIB:** *District Curriculum Guide:* Link Sections I–V to learning goals and information from your district curriculum guide that are informed by the results of the topic study.
Visit www.curriculumtopicstudy.org for updates or supplementary readings, Web sites, and videos.	

Matter

Primary Domain: Physical Science

Number of CTS Guides: 16

Overview: The primary focus of this section is the structure of matter and the changes it can undergo. Ideas such as the parts that make up matter and how they are arranged, types of matter and their combinations, properties and changes matter undergoes and factors that affect them, and the behavior of matter are developed through a study of the topics in this section.

Standards- and Research-Based Study of a Curricular Topic

ACIDS AND BASES

Section and Outcome	Selected Sources and Readings for Study and Reflection Read and examine *related parts* of:
I. Identify Adult Content Knowledge	**IA:** *Science for All Americans* ▸ Chapter 4, *Structure of Matter,* pages 46–49 **IB:** *Science Matters: Achieving Scientific Literacy* ▸ Chapter 18, *Acid Rain,* pages 269–270
II. Consider Instructional Implications	**IIA:** *Benchmarks for Science Literacy* ▸ 4D, *Structure of Matter* general essay, page 75; 6–8 and 9–12 grade span essays, pages 77–79 **IIB:** *National Science Education Standards* ▸ Grades 5–8, Standard B essay, page 149 ▸ Grades 9–12, Standard B essay, page 177
III. Identify Concepts and Specific Ideas	**IIIA:** *Benchmarks for Science Literacy* ▸ 4D, *Structure of Matter,* Grades 6–8 and 9–12, pages 78–80 **IIIB:** *National Science Education Standards* ▸ Grades 5–8, Standard B, *Properties and Changes of Properties in Matter,* page 154 ▸ Grades 9–12, Standard B, *Structure and Properties of Matter,* pages 178–179; *Chemical Reactions,* page 178
IV. Examine Research on Student Learning	**IVB:** *Making Sense of Secondary Science: Research Into Children's Ideas* ▸ Chapter 10, *Acids and Bases,* pages 90–91
V. Examine Coherency and Articulation	**V:** *Atlas of Science Literacy* ▸ *Chemical Reactions,* pages 60–61
VI. Clarify State Standards and District Curriculum	**VIA:** *State Standards:* Link Sections I–V to learning goals and information from your state standards or frameworks that are informed by the results of the topic study. **VIB:** *District Curriculum Guide:* Link Sections I–V to learning goals and information from your district curriculum guide that are informed by the results of the topic study.
Visit www.curriculumtopicstudy.org for updates or supplementary readings, Web sites, and videos.	

Standards- and Research-Based Study of a Curricular Topic

BEHAVIOR AND CHARACTERISTICS OF GASES

Section and Outcome	Selected Sources and Readings for Study and Reflection Read and examine *related parts* of:
I. Identify Adult Content Knowledge	**IA:** *Science for All Americans* ▸ Chapter 4, *Structure of Matter,* pages 46–48 **IB:** *Science Matters: Achieving Scientific Literacy* ▸ Chapter 7, *Gases,* pages 95–96
II. Consider Instructional Implications	**IIA:** *Benchmarks for Science Literacy* ▸ 4D, *Structure of Matter* general essay, page 75; grade span essays, pages 76–79 **IIB:** *National Science Education Standards* ▸ Grades K–4, Standard B essay, pages 123, 126 ▸ Grades 5–8, Standard B essay, page 149 ▸ Grades 9–12, Standard B essay, page 177
III. Identify Concepts and Specific Ideas	**IIIA:** *Benchmarks for Science Literacy* ▸ 4D, *Structure of Matter,* pages 76–80 **IIIB:** *National Science Education Standards* ▸ Grades K–4, Standard B, *Properties of Objects and Materials,* page 127 ▸ Grades 5–8, Standard B, *Properties and Changes of Properties in Matter,* page 154 ▸ Grades 9–12, Standard B, *Structure and Properties of Matter,* pages 178–179; *Conservation of Energy and the Increase in Disorder,* page 180
IV. Examine Research on Student Learning	**IVA:** *Benchmarks for Science Literacy* ▸ 4D, *Structure of Matter,* pages 336–337 **IVB:** *Making Sense of Secondary Science: Research Into Children's Ideas* ▸ Chapter 9, *The Gaseous State,* page 80; *Gaseous Solution,* page 84 ▸ Chapter 11, *Particle Ideas About Gases,* pages 93–94 ▸ Chapter 13, *Existence of Air,* pages 104–105
V. Examine Coherency and Articulation	**V:** *Atlas of Science Literacy* ▸ *States of Matter,* pages 58–59
VI. Clarify State Standards and District Curriculum	**VIA:** *State Standards:* Link Sections I–V to learning goals and information from your state standards or frameworks that are informed by the results of the topic study. **VIB:** *District Curriculum Guide:* Link Sections I–V to learning goals and information from your district curriculum guide that are informed by the results of the topic study.
Visit www.curriculumtopicstudy.org for updates or supplementary readings, Web sites, and videos.	

Standards- and Research-Based Study of a Curricular Topic

CHEMICAL BONDING

Section and Outcome	Selected Sources and Readings for Study and Reflection Read and examine *related parts* of:
I. Identify Adult Content Knowledge	**IA:** *Science for All Americans* ▸ Chapter 4, *Structure of Matter,* pages 46–49 **IB:** *Science Matters: Achieving Scientific Literacy* ▸ Chapter 6, *Chemical Bonding,* pages 75–83
II. Consider Instructional Implications	**IIA:** *Benchmarks for Science Literacy* ▸ 4D, *Structure of Matter* general essay, page 75; grades 6–8 and 9–12 essays, pages 77–79 **IIB:** *National Science Education Standards* ▸ Grades K–4, Standard B essay, pages 123, 126 ▸ Grades 5–8, Standard B essay, page 149 ▸ Grades 9–12, Standard B essay, page 177
III. Identify Concepts and Specific Ideas	**IIIA:** *Benchmarks for Science Literacy* ▸ 4D, *Structure of Matter,* Grades 6–8 and 9–12, pages 78–80 **IIIB:** *National Science Education Standards* ▸ Grades 5–8, Standard B, *Properties and Changes of Properties in Matter,* page 154 ▸ Grades 9–12, Standard B, *Structure and Properties of Matter,* pages 178–179; *Chemical Reactions,* page 179
IV. Examine Research on Student Learning	**IVA:** *Benchmarks for Science Literacy* ▸ 4D, *Chemical Changes,* page 337 **IVB:** *Making Sense of Secondary Science: Research Into Children's Ideas* ▸ Chapter 10, *Chemical Change,* pages 85–87 ▸ Chapter 11, *Conceptions of the Internal Structure of Molecules,* page 96; *Particle Models of Giant Ionic Lattices,* page 97
V. Examine Coherency and Articulation	**V:** *Atlas of Science Literacy* ▸ *Atoms and Molecules,* pages 54–55 ▸ *Chemical Reactions,* pages 60–61
VI. Clarify State Standards and District Curriculum	**VIA:** *State Standards:* Link Sections I–V to learning goals and information from your state standards or frameworks that are informed by the results of the topic study. **VIB:** *District Curriculum Guide:* Link Sections I–V to learning goals and information from your district curriculum guide that are informed by the results of the topic study.
Visit www.curriculumtopicstudy.org for updates or supplementary readings, Web sites, and videos.	

Standards- and Research-Based Study of a Curricular Topic
CHEMICAL PROPERTIES AND CHANGE

Section and Outcome	Selected Sources and Readings for Study and Reflection Read and examine *related parts* of:
I. Identify Adult Content Knowledge	**IA:** *Science for All Americans* ▸ Chapter 4, *Structure of Matter,* pages 46–49 ▸ Chapter 10, *Understanding Fire,* pages 153–155 **IB:** *Science Matters: Achieving Scientific Literacy* ▸ Chapter 6, *Elements in Combination,* pages 77–78 ▸ Chapter 7, *Atomic Architecture,* pages 94–95
II. Consider Instructional Implications	**IIA:** *Benchmarks for Science Literacy* ▸ 4D, *Structure of Matter* general essay, page 75; grade span essays, pages 76–79 ▸ 10F, *Understanding Fire* general essay, page 249; *Understanding Fire* grade span essays, pages 250–251 **IIB:** *National Science Education Standards* ▸ Grades K–4, Standard B essay, pages 123, 126 ▸ Grades 5–8, Standard B essay, page 149 ▸ Grades 9–12, Standard B essay, page 177
III. Identify Concepts and Specific Ideas	**IIIA:** *Benchmarks for Science Literacy* ▸ 4D, *Structure of Matter,* pages 76–80 ▸ 10F, *Understanding Fire,* pages 250–251 **IIIB:** *National Science Education Standards* ▸ Grades K–4, Standard B, *Properties of Objects and Materials,* page 127 ▸ Grades 5–8, Standard B, *Properties and Changes of Properties in Matter,* page 154 ▸ Grades 9–12, Standard B, *Structure and Properties of Matter,* pages 178–179, *Chemical Reactions,* page 179
IV. Examine Research on Student Learning	**IVA:** *Benchmarks for Science Literacy* ▸ 4D, *Structure of Matter,* pages 336–337 **IVB:** *Making Sense of Secondary Science: Research Into Children's Ideas* ▸ Chapter 10, *Chemical Change,* pages 85–91 ▸ Chapter 13, *Composition of Air and Chemical Interactions of Air,* page 110
V. Examine Coherency and Articulation	**V:** *Atlas of Science Literacy* ▸ *Conservation of Matter,* pages 56–57 ▸ *Chemical Reactions,* pages 60–61
VI. Clarify State Standards and District Curriculum	**VIA:** *State Standards:* Link Sections I–V to learning goals and information from your state standards or frameworks that are informed by the results of the topic study. **VIB:** *District Curriculum Guide:* Link Sections I–V to learning goals and information from your district curriculum guide that are informed by the results of the topic study.
Visit www.curriculumtopicstudy.org for updates or supplementary readings, Web sites, and videos.	

Standards- and Research-Based Study of a Curricular Topic

CLASSIFYING MATTER

Section and Outcome	Selected Sources and Readings for Study and Reflection Read and examine *related parts* of:
I. Identify Adult Content Knowledge	**IA:** *Science for All Americans* ▸ Chapter 4, *Structure of Matter,* pages 46–48 **IB:** *Science Matters: Achieving Scientific Literacy* ▸ Chapter 4, *The Periodic Table of Chemical Elements,* pages 60–63 ▸ Chapter 6, *Elements in Combination,* pages 77–78
II. Consider Instructional Implications	**IIA:** *Benchmarks for Science Literacy* ▸ 4D, *Structure of Matter* general essay, page 75; grade span essays, pages 76–79 **IIB:** *National Science Education Standards* ▸ Grades K–4, Standard B essay, pages 123, 126 ▸ Grades 5–8, Standard B essay, page 149 ▸ Grades 9–12, Standard B essay, page 177
III. Identify Concepts and Specific Ideas	**IIIA:** *Benchmarks for Science Literacy* ▸ 4D, *Structure of Matter,* pages 76–80 **IIIB:** *National Science Education Standards* ▸ Grades K–4, Standard B, *Properties of Objects and Materials,* page 127 ▸ Grades 5–8, Standard B, *Properties and Changes of Properties in Matter,* page 154 ▸ Grades 9–12, Standard B, *Structure and Properties of Matter,* pages 178–179
IV. Examine Research on Student Learning	**IVA:** *Benchmarks for Science Literacy* ▸ 4D, *Structure of Matter,* pages 336–337 **IVB:** *Making Sense of Secondary Science: Research Into Children's Ideas* ▸ Chapter 8, *Materials,* pages 74–77; *Classifying Materials,* page 78 ▸ Chapter 11, *Particle Models of Elements and Compounds,* pages 96–97
V. Examine Coherency and Articulation	**V:** *Atlas of Science Literacy* ▸ *Atoms and Molecules,* pages 54–55 ▸ *Chemical Reactions,* pages 60–61; note the conceptual strand *Basic Ingredients*
VI. Clarify State Standards and District Curriculum	**VIA:** *State Standards:* Link Sections I–V to learning goals and information from your state standards or frameworks that are informed by the results of the topic study. **VIB:** *District Curriculum Guide:* Link Sections I–V to learning goals and information from your district curriculum guide that are informed by the results of the topic study.
Visit www.curriculumtopicstudy.org for updates or supplementary readings, Web sites, and videos.	

Standards- and Research-Based Study of a Curricular Topic

CONSERVATION OF MATTER

Section and Outcome	Selected Sources and Readings for Study and Reflection Read and examine *related parts* of:
I. Identify Adult Content Knowledge	**IA:** **Science for All Americans** ▶ Chapter 5, *Flow of Matter and Energy*, pages 66–67 ▶ Chapter 10, *Understanding Fire*, pages 153–155
II. Consider Instructional Implications	**IIA:** **Benchmarks for Science Literacy** ▶ 4D, *Structure of Matter* general essay, page 75; grade span essays, pages 76–79 ▶ 10F, *Understanding Fire* general essay, page 249; grade span essays, pages 250–251
	IIB: **National Science Education Standards** ▶ Grades K–4, Standard B essay, pages 123, 126 ▶ Grades 5–8, Standard B essay, page 149 ▶ Grades 9–12, Standard B essay, page 177; Standard F, essay, pages 193, 197
III. Identify Concepts and Specific Ideas	**IIIA:** **Benchmarks for Science Literacy** ▶ 4D, *Structure of Matter*, pages 76–80 ▶ 10F, *Understanding Fire*, pages 250–251 **IIIB:** **National Science Education Standards** ▶ Grades K–4, Standard B, *Properties of Objects and Materials*, page 127 ▶ Grades 5–8, Standard B, *Properties and Changes of Properties in Matter*, page 154 ▶ Grades 9–12, Standard B, *Structure and Properties of Matter*, pages 178–179
IV. Examine Research on Student Learning	**IVA:** **Benchmarks for Science Literacy** ▶ 4D, *Conservation of Matter*, pages 336–337 **IVB:** **Making Sense of Secondary Science: Research Into Children's Ideas** ▶ Chapter 8, *Conservation of Matter*, page 77; *Mass*, pages 77–78 ▶ Chapter 9, *The Solid State*, page 79; *The Liquid State*, pages 79–80; *The Gaseous State*, page 80; *Melting*, page 80, *Evaporation*, page 81; *Dissolving*, pages 83–84 ▶ Chapter 10, *Combustion*, pages 87–88, *Conservation of Matter Through Change*, pages 88–89
V. Examine Coherency and Articulation	**V:** **Atlas of Science Literacy** ▶ *Conservation of Matter*, pages 56–57
VI. Clarify State Standards and District Curriculum	**VIA:** *State Standards:* Link Sections I–V to learning goals and information from your state standards or frameworks that are informed by the results of the topic study. **VIB:** *District Curriculum Guide:* Link Sections I–V to learning goals and information from your district curriculum guide that are informed by the results of the topic study.
Visit www.curriculumtopicstudy.org for updates or supplementary readings, Web sites, and videos.	

Standards- and Research-Based Study of a Curricular Topic

DENSITY

Section and Outcome	Selected Sources and Readings for Study and Reflection Read and examine *related parts* of:
I. Identify Adult Content Knowledge	**IA:** *Science for All Americans* ▸ Chapter 4, *Structure of Matter,* page 46
II. Consider Instructional Implications	**IIA:** *Benchmarks for Science Literacy* ▸ 4D, *Structure of Matter* general essay, page 75; grade span essays, pages 76–79 **IIB:** *National Science Education Standards* ▸ Grades K–4, Standard B essay, pages 123, 126 ▸ Grades 5–8, Standard B essay, page 149; Vignette *Funny Water,* pages 150–153 ▸ Grades 9–12, Standard B essay, page 177
III. Identify Concepts and Specific Ideas	**IIIA:** *Benchmarks for Science Literacy* ▸ 4D, *Structure of Matter,* pages 76–80 **IIIB:** *National Science Education Standards* ▸ Grades K–4, Standard B, *Properties of Objects and Materials,* page 127 ▸ Grades 5–8, Standard B, *Properties and Changes of Properties in Matter,* page 154 ▸ Grades 9–12, Standard B, *Structure and Properties of Matter,* pages 178–179
IV. Examine Research on Student Learning	**IVA:** *Benchmarks for Science Literacy* ▸ 4D, *Conservation of Matter,* pages 336–337 **IVB:** *Making Sense of Secondary Science: Research Into Children's Ideas* ▸ Chapter 8, *Mass,* pages 77–78; *Density,* page 78 ▸ Chapter 9, *The Gaseous State,* page 80 ▸ Chapter 12, *Floating and Sinking,* pages 102–103 ▸ Chapter 13, *Existence of Air,* pages 104–105
V. Examine Coherency and Articulation	**V:** *Atlas of Science Literacy* ▸ *Conservation of Matter,* pages 56–57; pay particular attention to the "air as a substance" idea
VI. Clarify State Standards and District Curriculum	**VIA:** *State Standards:* Link Sections I–V to learning goals and information from your state standards or frameworks that are informed by the results of the topic study. **VIB:** *District Curriculum Guide:* Link Sections I–V to learning goals and information from your district curriculum guide that are informed by the results of the topic study.
Visit www.curriculumtopicstudy.org for updates or supplementary readings, Web sites, and videos.		

Standards- and Research-Based Study of a Curricular Topic

ELEMENTS AND THE PERIODIC TABLE

Section and Outcome	Selected Sources and Readings for Study and Reflection Read and examine *related parts* of:
I. Identify Adult Content Knowledge	**IA:** *Science for All Americans* ▸ Chapter 4, *Structure of Matter*, pages 46–47 **IB:** *Science Matters: Achieving Scientific Literacy* ▸ Chapter 4, *The Periodic Table of Chemical Elements*, pages 60–63
II. Consider Instructional Implications	**IIA:** *Benchmarks for Science Literacy* ▸ 4D, *Structure of Matter* general essay, page 75; 6–8 and 9–12 grade span essays, pages 77–79 **IIB:** *National Science Education Standards* ▸ Grades 5–8, Standard B essay, page 149 ▸ Grades 9–12, Standard B essay, page 177
III. Identify Concepts and Specific Ideas	**IIIA:** *Benchmarks for Science Literacy* ▸ 4D, *Structure of Matter*, 6–8 and 9–12, pages 77–80 **IIIB:** *National Science Education Standards* ▸ Grades 5–8, Standard B, *Properties and Changes of Properties in Matter*, page 154 ▸ Grades 9–12, Standard B, *Structure and Properties of Matter*, pages 178–179
IV. Examine Research on Student Learning	**IVA:** *Benchmarks for Science Literacy* ▸ 4D, *Nature of Matter*, page 336 **IVB:** *Making Sense of Secondary Science: Research Into Children's Ideas* ▸ Chapter 8, *Elements*, pages 76–77
V. Examine Coherency and Articulation	**V:** *Atlas of Science Literacy* ▸ *Atoms and Molecules,* pages 54–55
VI. Clarify State Standards and District Curriculum	**VIA:** *State Standards:* Link Sections I–V to learning goals and information from your state standards or frameworks that are informed by the results of the topic study. **VIB:** *District Curriculum Guide:* Link Sections I–V to learning goals and information from your district curriculum guide that are informed by the results of the topic study.
Visit www.curriculumtopicstudy.org for updates or supplementary readings, Web sites, and videos.	

Standards- and Research-Based Study of a Curricular Topic

LIQUIDS

Section and Outcome	Selected Sources and Readings for Study and Reflection Read and examine *related parts* of:
I. Identify Adult Content Knowledge	**IA:** *Science for All Americans* ▸ Chapter 4, *Structure of Matter*, pages 46–49 **IB:** *Science Matters: Achieving Scientific Literacy* ▸ Chapter 7, *Liquids,* pages 96–97
II. Consider Instructional Implications	**IIA:** *Benchmarks for Science Literacy* ▸ 4D, *Structure of Matter* general essay, page 75; grade span essays, pages 76–79 **IIB:** *National Science Education Standards* ▸ Grades K–4, Standard B essay, pages 123, 126 ▸ Grades 5–8, Standard B essay, page 149 ▸ Grades 9–12, Standard B essay, pages 177–178
III. Identify Concepts and Specific Ideas	**IIIA:** *Benchmarks for Science Literacy* ▸ 4D, *Structure of Matter,* pages 76–80 **IIIB:** *National Science Education Standards* ▸ Grades K–4, Standard B, *Properties of Objects and Materials,* page 127 ▸ Grades 5–8, Standard B, *Properties and Changes of Properties in Matter,* page 154 ▸ Grades 9–12, Standard B, *Structure and Properties of Matter,* pages 178–179
IV. Examine Research on Student Learning	**IVB:** *Making Sense of Secondary Science: Research Into Children's Ideas* ▸ Chapter 9, *The Liquid State,* pages 79–80 ▸ Chapter 11, *Particle Ideas About Liquids,* page 93
V. Examine Coherency and Articulation	**V:** *Atlas of Science Literacy* ▸ *States of Matter,* pages 58–59
VI. Clarify State Standards and District Curriculum	**VIA:** *State Standards:* Link Sections I–V to learning goals and information from your state standards or frameworks that are informed by the results of the topic study. **VIB:** *District Curriculum Guide:* Link Sections I–V to learning goals and information from your district curriculum guide that are informed by the results of the topic study.
Visit www.curriculumtopicstudy.org for updates or supplementary readings, Web sites, and videos.	

Standards- and Research-Based Study of a Curricular Topic

MIXTURES AND SOLUTIONS

Section and Outcome	Selected Sources and Readings for Study and Reflection Read and examine *related parts* of:
I. Identify Adult Content Knowledge	**IA:** ***Science for All Americans*** ▸ Chapter 4, *Structure of Matter,* page 46
II. Consider Instructional Implications	**IIA:** ***Benchmarks for Science Literacy*** ▸ 4D, *Structure of Matter* general essay, page 75; grade span essays, pages 76–79 **IIB:** ***National Science Education Standards*** ▸ Grades K–4, Standard B essay, pages 123, 126 ▸ Grades 5–8, Standard B essay, page 149 ▸ Grades 9–12, Standard B essay, page 177
III. Identify Concepts and Specific Ideas	**IIIA:** ***Benchmarks for Science Literacy*** ▸ 4D, *Structure of Matter,* pages 76–80 **IIIB:** ***National Science Education Standards*** ▸ Grades K–4, Standard B, *Properties of Objects and Materials,* page 127 ▸ Grades 5–8, Standard B, *Properties and Changes of Properties in Matter,* page 154 ▸ Grades 9–12, Standard B, *Structure and Properties of Matter,* pages 178–179
IV. Examine Research on Student Learning	**IVA:** ***Benchmarks for Science Literacy*** ▸ 4D, *Structure of Matter,* pages 336–337 **IVB:** ***Making Sense of Secondary Science: Research Into Children's Ideas*** ▸ Chapter 8, *Mixtures of Substances,* pages 74–75 ▸ Chapter 9, *Dissolving,* pages 83–84 ▸ Chapter 10, *Mixtures of Substances,* page 85 ▸ Chapter 11, *Particle Ideas About Solutions,* page 95 ▸ Chapter 12, *Dissolving Substances in Water,* pages 100–101 ▸ Chapter 13, *Composition of Air and Chemical Interactions of Air,* page 110
V. Examine Coherency and Articulation	**V:** ***Atlas of Science Literacy*** ▸ *Conservation of Matter,* pages 56–57; note the conceptual strand *Parts and Wholes.*
VI. Clarify State Standards and District Curriculum	**VIA:** ***State Standards:*** Link Sections I–V to learning goals and information from your state standards or frameworks that are informed by the results of the topic study. **VIB:** ***District Curriculum Guide:*** Link Sections I–V to learning goals and information from your district curriculum guide that are informed by the results of the topic study.
Visit www.curriculumtopicstudy.org for updates or supplementary readings, Web sites, and videos.	

Standards- and Research-Based Study of a Curricular Topic

NUCLEAR CHEMISTRY

Section and Outcome	Selected Sources and Readings for Study and Reflection Read and examine *related parts* of:
I. Identify Adult Content Knowledge	**IA:** *Science for All Americans* ▸ Chapter 4, *Structure of Matter,* pages 46–49 ▸ Chapter 10, *Splitting the Atom,* pages 155–157 **IB:** *Science Matters: Achieving Scientific Literacy* ▸ Chapter 8, *Radioactivity,* pages 116–123
II. Consider Instructional Implications	**IIA:** *Benchmarks for Science Literacy* ▸ 4D, *Structure of Matter* general essay, page 75; 6–8 and 9–12 grade span essays, pages 77–79 ▸ 10G, *Splitting the Atom* general essay, page 252; grade span essays, pages 252–253 **IIB:** *National Science Education Standards* ▸ Grades K–4, Standard B essay, pages 123, 126 ▸ Grades 5–8, Standard B essay, page 149 ▸ Grades 9–12, Standard B essay, pages 177–178
III. Identify Concepts and Specific Ideas	**IIIA:** *Benchmarks for Science Literacy* ▸ 4D, *Structure of Matter,* 6–8 and 9–12, pages 77–80 ▸ 10G, *Splitting the Atom,* pages 252–253 **IIIB:** *National Science Education Standards* ▸ Grades 5–8, Standard B, *Properties and Changes of Properties in Matter,* page 154 ▸ Grades 9–12, Standard B, *Structure of Atoms,* page 178
IV. Examine Research on Student Learning	**IVA:** *Benchmarks for Science Literacy* ▸ 4D, *Particles,* page 337
V. Examine Coherency and Articulation	**V:** *Atlas of Science Literacy* ▸ *Atoms and Molecules,* pages 54–55
VI. Clarify State Standards and District Curriculum	**VIA:** *State Standards:* Link Sections I–V to learning goals and information from your state standards or frameworks that are informed by the results of the topic study. **VIB:** *District Curriculum Guide:* Link Sections I–V to learning goals and information from your district curriculum guide that are informed by the results of the topic study.
Visit www.curriculumtopicstudy.org for updates or supplementary readings, Web sites, and videos.	

Standards- and Research-Based Study of a Curricular Topic

PARTICULATE NATURE OF MATTER (ATOMS AND MOLECULES)

Section and Outcome	Selected Sources and Readings for Study and Reflection Read and examine *related parts* of:
I. Identify Adult Content Knowledge	**IA:** *Science for All Americans* ▸ Chapter 4, *Structure of Matter*, pages 46–49 ▸ Chapter 10, *Understanding Fire*, pages 153–155 **IB:** *Science Matters: Achieving Scientific Literacy* ▸ Chapter 4, *The Atom*, pages 54–64 ▸ Chapter 7, *Atomic Architecture*, pages 94–99
II. Consider Instructional Implications	**IIA:** *Benchmarks for Science Literacy* ▸ 4D, *Structure of Matter* general essay, page 75; grade span essays, pages 76–79 ▸ 10F, *Understanding Fire* general essay, page 249; grade span essays, pages 250–251 **IIB:** *National Science Education Standards* ▸ Grades K–4, Standard B essay, pages 123, 126 ▸ Grades 5–8, Standard B essay, page 149 ▸ Grades 9–12, Standard B essay, page 177
III. Identify Concepts and Specific Ideas	**IIIA:** *Benchmarks for Science Literacy* ▸ 4D, *Structure of Matter*, pages 76–80 ▸ 10F, *Understanding Fire*, pages 250–251 **IIIB:** *National Science Education Standards* ▸ Grades K–4, Standard B, *Properties of Objects and Materials*, page 127 ▸ Grades 5–8, Standard B, *Properties and Changes of Properties in Matter*, page 154 ▸ Grades 9–12, Standard B, *Structure of Atoms*, page 178; *Structure and Properties of Matter*, pages 178–179
IV. Examine Research on Student Learning	**IVA:** *Benchmarks for Science Literacy* ▸ 4D, *Particles*, page 337 **IVB:** *Making Sense of Secondary Science: Research Into Children's Ideas* ▸ Chapter 11, *Particles*, pages 92–97 ▸ Chapter 13, *Particle Ideas About Air*, page 106
V. Examine Coherency and Articulation	**V:** *Atlas of Science Literacy* ▸ *Atoms and Molecules*, pages 54–55
VI. Clarify State Standards and District Curriculum	**VIA:** *State Standards:* Link Sections I–V to learning goals and information from your state standards or frameworks that are informed by the results of the topic study. **VIB:** *District Curriculum Guide:* Link Sections I–V to learning goals and information from your district curriculum guide that are informed by the results of the topic study.

Visit www.curriculumtopicstudy.org for updates or supplementary readings, Web sites, and videos.

Standards- and Research-Based Study of a Curricular Topic

PHYSICAL PROPERTIES AND CHANGE

Section and Outcome	Selected Sources and Readings for Study and Reflection Read and examine *related parts* of:
I. Identify Adult Content Knowledge	**IA:** *Science for All Americans* ▸ Chapter 4, *Structure of Matter*, pages 46–49 **IB:** *Science Matters: Achieving Scientific Literacy* ▸ Chapter 7, *Atomic Architecture*, pages 94–109
II. Consider Instructional Implications	**IIA:** *Benchmarks for Science Literacy* ▸ 4D, *Structure of Matter* general essay, page 75; grade span essays, pages 76–79 **IIB:** *National Science Education Standards* ▸ Grades K–4, Standard B essay, pages 123, 126 ▸ Grades 5–8, Standard B essay, page 149; Vignette *Funny Water*, pages 150–153 ▸ Grades 9–12, Standard B essay, page 177
III. Identify Concepts and Specific Ideas	**IIIA:** *Benchmarks for Science Literacy* ▸ 4D, *Structure of Matter*, pages 76–80 **IIIB:** *National Science Education Standards* ▸ Grades K–4, Standard B, *Properties of Objects and Materials,* page 127 ▸ Grades 5–8, Standard B, *Properties and Changes of Properties in Matter,* page 154 ▸ Grades 9–12, Standard B, *Structure and Properties of Matter,* pages 178–179
IV. Examine Research on Student Learning	**IVA:** *Benchmarks for Science Literacy* ▸ 4B, *Water Cycle*, page 336 ▸ 4D, *Structure of Matter*, pages 336–337 **IVB:** *Making Sense of Secondary Science: Research Into Children's Ideas* ▸ Chapter 8, *Materials*, pages 73–78 ▸ Chapter 9, *Solids, Liquids, and Gases*, pages 79–84 ▸ Chapter 11, *Particle Ideas About Change in State*, pages 94–95 ▸ Chapter 12, *Water as a Liquid*, page 98, *Freezing Water and Melting Ice,* page 98; *Boiling Water*, pages 98–99; *Dissolving Substances in Water*, pages 100–101
V. Examine Coherency and Articulation	**V:** *Atlas of Science Literacy* ▸ *Atoms and Molecules*, pages 54–55 ▸ *Conservation of Matter*, pages 56–57; note the conceptual strand *Changing vs. Constant Properties.* ▸ *States of Matter*, pages 58–59
VI. Clarify State Standards and District Curriculum	**VIA:** *State Standards:* Link Sections I–V to learning goals and information from your state standards or frameworks that are informed by the results of the topic study **VIB:** *District Curriculum Guide:* Link Sections I–V to learning goals and information from your district curriculum guide that are informed by the results of the topic study.

Visit www.curriculumtopicstudy.org for updates or supplementary readings, Web sites, and videos.

Standards- and Research-Based Study of a Curricular Topic

PROPERTIES OF MATTER

Section and Outcome	Selected Sources and Readings for Study and Reflection Read and examine *related parts* of:
I. Identify Adult Content Knowledge	**IA:** ***Science for All Americans*** ▸ Chapter 4, *Structure of Matter*, pages 46–48 **IB:** ***Science Matters: Achieving Scientific Literacy*** ▸ Chapter 7, *Atomic Architecture*, pages 94–109
II. Consider Instructional Implications	**IIA:** ***Benchmarks for Science Literacy*** ▸ 4D, *Structure of Matter* general essay, page 75; grade span essays, pages 76–79 **IIB:** ***National Science Education Standards*** ▸ Grades K–4, Standard B essay, pages 123, 126 ▸ Grades 5–8, Standard B essay, page 149; Vignette *Funny Water*, pages 150–153 ▸ Grades 9–12, Standard B essay, page 177
III. Identify Concepts and Specific Ideas	**IIIA:** ***Benchmarks for Science Literacy*** ▸ 4D, *Structure of Matter*, pages 76–80 **IIIB:** ***National Science Education Standards*** ▸ Grades K–4, Standard B, *Properties of Objects and Materials*, page 127 ▸ Grades 5–8, Standard B, *Properties and Changes of Properties in Matter*, page 154 ▸ Grades 9–12, Standard B, *Structure and Properties of Matter*, pages 178–179
IV. Examine Research on Student Learning	**IVA:** ***Benchmarks for Science Literacy*** ▸ 4D, *Structure of Matter*, pages 336–337 **IVB:** ***Making Sense of Secondary Science: Research Into Children's Ideas*** ▸ Chapter 8, *Materials*, pages 73–78 ▸ Chapter 9, *Solids, Liquids, and Gases*, pages 79–84 ▸ Chapter 12, *Water*, pages 98–103 ▸ Chapter 13, *Summary of Ideas About the Physical Properties of Air*, pages 107–110
V. Examine Coherency and Articulation	**V:** ***Atlas of Science Literacy*** ▸ *Conservation of Matter*, pages 56–57; note the conceptual strand *Changing vs. Constant Properties* ▸ *States of Matter*, pages 58–59 ▸ *Chemical Reactions*, pages 60–61; note the conceptual strand *Changing Properties*.
VI. Clarify State Standards and District Curriculum	**VIA:** ***State Standards:*** Link Sections I–V to learning goals and information from your state standards or frameworks that are informed by the results of the topic study. **VIB:** ***District Curriculum Guide:*** Link Sections I–V to learning goals and information from your district curriculum guide that are informed by the results of the topic study.

Visit www.curriculumtopicstudy.org for updates or supplementary readings, Web sites, and videos.

Standards- and Research-Based Study of a Curricular Topic

SOLIDS

Section and Outcome	Selected Sources and Readings for Study and Reflection Read and examine *related parts* of:
I. Identify Adult Content Knowledge	**IA:** *Science for All Americans* ▸ Chapter 4, *Structure of Matter*, pages 46–49 **IB:** *Science Matters: Achieving Scientific Literacy* ▸ Chapter 7, *Solids,* pages 97–98
II. Consider Instructional Implications	**IIA:** *Benchmarks for Science Literacy* ▸ 4D, *Structure of Matter* general essay, page 75; grade span essays, pages 76–79 **IIB:** *National Science Education Standards* ▸ Grades K–4, Standard B essay, pages 123, 126 ▸ Grades 5–8, Standard B essay, page 149 ▸ Grades 9–12, Standard B essay, pages 177–178
III. Identify Concepts and Specific Ideas	**IIIA:** *Benchmarks for Science Literacy* ▸ 4D, *Structure of Matter,* pages 76–80 **IIIB:** *National Science Education Standards* ▸ Grades K–4, Standard B, *Properties of Objects and Materials,* page 127 ▸ Grades 5–8, Standard B, *Properties and Changes of Properties in Matter,* page 154 ▸ Grades 9–12, Standard B, *Structure and Properties of Matter,* pages 178–179
IV. Examine Research on Student Learning	**IVB:** *Making Sense of Secondary Science: Research Into Children's Ideas* ▸ Chapter 9, *The Solid State,* page 79 ▸ Chapter 11, *Particle Ideas About Solids,* pages 92–93
V. Examine Coherency and Articulation	**V:** *Atlas of Science Literacy* ▸ *States of Matter,* pages 58–59
VI. Clarify State Standards and District Curriculum	**VIA:** *State Standards:* Link Sections I–V to learning goals and information from your state standards or frameworks that are informed by the results of the topic study. **VIB:** *District Curriculum Guide:* Link Sections I–V to learning goals and information from your district curriculum guide that are informed by the results of the topic study.
Visit www.curriculumtopicstudy.org for updates or supplementary readings, Web sites, and videos.	

Standards- and Research-Based Study of a Curricular Topic

STATES OF MATTER

Section and Outcome	Selected Sources and Readings for Study and Reflection Read and examine *related parts* of:
I. Identify Adult Content Knowledge	**IA:** ***Science for All Americans*** ▸ Chapter 4, *Structure of Matter,* pages 46–49 **IB:** ***Science Matters: Achieving Scientific Literacy*** ▸ Chapter 7, *The States of Matter,* pages 95–99
II. Consider Instructional Implications	**IIA:** ***Benchmarks for Science Literacy*** ▸ 4D, *Structure of Matter* general essay, page 75; grade span essays, pages 76–79 **IIB:** ***National Science Education Standards*** ▸ Grades K–4, Standard B essay, pages 123, 126 ▸ Grades 5–8, Standard B essay, page 149 ▸ Grades 9–12, Standard B essay, pages 177–178
III. Identify Concepts and Specific Ideas	**IIIA:** ***Benchmarks for Science Literacy*** ▸ 4D, *Structure of Matter,* pages 76–80 **IIIB:** ***National Science Education Standards*** ▸ Grades K–4, Standard B, *Properties of Objects and Materials,* page 127 ▸ Grades 5–8, Standard B, *Properties and Changes of Properties in Matter,* page 154 ▸ Grades 9–12, Standard B, *Structure and Properties of Matter,* pages 178–179, *Conservation of Energy and the Increase in Disorder,* page 180
IV. Examine Research on Student Learning	**IVA:** ***Benchmarks for Science Literacy*** ▸ 4B, *Water Cycle,* page 336 ▸ 4D, *Structure of Matter,* pages 336–337 **IVB:** ***Making Sense of Secondary Science: Research Into Children's Ideas*** ▸ Chapter 9, *Solids, Liquids, and Gases,* pages 79–84 ▸ Chapter 11, *Development of Particle Ideas About Materials,* pages 92–94; *Particle Ideas About Change of State,* pages 94–95 ▸ Chapter 12, *Water as a Liquid,* page 98; *Freezing Water and Melting Ice,* page 98; *Boiling Water,* pages 98–99; *Evaporation,* pages 99–100; *Condensation,* page 100 ▸ Chapter 13, *Existence of Air,* pages 104–105
V. Examine Coherency and Articulation	**V:** ***Atlas of Science Literacy*** ▸ *States of Matter,* pages 58–59
VI. Clarify State Standards and District Curriculum	**VIA:** ***State Standards:*** Link Sections I–V to learning goals and information from your state standards or frameworks that are informed by the results of the topic study. **VIB:** ***District Curriculum Guide:*** Link Sections I–V to learning goals and information from your district curriculum guide that are informed by the results of the topic study.

Visit www.curriculumtopicstudy.org for updates or supplementary readings, Web sites, and videos.

Earth

Primary Domain: Earth and Space Science

Number of CTS Guides: 18

Overview: The primary focus of this section is on developing an understanding of the earth and its interconnected parts and processes. Ideas such as interacting earth systems (lithosphere, biosphere, hydrosphere, atmosphere, and heliosphere), structure of the earth system and the processes that affect those structures, cycles on earth, changes to the physical earth over time, and forces that affect the earth system are developed through a study of the topics in this section.

Standards- and Research-Based Study of a Curricular Topic

AIR AND ATMOSPHERE

Section and Outcome	Selected Sources and Readings for Study and Reflection Read and examine *related parts* of:
I. Identify Adult Content Knowledge	**IA:** *Science for All Americans* ▶ Chapter 4, *The Earth*, pages 42–44, *Processes That Change the Earth*, pages 44–46 **IB:** *Science Matters: Achieving Scientific Literacy* ▶ Chapter 14, *Earth Cycles*, pages 191–192; *The Atmospheric Cycle*, pages 202–205
II. Consider Instructional Implications	**IIA:** *Benchmarks for Science Literacy* ▶ 4B, *The Earth* general essay, page 66; grade span essay, pages 67–70 ▶ 4C, *Processes That Change the Earth* general essay, page 71; grade span essays, pages 72–74 **IIB:** *National Science Education Standards* ▶ Grades K–4, Standard D essay, pages 130, 134 ▶ Grades 5–8, Standard D essay, pages 158–159 ▶ Grades 9–12, Standard D essay, pages 187–189
III. Identify Concepts and Specific Ideas	**IIIA:** *Benchmarks for Science Literacy* ▶ 4B, *The Earth*, pages 67–70 ▶ 4C, *Processes That Change the Earth*, pages 72–74 **IIIB:** *National Science Education Standards* ▶ Grades K–4, Standard D, *Properties of Earth Materials*, page 134; *Changes in the Earth and Sky*, page 134 ▶ Grades 5–8, Standard D, *Structure of the Earth System*, pages 159–160; *Earth's History*, page 160 ▶ Grades 9–12, Standard D, *Energy in the Earth System*, page 189; *Geochemical Cycles*, page 189; *The Origin and Evolution of the Earth System*, pages 189–190
IV. Examine Research on Student Learning	**IVA:** *Benchmarks for Science Literacy* ▶ 4B, *Water Cycle*, page 336 ▶ 4C, *Processes That Shape the Earth*, page 336 **IVB:** *Making Sense of Secondary Science: Research Into Children's Ideas* ▶ Chapter 13, *Air*, pages 104–105
V. Examine Coherency and Articulation	**V:** *Atlas of Science Literacy* ▶ *Conservation of Matter*, pages 56–57 ▶ *States of Matter*, pages 58–59
VI. Clarify State Standards and District Curriculum	**VIA:** *State Standards:* Link Sections I–V to learning goals and information from your state standards or frameworks that are informed by the results of the topic study. **VIB:** *District Curriculum Guide:* Link Sections I–V to learning goals and information from your district curriculum guide that are informed by the results of the topic study.

Visit www.curriculumtopicstudy.org for updates or supplementary readings, Web sites, and videos.

Standards- and Research- Based Study of a Curricular Topic

EARTH HISTORY

Section and Outcome	Selected Sources and Readings for Study and Reflection Read and examine *related parts* of:	
I. Identify Adult Content Knowledge	**IA:**	***Science for All Americans*** ▸ Chapter 4, *Processes That Shape the Earth,* pages 44–46 ▸ Chapter 10, *Extending Time,* pages 151–152; *Moving the Continents,* pages 152–153
	IB:	***Science Matters: Achieving Scientific Literacy*** ▸ Chapter 13, *The Restless Earth,* pages 174–190 ▸ Chapter 17, *Fossils and Evolution,* page 252; *The Story of Evolution,* pages 252–255
II. Consider Instructional Implications	**IIA:**	***Benchmarks for Science Literacy*** ▸ 4C, *Processes That Shape the Earth* general essay, page 71; grade span essay, pages 72–74 ▸ 10D, *Extending Time* general essay, page 246; grade span essay, page 246 ▸ 10E, *Moving the Continents* general essay, page 247; grade span essay, page 248
	IIB:	***National Science Education Standards*** ▸ Grades K–4, Standard D essay, pages 130, 134 ▸ Grades 5–8, Standard D essay, pages 158–159 ▸ Grades 9–12, Standard D essay, pages 187–189; Vignette *Fossils,* pages 182–183
III. Identify Concepts and Specific Ideas	**IIIA:**	***Benchmarks for Science Literacy*** ▸ 4C, *Processes That Shape the Earth,* pages 72–74 ▸ 10D, *Extending Time,* page 246 ▸ 10E, *Moving the Continents,* page 248
	IIIB:	***National Science Education Standards*** ▸ Grades K–4, Standard D, *Changes in the Earth and Sky,* page 134 ▸ Grades 5–8, Standard D, *Structure of the Earth System,* pages 159–160; *Earth's History,* page 160 ▸ Grades 9–12, Standard C, Standard D, *The Origin and Evolution of the Earth System,* pages 189–190
IV. Examine Research on Student Learning	**IVA:**	***Benchmarks for Science Literacy*** ▸ 4C, *Processes That Shape the Earth,* page 336
V. Examine Coherency and Articulation	**V:**	**Atlas of Science Literacy** ▸ *Changes in the Earth's Surface,* pages 50–51 ▸ *Plate Tectonics,* pages 52–53 ▸ *Biological Evolution,* pages 80–81; note the *Fossil Evidence* conceptual strand.
VI. Clarify State Standards and District Curriculum	**VIA:**	***State Standards:*** Link Sections I–V to learning goals and information from your state standards or frameworks that are informed by the results of the topic study.
	VIB:	***District Curriculum Guide:*** Link Sections I–V to learning goals and information from your district curriculum guide that are informed by the results of the topic study.
Visit www.curriculumtopicstudy.org for updates or supplementary readings, Web sites, and videos.		

Standards- and Research-Based Study of a Curricular Topic

EARTHQUAKES AND VOLCANOES

Section and Outcome	Selected Sources and Readings for Study and Reflection Read and examine *related parts* of:
I. Identify Adult Content Knowledge	**IA:** *Science for All Americans* ▸ Chapter 4, *Processes That Shape the Earth,* pages 44–46 **IB:** *Science Matters: Achieving Scientific Literacy* ▸ Chapter 13, *The Restless Earth,* pages 174–189 ▸ Chapter 14, *Igneous Rocks,* pages 193–194
II. Consider Instructional Implications	**IIA:** *Benchmarks for Science Literacy* ▸ 4C, *Processes That Shape the Earth* general essay, page 71; grade span essays, pages 72–74 **IIB:** *National Science Education Standards* ▸ Grades K–4, Standard D essay, pages 130, 134 ▸ Grades 5–8, Standard D essay, pages 158–159 ▸ Grades 9–12, Standard D essay, pages 187–189
III. Identify Concepts and Specific Ideas	**IIIA:** *Benchmarks for Science Literacy* ▸ 4C, *Processes That Shape the Earth,* pages 72–74 **IIIB:** *National Science Education Standards* ▸ Grades K–4, Standard D, *Changes in the Earth and Sky,* page 134 ▸ Grades 5–8, Standard D, *Structure of the Earth System,* pages 159–160; Standard F, *Natural Hazards,* page 168 ▸ Grades 9–12, Standard D, *Energy in the Earth System,* page 189; *Geochemical Cycles,* page 189; *The Origin and Evolution of the Earth System,* page 189; Standard F, *Natural and Human: Induced Hazards,* pages 198–199
IV. Examine Research on Student Learning	**IVA:** *Benchmarks for Science Literacy* ▸ 4C, *Processes That Shape the Earth,* page 336 **IVB:** *Making Sense of Secondary Science: Research Into Children's Ideas* ▸ Chapter 14, *Igneous Rocks,* page 113; *Mountains and Volcanoes,* pages 113–114
V. Examine Coherency and Articulation	**V:** **Atlas of Science Literacy** ▸ *Changes in the Earth's Surface,* pages 50–51 ▸ *Plate Tectonics,* pages 52–53; note the conceptual strand *Earthquakes and Volcanoes.*
VI. Clarify State Standards and District Curriculum	**VIA:** *State Standards:* Link Sections I–V to learning goals and information from your state standards or frameworks that are informed by the results of the topic study. **VIB:** *District Curriculum Guide:* Link Sections I–V to learning goals and information from your district curriculum guide that are informed by the results of the topic study.
Visit www.curriculumtopicstudy.org for updates or supplementary readings, Web sites, and videos.	

Standards- and Research-Based Study of a Curricular Topic

EARTH'S GRAVITY

Section and Outcome	Selected Sources and Readings for Study and Reflection Read and examine *related parts* of:
I. Identify Adult Content Knowledge	**IA:** *Science for All Americans* ▸ Chapter 4, *The Earth,* page 42; *Forces of Nature,* pages 55–57 **IB:** *Science Matters: Achieving Scientific Literacy* ▸ Chapter 1, *Gravity,* pages 9–14
II. Consider Instructional Implications	**IIA:** *Benchmarks for Science Literacy* ▸ 4B, *The Earth* general essay, page 66; grade span essays, pages 67–70 ▸ 4G, *Forces of Nature* general essay, page 93; grade span essays, pages 94–96 **IIB:** *National Science Education Standards* ▸ Grades 5–8, Standard D essay, pages 158–159 ▸ Grades 9–12, Standard D essay, pages 188–189
III. Identify Concepts and Specific Ideas	**IIIA:** *Benchmarks for Science Literacy* ▸ 4B, *The Earth,* pages 67–70 ▸ 4G, *Forces of Nature,* pages 94–97 **IIIB:** *National Science Education Standards* ▸ Grades 5–8, Standard D, *Earth in the Solar System,* page 161 ▸ Grades 9–12, Standard B, *Motions and Forces,* page 180
IV. Examine Research on Student Learning	**IVA:** *Benchmarks for Science Literacy* ▸ 4B, *Shape of the Earth,* page 335 ▸ 4G, *Forces of Nature,* page 340 **IVB:** *Making Sense of Secondary Science: Research Into Children's Ideas* ▸ Chapter 23, *The Earth's Gravity,* pages 163–164
V. Examine Coherency and Articulation	**V:** *Atlas of Science Literacy* ▸ *Gravity,* pages 42–43
VI. Clarify State Standards and District Curriculum	**VIA:** *State Standards:* Link Sections I–V to learning goals and information from your state standards or frameworks that are informed by the results of the topic study. **VIB:** *District Curriculum Guide:* Link Sections I–V to learning goals and information from your district curriculum guide that are informed by the results of the topic study.
Visit www.curriculumtopicstudy.org for updates or supplementary readings, Web sites, and videos.	

Standards- and Research-Based Study of a Curricular Topic

EARTH'S NATURAL RESOURCES

Section and Outcome	Selected Sources and Readings for Study and Reflection Read and examine *related parts* of:
I. Identify Adult Content Knowledge	**IA:** ***Science for All Americans*** ▶ Chapter 4, *The Earth*, pages 42–44 ▶ Chapter 8, *Energy Sources*, pages 114–116; *Energy Use*, pages 116–118 **IB:** ***Science Matters: Achieving Scientific Literacy*** ▶ Chapter 13, *Searching for Buried Treasure*, pages 187–188
II. Consider Instructional Implications	**IIA:** ***Benchmarks for Science Literacy*** ▶ 4B, *The Earth* general essay, page 66; grade span essays, pages 67–70 ▶ 8C, *Energy Sources and Use* general essay, page 192; grade span essays, pages 193–195 **IIB:** ***National Science Education Standards*** ▶ Grades K–4, Standard D essay, pages 130, 134; Standard F essay, pages 138–140 ▶ Grades 5–8, Standard D essay, pages 158–159; Standard F essay, pages 167–168 ▶ Grades 9–12, Standard D essay, pages 187–189; Standard F Essay, pages 193, 197
III. Identify Concepts and Specific Ideas	**IIIA:** ***Benchmarks for Science Literacy*** ▶ 4B, *The Earth*, pages 67–70 ▶ 8C, *Energy Sources and Use*, pages 193–195 **IIIB:** ***National Science Education Standards*** ▶ Grades K–4, Standard D, *Properties of Earth Materials*, page 134; Standard F, *Types of Resources*, page 140 ▶ Grades 5–8, Standard D, *Structure of the Earth System*, pages 159–160; Standard F, *Populations, Resources, and Environments*, page 168 ▶ Grades 9–12, Standard D, *Energy in the Earth System*, page 189; Standard F, *Natural Resources*, page 198
IV. Examine Research on Student Learning	**IVB:** ***Making Sense of Secondary Science: Research Into Children's Ideas*** ▶ Chapter 7, *Pollution*, pages 68–69 ▶ Chapter 20, *Energy as a Fuel*, pages 145–146
V. Examine Coherency and Articulation	**V:** ***Atlas of Science Literacy:*** There are no maps for this topic in Volume 1.
VI. Clarify State Standards and District Curriculum	**VIA:** ***State Standards:*** Link Sections I–V to learning goals and information from your state standards or frameworks that are informed by the results of the topic study. **VIB:** ***District Curriculum Guide:*** Link Sections I–V to learning goals and information from your district curriculum guide that are informed by the results of the topic study.

Visit www.curriculumtopicstudy.org for updates or supplementary readings, Web sites, and videos.

Standards- and Research-Based Study of a Curricular Topic

LANDFORMS

Section and Outcome	Selected Sources and Readings for Study and Reflection Read and examine *related parts* of:
I. Identify Adult Content Knowledge	**IA:** *Science for All Americans* ▸ Chapter 4, *Processes That Shape the Earth,* pages 44–46 **IB:** *Science Matters: Achieving Scientific Literacy* ▸ Chapter 13, *Restless Earth,* pages 174–181 ▸ Chapter 14, *Earth Cycles,* pages 191–192; *The Rock Cycle,* pages 193–196
II. Consider Instructional Implications	**IIA:** *Benchmarks for Science Literacy* ▸ 4C, *Processes That Shape the Earth* general essay, page 71; grade span essays, pages 72–74 **IIB:** *National Science Education Standards* ▸ Grades K–4, Standard D essay, page 130, 134 ▸ Grades 5–8, Standard D essay, pages 158–159 ▸ Grades 9–12, Standard D essay, pages 187–189
III. Identify Concepts and Specific Ideas	**IIIA:** *Benchmarks for Science Literacy* ▸ 4C, *Processes That Shape the Earth,* pages 72–74 **IIIB:** *National Science Education Standards* ▸ Grades K–4, Standard D, *Properties of Earth Materials,* page 134 ▸ Grades 5–8, Standard D, *Structure of the Earth System,* pages 159–160; *Earth's History,* page 160 ▸ Grades 9–12, Standard D, *Origin and Evolution of the Earth System,* pages 189–190
IV. Examine Research on Student Learning	**IVA:** *Benchmarks for Science Literacy* ▸ 4C, *Processes That Shape the Earth,* page 336 **IVB:** *Making Sense of Secondary Science: Research Into Children's Ideas* ▸ Chapter 14, *Mountains and Volcanoes,* pages 113–114
V. Examine Coherency and Articulation	**V:** *Atlas of Science Literacy* ▸ *Changes in the Earth's Surface,* pages 50–51 ▸ *Plate Tectonics,* pages 52–53
VI. Clarify State Standards and District Curriculum	**VIA:** *State Standards:* Link Sections I–V to learning goals and information from your state standards or frameworks that are informed by the results of the topic study. **VIB:** *District Curriculum Guide:* Link Sections I–V to learning goals and information from your district curriculum guide that are informed by the results of the topic study.
Visit www.curriculumtopicstudy.org for updates or supplementary readings, Web sites, and videos.	

Standards- and Research-Based Study of a Curricular Topic

OCEANOGRAPHY

Section and Outcome	Selected Sources and Readings for Study and Reflection Read and examine *related parts* of:
I. Identify Adult Content Knowledge	**IA:** *Science for All Americans* ▸ Chapter 4, *The Earth*, pages 42–44; *Processes That Shape the Earth*, pages 44–46 **IB:** *Science Matters: Achieving Scientific Literacy* ▸ Chapter 14, *The Water Cycle*, pages 196–197; *The Oceans*, pages 197–198; *Frontiers*, page 205
II. Consider Instructional Implications	**IIA:** *Benchmarks for Science Literacy* ▸ 4B, *The Earth* general essay, page 66; grade span essays, pages 67–70 ▸ 4C, *Processes That Shape the Earth* general essay, page 71; grade span essays, pages 72–74 **IIB:** *National Science Education Standards* ▸ Grades K–4, Standard D essay, pages 130, 134 ▸ Grades 5–8, Standard D essay, pages 158–159 ▸ Grades 9–12, Standard D essay, pages 187–189
III. Identify Concepts and Specific Ideas	**IIIA:** *Benchmarks for Science Literacy* ▸ 4B, *The Earth,* pages 67–70 ▸ 4C, *Processes That Shape the Earth*, pages 72–74 **IIIB:** *National Science Education Standards* ▸ Grades K–4, Standard D, *Properties of Earth Materials,* page 134 ▸ Grades 5–8, Standard D, *Structure of the Earth System*, pages 159–160 ▸ Grades 9–12, Standard D, *Energy in the Earth System*, page 189; *Geochemical Cycles*, page 189; *The Origin and Evolution of the Earth System*, pages 189–190
IV. Examine Research on Student Learning	**IVB:** *Making Sense of Secondary Science: Research Into Children's Ideas* ▸ The research base does not explicitly address oceans and ocean processes, but it may be helpful to examine ideas related to water on pages 98–103
V. Examine Coherency and Articulation	**V:** *Atlas of Science Literacy* ▸ *Changes in the Earth's Surface*, pages 50–51
VI. Clarify State Standards and District Curriculum	**VIA:** *State Standards:* Link Sections I–V to learning goals and information from your state standards or frameworks that are informed by the results of the topic study. **VIB:** *District Curriculum Guide:* Link Sections I–V to learning goals and information from your district curriculum guide that are informed by the results of the topic study.
Visit www.curriculumtopicstudy.org for updates or supplementary readings, Web sites, and videos.	

Standards- and Research-Based Study of a Curricular Topic

PLATE TECTONICS

Section and Outcome	Selected Sources and Readings for Study and Reflection Read and examine *related parts* of:
I. Identify Adult Content Knowledge	**IA:** *Science for All Americans* ‣ Chapter 4, *Processes That Change the Earth*, pages 44–46 ‣ Chapter 10, *Moving the Continents*, pages 152–153 **IB:** *Science Matters: Achieving Scientific Literacy* ‣ Chapter 13, *Plate Tectonics*, pages 176–185
II. Consider Instructional Implications	**IIA:** *Benchmarks for Science Literacy* ‣ 4C, *Processes That Shape the Earth* general essay, page 71; grade span essays, pages 72–74 ‣ 10E, *Moving the Continents* general essay, page 247; grade span essay, page 248 **IIB:** *National Science Education Standards* ‣ Grades 5–8, Standard D essay, pages 158–159 ‣ Grades 9–12, Standard D essay, pages 187–189
III. Identify Concepts and Specific Ideas	**IIIA:** *Benchmarks for Science Literacy* ‣ 4C, *Processes That Shape the Earth*, pages 72–74 ‣ 10E, *Moving the Continents*, page 248 **IIIB:** *National Science Education Standards* ‣ Grades 5–8, Standard D, *Structure of the Earth System*, pages 159–160; *Earth History*, page 160 ‣ Grades 9–12, Standard D, *Energy in the Earth System*, page 189; *Geochemical Cycles*, page 189; *The Origin and Evolution of the Earth System*, pages 189–190
IV. Examine Research on Student Learning	**IVA:** *Benchmarks for Science Literacy* ‣ 4C, *Processes That Shape the Earth*, page 336 **IVB:** *Making Sense of Secondary Science: Research Into Children's Ideas* ‣ Chapter 14, *Mountains and Volcanoes*, pages 113–114
V. Examine Coherency and Articulation	**V:** *Atlas of Science Literacy* ‣ *Changes in the Earth's Surface*, pages 50–51 ‣ *Plate Tectonics*, pages 52–53
VI. Clarify State Standards and District Curriculum	**VIA:** *State Standards:* Link Sections I–V to learning goals and information from your state standards or frameworks that are informed by the results of the topic study. **VIB:** *District Curriculum Guide:* Link Sections I–V to learning goals and information from your district curriculum guide that are informed by the results of the topic study.
Visit www.curriculumtopicstudy.org for updates or supplementary readings, Web sites, and videos.	

Standards- and Research-Based Study of a Curricular Topic

PROCESSES THAT CHANGE THE SURFACE OF THE EARTH

Section and Outcome	Selected Sources and Readings for Study and Reflection Read and examine *related parts* of:
I. Identify Adult Content Knowledge	**IA:** *Science for All Americans* ▶ Chapter 4, *Processes That Shape the Earth*, pages 44–46 **IB:** *Science Matters: Achieving Scientific Literacy* ▶ Chapter 13, *The Restless Earth*, pages 174–185 ▶ Chapter 14, *Ice Caps and Glaciers*, pages 198–200
II. Consider Instructional Implications	**IIA:** *Benchmarks for Science Literacy* ▶ 4C, *Processes That Shape the Earth* general essay, page 71; grade span essays, pages 72–74 **IIB:** *National Science Education Standards* ▶ Grades K–4, Standard D essay, page 130, 134 ▶ Grades 5–8, Standard D essay, pages 158–159 ▶ Grades 9–12, Standard D essay, pages 187–189
III. Identify Concepts and Specific Ideas	**IIIA:** *Benchmarks for Science Literacy* ▶ 4C, *Processes That Shape the Earth*, pages 72–74 **IIIB:** *National Science Education Standards* ▶ Grades K–4, Standard D, *Changes in the Earth and Sky*, page 134 ▶ Grades 5–8, Standard D, *Structure of the Earth System*, pages 159–160; *Earth's History*, page 160; Standard F, *Natural Hazards*, pages 168–169 ▶ Grades 9–12, Standard D, *The Origin and Evolution of the Earth System*, pages 189–190; Standard F, *Natural and Human Induced Hazards*, pages 198–199
IV. Examine Research on Student Learning	**IVA:** *Benchmarks for Science Literacy* ▶ 4C, *Processes That Shape the Earth*, page 336 **IVB:** *Making Sense of Secondary Science: Research Into Children's Ideas* ▶ Chapter 14, *Mountains and Volcanoes*, pages 113–114; *Weathering*, Page 114
V. Examine Coherency and Articulation	**V:** *Atlas of Science Literacy* ▶ *Changes in the Earth's Surface*, pages 50–51 ▶ *Plate Tectonics*, pages 52–53
VI. Clarify State Standards and District Curriculum	**VIA:** *State Standards:* Link Sections I–V to learning goals and information from your state standards or frameworks that are informed by the results of the topic study. **VIB:** *District Curriculum Guide:* Link Sections I–V to learning goals and information from your district curriculum guide that are informed by the results of the topic study.
Visit www.curriculumtopicstudy.org for updates or supplementary readings, Web sites, and videos.	

Standards- and Research-Based Study of a Curricular Topic

ROCKS AND MINERALS

Section and Outcome	Selected Sources and Readings for Study and Reflection Read and examine *related parts* of:
I. Identify Adult Content Knowledge	**IA:** *Science for All Americans* ▸ Chapter 4, *The Earth*, page 44; *Processes That Shape the Earth*, pages 44–46 **IB:** *Science Matters: Achieving Scientific Literacy* ▸ Chapter 14, *Earth Cycles*, pages 191–192; *The Rock Cycle*, pages 193–196
II. Consider Instructional Implications	**IIA:** *Benchmarks for Science Literacy* ▸ 4B, *The Earth* general essay, page 66; grade span essay, pages 67–70 ▸ 4C, *Processes That Change the Earth* general essay, page 71; grade span essays, pages 72–74 **IIB:** *National Science Education Standards* ▸ Grades K–4, Standard D essay, pages 130, 134 ▸ Grades 5–8, Standard D essay, pages 158–159 ▸ Grades 9–12, Standard D essay, pages 187–189
III. Identify Concepts and Specific Ideas	**IIIA:** *Benchmarks for Science Literacy* ▸ 4B, *The Earth,* pages 67–70 ▸ 4C, *Processes That Shape the Earth*, pages 72–74 **IIIB:** *National Science Education Standards* ▸ Grades K–4, Standard D, *Properties of Earth Materials*, page 134 ▸ Grades 5–8, Standard D, *Structure of the Earth System*, pages 159–160 ▸ Grades 9–12, Standard D, *Geochemical Cycles*, page 189; *The Origin and Evolution of the Earth System*, pages 189–190
IV. Examine Research on Student Learning	**IVA:** *Benchmarks for Science Literacy* ▸ 4C, *Processes That Shape the Earth*, page 336 **IVB:** *Making Sense of Secondary Science: Research Into Children's Ideas* ▸ Chapter 14, *Rocks,* pages 112–114
V. Examine Coherency and Articulation	**V:** *Atlas of Science Literacy* ▸ *Changes in the Earth's Surface*, pages 50–51; note the *Rocks and Sediments* conceptual strand.
VI. Clarify State Standards and District Curriculum	**VIA:** *State Standards:* Link Sections I–V to learning goals and information from your state standards or frameworks that are informed by the results of the topic study. **VIB:** *District Curriculum Guide:* Link Sections I–V to learning goals and information from your district curriculum guide that are informed by the results of the topic study.
Visit www.curriculumtopicstudy.org for updates or supplementary readings, Web sites, and videos.	

Standards- and Research-Based Study of a Curricular Topic

SEASONS

Section and Outcome	Selected Sources and Readings for Study and Reflection Read and examine *related parts* of:
I. Identify Adult Content Knowledge	**IA:** *Science for All Americans* ▸ Chapter 4, *The Earth*, pages 42–44 **IB:** *Science Matters: Achieving Scientific Literacy* ▸ Chapter 14, *The Atmospheric Cycle*, page 202
II. Consider Instructional Implications	**IIA:** *Benchmarks for Science Literacy* ▸ 4B, *The Earth* general essay, page 66; grade span essays, pages 67–70 **IIB:** *National Science Education Standards* ▸ Grades K–4, Standard D essay, pages 130, 134 ▸ Grades 5–8, Standard D essay, pages 158–159 ▸ Grades 9–12, Standard D essay, pages 187–189
III. Identify Concepts and Specific Ideas	**IIIA:** *Benchmarks for Science Literacy* ▸ 4B, *The Earth*, pages 67–70 **IIIB:** *National Science Education Standards* ▸ Grades K–4, Standard D, *Objects in the Sky*, page 134; *Changes in the Earth and Sky*, page 134 ▸ Grades 5–8, Standard D, *Earth in the Solar System*, pages 160–161 ▸ Grades 9–12, Standard D, *Energy in the Earth System*, page 189
IV. Examine Research on Student Learning	**IVA:** *Benchmarks for Science Literacy* ▸ 4B, *Shape of the Earth*, page 335, and *Explanations of Astronomical Phenomena*, pages 335–336 **IVB:** *Making Sense of Secondary Science: Research Into Children's Ideas* ▸ Chapter 24, *The Changing Year*, pages 173–174
V. Examine Coherency and Articulation	**V:** *Atlas of Science Literacy* ▸ *Solar System*, pages 44–45
VI. Clarify State Standards and District Curriculum	**VIA:** *State Standards:* Link Sections I–V to learning goals and information from your state standards or frameworks that are informed by the results of the topic study. **VIB:** *District Curriculum Guide:* Link Sections I–V to learning goals and information from your district curriculum guide that are informed by the results of the topic study.
Visit www.curriculumtopicstudy.org for updates or supplementary readings, Web sites, and videos.	

Standards- and Research-Based Study of a Curricular Topic

SOIL

Section and Outcome	Selected Sources and Readings for Study and Reflection Read and examine *related parts* of:
I. Identify Adult Content Knowledge	**IA:** ***Science for All Americans*** ▸ Chapter 4, *Processes That Shape the Earth*, pages 44–46 ▸ Chapter 8, *Agriculture*, pages 109–110
II. Consider Instructional Implications	**IIA:** ***Benchmarks for Science Literacy*** ▸ 4C, *Processes That Shape the Earth* general essay, page 71; grade span essays, pages 72–74 ▸ 8A *Agriculture* general essay, page 183; grade span essays, pages 184–186
	IIB: ***National Science Education Standards*** ▸ Grades K–4, Standard D essay, page 130, 134 ▸ Grades 5–8, Standard D essay, pages 158–159 ▸ Grades 9–12, Standard D essay, pages 187–189
III. Identify Concepts and Specific Ideas	**IIIA:** ***Benchmarks for Science Literacy*** ▸ 4C, *Processes That Shape the Earth*, pages 72–74 ▸ 8A *Agriculture,* pages 184–186
	IIIB: ***National Science Education Standards*** ▸ Grades K–4, Standard D, *Properties of Earth Materials*, page 134; Standard F, *Types of Resources*, page 140 ▸ Grades 5–8, Standard D, *Structure of the Earth System*, pages 159–160; Standard F, *Risks and Benefits,* page 169 ▸ Grades 9–12, Standard D, *Geochemical Cycles*, page 189; Standard F, *Natural Resources,* page 198; *Environmental Quality*, page 198
IV. Examine Research on Student Learning	**IVA:** ***Benchmarks for Science Literacy*** ▸ 4C, *Processes That Shape the Earth*, page 336 **IVB:** ***Making Sense of Secondary Science: Research Into Children's Ideas*** ▸ Chapter 14, *Soil,* page 114
V. Examine Coherency and Articulation	**V:** ***Atlas of Science Literacy*** ▸ *Changes in the Earth's Surface,* pages 50–51; note the *Rocks and Sediments* conceptual strand.
VI. Clarify State Standards and District Curriculum	**VIA:** ***State Standards:*** Link Sections I–V to learning goals and information from your state standards or frameworks that are informed by the results of the topic study. **VIB:** ***District Curriculum Guide:*** Link Sections I–V to learning goals and information from your district curriculum guide that are informed by the results of the topic study.
Visit www.curriculumtopicstudy.org for updates or supplementary readings, Web sites, and videos.	

Standards- and Research-Based Study of a Curricular Topic

SOLAR ENERGY

Section and Outcome	Selected Sources and Readings for Study and Reflection Read and examine *related parts* of:
I. Identify Adult Content Knowledge	**IA:** *Science for All Americans* ▸ Chapter 8, *Energy Sources and Use,* page 114 **IB:** *Science Matters: Achieving Scientific Literacy* ▸ Chapter 6, *Microelectronics,* page 87
II. Consider Instructional Implications	**IIA:** *Benchmarks for Science Literacy* ▸ 8C, *Energy Sources and Use* general essay, page 192; grade span essays, pages 193–195 **IIB:** *National Science Education Standards* ▸ Grades K–4, Standard F essay, pages 138–139 ▸ Grades 5–8, Standard F essay, pages 167–168 ▸ Grades 9–12, Standard F essay, pages 193, 197
III. Identify Concepts and Specific Ideas	**IIIA:** *Benchmarks for Science Literacy* ▸ 8C, *Energy Sources and Use,* pages 193–195 **IIIB:** *National Science Education Standards* ▸ Grades K–4, Standard F, *Types of Resources,* page 140 ▸ Grades 5–8, Standard F, *Populations, Resources, and Environments,* page 168 ▸ Grades 9–12, Standard F, *Natural Resources,* page 198
IV. Examine Research on Student Learning	**IVB:** *Making Sense of Secondary Science: Research Into Children's Ideas* ▸ Chapter 20, *Energy,* pages 143–147
V. Examine Coherency and Articulation	**V:** *Atlas of Science Literacy:* ▸ There are no maps for this topic in Volume 1.
VI. Clarify State Standards and District Curriculum	**VIA:** *State Standards:* Link Sections I–V to learning goals and information from your state standards or frameworks that are informed by the results of the topic study. **VIB:** *District Curriculum Guide:* Link Sections I–V to learning goals and information from your district curriculum guide that are informed by the results of the topic study.
Visit www.curriculumtopicstudy.org for updates or supplementary readings, Web sites, and videos.	

Standards- and Research-Based Study of a Curricular Topic

STRUCTURE OF THE SOLID EARTH

Section and Outcome	Selected Sources and Readings for Study and Reflection Read and examine *related parts* of:	
I. Identify Adult Content Knowledge	**IA:**	***Science for All Americans*** ▸ Chapter 4, *The Earth*, pages 42–44; *Processes That Shape the Earth*, pages 44–46
	IB:	***Science Matters: Achieving Scientific Literacy*** ▸ Chapter 13, *Restless Earth*, pages 174–176; *A Window Into the Solid Earth*, pages 185–187; *The Earth's Deep Interior*, page 188; *Unstable Magnetic Poles*, pages 188–189 ▸ Chapter 14, *The Rock Cycle,* pages 193–196
II. Consider Instructional Implications	**IIA:**	***Benchmarks for Science Literacy*** ▸ 4B, *The Earth* general essay, page 66; grade span essays, pages 67–70 ▸ 4C, *Processes That Shape the Earth* general essay, page 71; grade span essays, pages 72–74
	IIB:	***National Science Education Standards*** ▸ Grades K–4, Standard D essay, pages 130, 134 ▸ Grades 5–8, Standard D essay, pages 158–159 ▸ Grades 9–12, Standard D essay, pages 187–189
III. Identify Concepts and Specific Ideas	**IIIA:**	***Benchmarks for Science Literacy*** ▸ 4B, *The Earth*, pages 67–70 ▸ 4C, *Processes That Shape the Earth*, pages 72–74
	IIIB:	***National Science Education Standards*** ▸ Grades K–4, Standard D, *Properties of Earth Materials*, page 134 ▸ Grades 5–8, Standard D, *Structure of the Earth System*, pages 159–160 ▸ Grades 9–12, Standard D, *Energy in the Earth System*, page 189, *Geochemical Cycles*, page 189
IV. Examine Research on Student Learning	**IVA:**	***Benchmarks for Science Literacy*** ▸ 4B, *Shape of the Earth*, page 335 ▸ 4C, *Processes That Shape the Earth*, page 336
	IVB:	***Making Sense of Secondary Science: Research Into Children's Ideas*** ▸ Chapter 14, *Rocks*, pages 112–114
V. Examine Coherency and Articulation	**V:**	***Atlas of Science Literacy*** ▸ *Changes in the Earth's Surface*, pages 50–51 ▸ *Plate Tectonics*, pages 52–53
VI. Clarify State Standards and District Curriculum	**VIA:**	***State Standards:*** Link Sections I–V to learning goals and information from your state standards or frameworks that are informed by the results of the topic study.
	VIB:	***District Curriculum Guide:*** Link Sections I–V to learning goals and information from your district curriculum guide that are informed by the results of the topic study.
Visit www.curriculumtopicstudy.org for updates or supplementary readings, Web sites, and videos.		

Standards- and Research-Based Study of a Curricular Topic

WATER CYCLE

Section and Outcome	Selected Sources and Readings for Study and Reflection Read and examine *related parts* of:
I. Identify Adult Content Knowledge	**IA:** ***Science for All Americans*** ▶ Chapter 4, *The Earth*, pages 42–44 **IB:** ***Science Matters: Achieving Scientific Literacy*** ▶ Chapter 14, *The Water Cycle*, pages 196–201
II. Consider Instructional Implications	**IIA:** ***Benchmarks for Science Literacy*** ▶ 4B, *The Earth* general essay, page 66; grade span essays, pages 67–70 **IIB:** ***National Science Education Standards*** ▶ Grades K–4, Standard D essay, pages 130, 134; Vignette *Willie the Hamster*, pages 124–125 ▶ Grades 5–8, Standard D essay, pages 158–159 ▶ Grades 9–12, Standard D essay, pages 187–189
III. Identify Concepts and Specific Ideas	**IIIA:** ***Benchmarks for Science Literacy*** ▶ 4B, *The Earth*, pages 67–70 **IIIB:** ***National Science Education Standards*** ▶ Grades K–4, Standard D, *Properties of Earth Materials*, page 134 ▶ Grades 5–8, Standard D, *Structure of the Earth System*, pages 159–160 ▶ Grades 9–12, Standard D, *Energy in the Earth System*, page 189
IV. Examine Research on Student Learning	**IVA:** ***Benchmarks for Science Literacy*** ▶ 4B, *Water Cycle*, page 336 **IVB:** ***Making Sense of Secondary Science: Research Into Children's Ideas*** ▶ Chapter 11, *Particle Ideas About Change of State*, pages 94–95 ▶ Chapter 12, *Evaporation*, pages 99–100; *Condensation*, page 100; *The Water Cycle*, pages 101–102
V. Examine Coherency and Articulation	**V:** ***Atlas of Science Literacy*** ▶ *States of Matter*, pages 58–59
VI. Clarify State Standards and District Curriculum	**VIA:** ***State Standards:*** Link Sections I–V to learning goals and information from your state standards or frameworks that are informed by the results of the topic study. **VIB:** ***District Curriculum Guide:*** Link Sections I–V to learning goals and information from your district curriculum guide that are informed by the results of the topic study
Visit www.curriculumtopicstudy.org for updates or supplementary readings, Web sites, and videos.	

Standards- and Research-Based Study of a Curricular Topic

WATER IN THE EARTH SYSTEM

Section and Outcome	Selected Sources and Readings for Study and Reflection Read and examine *related parts* of:
I. Identify Adult Content Knowledge	**IA:** *Science for All Americans* ▶ Chapter 4, *The Earth*, pages 42–44 ▶ Chapter 4, *Processes That Shape the Earth*, pages 44–46 **IB:** *Science Matters: Achieving Scientific Literacy* ▶ Chapter 14, *The Water Cycle*, pages 196–201
II. Consider Instructional Implications	**IIA:** *Benchmarks for Science Literacy* ▶ 4B, *The Earth* general essay, page 66; grade span essays, pages 67–70 ▶ 4C, *Processes That Shape the Earth* general essay, page 71; grade span essays, pages 72–74 **IIB:** *National Science Education Standards* ▶ Grades K–4, Standard D essay, pages 130, 134; Vignette *Willie the Hamster*, pages 124–125 ▶ Grades 5–8, Standard D essay, pages 158–159 ▶ Grades 9–12, Standard D essay, pages 187–189
III. Identify Concepts and Specific Ideas	**IIIA:** *Benchmarks for Science Literacy* ▶ 4B, *The Earth*, pages 67–70 **IIIB:** *National Science Education Standards* ▶ Grades K–4, Standard D, *Properties of Earth Materials*, page 134; Standard F, *Types of Resources*, page 140 ▶ Grades 5–8, Standard D, *Structure of the Earth System*, pages 159–160; *Earth in the Solar System*, pages 160–161; Standard F, *Populations, Resources, and Environments*, page 168 ▶ Grades 9–12, Standard D, *Energy in the Earth System*, page 189; *Geochemical Cycles*, page 189; *The Origin and Evolution of the Earth System*, pages 189–190; Standard F, *Natural Resources*, page 198; *Environmental Quality*, page 198
IV. Examine Research on Student Learning	**IVA:** *Benchmarks for Science Literacy* ▶ 4B, *Water Cycle*, page 336 **IVB:** *Making Sense of Secondary Science: Research Into Children's Ideas* ▶ Chapter 12, *Water*, pages 98–103
V. Examine Coherency and Articulation	**V:** *Atlas of Science Literacy* ▶ *Changes in the Earth's Surface*, pages 50–51 ▶ *States of Matter*, pages 58–59
VI. Clarify State Standards and District Curriculum	**VIA: State Standards:** Link Sections I–V to learning goals and information from your state standards or frameworks that are informed by the results of the topic study. **VIB: District Curriculum Guide:** Link Sections I–V to learning goals and information from your district curriculum guide that are informed by the results of the topic study.
Visit www.curriculumtopicstudy.org for updates or supplementary readings, Web sites, and videos.	

Standards- and Research-Based Study of a Curricular Topic

WEATHER AND CLIMATE

Section and Outcome	Selected Sources and Readings for Study and Reflection Read and examine *related parts* of:
I. Identify Adult Content Knowledge	**IA:** ***Science for All Americans*** ▸ Chapter 4, *The Earth*, pages 42–44 **IB:** ***Science Matters: Achieving Scientific Literacy*** ▸ Chapter 14, *The Atmospheric Cycle*, pages 202–205 ▸ Chapter 18, *The Greenhouse Effect*, pages 270–274
II. Consider Instructional Implications	**IIA:** ***Benchmarks for Science Literacy*** ▸ 4B, *The Earth* general essay, page 66; grade span essays, pages 67–70 **IIB:** ***National Science Education Standards*** ▸ Grades K–4, Standard D essay, pages 130, 134; Vignette *Weather,* pages 131–133, and *Weather Instruments*, page 136 ▸ Grades 5–8, Standard D essay, pages 158–159 ▸ Grades 9–12, Standard D essay, pages 187–189
III. Identify Concepts and Specific Ideas	**IIIA:** ***Benchmarks for Science Literacy*** ▸ 4B, *The Earth*, pages 67–70 **IIIB:** ***National Science Education Standards*** ▸ Grades K–4, Standard D, *Objects in the Sky*, page 134; *Changes in the Earth and Sky*, page 134 ▸ Grades 5–8, Standard D, *Structure of the Earth System*, pages 159–160; Standard F, *Natural Hazards*, pages 168–169; *Risks and Benefits*, page 169 ▸ Grades 9–12, Standard D, *Energy in the Earth System*, page 189; Standard F, *Natural and Human Induced Hazards*, pages 198–199
IV. Examine Research on Student Learning	**IVB:** ***Making Sense of Secondary Science: Research Into Children's Ideas*** ▸ Chapter 13, *Existence of Air*, pages 104–105; *Wind*, page 111
V. Examine Coherency and Articulation	**V.** ***Atlas of Science Literacy:*** There are no maps for this topic in Volume 1.
VI. Clarify State Standards and District Curriculum	**VIA:** ***State Standards:*** Link Sections I–V to learning goals and information from your state standards or frameworks that are informed by the results of the topic study. **VIB:** ***District Curriculum Guide:*** Link Sections I–V to learning goals and information from your district curriculum guide that are informed by the results of the topic study.
	Visit www.curriculumtopicstudy.org for updates or supplementary readings, Web sites, and videos.

Standards- and Research-Based Study of a Curricular Topic

WEATHERING AND EROSION

Section and Outcome	Selected Sources and Readings for Study and Reflection Read and examine *related parts* of:
I. Identify Adult Content Knowledge	**IA:** ***Science for All Americans*** ▸ Chapter 4, *Processes That Shape the Earth,* pages 44–46 **IB:** ***Science Matters: Achieving Scientific Literacy*** ▸ Chapter 14, *Earth Cycles,* pages 191–196
II. Consider Instructional Implications	**IIA:** ***Benchmarks for Science Literacy*** ▸ 4C, *Processes That Shape the Earth* general essay, page 71; grade span essays, pages 72–74 **IIB:** ***National Science Education Standards*** ▸ Grades K–4, Standard D essay, pages 130, 134 ▸ Grades 5–8, Standard D essay, pages 158–159 ▸ Grades 9–12, Standard D essay, pages 187–189
III. Identify Concepts and Specific Ideas	**IIIA:** ***Benchmarks for Science Literacy*** ▸ 4C, *Processes That Shape the Earth,* pages 72–74 **IIIB:** ***National Science Education Standards*** ▸ Grades K–4, Standard D, *Properties of Earth Materials,* page 134; *Changes in the Earth and Sky,* page 134 ▸ Grades 5–8, Standard D, *Structure of the Earth System,* pages 159–160; *Earth's History,* page 160 ▸ Grades 9–12, Standard D, *The Origin and Evolution of the Earth System,* pages 189–190
IV. Examine Research on Student Learning	**IVA:** ***Benchmarks for Science Literacy*** ▸ 4C, *Processes That Shape the Earth,* page 336 **IVB:** ***Making Sense of Secondary Science: Research Into Children's Ideas*** ▸ Chapter 14, *Rocks,* pages 112–114
V. Examine Coherency and Articulation	**V.** ***Atlas of Science Literacy*** ▸ *Changes in the Earth's Surface,* pages 50–51; note the *Weathering and Erosion* conceptual strand.
VI. Clarify State Standards and District Curriculum	**VIA:** ***State Standards:*** Link Sections I–V to learning goals and information from your state standards or frameworks that are informed by the results of the topic study. **VIB:** ***District Curriculum Guide:*** Link Sections I–V to learning goals and information from your district curriculum guide that are informed by the results of the topic study.
Visit www.curriculumtopicstudy.org for updates or supplementary readings, Web sites, and videos.	

Astronomy

Primary Domain: Earth and Space Science

Number of CTS Guides: 10

Overview: The primary focus of this section is on developing an understanding of the structure and evolution of our universe. Ideas such as objects in space and how they are arranged, interactions and relationships between objects in space, the magnitude of objects and distances in space, force and motion in space, and how we have come to understand space are developed through a study of the topics in this section.

Standards- and Research-Based Study of a Curricular Topic

EARTH, MOON, AND SUN SYSTEM

Section and Outcome	Selected Sources and Readings for Study and Reflection Read and examine *related parts* of:
I. Identify Adult Content Knowledge	**IA:** ***Science for All Americans*** ▸ Chapter 4, *The Earth*, pages 42–44 ▸ Chapter 10, *Displacing the Earth From the Center of the Universe*, pages 147–149; *Uniting the Heavens and Earth*, pages 149–150 **IB:** ***Science Matters: Achieving Scientific Literacy*** ▸ Chapter 1, *Gravity*, pages 9–14
II. Consider Instructional Implications	**IIA:** ***Benchmarks for Science Literacy*** ▸ 4A, *The Universe* general essay, page 61; grade span essays, pages 62–65 ▸ 4B, *The Earth* general essay, page 66; grade span essays, pages 67–70 ▸ 10A, *Displacing the Earth From the Center of the Universe* general essay, page 239; grade span essays, page 240 ▸ 10B, *Uniting the Heavens and Earth* general essay, page 242; grade span essays, page 243 **IIB:** ***National Science Education Standards*** ▸ Grades K–4, Standard D essay, page 130, 134 ▸ Grades 5–8, Standard D essay, pages 158–159 ▸ Grades 9–12, Standard D essay, pages 188–189
III. Identify Concepts and Specific Ideas	**IIIA:** ***Benchmarks for Science Literacy*** ▸ 4A, *The Universe*, pages 62–65 ▸ 4B, *The Earth*, pages 67–70 ▸ 10A, *Displacing the Earth From the Center of the Universe*, pages 240–241 ▸ 10B, *Uniting the Heavens and Earth*, page 243 **IIIB:** ***National Science Education Standards*** ▸ Grades K–4, Standard D, *Objects in the Sky*, page 134; *Changes in the Earth and Sky*, page 134 ▸ Grades 5–8, Standard D, *Earth in the Solar System*, pages 160–161 ▸ Grades 9–12, Standard D, *Energy in the Earth System*, page 189
IV. Examine Research on Student Learning	**IVA:** ***Benchmarks for Science Literacy*** ▸ 4A, *The Universe*, page 335 ▸ 4B, *Explanations of Astronomical Phenomena*, pages 335–336 **IVB:** ***Making Sense of Secondary Science: Research Into Children's Ideas*** ▸ Chapter 24, *The Earth in Space*, pages 168–175
V. Examine Coherency and Articulation	**V:** ***Atlas of Science Literacy*** ▸ *Solar System*, pages 44–45
VI. Clarify State Standards and District Curriculum	**VIA:** ***State Standards:*** Link Sections I–V to learning goals and information from your state standards or frameworks that are informed by the results of the topic study. **VIB:** ***District Curriculum Guide:*** Link Sections I–V to learning goals and information from your district curriculum guide that are informed by the results of the topic study.
Visit www.curriculumtopicstudy.org for updates or supplementary readings, Web sites, and videos.	

Standards- and Research-Based Study of a Curricular Topic

GRAVITY IN SPACE

Section and Outcome	Selected Sources and Readings for Study and Reflection Read and examine *related parts* of:
I. Identify Adult Content Knowledge	**IA:** *Science for All Americans* ▸ Chapter 4, *The Universe*, pages 40–42; *Forces of Nature*, pages 55–57 ▸ Chapter 10, *Uniting the Heavens and Earth*, pages 149–150; *Relating Matter and Energy and Time and Space*, pages 150–151 **IB:** *Science Matters: Achieving Scientific Literacy* ▸ Chapter 1, *Gravity*, pages 9–14 ▸ Chapter 10, *The Birth of Stars*, pages 135–136 ▸ Chapter 12, *General Relativity*, pages 167–170
II. Consider Instructional Implications	**IIA:** *Benchmarks for Science Literacy* ▸ 4A, *The Universe* general essay, page 61; grade span essays, pages 62–65 ▸ 4G, *Forces of Nature* general essay, page 93; grade span essays, pages 94–96 ▸ 10B, *Uniting the Heavens and Earth* general essay, page 242; grade span essay, page 243 ▸ 10C, *Relating Matter and Energy and Time and Space* general essay, page 244; grade span essay, page 245 **IIB:** *National Science Education Standards* ▸ Grades 5–8, Standard D essay, pages 158–159 ▸ Grades 9–12, Standard D essay, pages 188–189
III. Identify Concepts and Specific Ideas	**IIIA:** *Benchmarks for Science Literacy* ▸ 4A, *The Universe*, pages 62–65 ▸ 4G, *Forces of Nature*, pages 94–97 ▸ 10B, *Uniting the Heavens and Earth*, page 243 ▸ 10C, *Relating Matter and Energy and Time and Space*, page 245 **IIIB:** *National Science Education Standards* ▸ Grades 5–8, Standard D, *Earth in the Solar System*, page 161 ▸ Grades 9–12, Standard B, *Motions and Forces*, page 180; Standard D, *The Origin and Evolution of the Universe*, page 190
IV. Examine Research on Student Learning	**IVA:** *Benchmarks for Science Literacy* ▸ 4A, *Shape of the Earth*, page 335 ▸ 4G, *Forces of Nature*, page 340 **IVB:** *Making Sense of Secondary Science: Research Into Children's Ideas* ▸ Chapter 23, *Gravity in Space*, pages 166–167
V. Examine Coherency and Articulation	**V:** *Atlas of Science Literacy* ▸ *Gravity*, pages 42–43
VI. Clarify State Standards and District Curriculum	**VIA:** *State Standards:* Link Sections I–V to learning goals and information from your state standards or frameworks that are informed by the results of the topic study. **VIB:** *District Curriculum Guide:* Link Sections I–V to learning goals and information from your district curriculum guide that are informed by the results of the topic study.
Visit www.curriculumtopicstudy.org for updates or supplementary readings, Web sites, and videos.	

Standards- and Research-Based Study of a Curricular Topic

HISTORICAL EPISODES IN ASTRONOMY

Section and Outcome	Selected Sources and Readings for Study and Reflection Read and examine *related parts* of:
I. Identify Adult Content Knowledge	**IA:** ***Science for All Americans*** ‣ Chapter 10, *Displacing the Earth from the Center of the Universe*, pages 147–149; *Uniting the Heavens and Earth*, pages 149–150 **IB:** ***Science Matters: Achieving Scientific Literacy*** ‣ Chapter 1, *Knowing*, pages 1–16
II. Consider Instructional Implications	**IIA:** ***Benchmarks for Science Literacy*** ‣ Chapter 10, *Historical Perspectives* overview, pages 237–238 ‣ 10A, *Displacing the Earth from the Center of the Universe* general essay, page 239; grade span essays, page 240 ‣ 10B, *Uniting the Heavens and Earth* general essay, page 242; grade span essay, page 243 **IIB:** ***National Science Education Standards*** ‣ Grades K–4, Standard G essay, page 141 ‣ Grades 5–8, Standard G essay, page 170 ‣ Grades 9–12, Standard G essay, page 200
III. Identify Concepts and Specific Ideas	**IIIA:** ***Benchmarks for Science Literacy*** ‣ 10A, *Displacing the Earth From the Center of the Universe*, pages 240–241 ‣ 10B, *Uniting the Heavens and the Earth*, page 243 **IIIB:** ***National Science Education Standards*** ‣ Grades 5–8, Standard G, *History of Science*, page 171 ‣ Grades 9–12, Standard G, *Historical Perspectives*, pages 201, 203
IV. Examine Research on Student Learning	**IVA:** ***Benchmarks for Science Literacy*** ‣ 10, *Historical Perspectives*, pages 354–355
V. Examine Coherency and Articulation	**V:** ***Atlas of Science Literacy:*** There are no maps on historical episodes in astronomy in Volume 1. Some benchmark historical episode ideas are included in the four maps in the Universe cluster, pages 44–49.
VI. Clarify State Standards and District Curriculum	**VIA:** ***State Standards:*** Link Sections I–V to learning goals and information from your state standards or frameworks that are informed by the results of the topic study. **VIB:** ***District Curriculum Guide:*** Link Sections I–V to learning goals and information from your district curriculum guide that are informed by the results of the topic study.
	Visit www.curriculumtopicstudy.org for updates or supplementary readings, Web sites, and videos.

Standards- and Research-Based Study of a Curricular Topic
MOTION OF PLANETS, MOONS, AND STARS

Section and Outcome	Selected Sources and Readings for Study and Reflection Read and examine *related parts* of:
I. Identify Adult Content Knowledge	**IA:** *Science for All Americans* ▸ Chapter 4, *The Universe*, pages 40–42; *The Earth*, pages 42–43 ▸ Chapter 10, *Displacing the Earth From the Center of the Universe,* pages 147–149; *Uniting the Heavens and Earth,* pages 149–150 **IB:** *Science Matters: Achieving Scientific Literacy* ▸ Chapter 1, *Knowing*, pages 1–4; *The Clockwork Universe*, pages 5–14
II. Consider Instructional Implications	**IIA:** *Benchmarks for Science Literacy* ▸ 4A, *The Universe* general essay, page 61; grade span essays, pages 62–65 ▸ 4B, *The Earth* general essay, page 66, grade 3–5, 6–8 essays, pages 67–68 ▸ 10A, *Displacing the Earth From the Center of the Universe* general essay, page 239; grade span essays, page 240 ▸ 10B, *Uniting the Heavens and Earth* general essay, page 242; grade span essays, page 243 **IIB:** *National Science Education Standards* ▸ Standard D, *Earth and Space Science*, Grades K–4 essay, pages 130, 134; Grades 5–8 essay, pages 158–159; Grades 9–12 essay, pages 187–189
III. Identify Concepts and Specific Ideas	**IIIA:** *Benchmarks for Science Literacy* ▸ 4A, *The Universe*, pages 62–65 ▸ 4B, *The Earth*, pages 68–69 ▸ 10A, *Displacing the Earth From the Center of the Universe*, pages 240–241 ▸ 10B, *Uniting the Heavens and the Earth*, page 243 **IIIB:** *National Science Education Standards* ▸ Grades K–4, Standard D, *Objects in the Sky*, page 134; *Changes in the Earth and Sky*, page 134 ▸ Grades 5–8, Standard D, *Earth in the Solar System*, pages 160–161 ▸ Grades 9–12, Standard B, *Motions and Forces*, pages 179–180
IV. Examine Research on Student Learning	**IVA:** *Benchmarks for Science Literacy* ▸ 4A, *Explanations of Astronomical Phenomena*, pages 335–336 **IVB:** *Making Sense of Secondary Science: Research Into Children's Ideas* ▸ Chapter 24, *The Earth in Space*, pages 168–175
V. Examine Coherency and Articulation	**V:** *Atlas of Science Literacy* ▸ *Solar System*, pages 44–45 ▸ *Stars*, pages 46–47 ▸ *Laws of Motion*, pages 62–63
VI. Clarify State Standards and District Curriculum	**VIA:** *State Standards:* Link Sections I–V to learning goals and information from your state standards or frameworks that are informed by the results of the topic study. **VIB:** *District Curriculum Guide:* Link Sections I–V to learning goals and information from your district curriculum guide that are informed by the results of the topic study.
Visit www.curriculumtopicstudy.org for updates or supplementary readings, Web sites, and videos.	

Standards- and Research-Based Study of a Curricular Topic

ORIGIN AND EVOLUTION OF THE UNIVERSE

Section and Outcome	Selected Sources and Readings for Study and Reflection Read and examine *related parts* of:
I. Identify Adult Content Knowledge	**IA:** *Science for All Americans* ▸ Chapter 4, *The Universe*, pages 40–42 **IB:** *Science Matters: Achieving Scientific Literacy* ▸ Chapter 10, *The Solar System*, pages 140–141 ▸ Chapter 11, *The Cosmos*, pages 147–155
II. Consider Instructional Implications	**IIA:** *Benchmarks for Science Literacy* ▸ 4A, *The Universe* general essay, page 61; grade span essays, pages 62–65 **IIB:** *National Science Education Standards* ▸ Grades 9–12, Standard D essay, pages 187–189
III. Identify Concepts and Specific Ideas	**IIIA:** *Benchmarks for Science Literacy* ▸ 4A, *The Universe*, pages 62–65 **IIIB:** *National Science Education Standards* ▸ Grades 9–12, Standard D, *Origin and Evolution of the Earth System*, pages 189–190; *The Origin and Evolution of the Universe*, page 190
IV. Examine Research on Student Learning	**IV:** No related research in *Benchmarks* or Driver.
V. Examine Coherency and Articulation	**V:** *Atlas of Science Literacy* ▸ *Stars*, pages 46–47 ▸ *Galaxies and the Universe*, pages 48–49
VI. Clarify State Standards and District Curriculum	**VIA:** *State Standards:* Link Sections I–V to learning goals and information from your state standards or frameworks that are informed by the results of the topic study. **VIB:** *District Curriculum Guide:* Link Sections I–V to learning goals and information from your district curriculum guide that are informed by the results of the topic study.
Visit www.curriculumtopicstudy.org for updates or supplementary readings, Web sites, and videos.	

Standards- and Research-Based Study of a Curricular Topic

SCALE, SIZE, AND DISTANCE IN THE UNIVERSE

Section and Outcome	Selected Sources and Readings for Study and Reflection Read and examine *related parts* of:
I. Identify Adult Content Knowledge	**IA:** *Science for All Americans* ▶ Chapter 4, *The Universe*, page 40 ▶ Chapter 11, *Models*, pages 168–172; *Scale*, pages 179–181 **IB:** *Science Matters: Achieving Scientific Literacy* ▶ Chapter 10, *A Quick Tour of the Solar System*, pages 141–142; *Galaxies*, pages 142–144
II. Consider Instructional Implications	**IIA:** *Benchmarks for Science Literacy* ▶ 4A, *The Universe* general essay, page 61; grade span essays, pages 62–65 ▶ 11B, *Models* general essay, page 267; grade span essays, pages 268–270 ▶ 11D, *Scale* general essay, page 276; grade span essays, pages 277–279 **IIB:** *National Science Education Standards* ▶ Grades K–4, Standard D essay, pages 130, 134 ▶ Grades 5–8, Standard D essay, pages 158–159, Vignette *The Solar System*, pages 215–217 ▶ Grades 9–12, Standard D essay, pages 188–189
III. Identify Concepts and Specific Ideas	**IIIA:** *Benchmarks for Science Literacy* ▶ 4A, *The Universe*, pages 62–65 ▶ 11B, *Models*, pages 268–270 ▶ 11D, *Scale*, pages 277–279 **IIIB:** *National Science Education Standards* ▶ Grades K–4, Standard D, *Objects in the Sky*, page 134; *Changes in the Earth and Sky*, page 134 ▶ Grades 5–8, Standard D, *Earth in the Solar System*, pages 160–161 ▶ Grades 9–12, Standard D, *The Origin and Evolution of the Universe*, page 190
IV. Examine Research on Student Learning	**IVA:** *Benchmarks for Science Literacy* ▶ 4A, *The Universe*, page 335 ▶ 4B, *Shape of the Earth*, page 335 ▶ 11B, *Models*, page 357 ▶ 12B, *Proportional Reasoning*, page 360 **IVB:** *Making Sense of Secondary Science: Research Into Children's Ideas* ▶ Chapter 24, *The Earth in Space*, pages 168–175
V. Examine Coherency and Articulation	**V:** *Atlas of Science Literacy* ▶ *Mathematical Models*, pages 28–29 ▶ *Solar System*, pages 44–45 ▶ *Stars*, pages 46–47 ▶ *Galaxies and the Universe*, pages 48–49
VI. Clarify State Standards and District Curriculum	**VIA:** *State Standards:* Link Sections I–V to learning goals and information from your state standards or frameworks that are informed by the results of the topic study. **VIB:** *District Curriculum Guide:* Link Sections I–V to learning goals and information from your district curriculum guide that are informed by the results of the topic study.

Visit www.curriculumtopicstudy.org for updates or supplementary readings, Web sites, and videos.

Standards- and Research-Based Study of a Curricular Topic

SOLAR SYSTEM

Section and Outcome	Selected Sources and Readings for Study and Reflection Read and examine *related parts* of:
I. Identify Adult Content Knowledge	**IA:** *Science for All Americans* ▸ Chapter 4, *The Universe,* pages 40–42 ▸ Chapter 10, *Displacing the Earth From the Center of the Universe,* pages 147–149; *Uniting the Heavens and Earth,* pages 149–150 **IB:** *Science Matters: Achieving Scientific Literacy* ▸ Chapter 10, *A Quick Tour of the Solar System,* pages 141–142
II. Consider Instructional Implications	**IIA:** *Benchmarks for Science Literacy* ▸ 4A, *The Universe* general essay, page 61; grade span essays, pages 62–65 ▸ 10A, *Displacing the Earth From the Center of the Universe* general essay, page 239; grade span essays, page 240 ▸ 10B, *Uniting the Heavens and Earth* general essay, page 242; grade span essay, page 243 **IIB:** *National Science Education Standards* ▸ Grades K–4, Standard D essay, pages 130, 134 ▸ Grades 5–8, Standard D essay, pages 158–159, Vignette *The Solar System,* pages 215–217 ▸ Grades 9–12, Standard D essay, pages 188–189
III. Identify Concepts and Specific Ideas	**IIIA:** *Benchmarks for Science Literacy* ▸ 4A, *The Universe,* pages 62–65 ▸ 10A, *Displacing the Earth From the Center of the Universe,* pages 240–241 ▸ 10B, *Uniting the Heavens and the Earth,* page 243 **IIIB:** *National Science Education Standards* ▸ Grades K–4, Standard D, *Objects in the Sky,* page 134; *Changes in the Earth and Sky,* page 134 ▸ Grades 5–8, Standard D, *Earth in the Solar System,* pages 160–161 ▸ Grades 9–12, Standard D, *Origin and Evolution of the Earth System,* pages 189–190
IV. Examine Research on Student Learning	**IVA:** *Benchmarks for Science Literacy* ▸ 4A, *The Universe,* page 335 **IVB:** *Making Sense of Secondary Science: Research Into Children's Ideas* ▸ Chapter 24, *The Earth in Space,* pages 168–175
V. Examine Coherency and Articulation	**V:** *Atlas of Science Literacy* ▸ *Solar System,* pages 44–45
VI. Clarify State Standards and District Curriculum	**VIA:** *State Standards:* Link Sections I–V to learning goals and information from your state standards or frameworks that are informed by the results of the topic study. **VIB:** *District Curriculum Guide:* Link Sections I–V to learning goals and information from your district curriculum guide that are informed by the results of the topic study.

Visit www.curriculumtopicstudy.org for updates or supplementary readings, Web sites, and videos.

Standards- and Research-Based Study of a Curricular Topic

SPACE TECHNOLOGY AND EXPLORATION

Section and Outcome	Selected Sources and Readings for Study and Reflection Read and examine *related parts* of:
I. Identify Adult Content Knowledge	**IA:** **Science for All Americans** ▸ Chapter 3, *Technology and Science*, pages 26–28 ▸ Chapter 4, *The Universe*, pages 40–42 **IB:** **Science Matters: Achieving Scientific Literacy** ▸ Chapter 10, *Telescopes*, pages 144–145
II. Consider Instructional Implications	**IIA:** **Benchmarks for Science Literacy** ▸ 3A, *Technology and Science* general essay, page 43; grade span essays, pages 44–47 ▸ 4A, *The Universe* general essay, page 61; grade span essays, pages 62–65 **IIB:** **National Science Education Standards** ▸ Grades K–4, Standard D essay, pages 130, 134 ▸ Grades 5–8, Standard D essay, pages 158–159 ▸ Grades 9–12, Standard D essay, pages 188–189; Standard E essay, pages 190–192
III. Identify Concepts and Specific Ideas	**IIIA:** **Benchmarks for Science Literacy** ▸ 3A, *Technology and Science*, pages 44–47 ▸ 4A, *The Universe*, pages 62–65 **IIIB:** **National Science Education Standards** ▸ Grades K–4, Standard D, *Objects in the Sky*, page 134, Standard E, *Understanding About Science and Technology*, page 138 ▸ Grades 5–8, Standard D, *Earth in the Solar System*, pages 160–161; Standard E, *Understandings About Science and Technology*, page 166 ▸ Grades 9–12, Standard D, *The Origin and Evolution of the Universe*, page 190; Standard E, *Understandings About Science and Technology*, pages 192–193
IV. Examine Research on Student Learning	**IVA:** **Benchmarks for Science Literacy** ▸ 3A, *Technology and Science*, page 334
V. Examine Coherency and Articulation	**V:** **Atlas of Science Literacy** ▸ *Solar System*, pages 44–45 ▸ *Stars*, pages 46–47 ▸ *Galaxies and the Universe*, pages 48–49 Note the *Telescopes* conceptual strand in all 3 maps.
VI. Clarify State Standards and District Curriculum	**VIA:** **State Standards:** Link Sections I–V to learning goals and information from your state standards or frameworks that are informed by the results of the topic study. **VIB:** **District Curriculum Guide:** Link Sections I–V to learning goals and information from your district curriculum guide that are informed by the results of the topic study.
Visit www.curriculumtopicstudy.org for updates or supplementary readings, Web sites, and videos.	

Standards- and Research-Based Study of a Curricular Topic

STARS AND GALAXIES

Section and Outcome	Selected Sources and Readings for Study and Reflection Read and examine *related parts* of:
I. Identify Adult Content Knowledge	**IA:** ***Science for All Americans*** ▸ Chapter 4, *The Universe*, pages 40–42 ▸ Chapter 10, *Displacing the Earth From the Center of the Universe*, pages 147–149 **IB:** ***Science Matters: Achieving Scientific Literacy*** ▸ Chapter 10, *Stars Live and Die Like Everything Else*, page 134; *The Birth of Stars*, pages 135–136; *Stellar Lifetimes*, page 136; *The Death of Stars*, pages 137–138; *Supernovae and Their Consequences*, pages 138–139; *Galaxies*, pages 142–145 ▸ Chapter 11, *The Cosmos*, pages 147–155
II. Consider Instructional Implications	**IIA:** ***Benchmarks for Science Literacy*** ▸ 4A, *The Universe* general essay, page 61; grade span essays, pages 62–65 ▸ 10A, *Displacing the Earth From the Center of the Universe* general essay, page 239; grade span essays, page 240 **IIB:** ***National Science Education Standards*** ▸ Grades K–4, Standard D essay, pages 130, 134 ▸ Grades 5–8, Standard D essay, pages 158–159 ▸ Grades 9–12, Standard D essay, pages 188–189
III. Identify Concepts and Specific Ideas	**IIIA:** ***Benchmarks for Science Literacy*** ▸ 4A, *The Universe*, pages 62–65 ▸ 10A, *Displacing the Earth From the Center of the Universe*, pages 240–241 **IIIB:** ***National Science Education Standards*** ▸ Grades K–4, Standard D, *Objects in the Sky*, page 134; *Changes in the Earth and Sky*, page 134 ▸ Grades 5–8, Standard D, *Earth in the Solar System*, pages 160–161 ▸ Grades 9–12, Standard D, *Origin and Evolution of the Earth System*, pages 189–190; *The Origin and Evolution of the Universe*, page 190
IV. Examine Research on Student Learning	**IVA:** ***Benchmarks for Science Literacy*** ▸ 4A, *The Universe*, page 335 **IVB:** ***Making Sense of Secondary Science: Research Into Children's Ideas*** ▸ Chapter 24, *The Solar System and Beyond*, pages 174–175
V. Examine Coherency and Articulation	**V:** ***Atlas of Science Literacy*** ▸ *Stars*, pages 46–47 ▸ *Galaxies and the Universe*, pages 48–49
VI. Clarify State Standards and District Curriculum	**VIA:** ***State Standards:*** Link Sections I–V to learning goals and information from your state standards or frameworks that are informed by the results of the topic study. **VIB:** ***District Curriculum Guide:*** Link Sections I–V to learning goals and information from your district curriculum guide that are informed by the results of the topic study.

Visit www.curriculumtopicstudy.org for updates or supplementary readings, Web sites, and videos.

Standards- and Research-Based Study of a Curricular Topic

THE UNIVERSE

Section and Outcome	Selected Sources and Readings for Study and Reflection Read and examine *related parts* of:
I. Identify Adult Content Knowledge	**IA:** *Science for All Americans* ▸ Chapter 4, *The Universe,* pages 40–42 ▸ Chapter 10, *Displacing the Earth From the Center of the Universe,* pages 147–149; *Uniting the Heavens and Earth,* pages 149–150 **IB:** *Science Matters: Achieving Scientific Literacy* ▸ Chapter 10, *Astronomy,* pages 134–146 ▸ Chapter 11, *The Cosmos,* pages 147–155 ▸ Chapter 12, *Black Holes,* pages 171–172
II. Consider Instructional Implications	**IIA:** *Benchmarks for Science Literacy* ▸ 4A, *The Universe* general essay, page 61; grade span essays, pages 62–65 ▸ 10A, *Displacing the Earth from the Center of the Universe* general essay, page 239; grade span essays, page 240 ▸ 10B, *Uniting the Heavens and Earth* general essay, page 242; grade span essays, page 243 **IIB:** *National Science Education Standards* ▸ Grades K–4, Standard D essay, pages 130, 134 ▸ Grades 5–8, Standard D essay, pages 158–159 ▸ Grades 9–12, Standard D essay, pages 188–189
III. Identify Concepts and Specific Ideas	**IIIA:** *Benchmarks for Science Literacy* ▸ 4A, *The Universe,* pages 62–65 ▸ 10A, *Displacing the Earth From the Center of the Universe,* pages 240–241 ▸ 10B, *Uniting the Heavens and Earth,* page 243 **IIIB:** *National Science Education Standards* ▸ Grades K–4, Standard D, *Objects in the Sky,* page 134; *Changes in the Earth and Sky,* page 134 ▸ Grades 5–8, Standard D, *Earth in the Solar System,* pages 160–161 ▸ Grades 9–12, Standard D, *Origin and Evolution of the Earth System,* pages 189–190; *The Origin and Evolution of the Universe,* page 190
IV. Examine Research on Student Learning	**IVA:** *Benchmarks for Science Literacy* ▸ 4A, *The Universe,* page 335 **IVB:** *Making Sense of Secondary Science: Research Into Children's Ideas* ▸ Chapter 24, *The Earth in Space,* pages 168–175
V. Examine Coherency and Articulation	**V:** *Atlas of Science Literacy* ▸ *Solar System,* pages 44–45 ▸ *Stars,* pages 46–47 ▸ *Galaxies and the Universe,* pages 48–49
VI. Clarify State Standards and District Curriculum	**VIA:** *State Standards:* Link Sections I–V to learning goals and information from your state standards or frameworks that are informed by the results of the topic study. **VIB:** *District Curriculum Guide:* Link Sections I–V to learning goals and information from your district curriculum guide that are informed by the results of the topic study.
Visit www.curriculumtopicstudy.org for updates or supplementary readings, Web sites, and videos.	

Energy, Force, and Motion

Primary Domain: Physical Science

Number of CTS Guides: 23

Overview: The primary focus of this section is on developing ideas about the laws, interactions, and relationships that govern the natural world. Ideas about energy, force, and motion and their interaction with matter are developed through a study of the topics in this section.

Standards- and Research-Based Study of a Curricular Topic

CHEMICAL ENERGY

Section and Outcome	Selected Sources and Readings for Study and Reflection Read and examine *related parts* of:
I. Identify Adult Content Knowledge	**IA:** *Science for All Americans* ▸ Chapter 4, *Structure of Matter*, pages 46–49; *Energy Transformations*, pages 49–52 ▸ Chapter 5, *Flow of Matter and Energy*, pages 66–67 ▸ Chapter 8, *Energy Sources and Use*, pages 114–115 **IB:** *Science Matters: Achieving Scientific Literacy* ▸ Chapter 2, *Potential Energy*, pages 22–23 ▸ Chapter 15, *Power Plant*, pages 217–219
II. Consider Instructional Implications	**IIA:** *Benchmarks for Science Literacy* ▸ 4E, *Energy Transformations* general essay, pages 81–82; grade span essays, pages 83–86 ▸ 5E, *Flow of Matter and Energy* general essay, page 118; grade span essays, pages 119–121 ▸ 8C, *Energy Sources and Use* general essay, page 192; grade span essays, pages 193–195 **IIB:** *National Science Education Standards* ▸ Grades K–4, Standard B essay, pages 123, 126 ▸ Grades 5–8, Standard B essay, page 149, 154 ▸ Grades 9–12, Standard B essay, pages 177–178
III. Identify Concepts and Specific Ideas	**IIIA:** *Benchmarks for Science Literacy* ▸ 4E, *Energy Transformations*, pages 83–86 ▸ 5E, *Flow of Matter and Energy*, pages 119–121 ▸ 8C, *Energy Sources and Use*, pages 193–195 **IIIB:** *National Science Education Standards* ▸ Grades K–4, Standard B, *Light, Heat, Electricity, and Magnetism*, page 127 ▸ Grades 5–8, Standard B, *Transfer of Energy*, page 155 ▸ Grades 9–12, Standard B, *Chemical Reactions*, page 179; Standard C, *Matter, Energy, and Organization in Living Systems*, pages 186–187
IV. Examine Research on Student Learning	**IVA:** *Benchmarks for Science Literacy* ▸ 4E, *Energy Forms and Energy Transformation*, page 338 ▸ 5E, *Food*, page 342 **IVB:** *Making Sense of Secondary Science: Research Into Children's Ideas* ▸ Chapter 7, *Nutrition and Energy Flow*, pages 59–60 ▸ Chapter 10, *Energy and Chemical Change*, pages 89–90 ▸ Chapter 20, *Energy Stores*, page 144; *Energy as a Fuel*, pages 145–146
V. Examine Coherency and Articulation	**V:** *Atlas of Science Literacy* ▸ *Chemical Reactions*, pages 60–61 ▸ *Flow of Energy in Ecosystems*, pages 78–79
VI. Clarify State Standards and District Curriculum	**VIA:** *State Standards:* Link Sections I–V to learning goals and information from your state standards or frameworks that are informed by the results of the topic study. **VIB:** *District Curriculum Guide:* Link Sections I–V to learning goals and information from your district curriculum guide that are informed by the results of the topic study.

Visit www.curriculumtopicstudy.org for updates or supplementary readings, Web sites, and videos.

Standards- and Research-Based Study of a Curricular Topic

CONSERVATION OF ENERGY

Section and Outcome	Selected Sources and Readings for Study and Reflection Read and examine *related parts* of:		
I. Identify Adult Content Knowledge	**IA:**	***Science for All Americans*** ▸ Chapter 4, *Energy Transformations,* pages 49–52 ▸ Chapter 5, *Flow of Matter and Energy,* pages 66–67	
	IB:	***Science Matters: Achieving Scientific Literacy*** ▸ Chapter 2, *Energy is Conserved,* page 21; *Good News: The First Law,* pages 24–26	
II. Consider Instructional Implications	**IIA:**	***Benchmarks for Science Literacy*** ▸ 4E, *Energy Transformations* general essay, pages 81–82; grade span essays, pages 83–86	
	IIB:	***National Science Education Standards*** ▸ Grades 5–8, Standard B essay, pages 149, 154 ▸ Grades 9–12, Standard B essay, pages 177–178	
III. Identify Concepts and Specific Ideas	**IIIA:**	***Benchmarks for Science Literacy*** ▸ 4E, *Energy Transformations,* pages 83–86	
	IIIB:	***National Science Education Standards*** ▸ Grades 5–8, Standard B, *Transfer of Energy,* page 155 ▸ Grades 9–12, Standard B, *Conservation of Energy and the Increase in Disorder,* page 180	
IV. Examine Research on Student Learning	**IVA:**	***Benchmarks for Science Literacy*** ▸ 4E, *Energy Conservation,* page 338	
	IVB:	***Making Sense of Secondary Science: Research Into Children's Ideas*** ▸ Chapter 20, *Conservation of Energy,* page 146–147	
V. Examine Coherency and Articulation	**V:**	***Atlas of Science Literacy:*** There are no maps for this topic in Volume 1.	
VI. Clarify State Standards and District Curriculum	**VIA:**	***State Standards:*** Link Sections I–V to learning goals and information from your state standards or frameworks that are informed by the results of the topic study.	
	VIB:	***District Curriculum Guide:*** Link Sections I–V to learning goals and information from your district curriculum guide that are informed by the results of the topic study.	
Visit www.curriculumtopicstudy.org for updates or supplementary readings, Web sites, and videos.			

Standards- and Research-Based Study of a Curricular Topic

DESCRIBING POSITION AND MOTION

Section and Outcome	Selected Sources and Readings for Study and Reflection Read and examine *related parts* of:
I. Identify Adult Content Knowledge	**IA:** ***Science for All Americans*** ▸ Chapter 4, *Motion*, pages 52–55 **IB:** ***Science Matters: Achieving Scientific Literacy*** ▸ Chapter 1, *Motion*, pages 5–9
II. Consider Instructional Implications	**IIA:** ***Benchmarks for Science Literacy*** ▸ 4F *Motion* general essay, pages 87–88; grade span essays, pages 89–91 **IIB:** ***National Science Education Standards*** ▸ Grades K–4, Standard B essay, pages 123, 126; Vignette *Science Olympiad,* pages 39–40 ▸ Grades 5–8, Standard B essay, page 149, 154; Vignette *The Insect and the Spider,* pages 80–81 ▸ Grades 9–12, Standard B essay, pages 177–178
III. Identify Concepts and Specific Ideas	**IIIA:** ***Benchmarks for Science Literacy*** ▸ 4F, *Motion*, pages 89–92 **IIIB:** ***National Science Education Standards*** ▸ Grades K–4, Standard B, *Position and Motion of Objects,* page 127 ▸ Grades 5–8, Standard B, *Motion and Forces,* page 154 ▸ Grades 9–12, Standard B, *Motions and Forces,* pages 179–180
IV. Examine Research on Student Learning	**IVA:** ***Benchmarks for Science Literacy*** ▸ 4F, *The Concept of Force,* page 339; *Newton's Laws of Motion,* pages 339–340 **IVB:** ***Making Sense of Secondary Science: Research Into Children's Ideas*** ▸ Chapter 22, *Describing Motion,* pages 154–155; *Stationary Objects,* pages 155–156 ▸ Chapter 23, *Falling,* pages 165–166
V. Examine Coherency and Articulation	**V:** ***Atlas of Science Literacy*** ▸ *Laws of Motion,* pages 62–63
VI. Clarify State Standards and District Curriculum	**VIA:** ***State Standards:*** Link Sections I–V to learning goals and information from your state standards or frameworks that are informed by the results of the topic study. **VIB:** ***District Curriculum Guide:*** Link Sections I–V to learning goals and information from your district curriculum guide that are informed by the results of the topic study.
Visit www.curriculumtopicstudy.org for updates or supplementary readings, Web sites, and videos.	

Standards- and Research-Based Study of a Curricular Topic

ELECTRICAL CHARGE AND ENERGY

Section and Outcome	Selected Sources and Readings for Study and Reflection Read and examine *related parts* of:
I. Identify Adult Content Knowledge	**IA:** ***Science for All Americans*** ▸ Chapter 4, *Forces of Nature*, pages 55–56 **IB:** ***Science Matters: Achieving Scientific Literacy*** ▸ Chapter 3, *Electrical Charge and Coulomb's Law*, pages 36–38; *Electrical Circuits*, pages 44–45
II. Consider Instructional Implications	**IIA:** ***Benchmarks for Science Literacy*** ▸ 4G, *Forces of Nature* general essay, page 93; grade span essays, pages 94–96 **IIB:** ***National Science Education Standards*** ▸ Grades K–4, Standard B essay, pages 123, 126 ▸ Grades 5–8, Standard B essay, page 149, 154 ▸ Grades 9–12, Standard B essay, pages 177–178
III. Identify Concepts and Specific Ideas	**IIIA:** ***Benchmarks for Science Literacy*** ▸ 4G, *Forces of Nature,* pages 94–97 **IIIB:** ***National Science Education Standards*** ▸ Grades K–4, Standard B, *Light, Heat, Electricity, and Magnetism,* page 127 ▸ Grades 5–8, Standard B, *Transfer of Energy,* page 155 ▸ Grades 9–12, Standard B, *Motions and Forces,* pages 179–180; *Interactions of Energy and Matter,* page 181
IV. Examine Research on Student Learning	**IVB:** ***Making Sense of Secondary Science: Research Into Children's Ideas*** ▸ Chapter 15, *Electricity,* pages 117–125
V. Examine Coherency and Articulation	**V:** ***Atlas of Science Literacy:*** There are no maps for this topic in Volume 1.
VI. Clarify State Standards and District Curriculum	**VIA:** ***State Standards:*** Link Sections I–V to learning goals and information from your state standards or frameworks that are informed by the results of the topic study. **VIB:** ***District Curriculum Guide:*** Link Sections I–V to learning goals and information from your district curriculum guide that are informed by the results of the topic study.
Visit www.curriculumtopicstudy.org for updates or supplementary readings, Web sites, and videos.	

Standards- and Research-Based Study of a Curricular Topic

ELECTROMAGNETIC SPECTRUM

Section and Outcome	Selected Sources and Readings for Study and Reflection Read and examine *related parts* of:
I. Identify Adult Content Knowledge	**IA:** *Science for All Americans* ▸ Chapter 4, *Motion*, pages 52–55 **IB:** *Science Matters: Achieving Scientific Literacy* ▸ Chapter 3, *Electromagnetic Radiation*, pages 45–53
II. Consider Instructional Implications	**IIA:** *Benchmarks for Science Literacy* ▸ 4F, *Motion* general essay, pages 87–88; grade span essays, pages 89–91 **IIB:** *National Science Education Standards* ▸ Grades K–4, Standard B essay, pages 123, 126 ▸ Grades 5–8, Standard B essay, pages 149, 154 ▸ Grades 9–12, Standard B essay, pages 177–178
III. Identify Concepts and Specific Ideas	**IIIA:** *Benchmarks for Science Literacy* ▸ 4F, *Motion*, pages 89–92 **IIIB:** *National Science Education Standards* ▸ Grades K–4, Standard B, *Light, Heat, Electricity, and Magnetism*, page 127 ▸ Grades 5–8, Standard B, *Transfer of Energy*, page 155 ▸ Grades 9–12, Standard B, *Interactions of Energy and Matter*, page 180–181
IV. Examine Research on Student Learning	**IVA:** *Benchmarks for Science Literacy* ▸ 4F, *Light*, pages 338–339 **IVB:** *Making Sense of Secondary Science: Research Into Children's Ideas* ▸ Chapter 4, *Vision*, pages 41–45 ▸ Chapter 17, *Light*, pages 128–132
V. Examine Coherency and Articulation	**V:** *Atlas of Science Literacy* ▸ *Galaxies and the Universe*, pages 48–49 ▸ *Waves*, pages 64–65
VI. Clarify State Standards and District Curriculum	**VIA:** *State Standards:* Link Sections I–V to learning goals and information from your state standards or frameworks that are informed by the results of the topic study. **VIB:** *District Curriculum Guide:* Link Sections I–V to learning goals and information from your district curriculum guide that are informed by the results of the topic study.

Visit www.curriculumtopicstudy.org for updates or supplementary readings, Web sites, and videos.

Standards- and Research-Based Study of a Curricular Topic

ELECTROMAGNETISM

Section and Outcome	Selected Sources and Readings for Study and Reflection Read and examine *related parts* of:
I. Identify Adult Content Knowledge	**IA:** *Science for All Americans* ▸ Chapter 4, *Forces of Nature,* pages 55–56 **IB:** *Science Matters: Achieving Scientific Literacy* ▸ Chapter 3, *Electricity and Magnetism,* pages 35–53
II. Consider Instructional Implications	**IIA:** *Benchmarks for Science Literacy* ▸ 4G, *Forces of Nature* general essay, page 93; grade span essays, pages 94–96 **IIB:** *National Science Education Standards* ▸ Grades K–4, Standard B essay, pages 123, 126 ▸ Grades 5–8, Standard B essay, pages 149, 154 ▸ Grades 9–12, Standard B essay, pages 177–178
III. Identify Concepts and Specific Ideas	**IIIA:** *Benchmarks for Science Literacy* ▸ 4G, *Forces of Nature,* pages 94–97 **IIIB:** *National Science Education Standards* ▸ Grades K–4, Standard B, *Light, Heat, Electricity, and Magnetism,* page 127 ▸ Grades 5–8, Standard B, *Motion and Forces,* page 154 ▸ Grades 9–12, Standard B, *Motions and Forces,* pages 179–180
IV. Examine Research on Student Learning	**IVB:** *Making Sense of Secondary Science: Research Into Children's Ideas* ▸ Chapter 16, *Electromagnetism,* page 127
V. Examine Coherency and Articulation	**V:** *Atlas of Science Literacy:* There are no maps for this topic in Volume 1.
VI. Clarify State Standards and District Curriculum	**VIA:** *State Standards:* Link Sections I–V to learning goals and information from your state standards or frameworks that are informed by the results of the topic study. **VIB:** *District Curriculum Guide:* Link Sections I–V to learning goals and information from your district curriculum guide that are informed by the results of the topic study.
Visit www.curriculumtopicstudy.org for updates or supplementary readings, Web sites, and videos.	

Standards- and Research-Based Study of a Curricular Topic

ENERGY

Section and Outcome	Selected Sources and Readings for Study and Reflection Read and examine *related parts* of:	
I. Identify Adult Content Knowledge	**IA:**	***Science for All Americans*** ▸ Chapter 4, *Energy Transformations,* pages 49–52 ▸ Chapter 5, *Flow of Matter and Energy,* pages 66–67 ▸ Chapter 8, *Energy Sources and Use,* pages 114–116
	IB:	***Science Matters: Achieving Scientific Literacy*** ▸ Chapter 2, *Energy,* pages 20–34
II. Consider Instructional Implications	**IIA:**	***Benchmarks for Science Literacy*** ▸ 4E, *Energy Transformations* general essay, pages 81–82; grade span essays, pages 83–86 ▸ 5E, *Flow of Matter and Energy* general essay, page 118; grade span essays, pages 119–121 ▸ 8C, *Energy Sources and Use* general essay, page 192; grade span essays, pages 193–195
	IIB:	***National Science Education Standards*** ▸ Grades K–4 Standard B essay, pages 123, 126 ▸ Grades 5–8, Standard B essay, pages 149, 154 ▸ Grades 9–12 Standard B essay, pages 177–178
III. Identify Concepts and Specific Ideas	**IIIA:**	***Benchmarks for Science Literacy*** ▸ 4E, *Energy Transformations,* pages 83–86 ▸ 5E, *Flow of Matter and Energy,* pages 119–121 ▸ 8C, *Energy Sources and Use,* pages 193–195
	IIIB:	***National Science Education Standards*** ▸ Grades K–4, Standard B, *Light, Heat, Electricity, and Magnetism,* page 127; Standard F, *Types of Resources,* page 140 ▸ Grades 5–8, Standard B, *Transfer of Energy,* page 155; Standard C, *Populations and Ecosystems,* page 158 ▸ Grades 9–12, Standard B, *Conservation of Energy and the Increase in Disorder,* page 180; *Interactions of Energy and Matter,* pages 180–181; Standard C, *Matter, Energy, and Organization in Living Systems,* pages 186–187; Standard D, *Energy in the Earth System,* page 189; Standard F, *Natural Resources,* page 198
IV. Examine Research on Student Learning	**IVA:**	***Benchmarks for Science Literacy*** ▸ 4E, *Energy Transformations,* pages 337–338 ▸ 5E, *Flow of Matter and Energy,* pages 342–343
	IVB:	***Making Sense of Secondary Science: Research Into Children's Ideas*** ▸ Chapter 19, *Energy Transfer Processes,* pages 141–142 ▸ Chapter 20, *Energy,* pages 143–147
V. Examine Coherency and Articulation	**V:**	***Atlas of Science Literacy*** ▸ *States of Matter,* pages 58–59; note the conceptual strand *Heat Energy* ▸ *Chemical Reactions,* pages 60–61 ▸ *Flow of Energy in Ecosystems,* pages 78–79
VI. Clarify State Standards and District Curriculum	**VIA:**	***State Standards:*** Link Sections I–V to learning goals and information from your state standards or frameworks that are informed by the results of the topic study.
	VIB:	***District Curriculum Guide:*** Link Sections I–V to learning goals and information from your district curriculum guide that are informed by the results of the topic study.
Visit www.curriculumtopicstudy.org for updates or supplementary readings, Web sites, and videos.		

Standards- and Research-Based Study of a Curricular Topic

ENERGY RESOURCES AND USE

Section and Outcome	Selected Sources and Readings for Study and Reflection Read and examine *related parts* of:
I. Identify Adult Content Knowledge	**IA:** *Science for All Americans* ▸ Chapter 8, *Energy Sources and Use,* pages 114–118 **IB:** *Science Matters: Achieving Scientific Literacy* ▸ Chapter 2, *Frontiers: New Energy Sources,* pages 33–34
II. Consider Instructional Implications	**IIA:** *Benchmarks for Science Literacy* ▸ 8C, *Energy Sources and Use* general essay, page 192; grade span essays, pages 193–195 **IIB:** *National Science Education Standards* ▸ Grades K–4, Standard F essay, pages 138–139 ▸ Grades 5–8, Standard F essay, pages 167–168 ▸ Grades 9–12, Standard F essay, pages 193, 197
III. Identify Concepts and Specific Ideas	**IIIA:** *Benchmarks for Science Literacy* ▸ 8C, *Energy Sources and Use,* pages 193–195 **IIIB:** *National Science Education Standards* ▸ Grades K–4, Standard F, *Types of Resources,* page 140 ▸ Grades 5–8, Standard F, *Populations, Resources, and Environments,* page 168 ▸ Grades 9–12, Standard F, *Natural Resources,* page 198
IV. Examine Research on Student Learning	**IVB:** *Making Sense of Secondary Science: Research Into Children's Ideas* ▸ Chapter 20, *Energy,* pages 143–147
V. Examine Coherency and Articulation	**V:** *Atlas of Science Literacy:* There is no available map in Volume 1.
VI. Clarify State Standards and District Curriculum	**VIA:** *State Standards:* Link Sections I–V to learning goals and information from your state standards or frameworks that are informed by the results of the topic study. **VIB:** *District Curriculum Guide:* Link Sections I–V to learning goals and information from your district curriculum guide that are informed by the results of the topic study.
Visit www.curriculumtopicstudy.org for updates or supplementary readings, Web sites, and videos.	

Standards- and Research-Based Study of a Curricular Topic

ENERGY TRANSFORMATION

Section and Outcome	Selected Sources and Readings for Study and Reflection Read and examine *related parts* of:
I. Identify Adult Content Knowledge	**IA:** ***Science for All Americans*** ▸ Chapter 4, *Energy Transformations*, pages 49–52 **IB:** ***Science Matters: Achieving Scientific Literacy*** ▸ Chapter 2, *Energy*, pages 20–34
II. Consider Instructional Implications	**IIA:** ***Benchmarks for Science Literacy*** ▸ 4E, *Energy Transformations* general essay, pages 81–82; grade span essays, pages 83–86 **IIB:** ***National Science Education Standards*** ▸ Grades K–4, Standard B essay, pages 123, 126 ▸ Grades 5–8, Standard B essay, pages 149, 154 ▸ Grades 9–12, Standard B essay, pages 177–178
III. Identify Concepts and Specific Ideas	**IIIA:** ***Benchmarks for Science Literacy*** ▸ 4E, *Energy Transformations*, pages 83–86 **IIIB:** ***National Science Education Standards*** ▸ Grades K–4, Standard B, *Light, Heat, Electricity, and Magnetism,* page 127 ▸ Grades 5–8, Standard B, *Transfer of Energy,* page 155 ▸ Grades 9–12, Standard B, *Conservation of Energy and the Increase in Disorder,* page 180; *Interactions of Energy and Matter,* pages 180–181
IV. Examine Research on Student Learning	**IVA:** ***Benchmarks for Science Literacy*** ▸ 4E, *Heat Transfer,* page 337, *Energy Forms and Energy Transformation,* page 338 **IVB:** ***Making Sense of Secondary Science: Research Into Children's Ideas*** ▸ Chapter 19, *Energy Transfer Processes,* pages 141–142 ▸ Chapter 20, *Energy,* pages 143–147
V. Examine Coherency and Articulation	**V:** ***Atlas of Science Literacy*** ▸ *Flow of Energy in Ecosystems,* pages 78–79
VI. Clarify State Standards and District Curriculum	**VIA:** ***State Standards:*** Link Sections I–V to learning goals and information from your state standards or frameworks that are informed by the results of the topic study. **VIB:** ***District Curriculum Guide:*** Link Sections I–V to learning goals and information from your district curriculum guide that are informed by the results of the topic study.
Visit www.curriculumtopicstudy.org for updates or supplementary readings, Web sites, and videos.	

Standards- and Research-Based Study of a Curricular Topic

FORCES

Section and Outcome	Selected Sources and Readings for Study and Reflection Read and examine *related parts* of:
I. Identify Adult Content Knowledge	**IA:** *Science for All Americans* ▸ Chapter 4, *Forces of Nature*, pages 55–57 **IB:** *Science Matters: Achieving Scientific Literacy* ▸ Chapter 1, *The Clockwork Universe*, pages 5–14 ▸ Chapter 3, *Electricity and Magnetism,* pages 35–53 ▸ Chapter 9, *The Four Forces,* pages 127–131
II. Consider Instructional Implications	**IIA:** *Benchmarks for Science Literacy* ▸ 4G, *Forces of Nature* general essay, page 93; grade span essays, pages 94–96 **IIB:** *National Science Education Standards* ▸ Grades K–4, Standard B essay, pages 123, 126 ▸ Grades 5–8, Standard B essay, pages 149, 154 ▸ Grades 9–12, Standard B essay, pages 177–178
III. Identify Concepts and Specific Ideas	**IIIA:** *Benchmarks for Science Literacy* ▸ 4G, *Forces of Nature*, pages 94–97 **IIIB:** *National Science Education Standards* ▸ Grades K–4, Standard B, *Position and Motion of Objects*, page 127 ▸ Grades 5–8, Standard B, *Motion and Forces*, page 154 ▸ Grades 9–12, Standard B, *Motions and Forces*, pages 179–180
IV. Examine Research on Student Learning	**IVA:** *Benchmarks for Science Literacy* ▸ 4F, *The Concept of Force*, page 339 ▸ 4G, *Forces of Nature*, page 340 **IVB:** *Making Sense of Secondary Science: Research Into Children's Ideas* ▸ Chapter 21, *Forces*, pages 148–153 ▸ Chapter 22, *Forces*, page 156; *Forces Causing Changes in Motion*, pages 156–158; *Friction*, page 159 ▸ Chapter 23, *Gravity*, pages 163–167
V. Examine Coherency and Articulation	**V:** *Atlas of Science Literacy* ▸ *Gravity*, pages 42–43 ▸ *Laws of Motion*, pages 62–63; note the conceptual strand *Forces and Motion*.
VI. Clarify State Standards and District Curriculum	**VIA:** *State Standards:* Link Sections I–V to learning goals and information from your state standards or frameworks that are informed by the results of the topic study. **VIB:** *District Curriculum Guide:* Link Sections I–V to learning goals and information from your district curriculum guide that are informed by the results of the topic study.
	Visit www.curriculumtopicstudy.org for updates or supplementary readings, Web sites, and videos.

Standards- and Research-Based Study of a Curricular Topic
GRAVITATIONAL FORCE

Section and Outcome	Selected Sources and Readings for Study and Reflection Read and examine *related parts* of:
I. Identify Adult Content Knowledge	**IA:** *Science for All Americans* ▸ Chapter 4, *Forces of Nature,* pages 55–57 **IB:** *Science Matters: Achieving Scientific Literacy* ▸ Chapter 1, *Gravity,* pages 9–14 ▸ Chapter 9, *Quantum Gravity,* pages 132–133 ▸ Chapter 12, *General Relativity,* pages 167–171
II. Consider Instructional Implications	**IIA:** *Benchmarks for Science Literacy* ▸ 4G, *Forces of Nature* general essay, page 93; grade span essays, pages 94–96 **IIB:** *National Science Education Standards* ▸ Grades K–4, Standard B essay, pages 123, 126 ▸ Grades 5–8, Standard B essay, page 149, 154 ▸ Grades 9–12, Standard B essay, pages 177–178
III. Identify Concepts and Specific Ideas	**IIIA:** *Benchmarks for Science Literacy* ▸ 4G, *Forces of Nature,* pages 94–97 **IIIB:** *National Science Education Standards* ▸ Grades K–4, Standard B, *Position and Motion of Objects,* page 127 ▸ Grades 5–8, Standard B, *Motion and Forces,* page 154 ▸ Grades 9–12, Standard B, *Motions and Forces,* pages 179–180
IV. Examine Research on Student Learning	**IVA:** *Benchmarks for Science Literacy* ▸ 4G, *Forces of Nature,* page 340 **IVB:** *Making Sense of Secondary Science: Research Into Children's Ideas* ▸ Chapter 16, *Magnetism and Gravity,* page 126 ▸ Chapter 23, *Gravity,* pages 163–167
V. Examine Coherency and Articulation	**V:** *Atlas of Science Literacy* ▸ *Gravity,* pages 42–43 ▸ *Laws of Motion,* pages 62–63
VI. Clarify State Standards and District Curriculum	**VIA:** *State Standards:* Link Sections I–V to learning goals and information from your state standards or frameworks that are informed by the results of the topic study. **VIB:** *District Curriculum Guide:* Link Sections I–V to learning goals and information from your district curriculum guide that are informed by the results of the topic study.
Visit www.curriculumtopicstudy.org for updates or supplementary readings, Web sites, and videos.	

Standards- and Research-Based Study of a Curricular Topic

HEAT AND TEMPERATURE

Section and Outcome	Selected Sources and Readings for Study and Reflection Read and examine *related parts* of:
I. Identify Adult Content Knowledge	**IA:** *Science for All Americans* ▸ Chapter 4, *Energy Transformations,* pages 49–52 **IB:** *Science Matters: Achieving Scientific Literacy* ▸ Chapter 2, *Heat,* pages 26–28; *Bad News: The Second Law,* pages 29–33
II. Consider Instructional Implications	**IIA:** *Benchmarks for Science Literacy* ▸ 4E, *Energy Transformations* general essay, pages 81–82; grade span essays, pages 83–86 **IIB:** *National Science Education Standards* ▸ Grades K–4, Standard B essay, pages 123, 126 ▸ Grades 5–8, Standard B essay, page 149, 154 ▸ Grades 9–12, Standard B essay, pages 177–178
III. Identify Concepts and Specific Ideas	**IIIA:** *Benchmarks for Science Literacy* ▸ 4E, *Energy Transformations,* pages 83–86 **IIIB:** *National Science Education Standards* ▸ Grades K–4, Standard B, *Light, Heat, Electricity, and Magnetism,* page 127 ▸ Grades 5–8, Standard B, *Transfer of Energy,* page 155 ▸ Grades 9–12, Standard B, *Conservation of Energy and the Increase in Disorder,* page 180
IV. Examine Research on Student Learning	**IVA:** *Benchmarks for Science Literacy* ▸ 4E, *Heat and Temperature,* page 337; *Energy Forms and Transformation,* page 338 **IVB:** *Making Sense of Secondary Science: Research Into Children's Ideas* ▸ Chapter 19, *Heat and Temperature,* pages 138–141; *Energy Transfer Processes,* pages 141–142
V. Examine Coherency and Articulation	**V:** *Atlas of Science Literacy* ▸ *States of Matter,* pages 58–59; note the conceptual strand *Heat Energy.*
VI. Clarify State Standards and District Curriculum	**VIA:** *State Standards:* Link Sections I–V to learning goals and information from your state standards or frameworks that are informed by the results of the topic study. **VIB:** *District Curriculum Guide:* Link Sections I–V to learning goals and information from your district curriculum guide that are informed by the results of the topic study.
	Visit www.curriculumtopicstudy.org for updates or supplementary readings, Web sites, and videos.

Standards- and Research-Based Study of a Curricular Topic
KINETIC AND POTENTIAL ENERGY

Section and Outcome	Selected Sources and Readings for Study and Reflection Read and examine *related parts* of:
I. Identify Adult Content Knowledge	**IA:** *Science for All Americans* ▸ Chapter 4, *Energy Transformations*, pages 49–52 **IB:** *Science Matters: Achieving Scientific Literacy* ▸ Chapter 2, *Potential Energy*, pages 22–23; *Kinetic Energy*, page 23; *Other Kinds of Energy*, pages 23–24; *Good News: The First Law*, pages 24–26
II. Consider Instructional Implications	**IIA:** *Benchmarks for Science Literacy* ▸ 4E, *Energy Transformations* general essay, pages 81–82; 6–8 and 9–12 grade span essays, pages 84–86 **IIB:** *National Science Education Standards* ▸ Grades 5–8, Standard B essay, pages 149, 154 ▸ Grades 9–12, Standard B essay, pages 177–178
III. Identify Concepts and Specific Ideas	**IIIA:** *Benchmarks for Science Literacy* ▸ 4E, *Energy Forms and Energy Transformations*, 6–8 and 9–12, pages 85–86 **IIIB:** *National Science Education Standards* ▸ Grades 5–8, Standard B, *Transfer of Energy*, page 155 ▸ Grades 9–12, Standard B, *Conservation of Energy and the Increase in Disorder*, page 180
IV. Examine Research on Student Learning	**IVA:** *Benchmarks for Science Literacy* ▸ 4E, *Energy Forms and Energy Transformation*, page 338 **IVB:** *Making Sense of Secondary Science: Research Into Children's Ideas* ▸ Chapter 20, *Energy*, pages 143–147
V. Examine Coherency and Articulation	**V:** *Atlas of Science Literacy:* There is no related map in the current edition of the Atlas.
VI. Clarify State Standards and District Curriculum	**VIA:** *State Standards:* Link Sections I–V to learning goals and information from your state standards or frameworks that are informed by the results of the topic study. **VIB:** *District Curriculum Guide:* Link Sections I–V to learning goals and information from your district curriculum guide that are informed by the results of the topic study.
	Visit www.curriculumtopicstudy.org for updates or supplementary readings, Web sites, and videos.

Standards- and Research-Based Study of a Curricular Topic

LAWS OF MOTION

Section and Outcome	Selected Sources and Readings for Study and Reflection Read and examine *related parts* of:
I. Identify Adult Content Knowledge	**IA:** *Science for All Americans* ▸ Chapter 4, *Motion,* pages 52–55 ▸ Chapter 10, *Uniting the Heavens and Earth,* pages 149–150 **IB:** *Science Matters: Achieving Scientific Literacy* ▸ Chapter 1, *Motion,* pages 5–9
II. Consider Instructional Implications	**IIA:** *Benchmarks for Science Literacy* ▸ 4F, *Motion* general essay, pages 87–88; grade span essays, pages 89–91 ▸ 10B, *Uniting the Heavens and Earth* general essay, page 242; grade span essay, page 243 **IIB:** *National Science Education Standards* ▸ Grades K–4, Standard B essay, pages 123, 126 ▸ Grades 5–8, Standard B essay, page 149, 154 ▸ Grades 9–12, Standard B essay, pages 177–178
III. Identify Concepts and Specific Ideas	**IIIA:** *Benchmarks for Science Literacy* ▸ 4F, *Motion,* pages 89–92 ▸ 10B, *Uniting the Heavens and Earth,* page 243 **IIIB:** *National Science Education Standards* ▸ Grades K–4, Standard B, *Position and Motion of Objects,* page 127 ▸ Grades 5–8, Standard B, *Motion and Forces,* page 154 ▸ Grades 9–12, Standard B, *Motions and Forces,* pages 179–180
IV. Examine Research on Student Learning	**IVA:** *Benchmarks for Science Literacy* ▸ 4F, *Newton's Laws of Motion,* pages 339–340 **IVB:** *Making Sense of Secondary Science: Research Into Children's Ideas* ▸ Chapter 21, *Describing Forces,* pages 148–151 ▸ Chapter 22, *Horizontal Motion,* pages 154–162
V. Examine Coherency and Articulation	**V:** *Atlas of Science Literacy* ▸ *Laws of Motion,* pages 62–63
VI. Clarify State Standards and District Curriculum	**VIA:** *State Standards:* Link Sections I–V to learning goals and information from your state standards or frameworks that are informed by the results of the topic study. **VIB:** *District Curriculum Guide:* Link Sections I–V to learning goals and information from your district curriculum guide that are informed by the results of the topic study.

Visit www.curriculumtopicstudy.org for updates or supplementary readings, Web sites, and videos.

Standards- and Research-Based Study of a Curricular Topic

MAGNETISM

Section and Outcome	Selected Sources and Readings for Study and Reflection Read and examine *related parts* of:		
I. Identify Adult Content Knowledge	**IA:**	***Science for All Americans*** ▶ Chapter 4, *Forces of Nature*, pages 55–56	
	IB:	***Science Matters: Achieving Scientific Literacy*** ▶ Chapter 3 *Magnetism*, pages 38–39; *Two Sides of the Same Coin*, pages 39–42	
II. Consider Instructional Implications	**IIA:**	***Benchmarks for Science Literacy*** ▶ 4G, *Forces of Nature* general essay, page 93; grade span essays, pages 94–96	
	IIB:	***National Science Education Standards*** ▶ Grades K–4, Standard B essay, pages 123, 126 ▶ Grades 5–8, Standard B essay, pages 149, 154 ▶ Grades 9–12, Standard B essay, pages 177–178	
III. Identify Concepts and Specific Ideas	**IIIA:**	***Benchmarks for Science Literacy*** ▶ 4G, *Forces of Nature*, pages 94–97	
	IIIB:	***National Science Education Standards*** ▶ Grades K–4, Standard B, *Light, Heat, Electricity, and Magnetism*, page 127 ▶ Grades 5–8, Standard B, *Motion and Forces*, page 154 ▶ Grades 9–12, Standard B, *Motions and Forces*, pages 179–180	
IV. Examine Research on Student Learning	**IVB:**	***Making Sense of Secondary Science: Research Into Children's Ideas*** ▶ Chapter 16, *Magnetism*, pages 126–127	
V. Examine Coherency and Articulation	**V:**	***Atlas of Science Literacy:*** There are no maps for this topic in Volume 1.	
VI. Clarify State Standards and District Curriculum	**VIA:**	***State Standards:*** Link Sections I–V to learning goals and information from your state standards or frameworks that are informed by the results of the topic study.	
	VIB:	***District Curriculum Guide:*** Link Sections I–V to learning goals and information from your district curriculum guide that are informed by the results of the topic study.	
Visit www.curriculumtopicstudy.org for updates or supplementary readings, Web sites, and videos.			

Standards- and Research-Based Study of a Curricular Topic

MOTION

Section and Outcome	Selected Sources and Readings for Study and Reflection Read and examine *related parts* of:
I. Identify Adult Content Knowledge	**IA:** *Science for All Americans* ▸ Chapter 4, *Motion*, pages 52–55 **IB:** *Science Matters: Achieving Scientific Literacy* ▸ Chapter 1, *Motion*, pages 5–9
II. Consider Instructional Implications	**IIA:** *Benchmarks for Science Literacy* ▸ 4F, *Motion* general essay, pages 87–88; grade span essays, pages 89–91 **IIB:** *National Science Education Standards* ▸ Grades K–4, Standard B essay, pages 123, 126 ▸ Grades 5–8, Standard B essay, pages 149, 154; Vignette *The Insect and the Spider,* pages 80–81 ▸ Grades 9–12, Standard B essay, pages 177–178
III. Identify Concepts and Specific Ideas	**IIIA:** *Benchmarks for Science Literacy* ▸ 4F, *Motion*, pages 89–92 **IIIB:** *National Science Education Standards* ▸ Grades K–4, Standard B, *Position and Motion of Objects,* page 127 ▸ Grades 5–8, Standard B, *Motion and Forces,* page 154 ▸ Grades 9–12, Standard B, *Motions and Forces,* pages 179–180
IV. Examine Research on Student Learning	**IVA:** *Benchmarks for Science Literacy* ▸ 4F *The Concept of Force,* page 339; *Newton's Laws of Motion,* pages 339–340 **IVB:** *Making Sense of Secondary Science: Research Into Children's Ideas* ▸ Chapter 21, *Describing Forces,* pages 148–151 ▸ Chapter 22, *Horizontal Motion,* pages 154–162 ▸ Chapter 23, *Falling,* pages 165–166
V. Examine Coherency and Articulation	**V:** *Atlas of Science Literacy* ▸ *Laws of Motion,* pages 62–63
VI. Clarify State Standards and District Curriculum	**VIA:** *State Standards:* Link Sections I–V to learning goals and information from your state standards or frameworks that are informed by the results of the topic study. **VIB:** *District Curriculum Guide:* Link Sections I–V to learning goals and information from your district curriculum guide that are informed by the results of the topic study.
Visit www.curriculumtopicstudy.org for updates or supplementary readings, Web sites, and videos.	

Standards- and Research-Based Study of a Curricular Topic

NUCLEAR ENERGY

Section and Outcome	Selected Sources and Readings for Study and Reflection Read and examine *related parts* of:
I. Identify Adult Content Knowledge	**IA:** *Science for All Americans* ▸ Chapter 4, *Energy Transformations*, page 52 ▸ Chapter 8, *Energy Sources and Use*, pages 115–116 ▸ Chapter 10, *Splitting the Atom*, pages 155–157 **IB:** *Science Matters: Achieving Scientific Literacy* ▸ Chapter 8, *Nuclear Physics*, pages 110–116; *Fusion Research*, page 122
II. Consider Instructional Implications	**IIA:** *Benchmarks for Science Literacy* ▸ 4E, *Energy Transformations* general essay, pages 81–82; 6–8 and 9–12 grade span essays, pages 84–86 ▸ 8C, *Energy Sources and Use* general essay, page 192; grade span essays, pages 193–195 ▸ 10G, *Splitting the Atom* general essay, page 252; grade span essays, pages 252–253 **IIB:** *National Science Education Standards* ▸ Grades 5–8, Standard B essay, page 149, 154 ▸ Grades 9–12, Standard B essay, pages 177–178
III. Identify Concepts and Specific Ideas	**IIIA:** *Benchmarks for Science Literacy* ▸ 4E, *Energy Transformations*, 6–8 and 9–12, pages 84–86 ▸ 8C, *Energy Sources and Use*, 6–8, and 9–12, pages 194–195 ▸ 10C, *Splitting the Atom*, pages 252–253 **IIIB:** *National Science Education Standards* ▸ Grades 5–8, Standard B, *Transfer of Energy*, page 155 ▸ Grades 9–12, Standard B, *Structure of Atoms*, page 178; *Conservation of Energy and the Increase in Disorder*, page 180
IV. Examine Research on Student Learning	**IVA:** *Benchmarks for Science Literacy* ▸ 4E, *Energy Forms and Energy Transformation*, page 338 **IVB:** *Making Sense of Secondary Science: Research Into Children's Ideas* ▸ Chapter 20, *Energy*, pages 143–147
V. Examine Coherency and Articulation	**V:** *Atlas of Science Literacy:* There are no maps for this topic in Volume 1.
VI. Clarify State Standards and District Curriculum	**VIA:** *State Standards:* Link Sections I–V to learning goals and information from your state standards or frameworks that are informed by the results of the topic study. **VIB:** *District Curriculum Guide:* Link Sections I–V to learning goals and information from your district curriculum guide that are informed by the results of the topic study.

Visit www.curriculumtopicstudy.org for updates or supplementary readings, Web sites, and videos.

Standards- and Research-Based Study of a Curricular Topic

PRESSURE AND BUOYANCY

Section and Outcome	Selected Sources and Readings for Study and Reflection Read and examine *related parts* of:
I. Identify Adult Content Knowledge	**IA:** *Science for All Americans* ▸ Chapter 4, *Forces of Nature*, pages 55–57
II. Consider Instructional Implications	**IIA:** *Benchmarks for Science Literacy* ▸ 4G, *Forces of Nature* general essay, page 93; grade span essays, pages 94–96 **IIB:** *National Science Education Standards* ▸ Grades K–4, Standard B essay, pages 123, 126 ▸ Grades 5–8, Standard B essay, pages 149, 154 ▸ Grades 9–12, Standard B essay, pages 177–178
III. Identify Concepts and Specific Ideas	**IIIA:** *Benchmarks for Science Literacy* ▸ 4G, *Forces of Nature*, pages 94–97 **IIIB:** *National Science Education Standards* ▸ Grades K–4, Standard B, *Position and Motion of Objects*, page 127 ▸ Grades 5–8, Standard B, *Motion and Forces*, page 154 ▸ Grades 9–12, Standard B, *Motions and Forces*, pages 179–180
IV. Examine Research on Student Learning	**IVA:** *Benchmarks for Science Literacy* ▸ 4F, *The Concept of Force*, page 339 ▸ 4G, *Forces of Nature*, page 340 **IVB:** *Making Sense of Secondary Science: Research Into Children's Ideas* ▸ Chapter 12, *Floating and Sinking*, pages 102–103 ▸ Chapter 21, *Pressure*, page 152
V. Examine Coherency and Articulation	**V:** *Atlas of Science Literacy* ▸ *Laws of Motion*, pages 62–63; note the conceptual strand *Forces and Motion*.
VI. Clarify State Standards and District Curriculum	**VIA:** *State Standards:* Link Sections I–V to learning goals and information from your state standards or frameworks that are informed by the results of the topic study. **VIB:** *District Curriculum Guide:* Link Sections I–V to learning goals and information from your district curriculum guide that are informed by the results of the topic study.
Visit www.curriculumtopicstudy.org for updates or supplementary readings, Web sites, and videos.	

Standards- and Research-Based Study of a Curricular Topic

RELATIVITY

Section and Outcome	Selected Sources and Readings for Study and Reflection Read and examine *related parts* of:
I. Identify Adult Content Knowledge	**IA:** ***Science for All Americans*** ▶ Chapter 10, *Relating Matter and Energy and Time and Space,* pages 150–151 **IB:** ***Science Matters: Achieving Scientific Literacy*** ▶ Chapter 12, *Relativity,* pages 156–173
II. Consider Instructional Implications	**IIA:** ***Benchmarks for Science Literacy*** ▶ 10C, *Relating Matter and Energy and Time and Space* general essay, page 244; grade span essay, page 245 **IIB:** ***National Science Education Standards*** ▶ Grades 9–12, Standard B essay, pages 177–178
III. Identify Concepts and Specific Ideas	**IIIA:** ***Benchmarks for Science Literacy*** ▶ 10C, *Relating Matter and Energy and Time and Space,* page 245 **IIIB:** ***National Science Education Standards*** ▶ Grades 9–12, Standard B, *Interactions of Energy and Matter,* page 180
IV. Examine Research on Student Learning	**IV:** No research available in *Benchmarks* or Driver.
V. Examine Coherency and Articulation	**V:** ***Atlas of Science Literacy:*** There are no maps for this topic in Volume 1.
VI. Clarify State Standards and District Curriculum	**VIA:** ***State Standards:*** Link Sections I–V to learning goals and information from your state standards or frameworks that are informed by the results of the topic study. **VIB:** ***District Curriculum Guide:*** Link Sections I–V to learning goals and information from your district curriculum guide that are informed by the results of the topic study.
Visit www.curriculumtopicstudy.org for updates or supplementary readings, Web sites, and videos.	

Standards- and Research-Based Study of a Curricular Topic

SOUND

Section and Outcome	Selected Sources and Readings for Study and Reflection Read and examine *related parts* of:
I. Identify Adult Content Knowledge	**IA:** *Science for All Americans* ▶ Chapter 4, *Motion,* pages 52–55 **IB:** *Science Matters: Achieving Scientific Literacy* ▶ Chapter 2, *Other Kinds of Energy,* pages 23–24
II. Consider Instructional Implications	**IIA:** *Benchmarks for Science Literacy* ▶ 4F, *Motion* general essay, pages 87–88; grade span essays, pages 89–91 **IIB:** *National Science Education Standards* ▶ Grades K–4, Standard B essay, pages 123, 126; Vignette *Musical Instruments,* pages 47–49 ▶ Grades 5–8, Standard B essay, pages 149, 154 ▶ Grades 9–12, Standard B essay, pages 177–178
III. Identify Concepts and Specific Ideas	**IIIA:** *Benchmarks for Science Literacy* ▶ 4F, *Motion,* pages 89–92 **IIIB:** *National Science Education Standards* ▶ Grades K–4, Standard B, *Light, Heat, Electricity, and Magnetism,* page 127 ▶ Grades 5–8, Standard B, *Transfer of Energy,* page 155 ▶ Grades 9–12, Standard B, *Interactions of Energy and Matter,* page 180
IV. Examine Research on Student Learning	**IVA:** *Benchmarks for Science Literacy* ▶ 4E, *Energy Forms and Energy Transformation,* page 338 **IVB:** *Making Sense of Secondary Science: Research Into Children's Ideas* ▶ Chapter 4, *Hearing,* pages 45–46 ▶ Chapter 18, *Sound,* pages 133–137
V. Examine Coherency and Articulation	**V:** *Atlas of Science Literacy* ▶ *Waves,* pages 64–65
VI. Clarify State Standards and District Curriculum	**VIA:** *State Standards:* Link Sections I–V to learning goals and information from your state standards or frameworks that are informed by the results of the topic study. **VIB:** *District Curriculum Guide:* Link Sections I–V to learning goals and information from your district curriculum guide that are informed by the results of the topic study.
Visit www.curriculumtopicstudy.org for updates or supplementary readings, Web sites, and videos.	

Standards- and Research-Based Study of a Curricular Topic
VISIBLE LIGHT, COLOR, AND VISION

Section and Outcome	Selected Sources and Readings for Study and Reflection Read and examine *related parts* of:
I. Identify Adult Content Knowledge	**IA:** *Science for All Americans* ▸ Chapter 4, *Motion,* pages 52–55 **IB:** *Science Matters: Achieving Scientific Literacy* ▸ Chapter 3, *The Nature of Light,* pages 45–47; *Electromagnetic Spectrum,* pages 47–48; *Visible Light,* page 51
II. Consider Instructional Implications	**IIA:** *Benchmarks for Science Literacy* ▸ 4F, *Motion* general essay, pages 87–88; grade span essays, pages 89–91 **IIB:** *National Science Education Standards* ▸ Grades K–4, Standard B essay, pages 123, 126 ▸ Grades 5–8, Standard B essay, pages 149, 154 ▸ Grades 9–12, Standard B essay, pages 177–178
III. Identify Concepts and Specific Ideas	**IIIA:** *Benchmarks for Science Literacy* ▸ 4F, *Motion,* pages 89–92 **IIIB:** *National Science Education Standards* ▸ Grades K–4, Standard B, *Light, Heat, Electricity, and Magnetism,* page 127 ▸ Grades 5–8, Standard B, *Transfer of Energy,* page 155 ▸ Grades 9–12, Standard B, *Interactions of Energy and Matter,* page 180
IV. Examine Research on Student Learning	**IVA:** *Benchmarks for Science Literacy* ▸ 4F, *Light,* pages 338–339 **IVB:** *Making Sense of Secondary Science: Research Into Children's Ideas* ▸ Chapter 4, *Vision,* pages 41–45 ▸ Chapter 17, *Light,* pages 128–132
V. Examine Coherency and Articulation	**V:** *Atlas of Science Literacy* ▸ *Waves,* pages 64–65
VI. Clarify State Standards and District Curriculum	**VIA:** *State Standards:* Link Sections I–V to learning goals and information from your state standards or frameworks that are informed by the results of the topic study. **VIB:** *District Curriculum Guide:* Link Sections I–V to learning goals and information from your district curriculum guide that are informed by the results of the topic study.
Visit www.curriculumtopicstudy.org for updates or supplementary readings, Web sites, and videos.	

Standards- and Research-Based Study of a Curricular Topic

WAVES

Section and Outcome	Selected Sources and Readings for Study and Reflection Read and examine *related parts* of:
I. Identify Adult Content Knowledge	**IA:** *Science for All Americans* ▸ Chapter 4, *Motion,* pages 52–55 **IB:** *Science Matters: Achieving Scientific Literacy* ▸ Chapter 3, *Electromagnetic Radiation,* pages 45–53 ▸ Chapter 5, *Waves or Particles,* pages 69–71
II. Consider Instructional Implications	**IIA:** *Benchmarks for Science Literacy* ▸ 4F *Motion* general essay, pages 87–88; grade span essays, pages 89–91 **IIB:** *National Science Education Standards* ▸ Grades K–4, Standard B essay, pages 123, 126 ▸ Grades 5–8, Standard B essay, pages 149, 154 ▸ Grades 9–12, Standard B essay, pages 177–178
III. Identify Concepts and Specific Ideas	**IIIA:** *Benchmarks for Science Literacy* ▸ 4F *Motion,* pages 89–92 **IIIB:** *National Science Education Standards* ▸ Grades K–4, Standard B, *Light, Heat, Electricity, and Magnetism,* page 127 ▸ Grades 5–8, Standard B, *Transfer of Energy,* page 155 ▸ Grades 9–12, Standard B, *Interactions of Energy and Matter,* page 180
IV. Examine Research on Student Learning	**IVA:** *Benchmarks for Science Literacy* ▸ 4F *Light,* pages 338–339 **IVB:** *Making Sense of Secondary Science: Research Into Children's Ideas* ▸ Chapter 17 *Light,* pages 128–132 ▸ Chapter 18 *Sound,* pages 135–137
V. Examine Coherency and Articulation	**V:** *Atlas of Science Literacy* ▸ *Waves,* pages 64–65
VI. Clarify State Standards and District Curriculum	**VIA:** *State Standards:* Link Sections I–V to learning goals and information from your state standards or frameworks that are informed by the results of the topic study. **VIB:** *District Curriculum Guide:* Link Sections I–V to learning goals and information from your district curriculum guide that are informed by the results of the topic study.
Visit www.curriculumtopicstudy.org for updates or supplementary readings, Web sites, and videos.	

Standards- and Research-Based Study of a Curricular Topic

WORK, POWER, AND MACHINES

Section and Outcome	Selected Sources and Readings for Study and Reflection Read and examine *related parts* of:
I. Identify Adult Content Knowledge	**IA:** ***Science for All Americans*** ▸ Chapter 8, *Energy Sources and Use,* pages 114–116 ▸ Chapter 10, *Harnessing Power,* pages 161–163 **IB:** ***Science Matters: Achieving Scientific Literacy*** ▸ Chapter 2, *Work, Energy, and Power,* pages 21–22; *Bad News: The Second Law,* pages 29–33
II. Consider Instructional Implications	**IIA:** ***Benchmarks for Science Literacy*** ▸ 8C, *Energy Sources and Use* general essay, page 192; grade span essays, pages 193–195 ▸ 10J, *Harnessing Power* general essay, page 258; grade span essays, page 259 **IIB:** ***National Science Education Standards*** ▸ Grades 5–8 Standard B essay, pages 149, 154 ▸ Grades 9–12 Standard B essay, pages 177–178
III. Identify Concepts and Specific Ideas	**IIIA:** ***Benchmarks for Science Literacy*** ▸ 8C, *Energy Sources and Use,* pages 193–195 ▸ 10J, *Harnessing Power,* page 259 **IIIB:** ***National Science Education Standards*** ▸ Grades 5–8, Standard B, *Transfer of Energy,* page 155 ▸ Grades 9–12, Standard B, *Conservation of Energy and the Increase in Disorder,* page 180
IV. Examine Research on Student Learning	**IVA:** ***Benchmarks for Science Literacy*** ▸ 4E, *Energy Forms and Energy Transformation,* page 338 **IVB:** ***Making Sense of Secondary Science: Research Into Children's Ideas*** ▸ Chapter 20, *Energy,* pages 143–147
V. Examine Coherency and Articulation	**V:** ***Atlas of Science Literacy:*** There are no maps for this topic in Volume 1.
VI. Clarify State Standards and District Curriculum	**VIA:** ***State Standards:*** Link Sections I–V to learning goals and information from your state standards or frameworks that are informed by the results of the topic study. **VIB:** ***District Curriculum Guide:*** Link Sections I–V to learning goals and information from your district curriculum guide that are informed by the results of the topic study.
Visit www.curriculumtopicstudy.org for updates or supplementary readings, Web sites, and videos.	

Inquiry and the Nature of Science and Technology

Primary Domain: Science as Inquiry and Technology

Number of CTS Guides: 26

Overview: The primary focus of this section is the habits of mind, abilities, and understandings of science and technology. Abilities developed in this section include inquiry skills and technological design. Understandings include the nature of science and engineering as a discipline, the nature of scientific thought, how science and engineering are conducted, scientists and engineers, and the distinction between science and technology. Ideas developed through the study of the "cross-cutting" topics in this section are meant to be applied to the disciplinary content topics.

Standards- and Research-Based Study of a Curricular Topic

COMMUNICATING WITH DRAWINGS, MAPS, AND PHYSICAL MODELS

Section and Outcome	Selected Sources and Readings for Study and Reflection Read and examine *related parts* of:
I. Identify Adult Content Knowledge	**IA:** ***Science for All Americans*** ▶ Chapter 9, *Shapes*, pages 134–135 ▶ Chapter 11, *Physical Models*, pages 168–170 ▶ Chapter 12, *Communication*, pages 192–193
II. Consider Instructional Implications	**IIA:** ***Benchmarks for Science Literacy*** ▶ 9C, *Shapes* general essay, page 222; grade span essays, pages 223–225 ▶ 11B, *Models* general essay, page 267; grade span essays, pages 269–270 ▶ 12D, *Communication Skills* general essay, page 295 **IIB:** ***National Science Education Standards*** ▶ K–12, *Evidence, Models, and Explanation*, page 117 ▶ Grades K–4, Standard A essay, pages 121–122 ▶ Grades 5–8, Standard A essay, pages 143–145; Vignette *Pendulums*, pages 146–147, and *Solar System*, pages 215–217 ▶ Grades 9–12, Standard A essay, pages 173–175
III. Identify Concepts and Specific Ideas	**IIIA:** ***Benchmarks for Science Literacy*** ▶ 9C, *Shapes*, pages 223–225 ▶ 11B, *Models*, pages 268–270 ▶ 12D, *Communication Skills*, pages 296–297 **IIIB:** ***National Science Education Standards*** ▶ Grades K–4, Standard A, *Communicate Investigations and Explanations*, pages 122–123 ▶ Grades 5–8, Standard A, *Develop Descriptions, Explanations, Predictions, and Models Using Evidence*, page 145; *Communicate Scientific Procedures and Explanations*, page 148 ▶ Grades 9–12, Standard A, *Use Technology and Mathematics to Improve Investigations and Communications*, page 175; *Formulate and Revise Scientific Explanations and Models Using Logic and Evidence*, page 175; *Recognize and Analyze Alternative Explanations and Models*, page 175; *Communicate and Defend a Scientific Argument*, page 176
IV. Examine Research on Student Learning	**IVA:** ***Benchmarks for Science Literacy*** ▶ 11B, *Models*, page 357
V. Examine Coherency and Articulation	**V:** ***Atlas of Science Literacy*** ▶ *Scientific Theories*, pages 20–21 ▶ *Mathematical Models*, pages 28–29 ▶ *Graphic Representation*, pages 114–115; note the conceptual strand *Locating Points*.
VI. Clarify State Standards and District Curriculum	**VIA:** ***State Standards:*** Link Sections I–V to learning goals and information from your state standards or frameworks that are informed by the results of the topic study. **VIB:** ***District Curriculum Guide:*** Link Sections I–V to learning goals and information from your district curriculum guide that are informed by the results of the topic study.
Visit www.curriculumtopicstudy.org for updates or supplementary readings, Web sites, and videos.	

Standards- and Research-Based Study of a Curricular Topic

COMMUNICATION IN SCIENCE

Section and Outcome	Selected Sources and Readings for Study and Reflection Read and examine *related parts* of:
I. Identify Adult Content Knowledge	**IA:** *Science for All Americans* ▸ Chapter 12, *Communication*, pages 192–193
II. Consider Instructional Implications	**IIA:** *Benchmarks for Science Literacy* ▸ 12D, *Communication Skills* general essay, page 295 **IIB:** *National Science Education Standards* ▸ Grades K–4, Standard A essay, pages 121–122 ▸ Grades 5–8, Standard A essay, pages 143–145 ▸ Grades 9–12, Standard A essay, pages 173–175
III. Identify Concepts and Specific Ideas	**IIIA:** *Benchmarks for Science Literacy* ▸ 12D, *Communication Skills*, pages 296–297 **IIIB:** *National Science Education Standards* ▸ Grades K–4, Standard A, *Communicate Investigations and Explanations*, pages 122–123 ▸ Grades 5–8, Standard A, *Communicate Scientific Procedures and Explanations*, page 148 ▸ Grades 9–12, Standard A, *Use Technology and Mathematics to Improve Investigations and Communications*, page 175; *Communicate and Defend a Scientific Argument*, page 176
IV. Examine Research on Student Learning	**IV:** ▸ No research available in *Benchmarks* or Driver.
V. Examine Coherency and Articulation	**V:** *Atlas of Science Literacy* ▸ *Scientific Investigations*, pages 18–19 ▸ *Graphic Representation*, pages 114–115 ▸ *Averages and Comparisons*, pages 122–123
VI. Clarify State Standards and District Curriculum	**VIA:** *State Standards:* Link Sections I–V to learning goals and information from your state standards or frameworks that are informed by the results of the topic study. **VIB:** *District Curriculum Guide:* Link Sections I–V to learning goals and information from your district curriculum guide that are informed by the results of the topic study.
Visit www.curriculumtopicstudy.org for updates or supplementary readings, Web sites, and videos.	

Standards- and Research-Based Study of a Curricular Topic

CONTROLLING VARIABLES

Section and Outcome	Selected Sources and Readings for Study and Reflection Read and examine *related parts* of:	
I. Identify Adult Content Knowledge	**IA:**	***Science for All Americans*** ▸ Chapter 12, *Critical Response Skills,* pages 193–194
II. Consider Instructional Implications	**IIA:**	***Benchmarks for Science Literacy*** ▸ 1B *Scientific Inquiry* general essay, page 9; 6–8 and 9–12 grade span essays, pages 12–13
	IIB:	***National Science Education Standards*** ▸ Grades K–4, Standard A essay, pages 121–122 ▸ Grades 5–8, Standard A essay, pages 143–145, Vignette *Pendulums,* pages 146–147 ▸ Grades 9–12, Standard A essay, pages 173–175
III. Identify Concepts and Specific Ideas	**IIIA:**	***Benchmarks for Science Literacy*** ▸ 1B, *Scientific Inquiry* 6–8 and 9–12, pages 12–13 ▸ 12E, *Critical Response Skills,* page 299
	IIIB:	***National Science Education Standards*** ▸ Grades K–4, Standard A, *Plan and Conduct a Simple Investigation,* page 122 ▸ Grades 5–8, Standard A, *Design and Conduct a Scientific Investigation,* page 145 ▸ Grades 9–12, Standard A, *Design and Conduct Scientific Investigations,* page 175
IV. Examine Research on Student Learning	**IVA:**	***Benchmarks for Science Literacy*** ▸ 1B, *Experimentation,* page 332 ▸ 12E, *Control of Variables,* page 360
V. Examine Coherency and Articulation	**V:**	***Atlas of Science Literacy*** ▸ *Scientific Investigations,* pages 18–19 ▸ *Correlation,* pages 124–125; note the conceptual strand *Control and Conditions.*
VI. Clarify State Standards and District Curriculum	**VIA:**	***State Standards:*** Link Sections I–V to learning goals and information from your state standards or frameworks that are informed by the results of the topic study.
	VIB:	***District Curriculum Guide:*** Link Sections I–V to learning goals and information from your district curriculum guide that are informed by the results of the topic study.
Visit www.curriculumtopicstudy.org for updates or supplementary readings, Web sites, and videos.		

Standards- and Research-Based Study of a Curricular Topic

CORRELATION

Section and Outcome	Selected Sources and Readings for Study and Reflection Read and examine *related parts* of:
I. Identify Adult Content Knowledge	**IA:** *Science for All Americans* ▸ Chapter 9, *Symbolic Relationships,* pages 132–134; *Summarizing Data,* pages 137–139
II. Consider Instructional Implications	**IIA:** *Benchmarks for Science Literacy* ▸ 9B, *Symbolic Relationships* general essay, pages 215–216; grade span essays, pages 217–220 ▸ 9D, *Uncertainty* general essay, page 226; grade span essays, pages 227–230 **IIB:** *National Science Education Standards* ▸ Grades K–4, Standard A essay, pages 121–122 ▸ Grades 5–8, Standard A essay, pages 143–145 ▸ Grades 9–12, Standard A essay, pages 173–175
III. Identify Concepts and Specific Ideas	**IIIA:** *Benchmarks for Science Literacy* ▸ 9B, *Symbolic Relationships,* pages 217–221 ▸ 9D, *Uncertainty,* pages 227–230 **IIIB:** *National Science Education Standards* ▸ Grades K–4, Standard A, *Abilities Necessary to Do Scientific Inquiry,* page 122 ▸ Grades 5–8, *Use Mathematics in All Aspects of Scientific Inquiry,* page 148 ▸ Grades 9–12, Standard A, *Use Technology and Mathematics to Improve Investigations and Communications,* page 175
IV. Examine Research on Student Learning	**IVA:** *Benchmarks for Science Literacy* ▸ 12E, *Interpretation of Data,* page 361
V. Examine Coherency and Articulation	**V:** *Atlas of Science Literacy* ▸ *Correlation,* pages 124–125
VI. Clarify State Standards and District Curriculum	**VIA:** *State Standards:* Link Sections I–V to learning goals and information from your state standards or frameworks that are informed by the results of the topic study. **VIB:** *District Curriculum Guide:* Link Sections I–V to learning goals and information from your district curriculum guide that are informed by the results of the topic study.
Visit www.curriculumtopicstudy.org for updates or supplementary readings, Web sites, and videos.	

Standards- and Research-Based Study of a Curricular Topic
DATA COLLECTION AND ANALYSIS

Section and Outcome	Selected Sources and Readings for Study and Reflection Read and examine *related parts* of:
I. Identify Adult Content Knowledge	**IA:** ***Science for All Americans*** ▸ Chapter 1, *Scientific Inquiry*, pages 3–6 ▸ Chapter 9, *Summarizing Data*, pages 137–139; *Sampling*, pages 139–140
II. Consider Instructional Implications	**IIA:** ***Benchmarks for Science Literacy*** ▸ 1B, *Scientific Inquiry* general essay, page 9; grade span essays, pages 10–13 ▸ 9D, *Uncertainty* general essay, page 226; grade span essays, pages 227–230 **IIB:** ***National Science Education Standards*** ▸ Grades K–4, Standard A essay, pages 121–122; Vignette *Willie the Hamster,* pages 124–125 ▸ Grades 5–8, Standard A essay, pages 143–145; Vignette *Pendulums,* pages 146–147, and *Funny Water,* pages 150–153 ▸ Grades 9–12, Standard A essay, pages 173–175; Vignette *Fossils,* pages 182–183
III. Identify Concepts and Specific Ideas	**IIIA:** ***Benchmarks for Science Literacy*** ▸ 1B, *Scientific Inquiry*, pages 10–13 ▸ 9D, *Uncertainty*, pages 227–230 **IIIB:** ***National Science Education Standards*** ▸ Grades K–4, Standard A, *Employ Simple Equipment and Tools to Gather Data and Extend the Senses, Use Data to Construct a Reasonable Explanation*, page 122 ▸ Grades 5–8, Standard A, *Use Appropriate Tools and Techniques to Gather, Analyze, and Interpret Data*, page 145 ▸ Grades 9–12, Standard A, *Design and Conduct Scientific Investigations, Use Technology and Mathematics to Improve Investigations and Communications*, page 175
IV. Examine Research on Student Learning	**IVA:** ***Benchmarks for Science Literacy*** ▸ 9D, *Summarizing Data*, pages 353–354 ▸ 12E, *Interpretation of Data*, page 361
V. Examine Coherency and Articulation	**V:** ***Atlas of Science Literacy*** ▸ *Evidence and Reasoning in Inquiry*, pages 16–17 ▸ *Scientific Investigations*, pages 18–19 ▸ *Averages and Comparisons*, pages 122–123 ▸ *Correlation*, pages 124–125 ▸ *Statistical Reasoning*, pages 126–127; note the conceptual strand *Sampling*
VI. Clarify State Standards and District Curriculum	**VIA:** ***State Standards:*** Link Sections I–V to learning goals and information from your state standards or frameworks that are informed by the results of the topic study. **VIB:** ***District Curriculum Guide:*** Link Sections I–V to learning goals and information from your district curriculum guide that are informed by the results of the topic study.

Visit www.curriculumtopicstudy.org for updates or supplementary readings, Web sites, and videos.

Standards- and Research-Based Study of a Curricular Topic

EVIDENCE AND EXPLANATION

Section and Outcome	Selected Sources and Readings for Study and Reflection Read and examine *related parts* of:	
I. Identify Adult Content Knowledge	**IA:**	***Science for All Americans*** ▸ Chapter 1, *Scientific Inquiry*, pages 3–7 ▸ Chapter 12, *Communication*, pages 192–193; *Critical Response Skills*, pages 193–194
II. Consider Instructional Implications	**IIA:**	***Benchmarks for Science Literacy*** ▸ 1B, *Scientific Inquiry* general essay, page 9; grade span essays, pages 10–13 ▸ Chapter 12, *Habits of Mind* introductory essay, pages 282–283 12D *Communication Skills* general essay, page 295 12E *Critical Response Skills* general essay, page 298
	IIB:	***National Science Education Standards*** ▸ Grades K–4, Standard A essay, pages 121–122; Vignette *Willie the Hamster*, pages 124–125 ▸ Grades 5–8, Standard A essay, pages 143–145; Vignette *Pendulums*, pages 146–147 and *Funny Water*, pages 150–153 ▸ Grades 9–12, Standard A essay, pages 173–175; Vignette *Fossils*, pages 182–183 ▸ K–12, *Evidence, Models, and Explanation*, page 117
III. Identify Concepts and Specific Ideas	**IIIA:**	***Benchmarks for Science Literacy*** ▸ 1B *Scientific Inquiry*, pages 10–13 ▸ 12D *Communication Skills*, pages 296–297 ▸ 12E *Critical Response Skills*, pages 298–300
	IIIB:	***National Science Education Standards*** ▸ Grades K–4, Standard A, *Use Data to Construct a Reasonable Explanation*, page 122 ▸ Grades 5–8, Standard A, *Develop Descriptions, Explanations, Predictions, and Models Using Evidence* and *Think Critically and Logically to Make the Relationships Between Evidence and Explanations*, pages 145, 148 ▸ Grades 9–12, Standard A, *Formulate and Revise Scientific Explanations and Models Using Logic and Evidence* and *Recognize and Analyze Alternative Explanations and Models*, page 175
IV. Examine Research on Student Learning	**IVA:**	***Benchmarks for Science Literacy*** ▸ 1B, *Theory (Explanation) and Evidence*, page 332 ▸ *Theory and Evidence*, page 361; *Interpretation of Data*, page 361; *Inadequacies in Arguments*, page 361
V. Examine Coherency and Articulation	**V:**	***Atlas of Science Literacy*** ▸ *Evidence and Reasoning in Inquiry*, pages 16–17 ▸ *Scientific Investigations*, pages 18–19 ▸ *Scientific Theories*, pages 20–21 ▸ *Statistical Reasoning*, pages 126–127
VI. Clarify State Standards and District Curriculum	**VIA:**	**State Standards:** Link Sections I–V to learning goals and information from your state standards or frameworks that are informed by the results of the topic study.
	VIB:	**District Curriculum Guide:** Link Sections I–V to learning goals and information from your district curriculum guide that are informed by the results of the topic study.
Visit www.curriculumtopicstudy.org for updates or supplementary readings, Web sites, and videos.		

Standards- and Research-Based Study of a Curricular Topic

EXPERIMENTAL DESIGN

Section and Outcome	Selected Sources and Readings for Study and Reflection Read and examine *related parts* of:
I. Identify Adult Content Knowledge	**IA:** *Science for All Americans* ▶ Chapter 1, *Scientific Inquiry*, pages 3–7
II. Consider Instructional Implications	**IIA:** *Benchmarks for Science Literacy* ▶ 1B, *Scientific Inquiry* general essay, page 9; grade span essays, pages 10–13 **IIB:** *National Science Education Standards* ▶ Grades K–4, Standard A essay, pages 121–122; Vignette *Willie the Hamster*, pages 124–125 ▶ Grades 5–8, Standard A essay, pages 143–145; Vignette *Pendulums*, pages 146–147 ▶ Grades 9–12, Standard A essay, pages 173–175
III. Identify Concepts and Specific Ideas	**IIIA:** *Benchmarks for Science Literacy* ▶ 1B, *Scientific Inquiry*, pages 10–13 **IIIB:** *National Science Education Standards* ▶ Grades K–4, Standard A, *Abilities Necessary to Do Scientific Inquiry*, pages 122–123 ▶ Grades 5–8, Standard A, *Abilities Necessary to Do Scientific Inquiry*, pages 145, 148 ▶ Grades 9–12, Standard A, *Abilities Necessary to Do Scientific Inquiry*, pages 175–176
IV. Examine Research on Student Learning	**IVA:** *Benchmarks for Science Literacy* ▶ 1B, *Experimentation*, page 332 ▶ 12E, *Control of Variables*, page 360
V. Examine Coherency and Articulation	**V:** *Atlas of Science Literacy* ▶ *Scientific Investigations*, pages 18–19
VI. Clarify State Standards and District Curriculum	**VIA:** *State Standards:* Link Sections I–V to learning goals and information from your state standards or frameworks that are informed by the results of the topic study. **VIB:** *District Curriculum Guide:* Link Sections I–V to learning goals and information from your district curriculum guide that are informed by the results of the topic study.
Visit www.curriculumtopicstudy.org for updates or supplementary readings, Web sites, and videos.	

Standards- and Research-Based Study of a Curricular Topic

GRAPHS AND GRAPHING

Section and Outcome	Selected Sources and Readings for Study and Reflection Read and examine *related parts* of:
I. Identify Adult Content Knowledge	**IA:** *Science for All Americans* ▸ Chapter 9, *Symbolic Relationships*, pages 132–134; *Shapes*, pages 134–135 ▸ Chapter 12, *Communication*, pages 192–193
II. Consider Instructional Implications	**IIA:** *Benchmarks for Science Literacy* ▸ 9B, *Symbolic Relationships* general essay, pages 215–216; grade span essays, pages 217–220 ▸ 9C, *Shapes* general essay, page 222; grade span essays, pages 223–225 ▸ 12D, *Communication Skills* general essay, page 295 **IIB:** *National Science Education Standards* ▸ Grades K–4, Standard A essay, pages 121–122 ▸ Grades 5–8, Standard A essay, pages 143–145; Vignette *Pendulums*, pages 146–147, and *The Solar System*, pages 215–217 ▸ Grades 9–12, Standard A essay, pages 173–175; Vignette *Fossils*, pages 182–183
III. Identify Concepts and Specific Ideas	**IIIA:** *Benchmarks for Science Literacy* ▸ 9B, *Symbolic Relationships,* pages 217–221 ▸ 9C, *Shapes,* pages 223–225 ▸ 12D, *Communication Skills,* pages 296–297 **IIIB:** *National Science Education Standards* ▸ Grades K–4, Standard A, *Abilities Necessary to Do Scientific Inquiry,* pages 122–123 ▸ Grades 5–8, Standard A, *Abilities Necessary to Do Scientific Inquiry,* pages 145, 148 ▸ Grades 9–12, Standard A, *Abilities Necessary to Do Scientific Inquiry,* pages 175–176
IV. Examine Research on Student Learning	**IVA:** *Benchmarks for Science Literacy* ▸ 9B, *Graphs,* page 351
V. Examine Coherency and Articulation	**V:** *Atlas of Science Literacy* ▸ *Graphic Representation,* pages 114–115 ▸ *Symbolic Representation,* pages 116–117 ▸ *Describing Change,* pages 120–121
VI. Clarify State Standards and District Curriculum	**VIA:** *State Standards:* Link Sections I–V to learning goals and information from your state standards or frameworks that are informed by the results of the topic study. **VIB:** *District Curriculum Guide:* Link Sections I–V to learning goals and information from your district curriculum guide that are informed by the results of the topic study.

Visit www.curriculumtopicstudy.org for updates or supplementary readings, Web sites, and videos.

Standards- and Research-Based Study of a Curricular Topic

IDENTIFYING AND AVOIDING BIAS

Section and Outcome	Selected Sources and Readings for Study and Reflection Read and examine *related parts* of:
I. Identify Adult Content Knowledge	**IA:** *Science for All Americans* ▸ Chapter 1, *Scientists Try to Identify and Avoid Bias*, pages 6–7 ▸ Chapter 9, *Sampling*, pages 139–140
II. Consider Instructional Implications	**IIA:** *Benchmarks for Science Literacy* ▸ 1B, *Scientific Inquiry* general essay, page 9; grade span essays, pages 10–13 **IIB:** *National Science Education Standards* ▸ Grades K–4, Standard A essay, pages 121–122 ▸ Grades 5–8, Standard A essay, pages 143–145 ▸ Grades 9–12, Standard A essay, pages 173–175
III. Identify Concepts and Specific Ideas	**IIIA:** *Benchmarks for Science Literacy* ▸ 1B, *Scientific Inquiry*, pages 10–13 **IIIB:** *National Science Education Standards* ▸ Grades K–4, Standard A, *Understandings About Scientific Inquiry*, page 123 ▸ Grades 5–8, Standard A, *Understandings About Scientific Inquiry*, page 148 ▸ Grades 9–12 Standard A, *Understandings About Scientific Inquiry*, page 176
IV. Examine Research on Student Learning	**IVA:** *Benchmarks for Science Literacy* ▸ 1B, *Scientific Inquiry*, pages 332–333
V. Examine Coherency and Articulation	**V:** *Atlas of Science Literacy* ▸ *Avoiding Bias in Science*, pages 22–23
VI. Clarify State Standards and District Curriculum	**VIA:** *State Standards:* Link Sections I–V to learning goals and information from your state standards or frameworks that are informed by the results of the topic study. **VIB:** *District Curriculum Guide:* Link Sections I–V to learning goals and information from your district curriculum guide that are informed by the results of the topic study.
Visit www.curriculumtopicstudy.org for updates or supplementary readings, Web sites, and videos.	

Standards- and Research-Based Study of a Curricular Topic

INQUIRY SKILLS AND DISPOSITIONS

Section and Outcome	Selected Sources and Readings for Study and Reflection Read and examine *related parts* of:
I. Identify Adult Content Knowledge	**IA:** ***Science for All Americans*** ▸ Chapter 1, *Scientific Inquiry,* pages 3–7 ▸ Chapter 12, *Habits of Mind,* pages 183–194
II. Consider Instructional Implications	**IIA:** ***Benchmarks for Science Literacy*** ▸ 1B, *Scientific Inquiry* general essay, page 9; grade span essays, pages 10–13 ▸ Chapter 12, *Habits of Mind* general essay, pages 281–283; general and grade span essays, pages 284–298 **IIB:** ***National Science Education Standards*** ▸ Grades K–4, Standard A essay, pages 121–122; Vignette *Willie the Hamster,* pages 124–125 ▸ Grades 5–8, Standard A essay, pages 143–145; Vignette *Pendulums,* pages 146–147 ▸ Grades 9–12, Standard A essay, pages 173–175; Vignette *Photosynthesis,* pages 194–196
III. Identify Concepts and Specific Ideas	**IIIA:** ***Benchmarks for Science Literacy*** ▸ 1B, *Scientific Inquiry,* pages 10–13 ▸ Chapter 12, *Habits of Mind,* pages 285–300 **IIIB:** ***National Science Education Standards*** ▸ Grades K–4, Standard A, *Abilities Necessary to Do Scientific Inquiry,* pages 122–123 ▸ Grades 5–8, Standard A, *Abilities Necessary to Do Scientific Inquiry,* pages 145, 148 ▸ Grades 9–12, Standard A, *Abilities Necessary to Do Scientific Inquiry,* pages 175–176 ▸ *Changing Emphases to Promote Inquiry,* page 113
IV. Examine Research on Student Learning	**IVA:** ***Benchmarks for Science Literacy*** ▸ 1B, *Experimentation,* page 332; *Theory (Explanation) and Evidence,* page 332 ▸ 12C, *Manipulation and Observation,* page 360 ▸ 12E, *Control of Variables,* page 360; *Theory and Evidence,* page 361; *Interpretation of Data,* page 361; *Inadequacies in Arguments,* page 361
V. Examine Coherency and Articulation	**V:** ***Atlas of Science Literacy*** ▸ *Evidence and Reasoning in Inquiry,* pages 16–17 ▸ *Scientific Investigations,* pages 18–19 ▸ *Scientific Theories,* pages 20–21
VI. Clarify State Standards and District Curriculum	**VIA:** ***State Standards:*** Link Sections I–V to learning goals and information from your state standards or frameworks that are informed by the results of the topic study. **VIB:** ***District Curriculum Guide:*** Link Sections I–V to learning goals and information from your district curriculum guide that are informed by the results of the topic study.

Visit www.curriculumtopicstudy.org for updates or supplementary readings, Web sites, and videos.

Standards- and Research-Based Study of a Curricular Topic

MATHEMATICAL MODELING

Section and Outcome	Selected Sources and Readings for Study and Reflection Read and examine *related parts* of:
I. Identify Adult Content Knowledge	**IA:** *Science for All Americans* ▶ Chapter 11, *Mathematical Models*, pages 171–172
II. Consider Instructional Implications	**IIA:** *Benchmarks for Science Literacy* ▶ 11B, *Models* general essay, page 267; grade span essays, pages 268–270 **IIB:** *National Science Education Standards* ▶ Grades K–4, Standard A essay, pages 121–122 ▶ Grades 5–8, Standard A essay, pages 143–145 ▶ Grades 9–12, Standard A essay, pages 173–175
III. Identify Concepts and Specific Ideas	**IIIA:** *Benchmarks for Science Literacy* ▶ 11B, *Models*, pages 268–270 **IIIB:** *National Science Education Standards* ▶ Grades K–4, Standard A, *Abilities Necessary to Do Scientific Inquiry*, page 122; *Understandings About Scientific Inquiry*, page 123 ▶ Grades 5–8, *Develop Descriptions, Explanations, Predictions, and Models Using Evidence*, page 145; *Use Mathematics in All Aspects of Scientific Inquiry*, page 148; *Understandings About Scientific Inquiry*, page 148 ▶ Grades 9–12, Standard A, *Use Technology and Mathematics to Improve Investigations and Communications*, page 175; *Formulate and Revise Scientific Explanations and Models Using Logic and Evidence*, page 175; *Recognize and Analyze Alternative Explanations and Models*, page 175; *Understandings About Scientific Inquiry*, page 176
IV. Examine Research on Student Learning	**IVA:** *Benchmarks for Science Literacy* ▶ 11B, *Models*, page 357
V. Examine Coherency and Articulation	**V:** *Atlas of Science Literacy* ▶ *Mathematical Models*, pages 28–29
VI. Clarify State Standards and District Curriculum	**VIA:** *State Standards:* Link Sections I–V to learning goals and information from your state standards or frameworks that are informed by the results of the topic study. **VIB:** *District Curriculum Guide:* Link Sections I–V to learning goals and information from your district curriculum guide that are informed by the results of the topic study.
Visit www.curriculumtopicstudy.org for updates or supplementary readings, Web sites, and videos.	

Standards- and Research-Based Study of a Curricular Topic

MATHEMATICS IN SCIENCE AND TECHNOLOGY

Section and Outcome	Selected Sources and Readings for Study and Reflection Read and examine *related parts* of:
I. Identify Adult Content Knowledge	**IA:** *Science for All Americans* ▸ Chapter 2, *Mathematics, Science, and Technology*, pages 17–18
II. Consider Instructional Implications	**IIA** *Benchmarks for Science Literacy* ▸ 2B, *Mathematics, Science, and Technology* general essay, page 30; grade span essays, pages 31–33 **IIB:** *National Science Education Standards* ▸ Grades K–4, Standard A essay, pages 121–122 ▸ Grades 5–8, Standard A essay, pages 143–145; Vignette *Solar System*, pages 215–217 ▸ Grades 9–12, Standard A essay, pages 173–175
III. Identify Concepts and Specific Ideas	**IIIA:** *Benchmarks for Science Literacy* ▸ 2B, *Mathematics, Science, and Technology*, pages 31–33 **IIIB:** *National Science Education Standards* ▸ Grades K–4, Standard A, *Abilities Necessary to Do Scientific Inquiry*, page 122; *Understandings About Scientific Inquiry*, page 123 ▸ Grades 5–8, *Use Mathematics in All Aspects of Scientific Inquiry*, page 148; *Understandings About Scientific Inquiry*, page 148 ▸ Grades 9–12, Standard A, *Use Technology and Mathematics to Improve Investigations and Communications*, page 175; *Understandings About Scientific Inquiry*, page 176
IV. Examine Research on Student Learning	**IVA:** *Benchmarks for Science Literacy* ▸ 2B, *Mathematics, Science, and Technology*, page 334
V. Examine Coherency and Articulation	**V:** *Atlas of Science Literacy* ▸ *Designed Systems*, pages 34–35
VI. Clarify State Standards and District Curriculum	**VIA:** *State Standards:* Link Sections I–V to learning goals and information from your state standards or frameworks that are informed by the results of the topic study. **VIB:** *District Curriculum Guide:* Link Sections I–V to learning goals and information from your district curriculum guide that are informed by the results of the topic study.
Visit www.curriculumtopicstudy.org for updates or supplementary readings, Web sites, and videos.	

Standards- and Research-Based Study of a Curricular Topic

THE NATURE OF SCIENTIFIC THOUGHT AND DEVELOPMENT

Section and Outcome	Selected Sources and Readings for Study and Reflection Read and examine *related parts* of:
I. Identify Adult Content Knowledge	**IA:** *Science for All Americans* ▸ Chapter 1, *The Scientific World View*, pages 2–3
II. Consider Instructional Implications	**IIA:** *Benchmarks for Science Literacy* ▸ 1A, *The Scientific World View* general essay, page 5; grade span essays, pages 6–8 **IIB:** *National Science Education Standards* ▸ Grades K–4, Standard G essay, page 141 ▸ Grades 5–8, Standard G essay, page 170 ▸ Grades 9–12, Standard G essay, page 200; Vignette *An Analysis of a Scientific Inquiry*, pages 202–203
III. Identify Concepts and Specific Ideas	**IIIA:** *Benchmarks for Science Literacy* ▸ 1A, *The Scientific World View*, pages 6–8 **IIIB:** *National Science Education Standards* ▸ Grades 5–8, Standard G, *Nature of Science*, page 171 ▸ Grades 9–12, Standard G, *Nature of Scientific Knowledge*, page 201
IV. Examine Research on Student Learning	**IVA:** *Benchmarks for Science Literacy* ▸ 1, *Nature of Science*, pages 331–332 ▸ 1B, *Nature of Knowledge*, page 333
V. Examine Coherency and Articulation	**V:** *Atlas of Science Literacy* ▸ *Evidence and Reasoning in Inquiry*, pages 16–17 ▸ *Scientific Investigations*, pages 18–19 ▸ *Scientific Theories*, pages 20–21 ▸ *Avoiding Bias in Science*, pages 22–23
VI. Clarify State Standards and District Curriculum	**VIA:** *State Standards:* Link Sections I–V to learning goals and information from your state standards or frameworks that are informed by the results of the topic study. **VIB:** *District Curriculum Guide:* Link Sections I–V to learning goals and information from your district curriculum guide that are informed by the results of the topic study.
Visit www.curriculumtopicstudy.org for updates or supplementary readings, Web sites, and videos.	

Standards- and Research-Based Study of a Curricular Topic

OBSERVATION, MEASUREMENT, AND TOOLS

Section and Outcome	Selected Sources and Readings for Study and Reflection Read and examine *related parts* of:
I. Identify Adult Content Knowledge	**IA:** **Science for All Americans** ▸ Chapter 12, *Manipulation and Observation*, pages 191–192
II. Consider Instructional Implications	**IIA:** **Benchmarks for Science Literacy** ▸ 12C, *Manipulation and Observation* general essay, page 292 **IIB:** **National Science Education Standards** ▸ Grades K–4, Standard A essay, pages 121–122; Vignette *Science Olympiad,* pages 39–41 ▸ Grades 5–8, Standard A essay, pages 143–145; Vignette *Pendulums,* pages 146–147 ▸ Grades 9–12, Standard A essay, pages 173–175
III. Identify Concepts and Specific Ideas	**IIIA:** **Benchmarks for Science Literacy** ▸ 12C *Manipulation and Observation*, pages 293–294 **IIIB:** **National Science Education Standards** ▸ Grades K–4, Standard A, *Abilities Necessary to Do Scientific Inquiry,* pages 122–123 ▸ Grades 5–8, Standard A, *Abilities Necessary to Do Scientific Inquiry,* pages 145, 148 ▸ Grades 9–12, Standard A, *Abilities Necessary to Do Scientific Inquiry,* pages 175–176
IV. Examine Research on Student Learning	**IVA:** **Benchmarks for Science Literacy** ▸ 12C, *Manipulation and Observation*, page 360
V. Examine Coherency and Articulation	**V:** **Atlas of Science Literacy** ▸ *Evidence and Reasoning in Inquiry,* pages 16–17; note the *Observations and Evidence* strand.
VI. Clarify State Standards and District Curriculum	**VIA:** **State Standards:** Link Sections I–V to learning goals and information from your state standards or frameworks that are informed by the results of the topic study. **VIB:** **District Curriculum Guide:** Link Sections I–V to learning goals and information from your district curriculum guide that are informed by the results of the topic study.
	Visit www.curriculumtopicstudy.org for updates or supplementary readings, Web sites, and videos.

Standards- and Research-Based Study of a Curricular Topic

SCIENCE AND TECHNOLOGY

Section and Outcome	Selected Sources and Readings for Study and Reflection Read and examine *related parts* of:
I. Identify Adult Content Knowledge	**IA:** *Science for All Americans* ▶ Chapter 3, *Technology and Science*, pages 26–28
II. Consider Instructional Implications	**IIA:** *Benchmarks for Science Literacy* ▶ 3A, *Technology and Science* general essay, page 43; grade span essays, pages 44–47 **IIB:** *National Science Education Standards* ▶ Grades K–4, Standard E essay, pages 135, 137 ▶ Grades 5–8, Standard E essay, pages 161, 165 ▶ Grades 9–12, Standard E essay, pages 190–192
III. Identify Concepts and Specific Ideas	**IIIA:** *Benchmarks for Science Literacy* ▶ 3A, *Technology and Science*, pages 44–47 **IIIB:** *National Science Education Standards* ▶ Grades K–4, Standard E, *Understandings About Science and Technology*, page 138 ▶ Grades 5–8, Standard E, *Understandings About Science and Technology*, page 166 ▶ Grades 9–12, Standard E, *Understandings About Science and Technology*, pages 192–193
IV. Examine Research on Student Learning	**IVA:** *Benchmarks for Science Literacy* ▶ 3A, *Technology and Science*, page 334
V. Examine Coherency and Articulation	**V:** *Atlas of Science Literacy* ▶ *Design Constraints*, pages 32–33 ▶ *Interaction of Technology and Society*, pages 36–37
VI. Clarify State Standards and District Curriculum	**VIA:** *State Standards:* Link Sections I–V to learning goals and information from your state standards or frameworks that are informed by the results of the topic study. **VIB:** *District Curriculum Guide:* Link Sections I–V to learning goals and information from your district curriculum guide that are informed by the results of the topic study.
Visit www.curriculumtopicstudy.org for updates or supplementary readings, Web sites, and videos.	

Standards- and Research-Based Study of a Curricular Topic

SCIENCE AS A HUMAN ENDEAVOR

Section and Outcome	Selected Sources and Readings for Study and Reflection Read and examine *related parts* of:
I. Identify Adult Content Knowledge	**IA:** *Science for All Americans* ▸ Chapter 1, *The Scientific Enterprise*, pages 8–12 **IB:** *Science Matters: Achieving Scientific Literacy* ▸ Epilogue, *The Role of Science*, pages 277–278
II. Consider Instructional Implications	**IIA:** *Benchmarks for Science Literacy* ▸ 1C, *The Scientific Enterprise* general essay, page 14; grade span essays, pages 15–19 **IIB:** *National Science Education Standards* ▸ Grades K–4, Standard G essay, page 141 ▸ Grades 5–8, Standard G essay, page 170 ▸ Grades 9–12, Standard G essay, page 200; Vignette *An Analysis of a Scientific Inquiry*, pages 202–203
III. Identify Concepts and Specific Ideas	**IIIA:** *Benchmarks for Science Literacy* ▸ 1A, *The Scientific Enterprise*, pages 15–19 **IIIB:** *National Science Education Standards* ▸ Grades K–4, Standard G, *Science as a Human Endeavor,* page 141 ▸ Grades 5–8, Standard G, *Nature of Science,* page 171 ▸ Grades 9–12 Standard G, *Nature of Scientific Knowledge,* page 201
IV. Examine Research on Student Learning	**IVA:** *Benchmarks for Science Literacy* ▸ 1C, *The Scientific Enterprise*, page 333
V. Examine Coherency and Articulation	**V:** *Atlas of Science Literacy* ▸ *Scientific Investigations*, pages 18–19 ▸ *Avoiding Bias in Science*, pages 22–23
VI. Clarify State Standards and District Curriculum	**VIA:** *State Standards:* Link Sections I–V to learning goals and information from your state standards or frameworks that are informed by the results of the topic study. **VIB:** *District Curriculum Guide:* Link Sections I–V to learning goals and information from your district curriculum guide that are informed by the results of the topic study.
Visit www.curriculumtopicstudy.org for updates or supplementary readings, Web sites, and videos.	

Standards- and Research-Based Study of a Curricular Topic

SCIENCE AS INQUIRY

Section and Outcome	Selected Sources and Readings for Study and Reflection Read and examine *related parts* of:
I. Identify Adult Content Knowledge	**IA:** ***Science for All Americans*** ▸ Chapter 1, *The Scientific World View,* pages 2–3; *Scientific Inquiry,* pages 3–7 ▸ Chapter 12, *Critical Response Skills,* pages 193–194
II. Consider Instructional Implications	**IIA:** ***Benchmarks for Science Literacy*** ▸ 1A, *The Scientific World View* general essay, page 5; grade span essays, pages 6–8 ▸ 1B, *Scientific Inquiry* general essay, page 9; grade span essays, pages 10–13 ▸ Chapter 12, *Habits of Mind* overview essay, pages 281–283; general and grade span essays, pages 284–298 **IIB:** ***National Science Education Standards*** ▸ Grades K–4, Standard A essay, pages 121–122; Vignette *Willie the Hamster,* pages 124–125 ▸ Grades 5–8, Standard A essay, pages 143–145; Vignette *Pendulums,* pages 146–147 ▸ Grades 9–12, Standard A essay, pages 173–175; Vignette *Photosynthesis,* pages 194–196
III. Identify Concepts and Specific Ideas	**IIIA:** ***Benchmarks for Science Literacy*** ▸ 1A, *The Scientific World View,* pages 6–8 ▸ 1B, *Scientific Inquiry,* pages 10–13 ▸ Chapter 12, *Habits of Mind,* pages 285–300 **IIIB:** ***National Science Education Standards*** ▸ Grades K–4, Standard A, *Abilities Necessary to Do Scientific Inquiry,* pages 122–123; *Understanding About Scientific Inquiry,* page 123 ▸ Grades 5–8, Standard A, *Abilities Necessary to Do Scientific Inquiry,* pages 145, 148; *Understanding About Scientific Inquiry,* page 148 ▸ Grades 9–12, Standard A, *Abilities Necessary to Do Scientific Inquiry,* pages 175–176; *Understanding About Scientific Inquiry,* page 176
IV. Examine Research on Student Learning	**IVA:** ***Benchmarks for Science Literacy*** ▸ 1A, *The Scientific World View,* page 332 ▸ 1B, *Scientific Inquiry,* pages 332–333 ▸ 12C, *Manipulation and Observation,* page 360 ▸ 12E, *Critical Response Skills,* pages 360–361
V. Examine Coherency and Articulation	**V:** ***Atlas of Science Literacy*** ▸ *Evidence and Reasoning in Inquiry,* pages 16–17 ▸ *Scientific Investigations,* pages 18–19 ▸ *Scientific Theories,* pages 20–21 ▸ *Avoiding Bias in Science,* pages 22–23
VI. Clarify State Standards and District Curriculum	**VIA:** ***State Standards:*** Link Sections I–V to learning goals and information from your state standards or frameworks that are informed by the results of the topic study. **VIB** ***District Curriculum Guide:*** Link Sections I–V to learning goals and information from your district curriculum guide that are informed by the results of the topic study.
	Visit www.curriculumtopicstudy.org for updates or supplementary readings, Web sites, and videos.

Standards- and Research-Based Study of a Curricular Topic

SCIENTIFIC AND LOGICAL REASONING

Section and Outcome	Selected Sources and Readings for Study and Reflection Read and examine *related parts* of:
I. Identify Adult Content Knowledge	**IA:** *Science for All Americans* ▸ Chapter 9, *Reasoning,* pages 140–143 ▸ Chapter 12, *Critical Response Skills,* pages 193–194
II. Consider Instructional Implications	**IIA:** *Benchmarks for Science Literacy* ▸ 9E, *Reasoning* general essay, page 231; grade span essays, pages 232–234 ▸ 12E, *Critical Response Skills* general essay, page 298 **IIB:** *National Science Education Standards* ▸ Grades K–4, Standard A essay, pages 121–122 ▸ Grades 5–8, Standard A essay, pages 143–145 ▸ Grades 9–12, Standard A essay, pages 173–175
III. Identify Concepts and Specific Ideas	**IIIA:** *Benchmarks for Science Literacy* ▸ 9E, *Reasoning,* pages 232–234 ▸ 12E, *Critical Response Skills,* pages 298–300 **IIIB:** *National Science Education Standards* ▸ Grades K–4, Standard A, *Use Data to Construct a Reasonable Explanation,* page 122 ▸ Grades 5–8, Standard A, *Think Critically and Logically to Make the Relationship Between Evidence and Explanations,* pages 145; *Recognize and Analyze Alternative Explanations and Predictions,* page 148 ▸ Grades 9–12, Standard A, *Formulate and Revise Scientific Explanations and Models Using Logic and Evidence* and *Recognize and Analyze Alternative Explanations and Models,* pages 175–176
IV. Examine Research on Student Learning	**IVA:** *Benchmarks for Science Literacy* ▸ 1B, *Theory (Explanation) and Evidence,* page 332 ▸ 12B, *Proportional Reasoning,* page 360 ▸ 12E, *Theory and Evidence,* page 361; *Interpretation of Data,* page 361; *Inadequacies in Arguments,* page 361
V. Examine Coherency and Articulation	**V:** *Atlas of Science Literacy* ▸ *Evidence and Reasoning in Inquiry,* pages 16–17 ▸ *Scientific Theories,* pages 20–21 ▸ *Statistical Reasoning,* pages 126–127
VI. Clarify State Standards and District Curriculum	**VIA:** *State Standards:* Link Sections I–V to learning goals and information from your state standards or frameworks that are informed by the results of the topic study. **VIB:** *District Curriculum Guide:* Link Sections I–V to learning goals and information from your district curriculum guide that are informed by the results of the topic study.
Visit www.curriculumtopicstudy.org for updates or supplementary readings, Web sites, and videos.	

Standards- and Research-Based Study of a Curricular Topic

SCIENTIFIC SAMPLING

Section and Outcome	Selected Sources and Readings for Study and Reflection Read and examine *related parts* of:
I. Identify Adult Content Knowledge	**IA:** **Science for All Americans** ▶ Chapter 9, *Sampling,* pages 139–140
II. Consider Instructional Implications	**IIA:** **Benchmarks for Science Literacy** ▶ 9D, *Uncertainty* general essay, page 226; grade span essays, pages 227–230 **IIB:** **National Science Education Standards** ▶ Grades K–4, Standard A essay, pages 121–122 ▶ Grades 5–8, Standard A essay, pages 143–145 ▶ Grades 9–12, Standard A essay, pages 173–175
III. Identify Concepts and Specific Ideas	**IIIA:** **Benchmarks for Science Literacy** ▶ 9D, *Uncertainty,* pages 227–230 **IIIB:** **National Science Education Standards** ▶ Grades K–4, Standard A, *Abilities Necessary to Do Scientific Inquiry,* page 122 ▶ Grades 5–8, Standard A, *Use Mathematics in All Aspects of Scientific Inquiry,* page 148 ▶ Grades 9–12, Standard A, *Use Technology and Mathematics to Improve Investigations and Communications,* page 175
IV. Examine Research on Student Learning	**IVA:** **Benchmarks for Science Literacy** ▶ 9D, *Probability,* page 353 ▶ 12E, *Inadequacies in Arguments,* page 361
V. Examine Coherency and Articulation	**V:** **Atlas of Science Literacy** ▶ *Statistical Reasoning,* pages 126–127; note the conceptual strand *Sampling.*
VI. Clarify State Standards and District Curriculum	**VIA:** **State Standards:** Link Sections I–V to learning goals and information from your state standards or frameworks that are informed by the results of the topic study. **VIB:** **District Curriculum Guide:** Link Sections I–V to learning goals and information from your district curriculum guide that are informed by the results of the topic study.
Visit www.curriculumtopicstudy.org for updates or supplementary readings, Web sites, and videos.	

Standards- and Research-Based Study of a Curricular Topic

SCIENTIFIC VALUES AND ATTITUDES

Section and Outcome	Selected Sources and Readings for Study and Reflection Read and examine *related parts* of:
I. Identify Adult Content Knowledge	**IA:** ***Science for All Americans*** ▸ Chapter 12, *Values and Attitudes,* pages 184–187
II. Consider Instructional Implications	**IIA:** ***Benchmarks for Science Literacy*** ▸ 12A, *Values and Attitudes* general essay, page 284; grade span essays, pages 285–287 **IIB:** ***National Science Education Standards*** ▸ Grades K–4, Standard A essay, pages 121–122 ▸ Grades 5–8, Standard A essay, pages 143–145 ▸ Grades 9–12, Standard A essay, pages 173–175
III. Identify Concepts and Specific Ideas	**IIIA:** ***Benchmarks for Science Literacy*** ▸ 12A, *Values and Attitudes,* pages 285–287 **IIIB:** ***National Science Education Standards*** ▸ Grades K–4, Standard A, *Understanding About Scientific Inquiry,* page 123 ▸ Grades 5–8, Standard A, *Understanding About Scientific Inquiry,* page 148 ▸ Grades 9–12, Standard A, *Understanding About Scientific Inquiry,* page 176
IV. Examine Research on Student Learning	**IV:** No research available in *Benchmarks* or Driver.
V. Examine Coherency and Articulation	**V:** ***Atlas of Science Literacy*** ▸ *Evidence and Reasoning in Inquiry,* pages 16–17 ▸ *Scientific Theories,* pages 20–21
VI. Clarify State Standards and District Curriculum	**VIA:** *State Standards:* Link Sections I–V to learning goals and information from your state standards or frameworks that are informed by the results of the topic study. **VIB:** *District Curriculum Guide:* Link Sections I–V to learning goals and information from your district curriculum guide that are informed by the results of the topic study.
Visit www.curriculumtopicstudy.org for updates or supplementary readings, Web sites, and videos.	

Standards- and Research-Based Study of a Curricular Topic

SUMMARIZING AND REPRESENTING DATA

Section and Outcome	Selected Sources and Readings for Study and Reflection Read and examine *related parts* of:
I. Identify Adult Content Knowledge	**IA:** *Science for All Americans* ▸ Chapter 9, *Summarizing Data*, pages 137–139 ▸ Chapter 12, *Communication*, pages 192–193
II. Consider Instructional Implications	**IIA:** *Benchmarks for Science Literacy* ▸ 1B, *Scientific Inquiry* general essay, page 9; grade span essays, pages 10–13 ▸ 9B, *Symbolic Relationships* general essay, pages 215–216; grade span essays, pages 217–220 ▸ 9D, *Uncertainty* general essay, page 226; grade span essays, pages 227–230 ▸ 12D, *Communication Skills* general essay, page 295 **IIB:** *National Science Education Standards* ▸ Grades K–4, Standard A essay, pages 121–122 ▸ Grades 5–8, Standard A essay, pages 143–145; Vignette *Pendulums*, pages 146–147 ▸ Grades 9–12, Standard A essay, pages 173–175; Vignette *Fossils*, pages 182–183
III. Identify Concepts and Specific Ideas	**IIIA:** *Benchmarks for Science Literacy* ▸ 1B, *Scientific Inquiry*, pages 10–13 ▸ 9B, *Symbolic Relationships*, pages 217–221 ▸ 9D, *Uncertainty*, pages 227–230 ▸ 12D, *Communication Skills*, pages 296–297 **IIIB:** *National Science Education Standards* ▸ Grades K–4, Standard A, *Use Data to Construct a Reasonable Explanation*, page 122; *Communicate Investigations and Explanations*, pages 122–123 ▸ Grades 5–8, Standard A, *Use Appropriate Tools and Techniques to Gather, Analyze, and Interpret Data*, page 145; *Think Critically and Logically to Make the Relationships Between Evidence and Explanation*, pages 145, 148; *Communicate Scientific Procedures and Explanations*, page 148; *Use Mathematics in All Aspects of Scientific Inquiry*, page 148 ▸ Grades 9–12, Standard A, *Use Technology and Mathematics to Improve Investigations and Communications*, page 175; *Communicate and Defend a Scientific Argument*, page 176
IV. Examine Research on Student Learning	**IVA:** *Benchmarks for Science Literacy* ▸ 9B, *Graphs*, page 351 ▸ 9D, *Summarizing Data*, pages 353–354 ▸ 12E, *Interpretation of Data*, page 361
V. Examine Coherency and Articulation	**V:** *Atlas of Science Literacy* ▸ *Graphic Representation*, pages 114–115 ▸ *Symbolic Representation*, pages 116–117 ▸ *Describing Change*, pages 120–121 ▸ *Averages and Comparisons*, pages 122–123
VI. Clarify State Standards and District Curriculum	**VIA:** *State Standards:* Link Sections I–V to learning goals and information from your state standards or frameworks that are informed by the results of the topic study. **VIB:** *District Curriculum Guide:* Link Sections I–V to learning goals and information from your district curriculum guide that are informed by the results of the topic study.

Visit www.curriculumtopicstudy.org for updates or supplementary readings, Web sites, and videos.

Standards- and Research-Based Study of a Curricular Topic

TECHNOLOGICAL DESIGN

Section and Outcome	Selected Sources and Readings for Study and Reflection Read and examine *related parts* of:
I. Identify Adult Content Knowledge	**IA:** ***Science for All Americans*** ▸ Chapter 3, *Design and Systems*, pages 28–32
II. Consider Instructional Implications	**IIA:** ***Benchmarks for Science Literacy*** ▸ 3B, *Design and Systems* general essay, page 48; grade span essays, pages 49–52 ▸ 12C, *Manipulation and Observation* general essay, page 292 **IIB:** ***National Science Education Standards*** ▸ Grades K–4, Standard E essay, pages 135, 137; Vignette *Weather Instruments*, page 136 ▸ Grades 5–8, Standard E essay, pages 161, 165; Vignette *The Egg Drop*, pages 162–164 ▸ Grades 9–12, Standard E essay, pages 190–192
III. Identify Concepts and Specific Ideas	**IIIA:** ***Benchmarks for Science Literacy*** ▸ 3B, *Design and Systems*, pages 49–52 ▸ 12C, *Manipulation and Observation*, pages 293–294 **IIIB:** ***National Science Education Standards*** ▸ Grades K–4, Standard E, *Abilities of Technological Design*, pages 137–138 ▸ Grades 5–8, Standard E, *Abilities of Technological Design*, pages 165–166 ▸ Grades 9–12, Standard E, *Abilities of Technological Design*, page 192
IV. Examine Research on Student Learning	**IVA:** ***Benchmarks for Science Literacy*** ▸ 3A, *Technology and Science*, page 334
V. Examine Coherency and Articulation	**V:** ***Atlas of Science Literacy*** ▸ *Design Constraints*, pages 32–33 ▸ *Designed Systems*, pages 34–35
VI. Clarify State Standards and District Curriculum	**VIA:** ***State Standards:*** Link Sections I–V to learning goals and information from your state standards or frameworks that are informed by the results of the topic study. **VIB:** ***District Curriculum Guide:*** Link Sections I–V to learning goals and information from your district curriculum guide that are informed by the results of the topic study.
Visit www.curriculumtopicstudy.org for updates or supplementary readings, Web sites, and videos.	

Standards- and Research-Based Study of a Curricular Topic

TECHNOLOGY

Section and Outcome	Selected Sources and Readings for Study and Reflection Read and examine *related parts* of:
I. Identify Adult Content Knowledge	**IA:** *Science for All Americans* ▸ Chapter 3, *The Nature of Technology,* pages 26–37
II. Consider Instructional Implications	**IIA:** *Benchmarks for Science Literacy* ▸ 3A, *Technology and Science* general essay, page 43; grade span essays, pages 44–47 ▸ 3B, *Design and Systems* general essay, page 48; grade span essays, pages 49–51 ▸ 3C, *Issues in Technology* general essay, page 53; grade span essays, pages 54–56 **IIB:** *National Science Education Standards* ▸ Grades K–4, Standard E essay, pages 135, 137; Vignette *Weather Instruments,* page 136 ▸ Grades 5–8, Standard E essay, pages 161, 165; Vignette *The Egg Drop,* pages 162–164 ▸ Grades 9–12, Standard E essay, pages 190–192
III. Identify Concepts and Specific Ideas	**IIIA:** *Benchmarks for Science Literacy* ▸ 3A, *Technology and Science,* pages 44–47 ▸ 3B, *Design and Systems,* pages 49–52 ▸ 3C, *Issues in Technology,* pages 54–57 **IIIB:** *National Science Education Standards* ▸ Grades K–4, Standard E, *Abilities of Technological Design,* pages 137–138; *Understandings About Science and Technology,* page 138 ▸ Grades 5–8, Standard E, *Abilities of Technological Design,* pages 165–166; *Understandings About Science and Technology,* page 166 ▸ Grades 9–12, Standard E, *Abilities of Technological Design,* page 192; *Understandings About Science and Technology,* pages 192–193
IV. Examine Research on Student Learning	**IVA:** *Benchmarks for Science Literacy* ▸ Chapter 3, *The Nature of Technology,* pages 334–335
V. Examine Coherency and Articulation	**V:** *Atlas of Science Literacy* ▸ *Design Constraints,* pages 32–33 ▸ *Designed Systems,* pages 34–35 ▸ *Interaction of Technology and Society,* pages 36–37 ▸ *Decisions About Using Technology,* pages 38–39
VI. Clarify State Standards and District Curriculum	**VIA:** *State Standards:* Link Sections I–V to learning goals and information from your state standards or frameworks that are informed by the results of the topic study. **VIB:** *District Curriculum Guide:* Link Sections I–V to learning goals and information from your district curriculum guide that are informed by the results of the topic study.
Visit www.curriculumtopicstudy.org for updates or supplementary readings, Web sites, and videos.	

Standards- and Research-Based Study of a Curricular Topic

UNDERSTANDINGS ABOUT SCIENTIFIC INQUIRY

Section and Outcome	Selected Sources and Readings for Study and Reflection Read and examine *related parts* of:
I. Identify Adult Content Knowledge	**IA:** *Science for All Americans* ▸ Chapter 1, *The Scientific World View*, pages 2–3; *Scientific Inquiry*, pages 3–7
II. Consider Instructional Implications	**IIA:** *Benchmarks for Science Literacy* ▸ 1A, *The Scientific World View* general essay, page 5; grade span essays, pages 6–8 ▸ 1B, *Scientific Inquiry* general essay, page 9; grade span essays, pages 10–13 **IIB:** *National Science Education Standards* ▸ Grades K–4, Standard A essay, pages 121–122 ▸ Grades 5–8, Standard A essay, pages 143–145 ▸ Grades 9–12, Standard A essay, pages 173–175; Vignette *Photosynthesis,* pages 194–196
III. Identify Concepts and Specific Ideas	**IIIA:** *Benchmarks for Science Literacy* ▸ 1A, *The Scientific World View,* pages 6–8 ▸ 1B, *Scientific Inquiry,* pages 10–13 **IIIB** *National Science Education Standards* ▸ Grades K–4, Standard A, *Understanding About Scientific Inquiry,* page 123 ▸ Grades 5–8, Standard A, *Understanding About Scientific Inquiry,* page 148 ▸ Grades 9–12, Standard A, *Understanding About Scientific Inquiry,* page 176
IV. Examine Research on Student Learning	**IVA:** *Benchmarks for Science Literacy* ▸ 1A, *The Scientific World View,* page 332 ▸ 1B, *Scientific Inquiry,* pages 332–333
V. Examine Coherency and Articulation	**V:** *Atlas of Science Literacy* ▸ *Evidence and Reasoning in Inquiry,* pages 16–17 ▸ *Scientific Investigations,* pages 18–19 ▸ *Scientific Theories,* pages 20–21 ▸ *Avoiding Bias in Science,* pages 22–23
VI. Clarify State Standards and District Curriculum	**VIA:** *State Standards:* Link Sections I–V to learning goals and information from your state standards or frameworks that are informed by the results of the topic study. **VIB:** *District Curriculum Guide:* Link Sections I–V to learning goals and information from your district curriculum guide that are informed by the results of the topic study.
Visit www.curriculumtopicstudy.org for updates or supplementary readings, Web sites, and videos.	

Standards- and Research-Based Study of a Curricular Topic

UNDERSTANDINGS ABOUT TECHNOLOGY

Section and Outcome	Selected Sources and Readings for Study and Reflection Read and examine *related parts* of:
I. Identify Adult Content Knowledge	**IA:** *Science for All Americans* ▸ Chapter 3, *The Nature of Technology*, pages 26–37
II. Consider Instructional Implications	**IIA:** *Benchmarks for Science Literacy* ▸ 3A, *Technology and Science* general essay, page 43; grade span essays, pages 44–47 ▸ 3B, *Design and Systems* general essay, page 48; grade span essays, pages 49–51 ▸ 3C, *Issues in Technology* general essay, page 53; grade span essays, pages 54–56 **IIB:** *National Science Education Standards* ▸ Grades K–4, Standard E essay, pages 135, 137 ▸ Grades 5–8, Standard E essay, pages 161, 165 ▸ Grades 9–12, Standard E essay, pages 190–192
III. Identify Concepts and Specific Ideas	**IIIA:** *Benchmarks for Science Literacy* ▸ 3A, *Technology and Science*, pages 44–47 ▸ 3B, *Design and Systems*, pages 49–52 ▸ 3C, *Issues in Technology*, pages 54–57 **IIIB:** *National Science Education Standards* ▸ Grades K–4, Standard E, *Understandings About Science and Technology*, page 138 ▸ Grades 5–8, Standard E, *Understandings About Science and Technology*, page 166 ▸ Grades 9–12, Standard E, *Understandings About Science and Technology*, pages 192–193
IV. Examine Research on Student Learning	**IVA:** *Benchmarks for Science Literacy* ▸ Chapter 3, *The Nature of Technology*, pages 334–335
V. Examine Coherency and Articulation	**V:** *Atlas of Science Literacy* ▸ *Design Constraints*, pages 32–33 ▸ *Designed Systems*, pages 34–35 ▸ *Interaction of Technology and Society*, pages 36–37 ▸ *Decisions About Using Technology*, pages 38–39
VI. Clarify State Standards and District Curriculum	**VIA:** *State Standards:* Link Sections I–V to learning goals and information from your state standards or frameworks that are informed by the results of the topic study. **VIB:** *District Curriculum Guide:* Link Sections I–V to learning goals and information from your district curriculum guide that are informed by the results of the topic study.

Visit www.curriculumtopicstudy.org for updates or supplementary readings, Web sites, and videos.

Standards- and Research-Based Study of a Curricular Topic

USE OF COMPUTERS AND COMMUNICATION TECHNOLOGIES

Section and Outcome	Selected Sources and Readings for Study and Reflection Read and examine *related parts* of:
I. Identify Adult Content Knowledge	**IA:** ***Science for All Americans*** ▸ Chapter 8, *Communication*, page 118–120; *Information Processing*, pages 120–123 ▸ Chapter 11, *Mathematical Models*, pages 171–172
II. Consider Instructional Implications	**IIA:** ***Benchmarks for Science Literacy*** ▸ 8D, *Communication* general essay, page 196; grade span essays, pages 197–199 ▸ 8E, *Information Processing* general essay, page 200; grade span essays, pages 201–203 ▸ 11B, *Models* general essay, page 267; grade span essays, pages 268–270 **IIB:** ***National Science Education Standards*** ▸ Grades K–4, Standard A essay, pages 121–122 ▸ Grades 5–8, Standard A essay, pages 143–145 ▸ Grades 9–12, Standard A essay, pages 173–175; Vignette *Genetics*, pages 64–65
III. Identify Concepts and Specific Ideas	**IIIA:** ***Benchmarks for Science Literacy*** ▸ 8D, *Communication*, pages 197–199 ▸ 8E, *Information Processing*, pages 201–203 ▸ 11B, *Models*, pages 268–270 **IIIB:** ***National Science Education Standards*** ▸ Grades K–4, Standard A, *Abilities Necessary to Do Scientific Inquiry*, page 122; *Understandings About Scientific Inquiry*, page 123 ▸ Grades 5–8, Standard A, *Use Mathematics in All Aspects of Scientific Inquiry*, page 148; *Understandings About Scientific Inquiry*, page 148; *Develop Descriptions, Explanations, Predictions, and Models Using Evidence*, page 145 ▸ Grades 9–12, Standard A, *Use Technology and Mathematics to Improve Investigations and Communications*, page 175; *Formulate and Revise Scientific Explanations and Models Using Logic and Evidence*, page 175; *Recognize and Analyze Alternative Explanations and Models*, page 175; *Understandings About Scientific Inquiry*, page 176
IV. Examine Research on Student Learning	**IVA:** ***Benchmarks for Science Literacy*** ▸ 11B, *Models*, page 357
V. Examine Coherency and Articulation	**V:** ***Atlas of Science Literacy*** ▸ *Mathematical Models*, pages 28–29 ▸ *Computers*, pages 110–111
VI. Clarify State Standards and District Curriculum	**VIA:** ***State Standards:*** Link Sections I–V to learning goals and information from your state standards or frameworks that are informed by the results of the topic study. **VIB:** ***District Curriculum Guide:*** Link Sections I–V to learning goals and information from your district curriculum guide that are informed by the results of the topic study.
Visit www.curriculumtopicstudy.org for updates or supplementary readings, Web sites, and videos.	

Implications of Science and Technology

Primary Domain: Science and Technology

Number of CTS Guides: 11

Overview: The primary focus of this section is the various ways science and technology have impacted human life, the human environment, and human culture and beliefs. Ideas developed in this section include science in personal and social perspectives, ethics, applications of science and technology, and scientific episodes in history that have affected human knowledge and beliefs. Ideas developed through the study of the "cross-cutting" topics in this section can be applied to the disciplinary content topics.

Standards- and Research-Based Study of a Curricular Topic

AGRICULTURAL SCIENCE AND TECHNOLOGY

Section and Outcome	Selected Sources and Readings for Study and Reflection Read and examine *related parts* of:
I. Identify Adult Content Knowledge	**IA:** **Science for All Americans** ▸ Chapter 8, *Agriculture,* pages 108–110
II. Consider Instructional Implications	**IIA:** **Benchmarks for Science Literacy** ▸ 8A, *Agriculture* general essay, page 183; grade span essays, pages 184–186 **IIB:** **National Science Education Standards** ▸ Grades K–4, Standard F essay, pages 138–139 ▸ Grades 5–8, Standard F essay, pages 167–168 ▸ Grades 9–12, Standard F essay, pages 193, 197
III. Identify Concepts and Specific Ideas	**IIIA:** **Benchmarks for Science Literacy** ▸ 8A, *Agriculture,* pages 184–186 **IIIB:** **National Science Education Standards** ▸ Grades K–4, Standard F, *Science and Technology in Local Challenges,* pages 140–141 ▸ Grades 5–8, Standard F, *Science and Technology in Society,* page 169 ▸ Grades 9–12, Standard F, *Science and Technology in Local, National, and Global Challenges,* page 199
IV. Examine Research on Student Learning	**IVA:** **Benchmarks for Science Literacy** ▸ 1C, *The Scientific Enterprise,* page 333 ▸ 8, *The Designed World,* page 349
V. Examine Coherency and Articulation	**V:** **Atlas of Science Literacy** ▸ *Agricultural Technology,* pages 106–107
VI. Clarify State Standards and District Curriculum	**VIA:** **State Standards:** Link Sections I–V to learning goals and information from your state standards or frameworks that are informed by the results of the topic study. **VIB:** **District Curriculum Guide:** Link Sections I–V to learning goals and information from your district curriculum guide that are informed by the results of the topic study.
Visit www.curriculumtopicstudy.org for updates or supplementary readings, Web sites, and videos.	

Standards- and Research-Based Study of a Curricular Topic

BIOTECHNOLOGY

Section and Outcome	Selected Sources and Readings for Study and Reflection Read and examine *related parts* of:
I. Identify Adult Content Knowledge	**IA:** *Science for All Americans* ▶ Chapter 5, *Heredity*, pages 61–62; *Cells*, pages 62–64 ▶ Chapter 8, *Agriculture*, page 108; *Health Technology*, pages 123–126 **IB:** *Science Matters: Achieving Scientific Literacy* ▶ Chapter 16, *Genetic Engineering*, pages 238–240
II. Consider Instructional Implications	**IIA:** *Benchmarks for Science Literacy* ▶ 5B, *Heredity* general essay, page 106; 6–8, 9–12 grade span essays, page 108 ▶ 5C, *Cells* general essay, page 110; 9–12 grade span essay, page 113 ▶ 8A, *Agriculture* 9–12 grade span essay, page 186 ▶ 8F, *Health Technology* general essay, page 204; 9–12 grade span essay, page 207 **IIB:** *National Science Education Standards* ▶ Grades 9–12 Standard C essay, pages 181, 184; Standard E essay, pages 190–192; Standard F essay, pages 193, 197
III. Identify Concepts and Specific Ideas	**IIIA:** *Benchmarks for Science Literacy* ▶ 5B, *Heredity*, 6–8 and 9–12, pages 108–109 ▶ 5C, *Cells*, 9–12, page 114 ▶ 8A, *Agriculture*, 6–8 and 9–12, page 186 ▶ 8F, *Health Technology*, 6–8 and 9–12, pages 206–207 **IIIB:** *National Science Education Standards* ▶ Grades 9–12, Standard C, *The Cell*, pages 184–185; Standard E, *Understandings About Science and Technology*, pages 192–193; Standard F, *Science and Technology in Local, National, and Global Challenges*, page 199
IV. Examine Research on Student Learning	**IVB:** *Making Sense of Secondary Science: Research Into Children's Ideas* ▶ Chapter 6, *Biotechnology*, pages 57–58
V. Examine Coherency and Articulation	**V:** *Atlas of Science Literacy* ▶ *Interaction of Technology and Society*, pages 36–37 ▶ *Decisions About Using Technology*, pages 38–39 ▶ *DNA and Inherited Characteristics*, pages 68–69 ▶ *Agricultural Technology*, pages 106–107
VI. Clarify State Standards and District Curriculum	**VIA:** *State Standards:* Link Sections I–V to learning goals and information from your state standards or frameworks that are informed by the results of the topic study. **VIB:** *District Curriculum Guide:* Link Sections I–V to learning goals and information from your district curriculum guide that are informed by the results of the topic study.

Visit www.curriculumtopicstudy.org for updates or supplementary readings, Web sites, and videos.

Standards- and Research-Based Study of a Curricular Topic

ENVIRONMENTAL IMPACTS OF SCIENCE AND TECHNOLOGY

Section and Outcome	Selected Sources and Readings for Study and Reflection Read and examine *related parts* of:	
I. Identify Adult Content Knowledge	**IA:**	***Science for All Americans*** ▸ Chapter 3, *Technologies Always Have Side Effects,* pages 30–31 ▸ Chapter 5, *Interdependence of Life,* pages 65–66; *Flow of Matter and Energy,* page 67
II. Consider Instructional Implications	**IIA:**	***Benchmarks for Science Literacy*** ▸ 3C, *Issues in Technology* general essay, page 53; grade span essays, pages 54–56 ▸ 5D, *Interdependence of Life* general essay, page 115; grade span essays, pages 116–117
	IIB:	***National Science Education Standards*** ▸ Grades K–4, Standard F essay, pages 138–139 ▸ Grades 5–8, Standard F essay, pages 167–168 ▸ Grades 9–12, Standard F essay, pages 193, 197
III. Identify Concepts and Specific Ideas	**IIIA:**	***Benchmarks for Science Literacy*** ▸ 3C, *Issues in Technology,* pages 54–57 ▸ 5D, *Interdependence of Life,* pages 116–117
	IIIB:	***National Science Education Standards*** ▸ Grades K–4, Standard F, *Changes in Environments,* page 140 ▸ Grades 5–8, Standard F, *Populations, Resources, and Environments,* page 168 ▸ Grades 9–12, Standard F, *Environmental Quality,* page 198
IV. Examine Research on Student Learning	**IV:**	No research for this topic available in *Benchmarks* or Driver.
V. Examine Coherency and Articulation	**V:**	***Atlas of Science Literacy*** ▸ *Interaction of Technology and Society,* pages 36–37
VI. Clarify State Standards and District Curriculum	**VIA:**	***State Standards:*** Link Sections I–V to learning goals and information from your state standards or frameworks that are informed by the results of the topic study.
	VIB:	***District Curriculum Guide:*** Link Sections I–V to learning goals and information from your district curriculum guide that are informed by the results of the topic study.
Visit www.curriculumtopicstudy.org for updates or supplementary readings, Web sites, and videos.		

Standards- and Research-Based Study of a Curricular Topic

HISTORICAL EPISODES IN SCIENCE

Section and Outcome	Selected Sources and Readings for Study and Reflection Read and examine *related parts* of:
I. Identify Adult Content Knowledge	**IA:** *Science for All Americans* ▸ Chapter 10, *Historical Perspectives*, pages 145–163
II. Consider Instructional Implications	**IIA:** *Benchmarks for Science Literacy* ▸ Chapter 10, *Historical Perspectives* general essay, pages 237–238; grade span essays, pages 239–259 **IIB:** *National Science Education Standards* ▸ Grades K–4, Standard G essay, page 141 ▸ Grades 5–8, Standard G essay, page 170 ▸ Grades 9–12, Standard G essay, page 200; Vignette *Analysis of a Scientific Inquiry*, pages 202–203
III. Identify Concepts and Specific Ideas	**IIIA:** *Benchmarks for Science Literacy* ▸ Chapter 10, *Historical Perspectives*, pages 240–259 **IIIB:** *National Science Education Standards* ▸ Grades 5–8, Standard G, *History of Science*, page 171 ▸ Grades 9–12, Standard G, *Historical Perspectives*, page 201
IV. Examine Research on Student Learning	**IVA:** *Benchmarks for Science Literacy* ▸ Chapter 10, *Historical Perspectives*, pages 354–355
V. Examine Coherency and Articulation	**V:** *Atlas of Science Literacy:* No available maps in Volume 1 specifically on the topic of Historical Perspectives; however, many maps for other topics have connections to historical episodes.
VI. Clarify State Standards and District Curriculum	**VIA:** *State Standards:* Link Sections I–V to learning goals and information from your state standards or frameworks that are informed by the results of the topic study. **VIB:** *District Curriculum Guide:* Link Sections I–V to learning goals and information from your district curriculum guide that are informed by the results of the topic study.
Visit www.curriculumtopicstudy.org for updates or supplementary readings, Web sites, and videos.	

Standards- and Research-Based Study of a Curricular Topic

HUMAN POPULATION GROWTH AND IMPACT

Section and Outcome	Selected Sources and Readings for Study and Reflection Read and examine *related parts* of:
I. Identify Adult Content Knowledge	**IA:** ***Science for All Americans*** ▸ Chapter 7, *Social Change,* pages 94–95
II. Consider Instructional Implications	**IIA:** ***Benchmarks for Science Literacy*** ▸ 7C, *Social Change* general essay, page 161; 6–12 grade span essays, page 163 **IIB:** ***National Science Education Standards*** ▸ Grades K–4, Standard F essay, pages 138–139 ▸ Grades 5–8, Standard F essay, pages 167–168 ▸ Grades 9–12, Standard F essay, pages 193, 197
III. Identify Concepts and Specific Ideas	**IIIA:** ***Benchmarks for Science Literacy*** ▸ 7C, *Social Change,* page 162–163 **IIIB:** ***National Science Education Standards*** ▸ Grades K–4, Standard F, *Characteristics and Changes in Populations,* page 140 ▸ Grades 5–8, Standard F, *Populations, Resources, and Environments,* page 168 ▸ Grades 9–12, Standard F, *Population Growth,* page 198; *Natural Resources,* page 198
IV. Examine Research on Student Learning	**IV:** No research for this topic available in *Benchmarks* or Driver.
V. Examine Coherency and Articulation	**V:** ***Atlas of Science Literacy*** ▸ *Influences on Social Change,* pages 100–101
VI. Clarify State Standards and District Curriculum	**VIA:** *State Standards:* Link Sections I–V to learning goals and information from your state standards or frameworks that are informed by the results of the topic study. **VIB:** *District Curriculum Guide:* Link Sections I–V to learning goals and information from your district curriculum guide that are informed by the results of the topic study.
Visit www.curriculumtopicstudy.org for updates or supplementary readings, Web sites, and videos.	

Standards- and Research-Based Study of a Curricular Topic

MATERIALS AND MANUFACTURING SCIENCE AND TECHNOLOGY

Section and Outcome	Selected Sources and Readings for Study and Reflection Read and examine *related parts* of:
I. Identify Adult Content Knowledge	**IA:** ***Science for All Americans*** ▸ Chapter 8, *Materials and Manufacturing*, pages 111–114
II. Consider Instructional Implications	**IIA:** ***Benchmarks for Science Literacy*** ▸ 8B, *Materials and Manufacturing* general essay, page 187; grade span essays, pages 188–191 **IIB:** ***National Science Education Standards*** ▸ Grades K–4, Standard F essay, pages 138–139 ▸ Grades 5–8, Standard F essay, pages 167–168 ▸ Grades 9–12, Standard F essay, pages 193, 197
III. Identify Concepts and Specific Ideas	**IIIA:** ***Benchmarks for Science Literacy*** ▸ 8B, *Materials and Manufacturing*, pages 188–191 **IIIB:** ***National Science Education Standards*** ▸ Grades K–4, Standard F, *Science and Technology in Local Challenges*, pages 140–141 ▸ Grades 5–8, Standard F, *Science and Technology in Society*, page 169 ▸ Grades 9–12, Standard F, *Science and Technology in Local, National, and Global Challenges*, page 199
IV. Examine Research on Student Learning	**IVA:** ***Benchmarks for Science Literacy*** ▸ 1C, *The Scientific Enterprise*, page 333 ▸ 8, *The Designed World*, page 349
V. Examine Coherency and Articulation	**V:** ***Atlas of Science Literacy*** ▸ *Design Constraints*, pages 32–33
VI. Clarify State Standards and District Curriculum	**VIA:** ***State Standards:*** Link Sections I–V to learning goals and information from your state standards or frameworks that are informed by the results of the topic study. **VIB:** ***District Curriculum Guide:*** Link Sections I–V to learning goals and information from your district curriculum guide that are informed by the results of the topic study.
Visit www.curriculumtopicstudy.org for updates or supplementary readings, Web sites, and videos.	

Standards- and Research-Based Study of a Curricular Topic

MEDICAL SCIENCE AND TECHNOLOGY

Section and Outcome	Selected Sources and Readings for Study and Reflection Read and examine *related parts* of:
I. Identify Adult Content Knowledge	**IA:** ***Science for All Americans*** ▸ Chapter 8, *Health Technology,* pages 123–126
II. Consider Instructional Implications	**IIA:** ***Benchmarks for Science Literacy*** ▸ 8F, *Health Technology* general essay, page 204; grade span essays, pages 205–207 **IIB:** ***National Science Education Standards*** ▸ Grades K–4, Standard F essay, pages 138–139 ▸ Grades 5–8, Standard F essay, pages 167–168 ▸ Grades 9–12, Standard F essay, pages 193, 197
III. Identify Concepts and Specific Ideas	**IIIA:** ***Benchmarks for Science Literacy*** ▸ 8F, *Health Technology,* pages 205–207 **IIIB:** ***National Science Education Standards*** ▸ Grades K–4, Standard F, *Science and Technology in Local Challenges,* pages 140–141 ▸ Grades 5–8, Standard F, *Science and Technology in Society,* page 169 ▸ Grades 9–12, Standard F, *Science and Technology in Local, National, and Global Challenges,* page 199
IV. Examine Research on Student Learning	**IVA:** ***Benchmarks for Science Literacy*** ▸ 1C, *The Scientific Enterprise,* page 333 ▸ 8, *The Designed World,* page 349
V. Examine Coherency and Articulation	**V:** ***Atlas of Science Literacy*** ▸ *Maintainin Good Health,* pages 88–89
VI. Clarify State Standards and District Curriculum	**VIA:** ***State Standards:*** Link Sections I–V to learning goals and information from your state standards or frameworks that are informed by the results of the topic study. **VIB:** ***District Curriculum Guide:*** Link Sections I–V to learning goals and information from your district curriculum guide that are informed by the results of the topic study.
Visit www.curriculumtopicstudy.org for updates or supplementary readings, Web sites, and videos.	

Standards- and Research-Based Study of a Curricular Topic

PERSONAL AND COMMUNITY HEALTH

Section and Outcome	Selected Sources and Readings for Study and Reflection Read and examine *related parts* of:
I. Identify Adult Content Knowledge	**IA:** *Science for All Americans* ▸ Chapter 6, *Physical Health*, pages 80–82; *Mental Health*, pages 82–84
II. Consider Instructional Implications	**IIA:** *Benchmarks for Science Literacy* ▸ 6E, *Physical Health* general essay, page 143; grade span essays, pages 144–146 ▸ 6F, *Mental Health* general essay, page 147; grade span essays, pages 148–149 **IIB:** *National Science Education Standards* ▸ Grades K–4, Standard F essay, pages 138–139 ▸ Grades 5–8, Standard F essay, pages 167–168 ▸ Grades 9–12, Standard F essay, pages 193, 197
III. Identify Concepts and Specific Ideas	**IIIA:** *Benchmarks for Science Literacy* ▸ 6E, *Physical Health*, pages 144–146 ▸ 6F, *Mental Health*, pages 148–149 **IIIB:** *National Science Education Standards* ▸ Grades K–4, Standard F, *Personal Health*, pages 139–140 ▸ Grades 5–8, Standard F, *Personal Health*, page 168 ▸ Grades 9–12, Standard F, *Personal and Community Health*, pages 197–198
IV. Examine Research on Student Learning	**IVA:** *Benchmarks for Science Literacy* ▸ 6E, *Physical Health*, pages 345–346
V. Examine Coherency and Articulation	**V:** *Atlas of Science Literacy* ▸ *Disease*, pages 86–87 ▸ *Maintaining Good Health*, pages 88–89
VI. Clarify State Standards and District Curriculum	**VIA:** *State Standards:* Link Sections I–V to learning goals and information from your state standards or frameworks that are informed by the results of the topic study. **VIB:** *District Curriculum Guide:* Link Sections I–V to learning goals and information from your district curriculum guide that are informed by the results of the topic study.
Visit www.curriculumtopicstudy.org for updates or supplementary readings, Web sites, and videos.	

Standards- and Research-Based Study of a Curricular Topic

POLLUTION

Section and Outcome	Selected Sources and Readings for Study and Reflection Read and examine *related parts* of:
I. Identify Adult Content Knowledge	**IA:** *Science for All Americans* ▸ Chapter 3, *The Human Presence,* pages 32–33 ▸ Chapter 5, *Processes That Shape the Earth,* page 46 **IB:** *Science Matters: Achieving Scientific Literacy* ▸ Chapter 14, *Freshwater,* page 201; *Weather Report Jargon,* pages 203–205 ▸ Chapter 18, *Disposable Diapers,* pages 274–275; *Nuclear Waste,* pages 275–276
II. Consider Instructional Implications	**IIA:** *Benchmarks for Science Literacy* ▸ 5D, *Interdependence of Life* general essay, page 115; grade span essays, pages 116–117 **IIB:** *National Science Education Standards* ▸ Grades K–4, Standard F essay, pages 138–139 ▸ Grades 5–8, Standard F essay, pages 167–168 ▸ Grades 9–12, Standard F essay, page 193
III. Identify Concepts and Specific Ideas	**IIIA:** *Benchmarks for Science Literacy* ▸ 5D, *Interdependence of Life,* pages 116–117 **IIIB:** *National Science Education Standards* ▸ Grades K–4, Standard F, *Changes in Environments,* page 140 ▸ Grades 5–8, Standard F, *Populations, Resources, and Environments,* page 168; *Natural Hazards,* pages 168–169 ▸ Grades 9–12, Standard F, *Environmental Quality,* page 198; *Natural and Human-Induced Hazards,* pages 198–199
IV. Examine Research on Student Learning	**IVB:** *Making Sense of Secondary Science: Research Into Children's Ideas* ▸ Chapter 7, *Pollution,* pages 68–69
V. Examine Coherency and Articulation	**V:** *Atlas of Science Literacy:* There are no maps for this topic in Volume 1.
VI. Clarify State Standards and District Curriculum	**VIA:** *State Standards:* Link Sections I–V to learning goals and information from your state standards or frameworks that are informed by the results of the topic study. **VIB:** *District Curriculum Guide:* Link Sections I–V to learning goals and information from your district curriculum guide that are informed by the results of the topic study.
Visit www.curriculumtopicstudy.org for updates or supplementary readings, Web sites, and videos.	

Standards- and Research-Based Study of a Curricular Topic

RISKS AND BENEFITS OF SCIENCE AND TECHNOLOGY

Section and Outcome	Selected Sources and Readings for Study and Reflection Read and examine *related parts* of:
I. Identify Adult Content Knowledge	**IA:** ***Science for All Americans*** ▸ Chapter 3, *Technologies Always Have Side Effects,* pages 30–31; *Decisions About the Use of Technology Are Complex,* pages 35–37
II. Consider Instructional Implications	**IIA:** ***Benchmarks for Science Literacy*** ▸ 3B, *Design and Systems* general essay, page 48; grade span essays, pages 49–51 ▸ 3C, *Issues in Technology* general essay, page 53; grade span essays, pages 54–56 **IIB:** ***National Science Education Standards*** ▸ Grades K–4, Standard F essay, pages 138–139 ▸ Grades 5–8, Standard F essay, pages 167–168 ▸ Grades 9–12, Standard F essay, pages 193, 197
III. Identify Concepts and Specific Ideas	**IIIA:** ***Benchmarks for Science Literacy*** ▸ 3B, *Design and Systems,* pages 49–52 ▸ 3C, *Issues in Technology,* pages 54–57 **IIIB:** ***National Science Education Standards*** ▸ Grades K–4, Standard F, *Science and Technology in Local Challenges,* pages 140–141 ▸ Grades 5–8, Standard F, *Risks and Benefits,* page 169 ▸ Grades 9–12, Standard F, *Natural and Human-Induced Hazards,* pages 198–199
IV. Examine Research on Student Learning	**IVA:** ***Benchmarks for Science Literacy*** ▸ 3C, *Issues in Technology,* page 335
V. Examine Coherency and Articulation	**V:** ***Atlas of Science Literacy*** ▸ *Decisions About Using Technology,* pages 38–39
VI. Clarify State Standards and District Curriculum	**VIA:** *State Standards:* Link Sections I–V to learning goals and information from your state standards or frameworks that are informed by the results of the topic study. **VIB:** *District Curriculum Guide:* Link Sections I–V to learning goals and information from your district curriculum guide that are informed by the results of the topic study.
Visit www.curriculumtopicstudy.org for updates or supplementary readings, Web sites, and videos.	

Standards- and Research-Based Study of a Curricular Topic

SCIENCE AND TECHNOLOGY IN SOCIETY

Section and Outcome	Selected Sources and Readings for Study and Reflection Read and examine *related parts* of:
I. Identify Adult Content Knowledge	**IA:** *Science for All Americans* ▸ Chapter 1, *The Scientific Enterprise*, pages 8–12 ▸ Chapter 3, *Issues in Technology*, pages 32–37
II. Consider Instructional Implications	**IIA:** *Benchmarks for Science Literacy* ▸ 1C, *The Scientific Enterprise* general essay, page 14; grade span essays, pages 15–19 ▸ 3C, *Issues in Technology* general essay, page 53; grade span essays, pages 54–56 **IIB:** *National Science Education Standards* ▸ Grades K–4, Standard F essay, pages 138–139 ▸ Grades 5–8, Standard F essay, pages 167–168 ▸ Grades 9–12, Standard F essay, pages 193, 197
III. Identify Concepts and Specific Ideas	**IIIA:** *Benchmarks for Science Literacy* ▸ 1C, *The Scientific Enterprise*, pages 15–20 ▸ 3C, *Issues in Technology*, pages 54–57 **IIIB:** *National Science Education Standards* ▸ Grades K–4, Standard F, *Science and Technology in Local Challenges*, pages 140–141 ▸ Grades 5–8, Standard F, *Science and Technology in Society*, pages 169–170 ▸ Grades 9–12, Standard F, *Science and Technology in Local, National, and Global Challenges*, page 199
IV. Examine Research on Student Learning	**IVA:** *Benchmarks for Science Literacy* ▸ 1C, *The Scientific Enterprise*, page 333 ▸ 3C, *Issues in Technology*, page 335
V. Examine Coherency and Articulation	**V:** *Atlas of Science Literacy* ▸ *Interaction of Technology and Society*, pages 36–37 ▸ *Decisions About Using Technology*, pages 38–39 ▸ *Social Decisions*, pages 102–103
VI. Clarify State Standards and District Curriculum	**VIA:** *State Standards:* Link Sections I–V to learning goals and information from your state standards or frameworks that are informed by the results of the topic study. **VIB:** *District Curriculum Guide:* Link Sections I–V to learning goals and information from your district curriculum guide that are informed by the results of the topic study.
Visit www.curriculumtopicstudy.org for updates or supplementary readings, Web sites, and videos.	

Unifying Themes

Primary Domain: All domains

Number of CTS Guides: 4

Overview: The primary focus of this section is on developing an understanding of the pervading themes that transcend the boundaries of the individual scientific disciplines. Themes developed include systems, models, constancy, change, and scale. It is important to note that there are several unifying themes not included as guides in this section. The reason for this is that there are only limited sections in the common CTS resources in which to read about themes. Additional themes such as patterns, form and function, interactions, and so on are worthy to note and can be studied with the use of additional resources.

Standards- and Research-Based Study of a Curricular Topic

CONSTANCY, EQUILIBRIUM, AND CHANGE

Section and Outcome	Selected Sources and Readings for Study and Reflection Read and examine *related parts* of:	
I. Identify Adult Content Knowledge	**IA:**	***Science for All Americans*** ▸ Chapter 11, *Constancy and Change*, pages 172–179
II. Consider Instructional Implications	**IIA:**	***Benchmarks for Science Literacy*** ▸ 11C, *Constancy and Change* general essay, pages 271–272; grade span essays, pages 272–275
	IIB:	***National Science Education Standards*** ▸ K–12, *Unifying Concepts and Processes*, pages 115–116
III. Identify Concepts and Specific Ideas	**IIIA:**	***Benchmarks for Science Literacy*** ▸ 11C, *Constancy and Change*, pages 272–275
	IIIB:	***National Science Education Standards*** ▸ K–12, *Constancy, Change, and Measurement*, pages 117–118 ▸ K–12, *Evolution and Equilibrium*, page 119
IV. Examine Research on Student Learning	**IVA:**	***Benchmarks for Science Literacy*** ▸ 11C, *Constancy and Change*, pages 357–358
V. Examine Coherency and Articulation	**V:**	***Atlas of Science Literacy*** ▸ *Describing Change*, pages 120–121
VI. Clarify State Standards and District Curriculum	**VIA:**	**State Standards:** Link Sections I–V to learning goals and information from your state standards or frameworks that are informed by the results of the topic study.
	VIB:	***District Curriculum Guide:*** Link Sections I–V to learning goals and information from your district curriculum guide that are informed by the results of the topic study.
Visit www.curriculumtopicstudy.org for updates or supplementary readings, Web sites, and videos.		

Standards- and Research-Based Study of a Curricular Topic

MODELS

Section and Outcome	Selected Sources and Readings for Study and Reflection Read and examine *related parts* of:
I. Identify Adult Content Knowledge	**IA:** ***Science for All Americans*** ▸ Chapter 11, *Models*, pages 168–172
II. Consider Instructional Implications	**IIA:** ***Benchmarks for Science Literacy*** ▸ 11B, *Models* general essay, page 267; grade span essays, pages 268–270 **IIB:** ***National Science Education Standards*** ▸ K–12, *Unifying Concepts and Processes*, pages 115–116
III. Identify Concepts and Specific Ideas	**IIIA:** ***Benchmarks for Science Literacy*** ▸ 11B, *Models,* pages 268–270 **IIIB:** ***National Science Education Standards*** ▸ K–12, *Evidence, Models, and Explanation*, page 117
IV. Examine Research on Student Learning	**IVA:** ***Benchmarks for Science Literacy*** ▸ 11B, *Models,* page 357
V. Examine Coherency and Articulation	**V:** ***Atlas of Science Literacy*** ▸ *Scientific Theories*, pages 20–21 ▸ *Mathematical Models*, pages 28–29
VI. Clarify State Standards and District Curriculum	**VIA:** ***State Standards:*** Link Sections I–V to learning goals and information from your state standards or frameworks that are informed by the results of the topic study. **VIB:** ***District Curriculum Guide:*** Link Sections I–V to learning goals and information from your district curriculum guide that are informed by the results of the topic study.
Visit www.curriculumtopicstudy.org for updates or supplementary readings, Web sites, and videos.	

Standards- and Research-Based Study of a Curricular Topic

SCALE

Section and Outcome	Selected Sources and Readings for Study and Reflection Read and examine *related parts* of:	
I. Identify Adult Content Knowledge	**IA:**	***Science for All Americans*** ▸ Chapter 11, *Scale,* pages 179–181
II. Consider Instructional Implications	**IIA:**	***Benchmarks for Science Literacy*** ▸ 11D, *Scale* general essay, page 276; grade span essays, pages 277–279
	IIB:	***National Science Education Standards*** ▸ K–12, *Unifying Concepts and Processes,* pages 115–116
III. Identify Concepts and Specific Ideas	**IIIA:**	***Benchmarks for Science Literacy*** ▸ 11D, *Scale,* pages 277–279
	IIIB:	***National Science Education Standards*** ▸ K–12, *Constancy, Change, and Measurement,* pages 117–118
IV. Examine Research on Student Learning	**IV:**	No research findings available in *Benchmarks* or Driver.
V. Examine Coherency and Articulation	**V:**	***Atlas of Science Literacy:*** There are no maps for this topic in Volume 1.
VI. Clarify State Standards and District Curriculum	**VIA:**	***State Standards:*** Link Sections I–V to learning goals and information from your state standards or frameworks that are informed by the results of the topic study.
	VIB:	***District Curriculum Guide:*** Link Sections I–V to learning goals and information from your district curriculum guide that are informed by the results of the topic study.
Visit www.curriculumtopicstudy.org for updates or supplementary readings, Web sites, and videos.		

Standards- and Research-Based Study of a Curricular Topic

SYSTEMS

Section and Outcome	Selected Sources and Readings for Study and Reflection Read and examine *related parts* of:
I. Identify Adult Content Knowledge	**IA:** ***Science for All Americans*** ▸ Chapter 11, *Systems*, pages 166–168
II. Consider Instructional Implications	**IIA:** ***Benchmarks for Science Literacy*** ▸ 11A, *Systems* general essay, pages 262–263; grade span essays, pages 264–266 **IIB:** ***National Science Education Standards*** ▸ K–12, *Unifying Concepts and Processes*, pages 115–116
III. Identify Concepts and Specific Ideas	**IIIA:** ***Benchmarks for Science Literacy*** ▸ 11A, *Systems*, pages 264–266 **IIIB:** ***National Science Education Standards*** ▸ K–12, *Systems, Order, and Organization*, pages 116–117
IV. Examine Research on Student Learning	**IVA:** ***Benchmarks for Science Literacy*** ▸ 11A, *Systems*, pages 355–356
V. Examine Coherency and Articulation	**V:** ***Atlas of Science Literacy*** ▸ *Designed Systems*, pages 34–35 ▸ *Systems*, pages 132–133
VI. Clarify State Standards and District Curriculum	**VIA:** ***State Standards:*** Link Sections I–V to learning goals and information from your state standards or frameworks that are informed by the results of the topic study. **VIB:** ***District Curriculum Guide:*** Link Sections I–V to learning goals and information from your district curriculum guide that are informed by the results of the topic study.
Visit www.curriculumtopicstudy.org for updates or supplementary readings, Web sites, and videos.	

Resource A: Additional Resources to Support Curriculum Topic Study

CURRICULUM TOPIC STUDY WEB SITE

The Curriculum Topic Study Project maintains a project Web site at www
.curriculumtopicstudy.org. New information about CTS, updated guides, national
workshops, and new tools will be available here. A searchable database allows CTS
users to search by CTS guide for additional articles, videos, Web sites, and so on to
supplement readings from the CTS guides. Links to other national standards, such
as the *Standards for Technology Education,* are available for selected CTS guides.

MATHEMATICS CURRICULUM TOPIC STUDY

The Curriculum Topic Study Project funded by National Science Foundation (NSF)
is producing a mathematics version of the science CTS. This book will include
processes, contextual examples, vignettes, and a comprehensive set of study guides
for mathematics CTS. Information on the mathematics CTS guide is available on the
CTS Web site.

FACILITATOR'S GUIDE TO CURRICULUM TOPIC STUDY

The third book in the NSF-funded Curriculum Topic Project will be geared toward
professional developers, higher-education faculty, teacher leaders, and others who
facilitate group learning using CTS. The book will be developed in partnership with

WestEd and will utilize a national professional development and higher-education design team to produce tools, processes, and professional development materials to use with CTS. The book will also feature how CTS is used with study groups, action research, examining student work and thinking, lesson study, inquiry immersion, content immersion, curriculum and assessment development, online learning, mentoring and coaching, curriculum and assessment implementation, workshops and courses, case discussions, demonstration lessons, and other strategies. Information on the facilitator's guide is available on the CTS Web site.

OTHER PROJECT 2061 MATERIALS

Project 2061 produces several supporting resources to use with *Benchmarks for Science Literacy*, *Science for All Americans*, and *Atlas of Science Literacy*. Recommended resources to extend CTS and deepen understanding of individual benchmarks include *Designs for Science Literacy* (American Association for the Advancement of Science, 2000), the Project 2061 Curriculum Materials Analysis Procedure, and Project 2061's assessment resources. Information about these tools, including online versions of *Science for All Americans* and *Benchmarks* and ordering information for any of the Project 2061 materials used in CTS and other Project 2061 science literacy initiatives, are available at http://www.project2061.org.

OTHER NATIONAL RESEARCH COUNCIL RESOURCES

The National Research Council published several addenda to the *National Science Education Standards (NSES)* used in CTS. Companion resources that can be used to support CTS applications include *Inquiry and the National Science Education Standards* (2000), *Classroom Assessment and the National Science Education Standards* (2001), and *Selecting Instructional Materials* (1999). The materials along with the *NSES* can be read online or ordered at http://www.nap.edu.

NATIONAL SCIENCE TEACHERS ASSOCIATION

The National Science Teachers Association (NSTA) is the leading professional association in the United States for science educators. NSTA is a copublisher of this book, and various CTS workshop sessions will be held at their area and national conventions. The NSTA has an online bookstore that carries the materials used in CTS. You can visit the NSTA Web site and bookstore at http://www.nsta.org.

MAINE MATHEMATICS AND SCIENCE ALLIANCE

The Maine Mathematics and Science Alliance (MMSA) is a not-for-profit organization in Maine that supports standards- and research-based science education at the state, New England, and national levels. CTS was developed for use in several of the MMSA's teacher leadership and school-based science professional development initiatives, including the NSF-funded Northern New England Co-Mentoring Network (NNECN) at www.nnecn.org. The MMSA Web site features examples of projects and programs in science and mathematics that have been informed by CTS. For further information about CTS, CTS leadership training, and professional development or consultation on using CTS with your project or organization, please contact the author and project director, Page Keeley, at the MMSA www.mmsa.org.

CORWIN PRESS SPEAKERS BUREAU

Corwin Press maintains a Speakers Bureau for arranging presentations by Corwin authors, including CTS author Page Keeley. For information on arranging a CTS presentation, please visit the Corwin Press Web site at www.corwinpress.com.

Resource B:
Worksheets
for Curriculum
Topic Study

Resource B.1   Capture Your Thoughts

★ **Important Ideas**	👁 **Specific Insights**
? **Questions Raised**	⇨ **Implications for Action**

Resource B.2 CTS Content Summary Guide for Instructional Materials Review

CTS Topic: Grade Level:

Concepts for Teacher Background Information (Sec. I, II)	Students' Content Knowledge (Sec. III, V, VI)
Instructional Implications (Sec. II, IV)	Student Difficulties and Misconceptions (Sec. II, IV)
Prerequisite Knowledge (Sec. III, V)	Connections to Other Topics (Sec. II, V)

Resource B.3   Four-Square Elicitation Organizer

Prior Knowledge Related to the Topic

Adult Content Knowledge	Student Knowledge
Misconceptions or Difficulties	**Connections**

Resource B.4   CTS Content Summary Review Match for Instructional Materials

Unit: _____   Grade Level: _____   Developer: _____

Please rate the CTS summary categories, on a scale of 1–5, to the extent that the material showed evidence of matching the findings and recommendations in the CTS Summary Guide: **1-** No evidence; **2-** Minimal evidence; **3-** Sufficient evidence; **4-** Strong evidence; **5-** Strong evidence that includes additional useful and relevant material that exceeds the CTS findings and recommendations.

Concepts for Teacher Background Information

Evidence: 1   2   3   4   5
Comments:

Students' Content Knowledge

Evidence: 1   2   3   4   5
Comments:

Instructional Implications

Evidence: 1   2   3   4   5
Comments:

Student Difficulties and Misconceptions

Evidence: 1   2   3   4   5
Comments:

Prerequisite Knowledge

Evidence: 1   2   3   4   5
Comments:

Connections to Other Topics

Evidence: 1   2   3   4   5
Comments:

References

American Association for the Advancement of Science. (1990). *Science for all Americans.* New York: Oxford University Press.

American Association for the Advancement of Science. (1993). *Benchmarks for science literacy.* New York: Oxford University Press.

American Association for the Advancement of Science. (2000). *Designs for science literacy.* New York: Oxford University Press.

American Association for the Advancement of Science. (2001). *Atlas of science literacy.* Washington, DC: Author; Arlington, VA: National Science Teachers Association.

Asimov, I. (1970). *Photosynthesis.* London: George Allen & Unwin Ltd.

Audet, R., & Jordan, L. (2003). *Standards in the classroom: An implementation guide for teachers of science and mathematics.* Thousand Oaks, CA: Corwin Press.

Beane, J. (1995). Introduction: What is a coherent curriculum? In J. Beane (Ed.), *Toward a coherent curriculum: The 1995 ASCD yearbook.* Alexandria, VA: Association for Supervision and Curriculum Development.

Bransford, J., Brown, A., & Cocking, R. (2000). *How people learn.* Washington, DC: National Academy Press.

Bybee, R. (1997). *Achieving scientific literacy.* Portsmouth, NH: Heinemann.

Bybee, R. (Ed.). (2002). *Learning science and the science of learning.* Arlington, VA: National Science Teachers Association Press.

Chicago Science Group. (2004). Light. In *Science companion.* Chicago, IL: Pearson Scott Foresman.

Clermont, C. P., Krajcik, J. S., & Borko, H. (1993). The influence of an intensive inservice workshop on pedagogical content knowledge growth among novice teachers. *Journal of Research in Science Teaching, 30,* 21–43.

Cochran, K. F., DeRuiter, J. A., & King, R. A. (1993). Pedagogical content knowing: An integrative model for teacher preparation. *Journal of Teacher Education, 44,* 263–272.

Danielson, C. (1996). *Enhancing professional practice: A framework for teaching.* Alexandria, VA: Association for Supervision and Curriculum Development.

Darling-Hammond, L. (2000). Teacher quality and student achievement: A review of state policy and evidence. *Education Policy Archives, 8.* Available at http://epaa.asu.edu/epaa/v8n1/

Driver, R. (1989). Changing conceptions. In P. Adey (Ed.), *Adolescent development and school science.* London: Falmer Press.

Driver, R., Squires, A., Rushworth, P., & Wood-Robinson, V. (1994). *Making sense of secondary science.* New York: Routledge.

Erickson, L. (1998). *Concept-based curriculum and instruction.* Thousand Oaks, CA: Corwin Press.

Fernández-Balboa, J. M., & Stiehl, J. (1995). The generic nature of pedagogical content knowledge among college professors. *Teaching & Teacher Education, 11,* 293–306.

Gould, A., Willard, C., & Pompea, S. (2000). *Real reasons for seasons.* Berkeley, CA: Lawrence Hall of Science.

Gregory, G., & Chapman, C. (2002). *Differentiated instructional strategies: One size doesn't fit all.* Thousand Oaks, CA: Corwin Press.

Gregory, G., & Kuzmich, L. (2004). *Data driven differentiations in the standards based classroom.* Thousand Oaks, CA: Corwin Press.

Hazen, R., & Trefil, J. (1991). *Science matters: Achieving scientific literacy.* New York: Anchor Books.

Jacobs, H. (1997). *Mapping the big picture: Integrating curriculum and assessment K–12.* Alexandria, VA: Association for Supervision and Curriculum Development.

Jonassen, D. H. (1994). Thinking technology: Toward a constructivist design model. *Educational Technology, 34*(4), 34–37.

Kahle, J. B. (1999, June). Testimony, U.S. House of Representatives, Washington, DC.

Keeley, P., Eberle, F., & Farrin, L. (in press). *Probing students' ideas in science* (Vol. 1). Arlington, VA: National Science Teachers Association.

Leonard, W., Dufresne, R., Gerace, W., & Mestre, J. (1999). *Minds on physics: Conservation laws and concept-based problem solving.* Dubuque, IA: Kendall Hunt.

Loucks-Horsley, S., Love, N., Stiles, K., Mundry, S., & Hewson, P. (2003). *Designing professional development for teachers of science and mathematics.* Thousand Oaks, CA: Corwin Press.

Maine Department of Education. (1997). *Maine's learning results.* Augusta, ME: State of Maine Printing Office.

Maine NASALEARN. (2004). *Dark moons.* Available at http://www.nasalearn.org

Marzano, R., Pickering, D., & Pollock, J. (2001). *Classroom instruction that works: Research-based strategies for increasing student achievement.* Alexandria, VA: Association for Supervision and Curriculum Development.

Mezirow, J. (1997). Transformative learning: Theory to practice. In P. Cranton (Ed.), *Transformative learning in action: Insights from practice.* San Francisco: Jossey-Bass.

Monk, D. H. (1994). Subject area preparation of secondary mathematics and science teachers and student achievement. *Economics of Education Review, 13,* 125–145.

National Research Council. (1996). *National science education standards.* Washington, DC: National Academy Press.

National Research Council. (1999). *Selecting instructional materials: A guide for K–12 science.* Washington, DC: National Academy Press.

National Research Council. (2000). *Inquiry and the national science education standards.* Washington, DC: National Academy Press.

National Research Council. (2001). *Classroom assessment and the national science education standards.* Washington, DC: National Academy Press.

National Research Council. (2002). *Investigating the influence of standards.* Washington, DC: National Academy Press.

National Science Foundation. (2002). *Professional development that supports school mathematics reform* (Foundations Monograph, Vol. 3). Washington, DC: Author.

National Science Foundation. (2003). Teacher Professional Continuum Program grant solicitation. Available at http://www.nsf.gov/pubs/2003/nsf03534/nsf03534.htm

Pearson, P. D., & Fielding, L. (1991). Comprehension instruction. In B. Barr, M. Kamil, P. Mosenthal, & P. D. Pearson (Eds.), *Handbook of reading research* (Vol. 2, pp. 815–860). White Plains, NY: Longman.

Pratt, H. (2002). Introduction. In R. Bybee (Ed.), *Learning science and the science of learning.* Arlington, VA: National Science Teachers Association.

Rosenblatt, L. (1994). The transactional theory of reading and writing. In R. Ruddell, M. Ruddell, & H. Singer (Eds.), *Theoretical models and processes of reading* (4th ed., pp. 1057–1092). Newark, DE: International Reading Association.

Schmidt, W., McKnight, C., & Raizen, S. (1997). *A splintered vision: An investigation of U.S. science and mathematics education.* Norwell, MA: Kluwer Academic.

Shulman, L. S. (1986). Those who understand: Knowledge growth in teaching. *Educational Researcher, 15*(2), 4–14.

Siegel, M., Borasi, R., & Fonzi, J. (1998). Supporting students' mathematical inquiries through reading. *Journal for Research in Mathematics Education (USA), 30,* 378–413.

Stigler, J., & Hiebert, J. (1999). *The teaching gap: Best ideas from the world's teachers for improving education in the classroom.* New York: Free Press.

Van Driel, J. H., Verloop, N., & DeVos, W. (1998). Developing science teachers' pedagogical knowledge. *Journal of Teacher Education, 41,* 3–11.

York-Barr, J., Sommers, W., Ghere, G., & Montie, J. (2001). *Reflective practice to improve schools: An action guide for educators.* Thousand Oaks, CA: Corwin Press.

Weiss, I. R., Pasley, J. D., Smith, P. S., Banilower, E. R., & Heck, D. J. (2003). *Looking inside the classroom: A study of K–12 mathematics and science education in the United States.* Chapel Hill, NC: Horizon Research.

Wiggins, G., & McTighe, J. (1998). *Understanding by design.* Alexandria, VA: Association for Supervision and Curriculum Development.

Zembal-Saul, C., Blumenfeld, P., & Krajcik, J (2000). Influence of guided cycles of planning, teaching, and reflection on prospective elementary teachers' science content representations. *Journal of Research in Science Education, 37,* 295–317.

Index

**CORWIN
PRESS**

The Corwin Press logo—a raven striding across an open book—represents the union of courage and learning. Corwin Press is committed to improving education for all learners by publishing books and other professional development resources for those serving the field of K–12 education. By providing practical, hands-on materials, Corwin Press continues to carry out the promise of its motto: **"Helping Educators Do Their Work Better."**